A THEOLOGY OF LIBERATION

ORBIS BOOKS · MARYKNOLL, NEW YORK · 1973

A THEOLOGY
OF LIBERATION

History, Politics and Salvation

Gustavo Gutiérrez

Translated and edited by
Sister Caridad Inda and John Eagleson

*To José María Arguedas
and Henrique Pereira Neto*

Sixth Printing

Originally published as *Teología de la liberación, Perspectivas*
by CEP, Lima, 1971

Copyright © 1973 Orbis Books, Maryknoll, New York 10545

Library of Congress Catalog Card Number: 72-85790

Cloth: ISBN 0-88344-4771   Paper: ISBN: 0-88344-478X

Manufactured in the United States of America

CONTENTS

INTRODUCTION

This book is an attempt at reflection, based on the Gospel and
the experiences of men and women committed to the process
of liberation in the oppressed and exploited land of Latin
America. It is a theological reflection born of the experience
of shared efforts to abolish the current unjust situation and
to build a different society, freer and more human. Many in
Latin America have started along the path of a commitment
to liberation, and among them is a growing number of Christians;
whatever the validity of these pages, it is due to their experiences
and reflections. Our greatest desire is not to betray their experiences and efforts to elucidate the meaning of their solidarity
with the oppressed.

Our purpose is not to elaborate an ideology to justify postures
already taken, nor to undertake a feverish search for security
in the face of the radical challenges which confront the faith,
nor to fashion a theology from which political action is "deduced."
It is rather to let ourselves be judged by the Word of the Lord,
to think through our faith, to strengthen our love, and to give
reason for our hope from within a commitment which seeks to
become more radical, total, and efficacious. It is to reconsider
the great themes of the Christian life within this radically
changed perspective and with regard to the new questions posed
by this commitment. This is the goal of the so-called *theology
of liberation*.

Many significant efforts along these lines are being made in
Latin America. Insofar as we know about them, they have been
kept in mind and have contributed to this study. We wish to
avoid, however, the kind of reflection which—legitimately concerned with preventing the mechanical transfer of an approach
foreign to our historical and social coordinates—neglects the con-

tribution of the universal Christian community. It seems better, moreover, to acknowledge explicitly this contribution than to introduce surreptitiously and uncritically certain ideas elaborated in another context which can only be fruitful among us if they undergo a healthy and frank scrutiny.

A reflection on the theological meaning of the process of the liberation of man throughout history demands methodologically that we define our terms. The first part of this book is devoted to that purpose. This will enable us to indicate why we pay special attention in this work to the critical function of theology with respect to the presence and activity of man in history. The most important instance of this presence in our times, especially in underdeveloped and oppressed countries, is the struggle to construct a just and fraternal society, where people can live with dignity and be the agents of their own destiny. It is our opinion that the term *development* does not well express these profound aspirations. *Liberation*, on the other hand, seems to express them better. Moreover, in another way the notion of liberation is more exact and all-embracing: it emphasizes that man transforms himself by conquering his liberty throughout his existence and his history. The Bible presents liberation—salvation—in Christ as the total gift, which, by taking on the levels we indicate, gives the whole process of liberation its deepest meaning and its complete and unforeseeable fulfillment. Liberation can thus be approached as a single salvific process. This viewpoint, therefore, permits us to consider *the unity, without confusion,* of man's various dimensions, that is, his relationships with other men and with the Lord, which theology has been attempting to establish for some time; this approach will provide the framework for our reflection.

It is fitting, secondly, to show that the problem which the theology of liberation poses is simultaneously traditional and new. This twofold characteristic will be more evident if we analyze the different ways in which theology has historically responded to this problem. This will lead us to conclude that because the traditional approaches have been exhausted, new areas of theological reflection are being sought. Our examination should help us remove the obstacles from our path and move ahead more quickly. The second part of the work deals with this matter.

The preceding analysis leads us to reconsider the "practice" of the Church in today's world. The situation in Latin America, the only continent among the exploited and oppressed peoples where Christians are in the majority, is especially interesting. An attempt to describe and interpret the forms under which the Latin American Church is present in the process of liberation—especially among the most committed Christian groups—will allow us to establish the questions for an authentic theological reflection. These will be the first efforts along these lines. The third part of this treatise is devoted to this attempt.

The previous remarks make it clear that the question regarding the theological meaning of liberation is, in truth, a question *about the very meaning of Christianity and about the mission of the Church*. There was a time when the Church responded to any problem by calmly appealing to its doctrinal and vital resources. Today the seriousness and scope of the process which we call liberation is such that Christian faith and the Church are being radically challenged. They are being asked to show what significance they have for a human task which has reached adulthood. The greater part of our study is concerned with this aspect. We approach the subject within the framework of the unity and, at the same time, the complexity of the process of liberation centered in the salvific work of Christ. We are aware, however, that we can only sketch these considerations, or more precisely, outline the new questions—without claiming to give conclusive answers.

The novelty and shifting quality of the problems posed by the commitment to liberation make the use of adequate language and sufficiently precise concepts rather difficult. Nevertheless, we present this study in the hope that it will be useful, and especially because we are confident that the confrontation necessarily implied in publishing will allow us to improve and deepen these reflections.

The present study is based on a paper presented at the *Encuentro Nacional del Movimiento Sacerdotal ONIS*, July 1968, in Chimbote, Peru, published by the MIEC Documentation Service in Montevideo (1969) with the title *Hacia una teología de la liberación*. The original lecture was updated for a presentaton at the Consultation on Theology and Development organized by SODEPAX, November 1969, in Cartigny, Switzerland, and published as "Notes on a Theology of Liberation," in *In Search of a Theology of Development: A Sodepax Report* (Lausanne, 1970). This study follows the same line of thought.

PART 1

THEOLOGY AND LIBERATION

Theology and *liberation* are terms subject to a variety of interpretations. In order to present our study properly and clearly, we must examine critically the notion of *theology* which we will use throughout. Likewise, it is necessary to determine, at least in rough outline, what it is we understand by *liberation*. As we progress, various shades of meaning and deeper levels of understanding will complement this initial effort.

CHAPTER ONE

THEOLOGY: A CRITICAL REFLECTION

Theological reflection—that is, the understanding of the faith—arises spontaneously and inevitably in the believer, in all those who have accepted the gift of the Word of God. Theology is intrinsic to a life of faith seeking to be authentic and complete and is, therefore, essential to the common consideration of this faith in the ecclesial community. There is present in *all believers*—and more so in every Christian community—a rough outline of a theology. There is present an effort to understand the faith, something like a pre-understanding of that faith which is manifested in life, action, and concrete attitude. It is on this foundation, and only because of it, that the edifice of theology—in the precise and technical sense of the term—can be erected. This foundation is not merely a jumping-off point, but the soil into which theological reflection stubbornly and permanently sinks its roots and from which it derives its strength.[1]

But the focus of theological work, in the strict sense of the term, has undergone many transformations throughout the history of the Church. "Bound to the role of the Church, theology is dependent upon its historical development," writes Christian Duquoc.[2] Moreover, as Congar observed recently, this evolution has accelerated to a certain extent in recent years: "The theological work has changed in the past twenty-five years."[3]

THE CLASSICAL TASKS OF THEOLOGY

Theological study has fulfilled different functions throughout the history of the Christian community, but this does not necessarily mean that any of these different approaches has today been definitively superseded. Although expressed in different ways, the essential effort to understand the faith has remained. Moreover, the more penetrating and serious efforts have yielded decisive gains, opening paths along which all subsequent theological reflection must travel. In this perspective it is more accurate to speak of permanent tasks—although they have emerged at different moments in the history of the Church—than of historically successive stages of theology. Two of these functions are considered classical: theology as wisdom and theology as rational knowledge.

Theology as Wisdom

In the early centuries of the Church, what we now term theology was closely linked to the spiritual life.[4] It was essentially a meditation on the Bible,[5] geared toward spiritual growth. Distinctions were made between the "beginners," the faithful, and the "advanced," who sought perfection.[6] This theology was above all monastic and therefore characterized by a spiritual life removed from worldly concerns;[7] it offered a model for every Christian desirous of advancing along the narrow path of sanctity and seeking a life of spiritual perfection.

Anxious to dialogue with the thought of its time, this theology used Platonic and Neoplatonic categories. In these philosophies it found a metaphysics which stressed the existence of a higher world and the transcendence of an Absolute from which everything came and to which everything returned.[8] The present life, on the other hand, was regarded as essentially contingent and was not valued sufficiently.

It is important to remember, however, that at this same time the reflections of the Greek Fathers on the theology of the world—cosmos and history—go well beyond a mere personal spiritual meditation and place theology in a wider and more fruitful context.

Around the fourteenth century, a rift appears between theologians and masters of the spiritual life. This division can be seen, for example, in such books as *The Imitation of Christ*, which has made a deep impact upon Christian spirituality during past centuries. We are suffering from this dichotomy even today, although it is true that Biblical renewal and the need to reflect upon lay spirituality are providing us with the broad outlines of what might be considered a new spiritual theology.[9]

The spiritual function of theology, so important in the early centuries and later regarded as parenthetical, constitutes, nevertheless, a permanent dimension of theology.[10]

Theology as Rational Knowledge

From the twelfth century on, theology begins to establish itself as a science: "The transition has been made from *sacra pagina* to *theologia* in the modern sense which Abelard . . . was the first to use."[11] The process culminated with Albert the Great and Thomas Aquinas. On the basis of Aristotelian categories, theology was classified as a "subaltern science."[12] St. Thomas's view, nevertheless, was broad and synthetical: theology is not only a science, but also wisdom flowing from the charity which unites man to God.[13] But this balance is lost when the above-mentioned separation appears between theology and spirituality in the fourteenth century.

The Thomistic idea of science is unclear today because it does not correspond to the definition generally accepted by the modern mind. But the essential feature of St. Thomas Aquinas's work is that theology is an intellectual discipline, born of the meeting of faith and reason.[14] From this point of view, therefore, it is more accurate to regard the theological task not as a science, but as rational knowledge.

The function of theology as rational knowledge is also permanent—insofar as it is a meeting between faith and reason, not exclusively between faith and any one philosophy, nor even between faith and philosophy in general. Reason has, especially today, many other manifestations than philosophical ones. The understanding of the faith is also following along new paths in our day: the social, psychological, and biological sciences. The social sciences, for example, are extremely important for theological reflection in Latin America. Theological thought not characterized by such a rationality and disinterestedness would not be truly faithful to an understanding of the faith.

But it is well to remember, especially with respect to the outdated views which still persist in some quarters, that in Scholas-

tic theology after the thirteenth century there is a degradation
of the Thomistic concept of theology.[15] There arises at that time,
regardless of outward appearances, a very different way of
approaching the theological task. The demands of rational knowledge will be reduced to the need for systematization and clear
exposition.[16] Scholastic theology will thus gradually become,
especially after the Council of Trent, an ancillary discipline of
the magisterium of the Church. Its function will be "(1) to define,
present, and explain revealed truths; (2) to examine doctrine,
to denounce and condemn false doctrines, and to defend true
ones; (3) to teach revealed truths authoritatively."[17]

In summary, theology is of necessity both spirituality and
rational knowledge. These are permanent and indispensable
functions of all theological thinking. However, both functions
must be salvaged, at least partially, from the division and defor-
mations they have suffered throughout history. A reflective outlook and style especially must be retained, rather than one or
another specific achievement gained in a historical context different from ours.

THEOLOGY AS CRITICAL REFLECTION ON PRAXIS

The function of theology as critical reflection on praxis has
gradually become more clearly defined in recent years, but it
has its roots in the first centuries of the Church's life. The Augustinian theology of history which we find in *The City of God*,
for example, is based on a true analysis of the signs of the times
and the demands with which they challenge the Christian community.

Historical Praxis

For various reasons the existential and active aspects of the
Christian life have recently been stressed in a different way
than in the immediate past.

In the first place, *charity* has been fruitfully rediscovered as
the center of the Christian life. This has led to a more Biblical
view of the faith as an act of trust, a going out of one's self,
a commitment to God and neighbor, a relationship with others.[18]
It is in this sense that St. Paul tells us that faith works through

charity: love is the nourishment and the fullness of faith, the gift of one's self to the Other, and invariably to others. This is the foundation of the *praxis* of the Christian, of his active presence in history. According to the Bible, faith is the total response of man to God, who saves through love.[19] In this light, the understanding of the faith appears as the understanding not of the simple affirmation—almost memorization—of truths, but of a commitment, an overall attitude, a particular posture toward life.

In a parallel development, Christian *spirituality* has seen a significant evolution. In the early centuries of the Church there emerged the primacy, almost exclusiveness, of a certain kind of contemplative life, hermitical, monastic, characterized by withdrawal from the world, and presented as the model way to sanctity. About the twelfth century the possibility of sharing contemplation by means of preaching and other forms of apostolic activity began to be considered. This point of view was exemplified in the mixed life (contemplative and active) of the mendicant orders and was expressed in the formula: *contemplata aliis tradere* ("to transmit to others the fruits of contemplation").[20] Viewed historically this stage can be considered as a transition to Ignatian spirituality, which sought a difficult but fruitful synthesis between contemplation and action: *in actione contemplativus* ("contemplative in action").[21] This process, strengthened in recent years by the search for a spirituality of the laity, culminates today in the studies on the religious value of the profane and in the spirituality of the activity of the Christian in the world.[22]

Moreover, today there is a greater sensitivity to the *anthropological aspects* of revelation.[23] The Word about God is at the same time a promise to the world. In revealing God to us, the Gospel message reveals us to ourselves in our situation before the Lord and with other men. The God of Christian revelation is a God made man, hence the famous comment of Karl Barth regarding Christian anthropocentrism: "Man is the measure of all things, since God became man."[24] All this has caused the revaluation of the presence and the activity of man in the world, especially in relation to other men. On this subject Congar writes: "Seen as a whole, the direction of theological thinking has been characterized by a transference away from attention to the being *per se* of supernatural realities, and toward attention to their relationship with man, with the world, and with the problems and the affirmations of all those who for us represent the *Others.*"[25] There is no *horizontalism* in this approach.[26] It is simply a question of the rediscovery of the indissoluble unity of man and God.[27]

On the other hand, *the very life of the Church* appears ever more clearly as a *locus theologicus.* Regarding the participation of Christians in the important social movements of their time, Chenu wrote insightfully more than thirty years ago: "They are active *loci theologici* for the doctrines of grace, the Incarnation, and the redemption, as expressly promulgated and described in detail by the papal encyclicals. They are poor theologians who, wrapped up in their manuscripts and scholastic disputations, are not open to these amazing events, not only in the pious fervor of their hearts but formally in their science; there is a theological datum and an extremely fruitful one, in the *presence* of the Spirit."[28] The so-called "new theology" attempted to adopt this posture some decades ago. The fact that the life of the Church is a source for all theological analysis has been recalled to mind often since then. The Word of God gathers and is incarnated in the community of faith, which gives itself to the service of all men.

Vatican Council II has strongly reaffirmed the idea of a Church of service and not of power. This is a Church which is not centered upon itself and which does not "find itself" except when it "loses itself," when it lives "the joys and the hopes, the griefs and the anxieties of men of this age" (*Gaudium et spes,* no. 1). All of these trends provide a new focus for seeing the presence and activity of the Church in the world as a starting point for theological reflection.

What since John XXIII and Vatican Council II began to be called a theology of the *signs of the times*[29] can be characterized along the same lines, although this takes a step beyond narrow ecclesial limits. It must not be forgotten that the signs of the times are not only a call to intellectual analysis. They are above all a call to pastoral activity, to commitment, and to service. Studying the signs of the times includes both dimensions. Therefore, *Gaudium et spes,* no. 44, points out that discerning the signs of the times is the responsibility of every Christian, especially pastors and theologians, to hear, distinguish, and interpret the many voices of our age, and to judge them in the light of the divine Word. In this way, revealed truths can always be more deeply penetrated, better understood, and set forth to greater advantage." Attributing this role to every member of the People of God and singling out the pastors—charged with guiding the activity of the Church—highlights the call to commitment which the signs of the times imply. Necessarily connected with this consideration, the function of theologians will be to afford greater clarity regarding this commitment by means of intellectual analysis. (It is interesting to note that the inclusion of theologians in the above-mentioned text met opposition during the conciliar debates.)

Another factor, this time of a *philosophical* nature, reinforces the importance of human action as the point of departure for all reflection. The philosophical issues of our times are characterized by new relationships of man with nature, born of advances in science and technology. These new bonds affect the awareness man has of himself and of his active relationships with others.

Maurice Blondel, moving away from an empty and fruitless spirituality and attempting to make philosophical speculation more concrete and alive, presented it as a critical reflection on action. This reflection attempts to understand the internal logic of an action through which man seeks fulfillment by constantly transcending himself.[30] Blondel thus contributed to the elaboration of a new *apologetics* and became one of the most important thinkers of contemporary theology, including the most recent trends.

To these factors can be added the influence of *Marxist thought*, focusing on praxis and geared to the transformation of the world.[31] The Marxist influence began to be felt in the middle of the nineteenth century, but in recent times its cultural impact has becomes greater. Many agree with Sartre that "Marxism, as the formal framework of all contemporary philosophical thought, cannot be superseded."[32] Be that as it may, contemporary theology does in fact find itself in direct and fruitful confrontation with Marxism, and it is to a large extent due to Marxism's influence that theological thought, searching for its own sources, has begun to reflect on the meaning of the transformation of this world and the action of man in history.[33]

Further, this confrontation helps theology to perceive what its
efforts at understanding the faith receive from the historical
praxis of man in history as well as what its own reflection might
mean for the transformation of the world.

Finally, the rediscovery of the *eschatological dimension* in
theology has also led us to consider the central role of historical
praxis. Indeed, if human history is above all else an opening
to the future, then it is a task, a political occupation, through
which man orients and opens himself to the gift which gives
history its transcendent meaning: the full and definitive
encounter with the Lord and with other men. "To do the truth,"
as the Gospel says, thus acquires a precise and concrete meaning
in terms of the importance of action in Christian life. Faith in
a God who loves us and calls us to the gift of full communion
with him and brotherhood among men not only is not foreign
to the transformation of the world; it leads necessarily to the
building up of that brotherhood and communion in history.
Moreover, only by doing this truth will our faith be "veri-fied,"
in the etymological sense of the word. From this notion has
recently been derived the term *orthopraxis*, which still disturbs
the sensitivities of some. The intention, however, is not to deny
the meaning of *orthodoxy*, understood as a proclamation of and
reflection on statements considered to be true. Rather, the goal
is to balance and even to reject the primacy and almost exclusiveness which doctrine has enjoyed in Christian life and above all
to modify the emphasis, often obsessive, upon the attainment
of an orthodoxy which is often nothing more than fidelity to
an obsolete tradition or a debatable interpretation. In a more
positive vein, the intention is to recognize the work and importance of concrete behavior, of deeds, of action, of praxis in the
Christian life. "And this, it seems to me, has been the greatest
transformation which has taken place in the Christian conception of existence," said Edward Schillebeeckx in an interview.
"It is evident that thought is also necessary for action. But the
Church has for centuries devoted her attention to formulating
truths and meanwhile did almost nothing to better the world.
In other words, the Church focused on orthodoxy and left orthopraxis in the hands of nonmembers and nonbelievers."[34]

In the last analysis, this concern for praxis seeks to avoid
the practices which gave rise to Bernanos' sarcastic remark:

"God does not choose the same men to keep his word as to fulfill it."[35]

Critical Reflection

All the factors we have considered have been responsible for a more accurate understanding that communion with the Lord inescapably means a Christian life centered around a concrete and creative commitment of service to others. They have likewise led to the rediscovery or explicit formulation of the function of theology as critical reflection. It would be well at this point to define further our terms.

Theology must be man's critical reflection on himself, on his own basic principles. Only with this approach will theology be a serious discourse, aware of itself, in full possession of its conceptual elements. But we are not referring exclusively to this epistemological aspect when we talk about theology as critical reflection. We also refer to a clear and critical attitude regarding economic and socio-cultural issues in the life and reflection of the Christian community. To disregard these is to deceive both oneself and others. But above all, we intend this term to express the theory of a definite practice. Theological reflection would then necessarily be a criticism of society and the Church insofar as they are called and addressed by the Word of God; it would be a critical theory, worked out in the light of the Word accepted in faith and inspired by a practical purpose—and therefore indissolubly linked to historical praxis.[36]

By preaching the Gospel message, by its sacraments, and by the charity of its members, the Church proclaims and shelters the gift of the Kingdom of God in the heart of human history.[37] The Christian community professes a "faith which works through charity." It is—at least ought to be—real charity, action, and commitment to the service of men. Theology is reflection, a critical attitude. Theology *follows;* it is the second step.[38] What Hegel used to say about philosophy can likewise be applied to theology: it rises only at sundown. The pastoral activity of the Church does not flow as a conclusion from theological premises. Theology does not produce pastoral activity; rather it reflects upon it. Theology must be able to find in pastoral activity the presence of the Spirit inspiring the action of the Christian com-

munity.[39] A privileged *locus theologicus* for understanding the
faith will be the life, preaching, and historical commitment of
the Church.

To reflect upon the presence and action of the Christian in
the world means, moreover, to go beyond the visible boundaries
of the Church. This is of prime importance. It implies openness
to the world, gathering the questions it poses, being attentive
to its historical transformations. In the words of Congar, "If
the Church wishes to deal with the real questions of the modern
world and to attempt to respond to them, . . . it must open as
it were a new chapter of theologico-pastoral epistemology.
Instead of using only revelation and tradition as starting points,
as classical theology has generally done, it must start with facts
and questions derived from the world and from history."[40] It
is precisely this opening to the totality of human history that
allows theology to fulfill its critical function vis-à-vis ecclesial
praxis without narrowness.

This critical task is indispensable. Reflection in the light of
faith must constantly accompany the pastoral action of the
Church. By keeping historical events in their proper perspective,
theology helps safeguard society and the Church from regarding
as permanent what is only temporary. Critical reflection thus
always plays the inverse role of an ideology which rationalizes
and justifies a given social and ecclesial order. On the other
hand, theology, by pointing to the sources of revelation, helps
to orient pastoral activity; it puts it in a wider context and so
helps it to avoid activism and immediatism. Theology as critical
reflection thus fulfills a liberating function for man and the
Christian community, preserving them from fetishism and
idolatry, as well as from a pernicious and belittling narcissism.
Understood in this way, theology has a necessary and permanent
role in the liberation from every form of religious
alienation—which is often fostered by the ecclesiastical institution itself when it impedes an authentic approach to the Word
of the Lord.

As critical reflection on society and the Church, theology is
an understanding which both grows and, in a certain sense,
changes. If the commitment of the Christian community in fact
takes different forms throughout history, the understanding
which accompanies the vicissitudes of this commitment will be

constantly renewed and will take untrodden paths. A theology which has as its points of reference only "truths" which have been established once and for all—and not the Truth which is also the Way—can be only static and, in the long run, sterile. In this sense the often-quoted and misinterpreted words of Bouillard take on new validity: "A theology which is not up-to-date is a false theology."[41]

Finally, theology thus understood, that is to say as linked to praxis, fulfills a prophetic function insofar as it interprets historical events with the intention of revealing and proclaiming their profound meaning. According to Cullmann, this is the meaning of the prophetic role: "The prophet does not limit himself as does the fortune-teller to isolated revelations, but his prophecy becomes preaching, proclamation. He explains to the people the true meaning of all events; he informs them of the plan and will of God at the particular moment."[42] But if theology is based on this observation of historical events and contributes to the discovery of their meaning, it is with the purpose of making the Christians' commitment within them more radical and clear. Only with the exercise of the prophetic function understood in this way, will the theologian be—to borrow an expression from Antonio Gramsci—a new kind of "organic intellectual."[43] He will be someone personally and vitally engaged in historical realities with specific times and places. He will be engaged where nations, social classes, people struggle to free themselves from domination and oppression by other nations, classes, and people. In the last analysis, the true interpretation of the meaning revealed by theology is achieved only in historical praxis. "The hermeneutics of the Kingdom of God," observed Schillebeeckx, "consists especially in making the world a better place. Only in this way will I be able to discover what the Kingdom of God means."[44] We have here a political hermeneutics of the Gospel.[45]

CONCLUSION

Theology as a critical reflection on Christian praxis in the light of the Word does not replace the other functions of theology, such as wisdom and rational knowledge; rather it presupposes and needs them. But this is not all. We are not concerned here with a mere juxtaposition. The critical function of theology neces-

14   A THEOLOGY OF LIBERATION

sarily leads to redefinition of these other two tasks, Henceforth, wisdom and rational knowledge will more explicitly have ecclesial praxis as their point of departure and their context. It is in reference to this praxis that an understanding of spiritual growth based on Scripture should be developed, and it is through this same praxis that faith encounters the problems posed by human reason. Given the theme of the present work, we will be especially aware of this critical function of theology with the ramifications suggested above. This approach will lead us to pay special attention to the life of the Church and to commitments which Christians, impelled by the Spirit and in communion with other people, undertake in history. We will give special consideration to participation in the process of liberation, an outstanding phenomenon of our times, which takes on special meaning in the so-called Third World countries.

This kind of theology, arising from concern with a particular set of issues, will perhaps give us the solid and permanent albeit modest foundation for the *theology in a Latin American perspective* which is both desired and needed. This Latin American focus would not be due to a frivolous desire for originality, but rather to a fundamental sense of historical efficacy and also—why hide it?—to the desire to contribute to the life and reflection of the universal Christian community. But in order to make our contribution, this desire for universality—as well as input from the Christian community as a whole—must be present from the beginning. To concretize this desire would be to overcome particularistic tendencies—provincial and chauvinistic—and produce something *unique*, both particular and universal, and therefore fruitful.

"The only future that theology has, one might say, is to become the theology of the future," Harvey Cox has said.[46] But this theology of the future must necessarily be a critical appraisal of historical praxis, of the historical task in the sense we have attempted to sketch. Moltmann says that theological concepts "do not limp after reality .... They illuminate reality by displaying its future."[47] In our approach, to reflect critically on the praxis of liberation is not to "limp after" reality. The present in the praxis of liberation, in its deepest dimension, is pregnant with the future; hope must be an inherent part of our present commitment in history. Theology does not initiate this future which exists in the present. It does not create the vital attitude of hope out of nothing. Its role is more modest. It interprets and explains these as the true underpinnings of history. To reflect upon a forward-directed action is not to concentrate on the past. It does not mean being the caboose of the present. Rather it is to penetrate the present reality, the movement of history, that which is driving history toward the future. To reflect on the basis of the historical praxis of liberation is to reflect in the light of the future which is believed in and hoped for. It is to reflect with a view to action which transforms the present. But it does not mean doing this from an armchair; rather it means sinking roots where the pulse of history is beating at this moment and illuminating history with the Word of the Lord of history, who irreversibly commited himself to the present moment of mankind to carry it to its fulfillment.

It is for all these reasons that the theology of liberation offers us not so much a new theme for reflection as a *new way* to do theology. Theology as critical reflection on historical praxis is a liberating theology, a theology of the liberating transformation of the history of mankind and also therefore that part of mankind—gathered into *ecclesia*—which openly confesses Christ. This is a theology which does not stop with reflecting on the world, but rather tries to be part of the process through which the world is transformed. It is a theology which is open—in the protest against trampled human dignity, in the struggle against the plunder of the vast majority of people, in liberating love, and in the building of a new, just, and fraternal society—to the gift of the Kingdom of God.

NOTES

1. What Antonio Gramsci said of philosophy is also true of theology: "It is necessary to destroy the widely-held prejudice that philosophy is something extremely difficult because it is the intellectual activity proper to a certain category of scientific specialists or professional and systematic philosophers. It is necessary, therefore, to demonstrate first that all men are 'philosophers,' establishing the parameters and characteristics of this 'spontaneous philosophy' proper to 'every-man'" ("Avviamemento allo studio della filosofia e del materialismo storico, Saggio introduttivo" in *La formazione dell'uomo* [Rome: Editori Riuniti, 1969], p. 217).

2. "Théologie et mission de l'Église" in *Lumière et Vie* 14, no. 71 (January-February 1965), p. 55. See the well-known article of Congar, "Théologie" in *Dictionnaire de Théologie Catholique* (written in 1939, published in 1943); in English see Congar's *A History of Theology*, trans. and ed. Hunter Guthrie (Garden City, N.Y.: Doubleday, 1968), based on the *DTC* article. See also Congar's *La foi et la théologie* (Tournai: Desclée, 1962) and the thought-provoking study by José Comblin, *História da teologia católica* (São Paulo: Editôra Herder, 1969).

3. *Situation et tâches présentes de la théologie* (Paris: Les Éditions du Cerf, 1967), p. 11; see also Gustave Thils, *Orientations de la théologie* (Louvain: Éditions Ceuterick, 1958); Adolf Kolping, *Katholische Theologie gestern und heute; Thematik und Entfaltung deutscher katholischer Theologie vom I. Vaticanum bis zur Gegenwart* (Bremen: Carl Schuenemann, 1964); Walter Kasper, *The Methods of Dogmatic Theology*, trans. John Drury (New York: Paulist Press, Deus Books, 1969); P. Touilleux, *Introduction à une théologie critique* (Paris: Lethielleux, 1967).

4. The terms *learned* and *saintly* were interchangeable to a certain point. See Congar, "Théologie," *Foi et théologie*, *Situation et tâches*, and Louis Bouyer, *The Spirituality of the New Testament and the Fathers* (New York: Desclee Company, 1960).

5. Hence the term *sacra pagina* or *sacra eruditio*. See Joseph de Ghellinck, *"Pagina et Sacra Pagina*, Histoire d'un mot et transformation de l'objet primitivement désigné" in *Mélanges Auguste Pelzer* (Louvain: Éditions de l'Institut Supérieur de Philosophie,1947), pp. 23-59.

6. See Henri de Lubac, *Exégèse médiévale: Les quatre sens de l'Écriture*, 4 vols. (Paris: Aubier, 1959-64).

7. See the works of R. Bultot on "contempt for the world"; a good overall view of the controversy they stirred is found in L.J. Bataillon and J.P. Jossua, "Le mépris du monde," *Revue des Sciences Philosophiques et Théologiques* 51, no. 1 (January 1967): 23-28.

8. See *Dictionnaire de Théologie Catholique*, s.v. "Platonisme des Pères."

9. The works of Guardini, Congar, Voillume, Evely, Paoli, Régamey and many others are examples of this effort.

10. Hans Urs von Balthasar pointed this out years ago: "Théologie et sainteté," *Dieu Vivant*, no. 12, pp. 15-31; see also by the same author, "Spirituality," in *Word and Redemption: Essays in Theology II* (New York: Herder and Herder, 1965), pp. 87-108.

11. See Congar, *Foi et théologie*, p. 238.

12. *Summa Theologica*, I, q. 1; see also Congar, "Théologie," *Foi et théologie*, and *Situations et tâches;* Comblin, *Teologia católica;* and M.D. Chenu, O.P., *Is Theology a Science?*, trans. A.H.N. Green Armytage (New York: Hawthorn Books, 1959).

13. See in this regard the strong commentary on *Summa Theologica*, I, q. 1, of Michel Corbin, "La fonction et les principes de la théologie selon la Somme Théologique de saint Thomas d'Aquin," *Recherches de Science Religieuse* 55, no. 3 (July-September 1967): 321-66.

14. A point well developed by C. Dumont, S.J., in "La réflexion sur la méthode théologique," *Nouvelle Revue Théologique* 83, no. 10 (December 1961): 1034-50 and 84, no. 1 (January 1962): 17-35.

15. See also *ibid.*

16. "According to classical scholastic theology, the scientific character of theology consists in its systematization . . . . The role of reason is confined to clarity of exposition" (Comblin, *Teologia católica*, p. 71).

17. *Ibid.*, p. 10. Because of this the theological centers close to the magisterium, especially the Roman universities, were invested with greater authority.

18. See also among others Gérard Gilleman, *The Primacy of Charity in Moral Theology*, trans. William F. Ryan and André Vachen (Westminster, Md.: The Newman Press, 1959); Jean Mouroux, *I Believe, The Personal Structure of Faith*, trans. Michael Turner (New York: Sheed and Ward, 1959); Bernard Haring, C.Ss.R., *The Law of Christ*, trans. Edwin G. Kaiser, C.Pp.S., 3 vols. (Westminster, Md.: The Newman Press, 1966); Pierre-André Liégé, O.P., *Consider Christian Maturity*, trans. and intr. Thomas C. Donlan, O.P. (Chicago: The Priory Press, 1965); Joseph Ratzinger, *The Open Circle, The Meaning of Brotherhood*, trans. W. A. Glen-Doeple (New York: Sheed and Ward, 1966); C. Spicq, O.P., *Théologie morale du nouveau testament*, 2 vols. (Paris: J. Gabalda et Cie, Éditeurs, 1965).

19. See also Iohannes Alfaro, S.I., "Fides in terminologia biblica," *Gregorianum* 42, no. 3 (1961): 463-505.

20. See *Summa Theologica*, II-II, q. 188.

21. It is common knowledge that the phrase is Nadal's, but it expresses well the intuition of Ignatius of Loyola. See Maurice Giuliani, S.J., "Trouver Dieu en toutes choses," *Christus*, no. 6 (April 1955): 172-94, and G. Fessard, *La Dialectique des "Exercises Spirituels" de s. Ignace de Loyola* (Paris: Aubier, 1958).

22. See Yves M.J. Congar, O.P., *Lay People in the Church*, trans. Donald Attwater (Westminster, Md.: The Newman Press, 1965), especially Chapter 9, "In the World and Not of the World"; Olivier A. Rabut, *Valeur spirituelle du profane* (Paris: Les Éditions du Cerf, 1963); P. Roquelo, *Expérience du monde: expérience de Dieu?* (Paris: Les Éditions du Cerf, 1968).

23. Karl Rahner writes, "Dogmatic theology today has to be theological anthropology, and . . . such an anthropocentric orientation of theology is both necessary and fruitful" ("Theology and Anthropology," in *The Word in History*, ed. T. Patrick Burke [New York: Sheed and Ward, 1966], p. 1). See also J.B. Metz, *Christliche Anthropozentrik: Ueber die Denkform des Thomas von Aquin* (Munich: Kösel Verlag, 1962); C. Dumont, S.J., "Pour une conversion 'anthropocentrique' dans la formation des clercs," *Nouvelle Revue Théologique* 87, no. 5 (May 1965): 449-65; L. Malevez, S.J., "Présence de la théologie à Dieu et à l'homme, *Nouvelle Revue Théologique* 90, no. 8 (October 1968), 785-800.

24. *Christengemeinde und Bürgergemeinde* (Zollikon-Zurich: Evangelischer Verlag, 1946), p. 36; English version: *Against the Stream: Shorter Post-War Writings, 1946-52* (New York: Philosophical Library, 1954).

25. *Situation et tâches*, p. 27.

26. See the debate between Congar (*ibid.*, pp. 62-67) and the periodical *Frères du Monde*, nos. 46-47 and 49-50 (1967); for an over-all view of this subject see Jean-Pierre Jossua, "Christianisme horizontal ou vertical?" *Parole et Mission* 11, no. 41 (April 1968): 245-55.

27. See below Chapter 10.

28. M. D. Chenu, O.P., "La théologie au Saulchoir" (1937 text), *La Parole de Dieu*, vol. 1, *La foi dans l'intelligence* (Paris: Les Éditions du Cerf, 1964), p. 259. René Laurentin has rightly recalled this character of *locus theologicus* proper to the Church in *Liberation, Development and Salvation*, trans. Charles Underhill Quinn (Maryknoll, New York: Orbis Books, 1972), pp. 7-8.

29. Despite its great interest, the notion of the signs of the times is far from being a clear and well-defined area. *Gaudium et spes* does not attempt to define it; it only provides a description and some consequences for the life of faith. See M. D. Chenu, "Les signes des temps: Réflexion théologique," *L'Église dans le monde*

de ce temps, ed. Y.M.J. Congar, O.P., and M. Peuchmaurd, O.P., 3 vols. (Paris: Les Éditions du Cerf, 1967), 2:205-25; see also the documentation of the "Signs of the Times" in *Understanding the Signs of the Times*, ed. Franz Bockle, Concilium 25 (New York: Paulist Press, 1967), pp. 143-52; from a more Latin American viewpoint see Marcos McGrath, "The Signs of the Times in Latin America Today" and Eduardo F. Pironio, "Christian Interpretation of the Signs of the Times in Latin America Today," *The Church in the Present-day Transformation of Latin America in the Light of the Council*, vol. 1, Position Papers of the Second General Conference of Latin American Bishops, Medellín, Colombia, 1968 (Bogota: General Secretariat of CELAM, 1970), pp. 79-106 and 107-28.

30. See Maurice Blondel, *L'Action* (Paris: Alcan, 1893); for a good treatment of Blondelian methodology, see Henry Duméry, *Critique et religion* (Paris: SEDES, 1957) and by the same author, *Raison et religion dans la philosophie de l'action* (Paris: Les Éditions du Seuil, 1963); in English see James M. Somerville, ed., *Total Commitment: Blondel's L'Action* (Washington, D.C.: Corpus Books, 1968).

31. The Marxian text is well known: "The Philosophers have only *interpreted* the world, in various ways; the point, however, is to *change* it" ("Theses on Feuerbach," no. 11, in Karl Marx and Friedrich Engels, *On Religion* [New York: Schocken Books, 1964], p. 72). The exact role of the idea of praxis in Marxian thought is a controversial subject; for a quick review of the different positions see Adolfo Sánchez Vázquez, *Filosofía de la praxis* (Mexico, D.F.: Grijalbo, 1967), pp. 43-45.

32. "Marxisme et philosophie de l'existence," a letter quoted in Roger Garaudy, *Perspectives de l'homme*, 3rd ed. (Paris: Presses Universitaires de France, 1961), p. 112.

33. See the collective work *Christentum und Marxismus-heute*, ed. Erich Kellner (Vienna: Europa Verlag, 1966); *Marxism and Christianity*, trans. Kevin Traynor (New York: The Macmillan Company, 1968); Georges M.-M. Cottier, *Chrétiens et marxistes* (Tours: Maison Mame, 1967); Roger Garaudy, *From Anathema to Dialogue*, trans. Luke O'Neill (New York: Herder and Herder, 1966). A high-level theoretical and practical confrontation is needed, however, to get away from the well-trodden paths of "dialogue" and explore the possibilities for creative innovation. To this end, grassroots experiences in social praxis are fundamental. Experiments up to this point have not been of sufficient duration or number. For this purpose what is happening in all of Latin America—and not only in Cuba and Chile—can be regarded as laboratory experiments.

34. "La teología," in *Los católicos holandeses* (Bilbao: Desclée deBrouwer, 1970). See also the interesting article of Michel de Certeau, "La rupture instauratrice ou le christianisme dans la culture," *Éspirit* 39, no. 6 (June 1971): 1177-1214.

35. *Lettre aux anglais* (Paris: Gallimard, 1948), p. 245; English version: *Plea for Liberty: Letters to the English, the Americans, the Europeans* (New York: Pantheon Books, Inc., 1944). Regarding the—in a certain sense—traditional character of the importance of praxis, see the observations of C. Dumont, "De trois dimensions retrouvées en théologie," *Nouvelle Revue Théologique* 92, no. 6 (June-July 1970): 570-80.

36. What José Carlos Mariátegui wrote in another context is definitely valid for a theology so conceived: "The ability to think history and the ability to make it or create it become one" *(Peruanicemos al Perú* [Lima: Empresa Editora Amauta, 1970], p. 119). This approach of theology as critical reflection is found in our work, *La pastoral de la Iglesia en América Latina* (Montevideo: Ediciones del Centro de Documentación MIEC-JECI, 1968), p. 15.

37. See the relevant remarks of Rudolf Schnackenburg on expressions such as "building up the Kingdom of God" or "spreading the Kingdom of God on earth" *(God's Rule and Kingdom*[New York: Herder and Herder, 1963], p. 354). Criticism on this subject has been gathered by Hans Küng, *The Church* (New York: Sheed and Ward, 1967), pp. 90-92.

38. "All bodies together, and all minds together, and all their products, are not equal to the least feeling of charity. . . . From all bodies and minds, we cannot produce a feeling of true charity" (Blaise Pascal, "Pensées," no. 793, in *Pascal*, Great Books of the Western World, vol. 33 [Chicago: William Benton, Publishers; Encyclopaedia Britannica, Inc., 1952], p. 327).

39. "Theology," wrote Karl Barth in another context, "follows the language of the Church, so far as, in its question as to the correctness of the Church's procedure therein, it measures it, not by a standard foreign to her, but by her very own source and object" *(Church Dogmatics*, vol. 1, part 1, *The Doctrine of the Word of God* [Edinburgh: T. & T. Clark, 1936], p. 2).

40. *Situation et tâches*, p. 72.

41. Henri Bouillard, *Conversion et grace chez S. Thomas d'Aquin* (Paris: Aubier, 1944), p. 219.

42. Oscar Cullmann, *The Christology of the New Testament*, rev. ed., trans. Shirley C. Guthrie and Charles A. M. Hall (Philadelphia: The Westminster Press, 1963), p. 14.

43. See "La formazione degli intellettuali," *Scritti politici* (Rome: Editori Riuniti, 1967), pp. 830-40.

44. *Católicos holandeses*, p. 29. Just previously the author acknowledges that the hermeneutics of the Kingdom of God also presupposes a reinterpretation of the Bible.

45. See Jürgen Moltmann's interesting article entitled "Towards a Political Hermeneutics of the Gospel," in *Union Seminary Quarterly Review* 23, no. 4 (Summer 1968): 303-23, and in a slightly different form in Moltmann's *Religion, Revolution, and the Future*, trans. M. Douglas Meeks (New York: Charles Scribner's Sons, 1969), pp. 83-107.

46. *On Not Leaving It to the Snake* (New York: The Macmillan Company, 1967), p. 12.

47. *Theology of Hope* (New York: Harper & Row, Publishers, 1967), p. 36.

CHAPTER TWO

LIBERATION AND DEVELOPMENT

The world today is experiencing a profound and rapid socio-cultural transformation. But the changes do not occur at a uniform pace, and the discrepancies in the change process have differentiated the various countries and regions of our planet.

Contemporary man has become clearly aware of this unequal process of transformation, of its economic causes, and of the basic relationships which combine to determine conditions and approaches. He examines his own circumstances and compares them to those of others; since he lives in a world where communication is fast and efficient, the conditions in which others live are no longer distant and unknown. But man goes beyond the limited expectations which such a comparison might create. He sees the process of transformation as a quest to satisfy the most fundamental human aspirations—liberty, dignity, the possibility of personal fulfillment for all. Or at least he would like the process to be moving toward these goals. He feels that the satisfaction of these aspiratons should be the purpose of all organization and social activity. He knows also that all his plans are possible, able to be at least partially implemented.

Finally, history demonstrates that the achievements of humanity are cumulative; their effects and the collective experience of the generations open new perspectives and allow for even greater achievements in the generations yet to come.

The phenomenon of the awareness of differences among countries characterizes our era, due to the bourgeoning of communications media; it is particularly acute in those countries less favored by the evolution of the world economy—the poor countries where the vast majority of people live. The inhabitants of these countries are aware of the unacceptable living conditions of most of their countrymen. They confirm the explanation that these inequalities are caused by a type of relationship which often has been imposed upon them. For these reasons, the efforts for social change in these areas are characterized both by a great urgency and by conflicts stemming from differences of expectations, degrees of pressure, and existing systems of relationships and power. It is well to clarify, on the one hand, that the current (and very recent) level of expectations of the poor countries goes far beyond a mere imitation of the rich countries and is of necessity somewhat indistinct and imprecise. On the other hand, both the internal heterogeneity and the presence of external determinants in these societies contribute to defining different needs in different groups. All of this causes a dynamics of action which is inevitably conflictual.

The poor countries are not interested in modeling themselves after the rich countries, among other reasons because they are increasingly more convinced that the status of the latter is the fruit of injustice and coercion. It is true that the poor countries are attempting to overcome material insufficiency and misery, but it is in order to achieve a more human society.

THE CONCEPT OF DEVELOPMENT

The term *development* seems tentatively to have synthesized the aspirations of people today for more human living conditions. The term itself is not new, but its current usage in the social sciences is new, for it responds to a different set of issues which has emerged only recently. Indeed, the old wealth-poverty antinomy no longer expresses all the problems and contemporary aspirations of mankind.

Origin

For some, the origin of the term *development* is, in a sense, negative. They consider it to have appeared in opposition to the term *underdevelopment*, which expressed the situation—and anguish—of the poor countries compared with the rich countries.[1]

It would perhaps be helpful to recall some of the more important trends which helped clarify the concept of development.

First of all, there is the work of Joseph A. Schumpeter,[2] the first economist after the English classics and Marx to concern himself with long-term processes. Schumpeter studied a capitalism characterized by a "circular flow," that is, a system which repeats itself from one period to the next and does not suffer appreciable structural change. The element which breaks this equilibrium and introduces a new dynamism is an *innovation*. Innovations are on the one hand technico-economic, since they are supposed to have originated in these areas; but they are simultaneously politico-social, because they imply contradicting and overcoming the prevailing system. Schumpeter calls this process *Entwicklung*, which today is translated as "development," although earlier renderings were "evolution"[3] or "unfolding."[4]

The work of the Australian economist Colin Clark represents another important contribution.[5] Clark affirms that the objective of economic activity is not wealth, but well-being, a term understood to mean the satisfaction derived from the resources at one's disposal. He proposes to measure well-being by making comparisons in time and space. The differences among countries are shown by various indicators. His calculations show that the highest levels of well-being are found in the industrialized countries. Clark designated the road toward industrialization which poor countries are to follow as "progress" (not development).

The Bandung Conference of 1955 also played an important role in the evolution of the term, although on a different level. A large number of countries met there, especially Asian and African countries. They recognized their common membership in a Third World—underdeveloped and facing two developed worlds, the capitalist and the socialist. This conference marked the beginning of a policy which was supposed to lead out of this state of affairs. Although the deeds that followed did not always correspond to the expectations aroused, Bandung nevertheless signalled a deepened awareness of the fact of underdevelopment and a proclamation of its unacceptability.[6]

Approaches

The concept of development has no clear definition;[7] there are a variety of ways to regard it. Rather than reviewing them all at length, we will recall briefly the general areas involved.

Development can be regarded as purely economic, and in that sense it would be synonymous with *economic growth*.

The degree of development of a country could be measured, for example, by comparing its gross national product or its per capita income with those of a country regarded as highly developed. It is also possible to refine this gauge and make it more complex, but the presuppositions would still be the same: development consists above all in increased wealth or, at most, a higher level of well-being.

Historically, this is the meaning which appears first. What led to this point of view was perhaps the consideration of the process in England, the first country to develop and, understandably enough, the first to be studied by economists. This viewpoint was later reinforced by the mirage which the well-being of the rich nations produced.

Those who champion this view today, at least explicitly, are few in number.[8] Currently its value lies in serving as a yardstick to measure more integral notions. However, this focus continues to exist in a more or less subtle form in the capitalistic view of development.

The deficiencies of the above-mentioned view have led to another more important and more frequently held one. According to it, development is a *total social process*, which includes economic, social, political, and cultural aspects. This notion stresses the interdependence of the different factors. Advances in one area imply advances in all of them and, conversely, the stagnation of one retards the growth of the rest.[9]

A consideration of development as a total process leads one to consider also all the external and internal factors which affect the economic evolution of a nation as well as to evaluate the distribution of goods and services and the system of relationships among the agents of its economic life. This has been carefully worked out by social scientists concerned with so-called Third World countries. They have reached the conclusion that the dynamics of world economics leads simultaneously to the creation of greater wealth for the few and greater poverty for the many.[10]

From all this flows a strategy of development which, taking into account the different factors, will allow a country to advance both totally and harmoniously and to avoid dangerous setbacks.

To view development as a total social process necessarily implies for some an ethical dimension, which presupposes a concern for human values. The step toward an elaboration of a *humanistic perspective* of development is thus taken unconsciously, and it prolongs the former point of view without contradicting it.

François Perroux worked consistently along these lines. Development for him means "the combination of mental and social changes of a people which enable them to increase, cumulatively and permanently, their total real production." Going even further, he says, "Development is achieved fully in the measure that, by reciprocity of services, it prepares the way for reciprocity of consciousness."[11]

It would be a mistake to think that this point of view, which is concerned with human values, is the exclusive preserve of scholars of a Christian inspiration. Converging viewpoints are found in Marxist-inspired positions.[12]

This humanistic approach attempts to place the notion of development in a wider context: a historical vision in which mankind assumes control of it own destiny.[13] But this leads precisely to a change of perspective which—after certain additions and corrections—we would prefer to call liberation. We shall attempt to clarify this below.

THE PROCESS OF LIBERATION

From the Critique of Developmentalism to Social Revolution

The term *development* has synthesized the aspirations of poor peoples during the last few decades. Recently, however, it has become the object of severe criticism due both to the deficiencies of the development policies proposed to the poor countries to lead them out of their underdevelopment and also to the lack of concrete achievements of the interested governments. This

is the reason why *developmentalism (desarrollismo)*, a term
derived from *development (desarrollo)*, is now used in a pejorative
sense, especially in Latin America.[14]

Much has been said in recent times about development. Poor
countries competed for the help of the rich countries. There were
even attempts to create a certain development mystique. Support for development was intense in Latin America in the '50s,
producing high expectations. But since the supporters of
development did not attack the roots of the evil, they failed and
caused instead confusion and frustration.[15]

One of the most important reasons for this turn of events is
that development—approached from an economic and modernizing point of view—has been frequently promoted by international organizations closely linked to groups and governments
which control the world economy.[16] The changes encouraged
were to be achieved within the formal structure of the existing
institutions without challenging them. Great care was exercised,
therefore, not to attack the interests of large international
economic powers nor those of their natural allies, the ruling
domestic interest groups. Furthermore, the so-called changes
were often nothing more than new and underhanded ways of
increasing the power of strong economic groups.

Developmentalism thus came to be synonymous with *reformism* and modernization, that is to say, synonymous with timid
measures, really ineffective in the long run and counterproductive to achieving a real transformation. The poor countries are
becoming ever more clearly aware that their underdevelopment
is only the by-product of the development of other countries,
because of the kind of relationship which exists between the
rich and the poor countries. Moreover, they are realizing that
their own development will come about only with a struggle
to break the domination of the rich countries.

This perception sees the conflict implicit in the process.
Development must attack the root causes of the problems and
among them the deepest is economic, social, political and cultural
dependence of some countries upon others—an expression of the
domination of some social classes over others. Attempts to bring
about changes within the existing order have proven futile. This
analysis of the situation is at the level of scientific rationality.
Only a radical break from the status quo, that is, a profound
transformation of the private property system, access to
power of the exploited class, and a social revolution that would

break this dependence would allow for the change to a new society, a socialist society—or at least allow that such a society might be possible.[17]

In this light, to speak about the process of *liberation* begins to appear more appropriate and richer in human content. Liberation in fact expresses the inescapable moment of radical change which is foreign to the ordinary use of the term *development*. Only in the context of such a process can a policy of development be effectively implemented, have any real meaning, and avoid misleading formulations.

Man, the Master of his Own Destiny

To characterize the situation of the poor countries as dominated and oppressed leads one to speak of economic, social, and political liberation. But we are dealing here with a much more integral and profound understanding of human existence and its historical future.

A broad and deep aspiration for liberation inflames the history of mankind in our day, liberation from all that limits or keeps man from self-fulfillment, liberation from all impediments to the exercise of his freedom. Proof of this is the awareness of new and subtle forms of oppression in the heart of advanced industrial societies, which often offer themselves as models to the underdeveloped countries. In them subversion does not appear as a protest against poverty, but rather against wealth.[18] The context in the rich countries, however, is quite different from that of the poor countries: we must beware of all kinds of imitations as well as new forms of imperialism—revolutionary this time—of the rich countries, which consider themselves central to the history of mankind. Such mimicry would only lead the revolutionary groups of the Third World to a new deception regarding their own reality. They would be led to fight against windmills.

But, having acknowledged this danger, it is important to remember also that the poor countries would err in not following these events closely since their future depends at least partially upon what happens on the domestic scene in the dominant countries. Their own efforts at liberation cannot be indifferent to that proclaimed by growing minorities in rich nations. There are, moreover, valuable lessons to be learned by the revolutionaries of the countries on the periphery, who could in turn use them as corrective measures in the difficult task of building a new society.

What is at stake in the South as well as in the North, in the West as well as the East, on the periphery and in the center is the possibility of enjoying a truly human existence, a free life, a dynamic liberty which is related to history as a conquest. We have today an ever-clearer vision of this dynamism and this conquest, but their roots stretch into the past.

The fifteenth and sixteenth centuries are important milestones in man's understanding of himself. His relationship with nature changed substantially with the emergence of experimental science and the techniques of manipulation derived from it. Relying on these achievements, man abandoned his former image of the world and himself. Gilson expresses this idea in a well-known phrase: "It is because of its physics that metaphysics grows old." Because of science man took a step forward and began to regard himself in a different way.[19] This process indicates why the best philosophical tradition is not merely an armchair product; it is rather the reflective and thematic awareness of man's experience of his relationships with nature and with other men. And these relationships are interpreted and at the same time modified by advances in technological and scientific knowledge.[20]

Descartes is one of the great names of the new physics which altered man's relationship to nature. He laid the cornerstone of a philosophical reflection which stressed the primacy of thought and of "clear and distinct ideas," and so highlighted the creative aspects of human subjectivity.[21] Kant's "Copernican Revolution" strengthened and systematized this point of view. For him our concept ought not to conform to the objects, but rather "the objects, or, in which is the same thing, that experience, which alone as given objects they are *cognized*, must conform to my conceptions." The reason is that "we only cognize in things *a priori* that which we ourselves place in them."[22] Kant was aware that this leads to a "new method" of thought, to a knowledge which is critical of its foundations and thus abandons its naiveté and enters an adult stage.

Hegel followed this approach, introducing with vitality and urgency the theme of history.[23] To a great extent his philosophy is a reflection on the French Revolution. This historical event had vast repercussions, for it proclaimed the right of every man to participate in the direction of the society to which he belongs. For Hegel man is aware of himself "only by being acknowledged or 'recognized' " by another consciousness. But this being recognized by another presupposes an initial conflict, "a life-and-death struggle," because it is "solely by risking life that freedom is obtained."[24]

Through the lord-bondsman dialectic (resulting from this original confrontation), the historical process will then appear as the genesis of consciousness and therefore of the gradual liberation of man.[25] Through the dialectical process man constructs himself and attains a real awareness of his own being; he liberates himself in the acquisition of genuine freedom which through work transforms the world and educates man.[26] For Hegel "world history is the progression of the awareness of freedom." Moreover, the driving force of history is the difficult conquest of freedom, hardly perceptible in its initial stages. It is the passage from awareness of freedom to real freedom. "It is Freedom in itself that comprises within itself the infinite necessity of bringing itself to consciousness and thereby, since knowledge about itself is its very nature, to reality."[27] Thus man gradually takes hold of the reins of his own destiny. He looks ahead and turns towards a society in which he will be free of all alienation and servitude. This focus will initiate a new dimension in philosophy: social criticism.[28]

Marx deepened and renewed this line of thought in his unique way.[29] But this required what has been called an "epistemological break" (a notion taken from Gaston Bachelard) with previous thought. The new attitude was expressed clearly in the famous *Theses on Feuerbach*, in which Marx presented concisely but penetratingly the essential elements of his approach. In them, especially in the First Thesis, Marx situated himself equidistant between the old materialism and idealism; more precisely, he presented his position as the dialectical transcendence of both. Of the first he retained the affirmation of the objectivity of the external world; of the second he kept man's transforming capacity. For Marx, to know was something indissolubly linked to the transformation of the world through work. Basing his thought on these first intuitions, he went on to construct a scientific understanding of historical reality. He analyzed capitalistic society, in which were found concrete instances of the exploitation of man by his fellows and of one social class by another. Pointing the way towards an era in history when man can live humanly, Marx created categories which allowed for the elaboration of a science of history.[30]

The door was opened for science to help man take one more step on the road of critical thinking. It made him more aware of the socio-economic determinants of his ideological creations and therefore freer and more lucid in relation to them. But at the same time these new insights enabled man to have greater control and rational grasp of his historical initiatives. (This interpretation is valid unless of course one holds a dogmatic and mechanistic interpretation of history.) These initiatives ought to assure the change from the capitalistic mode of production to the socialistic mode, that is to say, to one oriented towards a society in which man can begin to live freely and humanly. He will have controlled nature, created the conditions for a socialized production of wealth, done away with private acquisition of excessive wealth, and established socialism.

But modern man's aspirations include not only liberation from *exterior* pressures which prevent his fulfillment as a member of a certain social class, country, or society. He seeks likewise an *interior* liberation, in an individual and intimate dimension; he seeks liberation not only on a social plane but also on a psychological. He seeks an interior freedom understood however not as an ideological evasion from social confrontation or as the internalization of a situation of dependency.[31] Rather it must be in relation to the real world of the human psyche as understood since Freud.

A new frontier was in effect opened up when Freud highlighted the unconscious determinants of human behavior, with repression as the central element of man's psychic make-up. Repression is the result of the conflict between instinctive drives and the cultural and ethical demands of the social environment.[32] For Freud, unconscious motivations exercise a tyrannical power and can produce aberrant behavior. This behavior is controllable only if the subject becomes aware of these motivations through an accurate reading of the new language of meanings created by the unconscious. Since Hegel we have seen *conflict* used as a germinal explanatory category and *awareness* as a step in the conquest of freedom. In Freud however they appear in a psychological process which ought also to lead to a fuller liberation of man.

The scope of liberation on the collective and historical level does not always and satisfactorily include psychological liberation. Psychological liberation includes dimensions which do not exist in or are not sufficiently integrated with collective, historical liberation.[33] We are not speaking here, however, of facilely separating them or putting them in opposition to one another. "It seems to me," writes David Cooper, "that a cardinal failure of all past revolutions has been the dissociation of liberation on the mass social level, i.e. liberation of whole classes in economic and political terms, and liberation on the level of the individual and the concrete groups in which he is directly engaged. If we are to talk of revolution today our talk will be meaningless unless we effect some union between the macro-social and micro-social, and between 'inner reality' and 'outer reality.' "[34] Moreover, alienation and exploitation as well as the very struggle for liberation from them have ramifications on the personal and psychological planes which it would be dangerous to overlook in the process of constructing a new society and a new man.[35] These personal aspects—considered not as excessively privatized, but rather as encompassing all human dimensions—are also under consideration in the contemporary debate concerning greater participation of all in political activity. This is so even in a socialist society.

In this area, Marcuse's attempt, under the influence of Hegel and Marx, to use the psychoanalytical categories for social criticism is important. Basing his observations on a work which Freud himself did not hold in high regard, *Civilization and its Discontents*,[36] Marcuse analyzes the *over-repressive* character of the affluent society and envisions the possibility of a non-repressive society,[37] a possibility skeptically denied by Freud. Marcuse's analyses of advanced industrial society, capitalistic or socialistic, lead him to denounce the emergence of a one-dimensional and oppressive society.[38] In order to achieve this non-repressive society, however, it will be necessary to challenge the values espoused by the society which denies man the possibility of living freely. Marcuse labels this the Great Refusal: "the specter of a revolution which subordinates the development of the productive forces and higher standards of living to the requirements of creating solidarity for the human species, for abolishing poverty and misery beyond all national frontiers and spheres of interest, for the attainment of peace."[39]

We are not suggesting, of course, that we should endorse without question every aspect of this development of ideas. There are ambiguities, critical observations to be made, and points to be clarified. Many ideas must be reconsidered in the light of a history that advances inexorably, simultaneously confirming and rejecting previous assertions. Ideas must be reconsidered too in light of praxis, which is the proving ground of all theory, and in light of socio-cultural realities very different from those from which the ideas emerged. But all this should not lead us to an attitude of distrustful reserve toward these ideas; rather it should suggest that the task to be undertaken is formidable. And the task is all the more urgent because these reflections are attempts to express a deeply-rooted sentiment in today's masses: the aspiration to liberation. This aspiration is still confusedly perceived, but there is an ever greater awareness of it. Furthermore, for many people in various ways this aspiration—in Vietnam or Brazil, New York or Prague—has become a norm for their behavior and a sufficient reason to lead lives of dedication. Their commitment is the backbone which validates and gives historical viability to the development of the ideas outlined above.

To conceive of history as a process of the liberation of man is to consider freedom as a historical conquest; it is to understand that the step from an abstract to a real freedom is not taken without a struggle against all the forces that oppress man, a struggle full of pitfalls, detours, and temptations to run away. The goal is not only better living conditions, a radical change of structures, a social revolution; it is much more: the continuous creation, never ending, of a new way to be a man, a *permanent cultural revolution.*

In other words, what is at stake above all is a dynamic and historical conception of man, oriented definitively and creatively toward his future, acting in the present for the sake of tomorrow.[40] Teilhard de Chardin has remarked that man has taken hold of the reins of evolution. History, contrary to essentialist and static thinking, is not the development of potentialities preexistent in man; it is rather the conquest of new, qualitatively different ways of being a man in order to achieve an ever more total and   complete fulfillment of the individual in solidarity with all mankind.

The Concept of Liberation Theologically Considered

Although we will consider liberation from a theological perspective more extensively later,[41] it is important at this time to attempt an initial treatment in the light of what we have just discussed.

The term *development* is relatively new in the texts of the ecclesiastical magisterium.[42] Except for a brief reference by Pius XII,[43] the subject is broached for the first time by John XXIII in the encyclical letter *Mater et Magistra*.[44] *Pacem in terris* gives the term special attention. *Gaudium et spes* dedicates a whole section to it, though the treatment is not original. All these documents stress the urgency of eliminating the existing injustices and the need for an economic development geared to the service of man. Finally, *Populorum progressio* discusses development as its central theme. Here the language and ideas are clearer; the adjective *integral* is added to development, putting things in a different context and opening new perspectives.

These new viewpoints were already hinted at in the sketchy discussion of Vatican Council II on dependence and liberation. *Gaudium et spes* points out that "nations on the road to progress . . . continually fall behind while very often their *dependence* on wealthier nations deepens more rapidly, even in the economic sphere" (no. 9). Later it acknowledges that "although nearly all peoples have gained their independence, it is still far from true that they are free from excessive inequalities and from every form of *undue dependence*" (no. 85).

These assertions should lead to a discernment of the need to be free from the dependence, to be liberated from it. The same *Gaudium et spes* on two occasions touches on liberation and laments the fact that it is seen exclusively as the fruit of human effort: "Many look forward to a genuine and total *emancipation* of humanity wrought solely by human effort. They are convinced that the future rule of man over the earth will satisfy every desire of his heart" (no. 10). Or it is concerned that liberation be reduced to a purely economic and social level: "Among the forms of modern atheism is that which anticipates the *liberation* of man especially through his economic and social emancipation" (no. 20).[45] These assertions presuppose, negatively speaking, that liberation must be placed in a wider context; they criticize a narrow vision. They allow, therefore, for the possibility of a "genuine and total" liberation.

Unfortunately, this wider perspective is not elaborated. We find some indications, however, in the texts in which *Gaudium et spes* speaks of the birth of a "new humanism, one in which man is defined first of all by his responsibility toward his brothers and toward history" (no. 55). There is a need for men who are makers of history, "men who are truly new and artisans of a new humanity" (no. 30), men moved by the desire to build a really new society. Indeed, the conciliar document asserts that beneath economic and political demands "lies a deeper and more widespread longing. Persons and societies thirst for a full and free life worthy of man—one in which they can subject to their own welfare all that the modern world can offer them so abundantly" (no. 9).

All this is but a beginning. It is an oft-noted fact that *Gaudium et spes* in general offers a rather irenic description of the human situation; it touches up the uneven spots, smoothes the rough edges, avoids the more conflictual aspects, and stays away from the sharper confrontations among social classes and countries.

The encyclical *Populorum progressio* goes a step further. In a somewhat isolated text it speaks clearly of "building a world where every man, no matter what his race, religion or nationality, can live a fully human life, freed from servitude imposed on him by other men or by natural forces over which he has not sufficient control" (no. 47).[46] It is unfortunate, however, that this idea was not expanded in the encyclical. From this point of view, *Populorum progressio* is a transitional document. Although it energetically denounces the "international imperialism of money," "situations whose injustice cries to heaven," and the growing gap between rich and poor countries, ultimately it addresses itself to the great ones of this world urging them to carry out the necessary changes.[47] The outright use of the language of liberation, instead of its mere suggestion, would have given a more decided and direct thrust in favor of the

oppressed, encouraging them to break with their present situation and take control of their own destiny.[48]

The theme of liberation appears more completely discussed
in the message from eighteen bishops of the Third World, published as a specific response to the call made by *Populorum progressio.*[49] It is also treated frequently—almost to the point of
being a synthesis of its message—in the conclusions of the Second
General Conference of Latin American Bishops held in Medellín,
Colombia, in 1968,[50] which have more doctrinal authority than
the eighteen bishops' message. In both these documents the focus
has changed. The situation is not judged from the point of view
of the countries at the center, but rather of those on the
periphery, providing insiders' experience of their anguish and
aspirations.

The product of a profound historical movement, this aspiration
to liberation is beginning to be accepted by the Christian community as a sign of the times, as a call to commitment and
interpretation. The Biblical message, which presents the work
of Christ as a liberation, provides the framework for this interpretation. Theology seems to have avoided for a long time reflecting
on the conflictual character of human history, the confrontations
among men, social classes, and countries. St. Paul continuously
reminds us, however, of the paschal core of Christian existence
and of all of human life: the passage from the old man to the
new, from sin to grace, from slavery to freedom.

"For freedom Christ has set us free" (Gal. 5:1), St. Paul tells
us. He refers here to liberation from sin insofar as it represents
a selfish turning in upon oneself. To sin is to refuse to love one's
neighbors and, therefore, the Lord himself. Sin—a breach of
friendship with God and others—is according to the Bible the
ultimate cause of poverty, injustice, and the oppression in which
men live. In describing sin as the ultimate cause we do not in
any way negate the structural reasons and the objective determinants leading to these situations. It does, however, emphasize
the fact that things do not happen by chance and that behind
an unjust structure there is a personal or collective will responsible—a willingness to reject God and neighbor. It suggests,
likewise, that a social transformation, no matter how radical
it may be, does not automatically achieve the suppression of
all evils.

But St. Paul asserts not only that Christ liberated us; he also
tells us that he did it in order that we might be free. Free for
what? Free to love. "In the language of the Bible," writes
Bonhoeffer, "freedom is not something man has for himself but
something he has for others .... It is not a possession, a presence,
an object, ... but a relationship and nothing else. In truth, freedom is a relationship between two persons. Being free means
'being free for the other,' because the other has bound me to
him. Only in relationship with the other am I free."[51] The freedom
to which we are called presupposes the going out of oneself,
the breaking down of our selfishness and of all the structures
that support our selfishness; the foundation of this freedom is
openness to others. The fullness of liberation—a free gift from
Christ—is communion with God and with other men.

CONCLUSION

Summarizing what has been said above, we can distinguish
three reciprocally interpenetrating levels of meaning of the term
liberation, or in other words, three approaches to the process
of liberation.

In the first place, *liberation* expresses the aspirations of
oppressed peoples and social classes, emphasizing the conflictual
aspect of the economic, social, and political process which puts
them at odds with wealthy nations and oppressive classes. In
contrast, the word *development*, and above all the policies characterized as developmentalist [*desarrollista*], appear somewhat
aseptic, giving a false picture of a tragic and conflictual reality.
The issue of development does in fact find its true place in the
more universal, profound, and radical perspective of liberation.
It is only within this framework that *development* finds its true
meaning and possibilities of accomplishing something worth-
while.

At a deeper level, *liberation* can be applied to an understanding
of history. Man is seen as assuming conscious responsibility for
his own destiny. This understanding provides a dynamic context
and broadens the horizons of the desired social changes. In this
perspective the unfolding of all of man's dimensions is demand-
ed—a man who makes himself throughout his life and throughout
history. The gradual conquest of true freedom leads to the cre-

ation of a new man and a qualitatively different society. This vision provides, therefore, a better understanding of what in fact is at stake in our times.

Finally, the world *development* to a certain extent limits and obscures the theological problems implied in the process designated by this term.[52] On the contrary the word *liberation* allows for another approach leading to the Biblical sources which inspire the presence and action of man in history. In the Bible, Christ is presented as the one who brings us liberation. Christ the Savior liberates man from sin, which is the ultimate root of all disruption of friendship and of all injustice and oppression. Christ makes man truly free, that is to say, he enables man to live in communion with him; and this is the basis for all human brotherhood.

This is not a matter of three parallel or chronologically successive processes, however. There are three levels of meaning of a single, complex process, which finds its deepest sense and its full realization in the saving work of Christ. These levels of meaning, therefore, are interdependent. A comprehensive view of the matter presupposes that all three aspects can be considered together. In this way two pitfalls will be avoided: first, *idealist* or *spiritualist* approaches, which are nothing but ways of evading a harsh and demanding reality, and second, shallow analyses and programs of short-term effect initiated under the pretext of meeting immediate needs.[53]

NOTES

1. See Thomas Suavet, "Développement," in *Dictionnaire économique et social*, 2nd ed. (Paris: Économie et Humanisme, Les Éditions Ouvrières, 1962). For L. J. Lebret, "the idea of development originates in 1945" (*Dynamique concrète du développement* [Paris: Les Éditions Ouvrières, 1967], p. 38), but he does not indicate the source of this information. See also the systematic study of Jacques Freyssinet, *Le concept du sousdéveloppement* (Paris: Mouton, 1966).

2. See *Theorie der Wirtschaftlichen Entwicklung* (Leipzig: Dunker & Humblot, 1912); English edition: *The Theory of Economic Development: An Inquiry into Profits, Capital, Credit, Interest, and the Business Cycle*, trans. Redvers Opie (Cambridge: Harvard University Press, 1934).

3. *Théorie de l'évolution économique* [French translation] (Paris: Dalloz, 1935).

4. *Teoría del desenvolvimiento económico* [Spanish translation] (Mexico, D.F.: Fondo de Cultura Económica, 1944).

5. *The Conditions of Economic Progress* (London: Macmillan and Co., 1940).

6. See in this regard Odette Guitard, *Bandoeng et le réveil des anciens peuples colonisés* (Paris: Presses Universitaires de France, 1961).

7. "The word *development* has not been in use long enough for its meaning to have become absolutely determined" (Suavet, "Développement").

8. Among them is a work which due to special circumstances and carefully planned methods of distribution became widely known in the underdeveloped countries: Walt W. Rostow's *The Stages of Economic Growth: A Non-Communist Manifesto* (New York: Cambridge University Press, 1960).

9. "Development is a total social process, and only for methodological convenience or in a partial sense can one speak of economic, political, cultural, and social development" (Helio Jaguaribe, *Economic & Political Development: A Theoretical Approach & a Brazilian Case Study* [Cambridge: Harvard University Press, 1968], p. 4). See also Giorgio Ceriani Sebregondi, *Sullo sviluppo della società italiana* (Turin: Boringhieri, 1965); Raymond Barre, *Le développement économique: Analyse et politique* (Paris: Cahiers de l'Institute de Science Économique Apliquée, 1958).

10. See below Chapter 6.

11. "La notion de développement," in *L'économie de XXe siècle*, 2nd ed., enl., (Paris: Presses Universitaires de France, 1964), pp. 155 and 171. Perroux had already addressed himself to this perspective in "From the Avarice of Nations to an Economy for Mankind," *Cross Currents* 3, no. 3 (Spring 1953): 193-207. "Development for us," writes Lebret, "is *the object itself of human economics* .... This is the discipline of the transition ... from a less human to a more human condition as fast and as cheaply as possible, bearing in mind the solidarity among subpopulations and populations ..." (*Dynamique concrète*, p. 28). The same idea is expressed in another definition of development by the same author: "To have more in order to be more." As is well known, both of these expressions were used in the encyclical *Populorum progressio*. See also Luis Velaochaga, *Concepción integral del desarrollo*, pamphlet (Lima: Universidad Católica, 1967).

12. See the themes of the "new man" and the "whole man" of communist society. In it, according to an early text of Karl Marx, man will be defined not by what he has but by what he is: "... The positive transcendence of private property ... should not be conceived merely in the sense of *immediate, one-sided gratification*—merely in the sense of *possession*, of *having*. Man appropriates his total *essence* in a total manner, that is to say, as a whole man" (*Economic and Philosophic Manuscripts of 1844*, ed. Dirk J. Struik, trans. Martin Milligan [New York: International Publishers, 1964], p. 138; the final italics are ours). See also Garaudy, *Perspectives*, pp. 347-51; Henri Lefebvre, *Dialectical Materialism*, trans. John Sturrock (London: Jonathan Cape, 1968), pp. 148-66; Karel Kosik, *Dialéctica de lo concreto* (Mexico D.F.: Grijalbo, 1963), translated from the Czech, especially pp. 235-69.

13. An example of this inevitable progression to a wider context is the following paragraph of Vincent Cosmao: "We are therefore led beyond the integration of social development with economic development, or in other words of the noneconomic factors with economic development, to a vision of history in which mankind collectively takes hold of its collective destiny, humanizing it for the benefit of the whole man and of all men" ("Les exigences du développement au service de l'homme," *Parole et Mission* 10, no. 39 [October 15, 1967]: 581).

14. See the anthology *Del desarrollo al desarrollismo* (Buenos Aires: Galerna,

1969), especially the article by Juan Pablo Franco, "Relexiones críticas en torno al desarrollismo."

15. See Chapter 6 below.

16. As regards Latin America, the International Monetary Fund (IMF), the Inter-American Development Bank (IBD), the Alliance for Progress, and on another level the Economic Commission for Latin America (ECLA), especially in its first period.

17. Related aspects of this problem as they apply specifically to Latin America will be dealt with in Chapter 6 below.

18. In connection with the events in France of May 1968, Marcuse has said, "The students have not rebelled against a poor and badly organized society, but against a quite wealthy one; it is well organized in its luxury and its wastefulness, although 25% of the population of the country live in poverty-ridden ghettos. The rebellion does not oppose the grief caused by this society, but its benefits. It is a new phenomenon, peculiar to what is called the affluent society." (Quoted in J. M. Palmier, *Sur Marcuse* [Paris: Union Générale d'Éditions, 1968] p. 167). In a similar vein Paul Ricoeur writes, "This revolution attacks capitalism, not only because of its failure to achieve social justice, but also because of its success in seducing people into its inhuman design for quantitative well-being .... In the face of this meaningless society, the revolution hopes to give more importance to the creation of well-being, of ideas, of values, rather than to their consumption" ("Réforme et révolution dans l'Université," *Esprit* 36, no. 372 [June-July 1968] 987).

19. Concerning the dependence of man's self-understanding on the man-nature relationship, see Edward Schillebeeckx, "L'immagine di Dio in un mondo secolarizzato," *Ricerca* (Rome), March 31, 1969; reproduced in *Processo alla religione* (Rome: IDOC, 1968). This point has been heavily emphasized by Marx.

20. "For philosophy to be born or reborn it is necessary that the sciences be. This is perhaps why philosophy in the strict sense did not come into being until Plato's time, stimulated by the existence of Greek mathematics; it was tranformed by Descartes, its modern revolution having been provoked by the physics of Galileo; Kant made it over under the influence of the Newtonian discovery; it was remodeled by Husserl, prompted by the first axiomatics, etc." (Louis Althusser, *Lénine et la philosophie* [Paris: François Maspero, 1969], p. 27). For a severe critique of the historical aspects of the relationship between science and philosophy according to Althusser, see André Regnier, "Les surprises de l'idéologie: Heisenberg et Althusser," *L'Homme et la Société*, no. 15 (January-March, 1970), pp. 247-50.

21. According to J. B. Metz, St. Thomas Aquinas initiated the anthropological viewpoint in opposition to the cosmological vision of the ancient world; see *Christliche Anthropozentrik: Üeber die Denkform des Thomas von Aquin* (Munich: Kösel, 1962).

22. "The Critique of Pure Reason," Preface to the second edition, 1787, in *Kant*, Great Books of the Western World, vol. 24, p. 7.

23. The point of view of a philosophy of history is already present in Kant (orientation toward the realm of ends) and even before him. But the systematic organization of the subject was done by Hegel. After Hegel, modern awareness will be a "historical awareness." See Henrique de Lima Vaz, *Cristianismo e conciencia histórica* (São Paulo, 1963), p. 20, reproduced in a collection of articles by the same author, *Ontologia e história* (São Paulo: Duas Cidades, 1968).

24. *The Phenomenology of Mind*, trans. J. B. Baillie (New York: The Humanities Press, Inc., 1964), pp. 229, 232-33.

25. This view has been especially stressed by Alexandre Kojève, *Introduction to the Reading of Hegel*, ed. Allan Bloom, trans. James H. Nichols, Jr. (New York: Basic Books, Inc., 1969).

26. Hegel, *Phenomenology*, pp. 238-39. See Kojève's commentary on this passage in *Introduction*, pp. 48 ff. Karl Marx in an early work praised this Hegelian intuition: "The outstanding achievement of Hegel's *Phenomenology* ... is ... that Hegel conceives the self-creation of man as a process.... He thus grasps the essence of *labor* and comprehends objective man—true, because real man—as the outcome of man's *own labor (Manuscripts of 1844*, p. 177).

27. *Reason in History*, trans. Robert S. Hartman (New York: Liberal Arts Press, 1953), p. 25. "Universal history ... shows the development of the consciousness of freedom ... " ("The Philosophy of History" in *Hegel*, Great Books, p. 182).

28. This matter is studied by Marcuse from the perspective of a history of ideas and in a personal fashion (Herbert Marcuse, *Reason and Revolution: Hegel and the Rise of Social Theory* [Boston: Beacon Press, 1941]).

29. We are not implying that Marx's work is but a socio-economic presentation of Hegelian thought. His originality is indisputable, although it has given rise to a variety of interpretations. See for example the different positions of Louis Althusser, *For Marx*, trans. Ben Brewster (New York: Pantheon Books, 1969); Ernest Mandel, *The Formation of the Economic Thought of Karl Marx*, trans. Brian Pearce (New York: Monthly Review Press, 1971); Kosik, *Dialéctica*.

30. It is common knowledge that Hegel did not deal with economics, especially in his youth. See György Lukács, *Der junge Hegel und die Probleme der kapitalistischen Gesselschaft* (Berlin: Aufbau-Verlag, 1954). See also Jean Hyppolite, *Studies on Marx and Hegel*, trans. John O'Neill (New York: Basic Books, Inc., 1969). At no time is this part of his work as rigorous as Marx's; furthermore, it can be stated that it is thanks to the latter that the works of Hegel's youth have been reevaluated.

31. This is the kind of evasion Georges Politzer referred to in his polemical essay on Bergson's philosophy: "In a word, the slave is freer insofar as he is more a slave, that is to say, the more interior and profound in his submission. It is not by escaping that the prisoner recovers his freedom, but by becoming a voluntary prisoner. It is not by preaching rebellion that one propagandizes freedom, but by preaching total submission. Freedom will reign only when slaves have the souls of slaves" (*Le Bergsonisme: Une mystification philosophique* [Paris: Éditions Sociales, 1949], p. 77).

32. The idea of psychic conflict is sketched for the first time by Freud in 1892 (J. M. Charcot, *Poliklinische Vorträge*, trans., intr., and notes by Sigmund Freud [Leipzig and Vienna: Deuticke, 1892-94], p. 137, translator's note; included in *The Standard Edition of the Complete Psychological Works of Sigmund Freud*, ed. James Strachey, vol. 1, *Pre-Psycho-Analytic Publications and Unpublished Drafts* [London: The Hogarth Press and the Institute of Psycho-Analysis, 1966], p. 138). The idea grew and gained precision in the years immediately following. It was an important and definitive gain. The forces involved in this confrontation were initially described in terms of instinctive drives and social pressures; later, after much correction, they were expressed in the statements of the pleasure principle and the reality principle.

33. See in this connection the observations of Harvey Cox in "Political Theology for the United States," in *Projections: Shaping an American Theology for the Future*, ed. Thomas F. O'Meara and Donald M. Weisser (Garden City, N.Y.: Doubleday & Company, Inc., 1970), pp. 41-49.

34. "Introduction" in the anthology (Stokely Carmichael, John Gerassi, Paul Sweezy, Herbert Marcuse, Lucien Goldmann et al.) *To Free a Generation: The Dialectics of Liberation*, ed. David Cooper (London: Collier Books, 1968), pp. 9-10.

35. The life and work of Frantz Fanon were generously and creatively dedicated to this problem; see *The Wretched of the Earth*, trans. Constance Farrington (New York: Grove Press, 1963) and *Studies in a Dying Colonialism*, trans. Haakon Chevalier (New York: Monthly Review Press, 1965). For a study of Fanon, see Renate Zahar, *Colonialismo y enajenación: Contribución a la teoría política de Frantz Fanon* (Mexico, D.F.: Siglo Veintiuno, 1970).

36. See Freud's letter of July 28, 1929, included in Ernst Jones, M.D., *The Life and Work of Sigmund Freud*, 3 vols. (New York: Basic Books, Inc., 1957), 3: 448.

37. *Eros and Civilization* (Boston: Beacon Press, 1955).

38. *One Dimensional Man* (Boston: Beacon press, 1964).

39. *An Essay on Liberation* (Boston: Beacon Press, 1969), pp. ix-x.

40. See among recent authors the inspiring studies of Ernst Bloch, *Das Prinzip Hoffnung* (Franfurt: Suhrkamp Verlag, 1959); in English see his *Man on his Own* (New York: Herder and Herder, 1970), and *On Karl Marx*, trans. John Maxwell (New York: Herder and Herder, 1971). See also Jürgen Moltmann, *Theology of Hope*, referred to below in Chapter 11.

41. See Chapter 9.

42. The work of Jean-Yves Calvez, S.J., and Jacques Perrin, S.J., *The Church and Social Justice: The Social Teaching of the Popes from Leo XIII to Pius XII (1878-1958)* (Chicago: Regnery Company, 1961), contains no reference to this idea.

43. See René Laurentin, *Liberation, Development, and Salvation*, pp. 102-03.

44. There is an entire chapter devoted to it in the sequel to the work cited in note 42—first published four years later and dedicated to John XXIII: Jean-Yves Calvez, S.J., *The Social Thought of John XXIII: Mater et Magistra*, trans. George J. M. McKenzie, S.M. (Chicago: Henry Regnery Company, 1964).

45. In the texts quoted here the italics are ours.

46. In a less important statement of two years before, there is an interesting text of Paul VI regarding the consequences of technological progress on work styles: "No one foresaw that new work styles would awaken in the worker the awareness of his *alienation*, that is to say, the will no longer to work for others, with instruments belonging to others, not alone but with others. Did no one think that the desire for an economic and *social* liberation would arise, hindering his appreciation of the moral and spiritual redemption offered through faith in Christ?" (Allocuation of May 1, 1965, in *L'Osservatore Romano*, May 3, 1965; the italics are ours).

47. See the analyses of René Dumont in "Populorum Progressio: Un pas en avant, trop timide," *Esprit* 35, no. 361 (June 1967): 1092-96; Raymundo Ozanam de Andrade, " 'Populorum Progressio': Neocapitalismo ou revolução," *Paz e Terra* (Rio de Janeiro), no. 4 (August 1967), pp. 209-21; François Perroux, " 'Populorum Progressio': L'encyclique de la Résurrection," *L'Église dans le monde de ce temps*, 3:201-12; Herné Chaigne, "Force et faiblesse de l'encyclique," *Frères du Monde*, nos. 46-47 (1967), pp. 58-74, which proposes "to radicalize the encyclical."

48. It is not our intention to negate the values of *Populorum progressio*, highlighted for example by Ricardo Cetrulo, S.J., " 'Populorum progressio': De la 'animación' de la socieded al análisis de situación," *Vispera* (Montevideo), no. 3 (October 1967), pp. 5-10. The author comments perceptively on the change of style and perspective in relation to preceding encyclicals. Regarding the encyclical's step forward in the doctrine of the ownership of means of production, see *Comen-*

tarios de cuadernos para el diálogo a la Populorum progressio (Madrid :Ed. Cuadernos para el Diálogo, 1967), especially the observations of Joaquín Ruiz-Giménez (pp. 16-20) and Eduardo Cierco (pp. 31-49). See also the thought-provoking and warm commentary of the Italian Marxist Lucio Lombardo Radice, *Socialismo e libertà* (Rome: Editori Riuniti, 1968), pp. 136-48. Pope Paul VI has taken up these subjects in his recent and in many ways innovative letter to Cardinal Roy, *Octogesima adveniens.* There he says that "today men yearn to *free* themselves from need and dependence" (no. 45; our italics).

49. Reprinted, among others, in *Between Honesty and Hope: Documents from and about the Church in Latin America. Issued at Lima by the Peruvian Bishops' Commission for Social Action,* trans. John Drury (Maryknoll, New York: Maryknoll Publications, 1970), pp. 3-12.

50. We will study these texts in greater detail in Chapter 7.

51. *Creation and Fall, Temptation* (New York: The Macmillan Company, 1966), p. 37. Paul VI suggestively points out that freedom "will develop in its deepest human reality: to involve itself and to spend itself in building up active and lived solidarity." And he adds, "It is by losing himself in God who sets him free that man finds true freedom, renewed in the death and resurrection of the Lord" *Octogesima adveniens,* no. 47).

52. See Laurentin, *Liberation, Development, and Salvation,* p. 63 and also p. 39.

53. An old comparison unexpectedly presented by St. Augustine of Hippo in his own inimitable style is related to the intimate relationship of the different levels of meaning of the term *liberation:* the soul under the control of sin, he says, resembles a country subdued by the enemy. See his commentary on Psalm 9, no. 8, quoted by Congar in "Christianisme et liberation de l'homme," *Masses Ouvrières* (Paris), no. 258, (December, 1969), p. 3.

PART 2

POSING THE PROBLEM

The foregoing comments lead us to reflect, in the light of the Word of the Lord, on the complex process of liberation which we have attempted to sketch; that is to say, they lead us to a *theology of liberation.*

This reflection must be rooted in the presence and action of Christians—in solidarity with others—in the world today, especially as participants in the process of liberation which is being effected in Latin America. But first we will attempt to state the problem we are considering as precisely as possible. Throughout the life of the Church, this problem has received different responses which are still in one way or another significant because of the part they play in the concrete activity of many Christians. An analysis of these responses can therefore help us to understand the features which currently characterize the problem.

CHAPTER THREE

THE PROBLEM

To speak about a theology of liberation is to seek an answer to the following question: what relation is there between salvation and the historical process of the liberation of man? In other words, we must attempt to discern the interrelationship among the different meanings of the term *liberation* which we indicated above. The scope of the problem will be clarified in the course of this work, but it might be helpful to point out at this stage some of its fundamental features.

The question is essentially traditional. Theological reflection has always at least implicitly addressed itself to it. In recent years the theology of temporal realities[1]—an expression which was never fully accepted—attempted to deal with it in its own way. Other attempts have been the theology of history[2] and, more recently, the theology of development.[3] From another viewpoint, the question is also considered by "political theology";[4] and it is partially treated by the much-debated—and debatable—theology of revolution.[5]

We are dealing here with the classic question of the relation between faith and human existence, between faith and social reality, between faith and political action, or in other words, between the Kingdom of God and the building up of the world. Within the scope of this problem the classical theme of the Church-society or Church-world relationship is also considered.

Its perennial quality, however, must not make us forget the new aspects which the traditional question takes on today.

Under new forms it maintains all its topicality. J.B. Metz asserted recently that, "despite the many discussions about the Church and the world, there is nothing more unclear than the nature of their relationship to one another."[6] But if this is so, if the problem continues to be current and yet the attempted responses are not wholly satisfactory, it is perhaps because as traditionally stated the problem has become tangential to a new and changing reality; as traditionally stated the problem does not go deep enough. In studying these questions, the texts and especially the spirit of Vatican II are undoubtedly necessary as points of reference. Nevertheless, the new design of the problem was—and could only be—partially present in the conciliar documents. "It seems to me of utmost importance," said Karl Rahner recently, "to agree on the fact that the ideas explicitly considered during Vatican Council II do not actually represent the central problems of the postconciliar Church."[7] It is not enough to say that Christians should not "shirk" their earthly responsibilties or that these have a "certain relationship" to salvation. *Gaudium et spes* itself sometimes gives the impression of remaining at this level of generalization.[8] More regrettably, the same is true of a considerable number of commentators. The task of contemporary theology is to elucidate the current state of these problems, drawing with sharper lines the terms in which they are expressed.[9] Only thus will it be possible to confront the concrete challenges of the present.[10]

In the current statement of the problem, one fact is evident: the social praxis of contemporary man has begun to reach maturity. It is the behavior of man ever more conscious of being an active subject of history; he is ever more articulate in the face of social injustice and of all repressive forces which stand in the way of his fulfillment; he is ever more determined to participate both in the transformation of social structures and in effective political action. It was above all the great social revolutions—the French and the Russian, for example, to mention only two important milestones—together with the whole process of revolutionary ferment that they initiated which wrested—or at least began to—political decisions from the hands of an elite who were "destined" to rule. Up to that time the great majority of people did not participate in political decisions or did so only sporadically and formally. Although it is true that the majority of people are far from this level of awareness, it is also certain that they have had confused glimpses of it and are oriented in its direction. The phenomenon that we designate with the term "politicization"—which is increasing in breadth and depth in Latin America—is one of the manifestations of this complex process. And in the struggle for the liberation of the oppressed classes on this continent—which is implicit in the effective and human political responsibility of all—people are searching out new paths.

Human reason has become political reason. For the contemporary historical consciousness, things political are not only those which one attends to during the free time afforded by his private life; nor are they even a well-defined area of human existence. The construction—from its economic bases—of the "polis," of a society in which people can live in solidarity, is a dimension which encompasses and severely conditions all of man's activity. It is the sphere for the exercise of a critical freedom which is won down through history. It is the universal determinant and the collective arena for human fulfillment.[11] Only within this broad meaning of the political sphere can we situate the more precise notion of "politics," as an orientation to power. For Max Weber this orientation constitutes the typical characteristics of political activity. The concrete forms taken on by this quest for and exercise of political power are varied. But they are all based on the profound aspiration of man, who wants to take hold of the reins of his own life and be the artisan of his own destiny. Nothing lies outside the political sphere understood in this way. Everything has a political color. It is always in the political fabric—and never outside of it—that a person emerges as a free and responsible being, as a person in relationship with other people, as someone who takes on a historical task. Personal relationships themselves acquire an ever-increasing political dimension. Men enter into relationships among themselves through political means. This is what Ricoeur calls the "lasting and stable" relationships of the socius, as opposed to the "fleeting and fragile" relationships of the neighbor.[12] To this effect, M.D. Chenu writes: "Man has always enjoyed this social dimension, since he is social by his very nature. But today, not accidentally but structurally, the collective event lends scope and intensity to the social dimension. What is collective as such has human value and is, therefore, a means and object of love. Human love treads these 'lasting' paths, these organizations of distributive justice, and these administrative systems."[13]

In addition to this universality of the political sphere, we are faced with an increasing radicalization of social praxis. Contemporary man has begun to lose his naiveté as he confronts economic and socio-cultural determinants; the deep causes of the situation in which he finds himself are becoming clearer. He realizes that to attack these deep causes is the indispensable prerequisite for radical change. And so he has gradually abandoned a simple reformist attitude regarding the existing social order, for, by its very shallownesss this reformism perpetuates the existing system. The revolutionary situation which prevails today, especially in the Third World, is an expression of this growing radicalization. To support the social revolution means to abolish the present status quo and to attempt to replace it with a qualitatively different one; it means to build a just society based on new relationships of production; it means to attempt to put an end to the domination of some countries by others, of some social classes by others, of some people by others. The liberation of these countries, social classes and people undermines the very foundation of the present order; it is the greatest challenge of our time.

This radicality has led us to see quite clearly that the political arena is necessarily conflictual. More precisely, the building of a just society means the confrontation—in which different kinds of violence are present—between groups with different interests and opinions. The building of a just society means overcoming every obstacle to the creation of an authentic peace among people. Concretely, in Latin America this conflict revolves around the *oppression-liberation axis*. Social praxis makes demands which may seem difficult or disturbing to those who wish to achieve—or maintain—a low-cost conciliation. Such a conciliation can be only a justifying ideology for a profound disorder, a device for the few to keep living off the poverty of the many. But to become aware of the conflictual nature of the political sphere should not mean to become complacent. On the contrary, it should mean struggling—with clarity and courage, deceiving neither oneself nor others—for the establishment of peace and justice among all people.

In the past, concern for social praxis in theological thought did not sufficiently take into account the political dimension. In Christian circles there was—and continues to be—difficulty in perceiving the originality and specificity of the political sphere. Stress was placed on private life and on the cultivation of private values; things political were relegated to a lower plane, to the elusive and undemanding area of a misunderstood "common good." At most, this viewpoint provided a basis for "social pastoral planning," grounded on the "social emotion" which every self-respecting Christian ought to experience. Hence there developed the complacency with a very general and "humanizing" vision of reality, to the detriment of a scientific and structural knowledge of socio-economic mechanisms and historical dynamics. Hence also there came the insistence on the personal and conciliatory aspects of the Gospel message rather than on its political and conflictual dimensions. We must take a new look at Christian life; we must see how these emphases in the past have conditioned and challenged the historical presence of the Church. This presence has an inescapable political dimension. It has always been so, but because of new circumstances it is more urgent that we come to terms with it. Indeed, there is a greater awareness of it, even among Christians. It is impossible to think of or live in the Church without taking into account this political dimension.

What we have discussed above leads us to understand why for Christians social praxis is becoming less and less merely a duty imposed by their moral conscience or a reaction to an attack on Church interests. The characteristics of totality, radicalness, and conflict which we have attributed to the political sphere preclude any compartmentalized approach and lead us to see its deepest human dimensions. Social praxis is gradually becoming more of the arena itself in which the Christian works out—along with others—both his destiny as man and his life of faith in the Lord of history. Participation in the process of liberation is an obligatory and privileged *locus* for Christian life and reflection. In this participation will be heard nuances of the Word of God which are imperceptible in other existential situations and without which there can be no authentic and fruitful faithfulness to the Lord.

If we look more deeply into the question of the value of salvation which emerges from our understanding of history—that is, a liberating praxis—we see that at issue is a question concerning *the very meaning of Christianity*. To be a Christian is to accept and to live—in solidarity, in faith, hope and charity—the meaning that the Word of the Lord and our encounter with him give to the historical becoming of mankind on the way toward total communion. To regard the unique and absolute relationship with God as the horizon of every human action is to place oneself, from the outset, in a wider and more profound context. It is likewise more demanding. We are faced in our day with the bare, central theologico-pastoral question: *What does it mean to be a Christian? What does it mean to be Church in the unknown circumstances of the future?* [14] In the last instance, we must search the Gospel message for the answer to what according to Camus constitutes the most important question facing all people: "To decide whether life deserves to be lived or not." [15]

These elements lend perhaps greater depth and a new dimension to the traditional problem. Not to acknowledge the newness of the issues raised under the pretext that in one way or another the problem has always been present is to detach oneself dangerously from reality; it is to risk falling into generalities, solutions without commitment, and, finally, evasive attitudes. But, on the other hand, to acknowledge nothing but the new aspects of the contemporary statement of the problem is to forego the contribution of the life and reflection of the Christian community in its historical pilgrimage. Its successes, its omissions, and its errors are our heritage. They should not, however, delimit our boundaries. The People of God march on "acccounting for their hope" toward "a new heaven and a new earth."

The question as it is posed today is not really dealt with by the attempted responses we will look at in the next chapter. But the positive achievements of these efforts with regard to the permanent elements of the problem as well as their deficiencies and limitations can help us to sketch—often by showing us pitfalls to avoid—the itinerary which we must follow.

NOTES

1. See Gustave Thils, *Théologie des realités terrestres*, vol. 1, *Préludes* (Paris: Desclée de Brouwer, 1947). For Congar this remains an open question: "There are some chapters of theology which still need to be worked out: together with the one on the relationship between creation and redemption, there is the problem of the so-called theology of temporal realities" (*Situation et tâches*, p, 79).

2. For a statement of this question and some bibliographical comments, see Joseph Comblin, *Vers une théologie de l'action*, Études Religieuses, no. 767 (Brussels: La Pensée Catholique, 1964), pp. 87-108.

3. For a presentation of the scope of this effort see Vincent Cosmão, "Towards a Theology of Development," *IDOC International, North American Edition*, no. 5 (June 13, 1970), pp. 86-96. See also the abundant bibliography on this and related subjects prepared by Gerhard Bauer and published by the Committee on Society, Development and Peace (SODEPAX), *Towards a Theology of Development: An Annotated Bibliography*, (Geneva, 1970).

4. The position of J.B. Metz will be studied in Chapter 11.

5. Writing on this subject is increasing, but quality varies. See Hugo Assman, "Caracterização de uma Teologia de Revolução," *Ponto Homem*, no. 4 (September-October 1968), pp. 6-45; Richard Shaull, "Hacia una perspectiva cristiana de la revolución social," *Cristianismo y Sociedad* 3, no. 7, pp. 6-16; in English see Shaull's "Revolutionary Change in Theological Perspective," *Christian Social Ethics in a Changing World*, ed. J.C. Bennett (New York: Association Press, 1966), pp. 23-43. See also Richard A. McCormick, S.J., "The Theology of Revolution," *Theological Studies* 29, no. 4 (December 1968): 685-97; Joseph Smolik and Concilium General Secretariat, "Revolution and Desacralization," *Sacralization and Secularization*, ed. Roger Aubert, Concilium 47 (New York: Paulist Press, 1969), pp. 163-79; on the impasses implicit in a theology of revolution, see the interesting articles of Paul Blanquart, "Foi chrétienne et révolution," *A la recherche d'une théologie de la violence* (Paris: Les Éditions du Cerf, 1968), pp. 138-55; see also the anthology *Christianisme et révolution*, a colloquium organized by "Lettre" and IDOC International (Paris: Éditions La Lettre, 1968); *When All Else Fails: Christian Arguments on Violent Revolution*, ed. IDOC (Philadelphia: Pilgrim Press, 1970), includes several of these articles; see also Ernst Feil and Rudolf Weth, *Diskussion zur Theologie der Revolution* (Munich-Mainz:Kaiser-Grünewald, 1969). A related topic is theological reflection on violence; see *Recherche* mentioned above and another anthology, *La violenza dei cristiani* (Assisi: Cittadella, 1969), especially Giulio Girardi's article, "Amore cristiano e violenza rivoluzionaria."

6. Johannes B. Metz, *Theology of the World*, trans. William Glen-Doepel (New York: Herder and Herder, 1969), p. 93. Christian Duquoc, O.P., wrote in the same vein some years ago: "The question of the Church and the world is irritatingly complex" ("L'Église et le Monde," *Lumière et Vie* 14, no. 73 [May-July 1955]:49).

7. *La risposta dei teologi* (Brescia: Queriniana, 1969), p. 61.

8. See for example nos. 39 and 43.

9. Moreover, this approach will be truer to the spirit of the Council: "Conciliar renewal," said Paul VI, "is not measured so much by changes in exterior practices, regulations, and customs as by changes in habitual behavior and by the rejection of a kind of inertia, a kind of heartfelt resistance to a truly Christian spirit. We

must think *in a new way:* this is the beginning of reform and *aggiornamento*"
(Allocution at a general audience in January 1966; italics are ours).

10. See below Chapter 8.

11. The political sphere, however, remains ambiguous. Although universal in
its significance, its empirical reality cannot be entirely separated from particular
instances.

12. "The *Socius* and the Neighbor," *History and Truth,* trans. Charles A. Kelbley
(Evanston, Ill.: Northwestern University Press, 1965), pp. 98-109. We should clarify
that to affirm that all human reality has a political dimension in no way means,
as the term itself indicates, to *reduce* everything to this dimension.

13. "Les masses pauvres," in G. Cottier et al., *Église et pauvreté* (Paris: Les
Éditions du Cerf, 1965), p. 174. See also the interesting observations concerning
the political sphere in Pierre Eyt, "Pour une réflexion en matière politique,"
Nouvelle Revue Théologique 93, no. 10 [December 1971]: 1055-75).

14. Many Christians have sought answers to these questions in relatively novel
ways. This search has produced many experiences, sometimes confused. See in
this connection René Laurentin's *Enjeu du IIe Synode et contestation dans l'Église*
(Paris: Éditions du Seuil, 1969); see also *A la recherche d'une Église,* special issue
of *Parole et Mission* 12, no. 46 (July 15, 1969); *Le due chiese,* (Rome: IDOC, 1969);
and the collection edited by Malcolm Boyd, *The Underground Church* (New York:
Sheed and Ward, 1968).

15. In this context the starting point would be what P.-A. Liégé called some
time ago "the human credibility of Christianity" ("Bulletin d'Apologétique," *Revue
des Sciences Philosophiques et Théologiques* 33 [1949]: 67).

CHAPTER FOUR

DIFFERENT RESPONSES

The different responses given throughout history to the question of the relationship between faith and temporal realities, between the Church and the world, are still pertinent in one form or another. It is because they are germane to the ecclesial present and not merely because of their historical interest that we recall these points of view.[1]

THE CHRISTENDOM MENTALITY

Christendom is not primarily a mental construct. It is above all a fact, indeed the longest historical experience the Church has had. Hence the deep impact it has made on her life and thought.

In the Christendom mentality, and in the point of view which prolongs it, temporal realities lack autonomy. They are not regarded by the Church as having an authentic existence. It therefore uses them for her own ends. This is the sequel of the so-called "Political Augustinism."[2] The plan for the Kingdom of God has no room for a profane, historical plan.[3]

The Church is regarded substantially as the exclusive depository of salvation: "Outside the Church there is no salvation." Because of this exclusiveness, notwithstanding certain qualifications which do not change the overall picture, the Church feels justified in considering itself as the center of the economy of salvation and therefore presenting itself as a powerful force in relation to the world. This power will spontaneously and inevitably seek to express itself in the political arena.

Under these circumstances, participation in temporal tasks has a very precise meaning for the Christian: to work for the direct and immediate benefit of the Church. A historical example typical of this point of view is to be found in the well-known ban (*Non possumus*) upon Italian Catholics, which prohibited them from participating—until a few decades ago—in the political life of their country. "Christian politics," therefore, will mean assisting the Church in its evangelizing mission and safeguarding the Church's interests. This was the mentality which inspired the confessional parties in Europe and Latin America toward the end of the nineteenth century and the beginning of the twentieth. This is the role which in certain places Catholics in public office are still expected to play. The interests of the ecclesiastical institution are represented especially by the bishops and the clergy; laymen, given their situation in political society, will normally act in an auxiliary capacity.[4]

The theological categories we have mentioned were formulated—at least essentially—in that era of the history of the Christian community characterized by close unity between faith and social life. In our day, since this unity no longer exists, those categories have become dysfunctional and engender pastoral attitudes out of touch with reality;[5] worse yet, they engender conservative political positions, tending towards the restoration of an obsolete social order or the shoring up of what is left of it.

Let us not too easily dismiss this mentality as extinct. It survives today implicitly or explicitly in large and important sectors of the Church. It is the cause of conflict and resistance to change in the Church today which cannot otherwise be explained. The conciliar debates[6] and perhaps above all the postconciliar era provide sufficient proof of this.

NEW CHRISTENDOM

The grave problems facing the Church which arose from the new historical circumstances of the sixteenth century and were made more acute by the French Revolution slowly gave way to another pastoral approach and another theological mentality. Thanks to Jacques Maritain, this new approach was to be known as New Christendom.[7] It attempted to learn from the separation between faith and social life, which had been so intimately linked during the era of Christendom. This attempt, however, was to use categories which were not able to shake off completely the traditional mentality, as we can see better with the help of hindsight. A century before a similar effort had taken place, although it was perhaps less solid and coherent from a doctrinal point of view. We refer to the so-called "Catholic liberalism," which sought to take into account the situation created a short time before by the ideas of French Revolution. Although it created a clamor, this movement was neutralized by the misunderstanding of the majority of the Christian community and the hostility of the ecclesiastical authorities.

The theses of New Christendom mark another stage in the life of the Church. This is a first and well-structured effort, which attempts moreover to root itself in the traditional thought of the Church. If Augustinian theology predominated in the previous approach, Thomism does in the latter. St. Thomas Aquinas's teaching that grace does not suppress or replace nature, but rather perfects it, opened the door to possibilities of a more autonomous and disinterested political action. On this foundation, Maritain fashioned a political philosophy which also sought to integrate certain modern elements.[8] The task of constructing the city of man would consist above all in the search for a society based upon justice, respect for the rights of others, and human brotherhood. Its meaning would not flow, as in the approach we considered above, directly from religion or the defense of Church interests. Consequently, the autonomy of the temporal sphere is asserted especially in relation to the ecclesiastical hierarchy, thus preventing their later interference in an area considered outside their competence.[9]

The view of the Church as a power in relation to the world has been profoundly modified. But she continues to be, in a certain way, at the center of the work of salvation. A certain ecclesiastical narcissism is still evident. In fact, this approach seeks—by means of the creation of a just and democratic society—to achieve conditions favorable to the activity of the Church in the world. It is necessary to build a "profane Christendom," in other words, a society inspired by Christian principles.

Once the autonomy of the world is asserted, the layman acquires a proper function which was not recognized as his before. This function is facilitated by the famous distinction between acting "as a Christian as such" and acting "as a Christian."[10] In the first case, the Christian acts as a member of the Church, and his actions represent the ecclesial community. (This is what happened with the leaders of "Catholic Action" groups.) In the second case the Christian acts under the inspiration of Christian principles but assumes exclusive personal responsibility for his actions; this gives him greater freedom in his political commitments. Therefore, the special task of the layman will be to create this New Christendom in the temporal sphere. To this end he will find it useful to join organizations inspired by Christian principles—and carrying a Christian name.[11]

This position represents an initial effort to evaluate temporal tasks with the eyes of faith as well as to situate better the Church in the modern world. This approach led many Christians to commit themselves authentically and generously to the construction of a just society. Those Christians who supported this position often had to endure the enmity of the faithful and the Church authorities, both of whom were of a conservative mentality. In fact, nevertheless, this approach amounted only to a timid and basically ambiguous attempt.[12] It gave rise to fundamentally moderate political attitudes—at least in the beginning— which combined a certain nostalgia for the past (re-establishment of guilds, for example) with a modernizing mentality. It is a long way, therefore, from a desire to become oriented towards radically new social forms.

THE DISTINCTION OF PLANES

The focus provided by New Christendom made possible an advance from the traditional viewpoint towards a position in which the terms of the Church-world relationship are better defined. The first attempts to distinguish these two levels without separating them comes from Maritain. Later the theme was quickly enriched and radicalized, losing every trace of "Christendom." In the years prior to the Council the pastoral and theological thinking of some sectors of the Church tended to draw a very clear distinction between the Church and the world, within the unity of God's plan.[13]

Much more clearly than in the past, the world emerged as autonomous, distinct from the Church and having its own ends.[14] The autonomy of the temporal sphere was asserted not only with regard to ecclesiastical authority but also with regard to

the Church's very mission. She was not to interfere, as institution, in temporal matters, except—according to the most vener-
able tradition—through moral teaching. In practice this would
mean, as we will see later, acting through the mediation of the
conscience of the individual Christian.[15] The building up of the
earthly city, then, is an endeavor which exists in its own right.

As a result, the function of the Church in the world becomes
clearer. The Church, it was said, has two missions: evangelization
and the inspiration of the temporal sphere.[16] "By converting
men to faith and baptizing them," wrote Congar, "according to
the mission she has received from the Lord, the Church presents
and actualises herself as the 'order apart' of salvation and holiness in the world. By acting in the sphere of civilization, which
means in the temporal order and in history, she fulfills her mission to be the soul of human society."[17] The Church is not responsible for constructing the world; hence the lack of sympathy
for this point of view from temporal institutions of Christian
inspiration, especially those considered "powerful."[18] (Institutions of this sort do in fact give the impression that Christianity
is an ideology for the building up of the world.)[19] The planes
are thus clearly differentiated. The Kingdom of God provides
the unity; the Church and the world, each in its own way, contribute to its edification.[20]

The functions of the priest and the layman can be differentiated in like manner. The priest breaks off his point of insertion
in the world. His mission is identified with that of the Church:
to evangelize and to inspire the temporal order. To intervene
directly in political action is to betray his function. The layman's
position in the Church, on the other hand, does not require him
to abandon his insertion in the world. It is his responsibility
to build up both the Church and the world.[21] In his temporal
endeavors, the layman will seek to create with other men, Christian or not, a more just and more human society; he will be
well aware that in so doing he is ultimately building up a society
in which man will be able to respond freely to the call of God.[22]
He will have, nevertheless, the fullest respect for the autonomy
of temporal society.

The mission of lay apostolic movements, on the other hand,
should not go beyond the mission of the Church and the priest:
to evangelize and to inspire the temporal order.[23] To this theology
corresponds *a particular way* of approaching the *Revision de*

Vie technique, which assures an authentically Christian presence in the world. Christians meet, as Christians, only to share and celebrate their faith and to examine in the light of faith their own political options—or other options, which might be different and even opposing.[24]

This theological perspective predominated in the specialized apostolic movements of Europe, the French in particular, around 1950 and a few years later in the Latin American movements. But in Latin America, contrary to the European experience, this approach did not extend beyond the members of the movements and certain pastoral circles. In practice, the greater part of the Church remained untouched by this Church-world distinction, for it was contradicted by the strong bonds which consciously or unconsciously tied the Church to the existing social order.

This model has the advantage of being clear and achieving a difficult balance between the unity of God's plan and the distinction between Church and world. By and large, this is the theological approach of many of the texts of Vatican II. There are, however, emphases and insights which go beyond this, for example in *Gaudium et spes*. Congar explains that because the inductive method was used, *Gaudium et spes* does not clearly distinguish between two missions of the Church: this relationship "could have been stated from the beginning after the fashion of a doctrinal thesis," he said.[25] But it is interesting to observe that due precisely to the dynamics of the inductive method, the constitution *Lumen gentium* at times transcends a rigid distinction of planes.[26]

NOTES

1. We express here some ideas we have had an opportunity to develop more fully in Gustavo Gutiérrez, *La pastoral en la Iglesia en América Latina* (Montevideo: Ediciones del Centro de Documentación MIEC-JECI, 1968), re-edited as *Líneas pastorales de la Iglesia en América Latina, Análisis Teológico* (Lima: Centro de Estudios y Publicaciones and Santiago de Chile: Instituto Catequístico Latinoamericano, 1970). This work is a series of talks to university students and is an attempt to present a typology of pastoral thinking in the Latin American Church, subject of course to further study and more precise delineations.

2. See the historical study of H.-X Arquillère, *L'Augustinisme politique,* 2nd

ed. rev. and enl. (Paris: Librairie Philosophique J. Vrin, 1955); see also, regarding this work, the critical observations and clarifications proposed by Henri de Lubac, S.J., in *Augustinianism and Modern Theology*, trans. Lancelot Sheppard (New York: Herder and Herder, 1969).

3. "The Church did not face an autonomous world, since society was ordered towards serving the ends of eternal salvation according to rules determined by the Church" (Yves Congar, "Église et Monde," *Le Concile au jour le jour, troisième session* (Paris: Éditions du Cerf , 1965), p. 143.

4. This point of view is evident in a classic work of another period by Luigi Civardi, *A Manual of Catholic Action*, trans. C. C. Martindale, S.J. (New York: Sheed and Ward, 1943); see especially Chapters 6 and 8.

5. It was only with Vatican II that the Church began to abandon in any real sense the mentality of Christendom, a historical period which had already ended—four centuries before.

6. See for example the case of the most widely discussed schema of the Council: Religious Freedom. In this regard see our study "Libertad religiosa y diálogo salvador" in *Salvación y construcción del mundo* (Barcelona: Nova Terra, 1968), pp. 11-43.

7. This idea is explained fully in his well-known work *True Humanism* (New York: Charles Scribner's Sons, 1938).

8. Maritain's thought was very influential in certain Christian sectors of Latin America. Argentina was one of the most significant examples. See Fernando Martínez Paz, *Maritain, política e ideología: Revolución cristiana en la Argentina* (Buenos Aires: Editorial Nahuel, 1966). Furthermore, Maritain's ideas provoked strong controversies in which Maritain himself took part; see Luis Arturo Pérez, *Estudio de filosofía político-social* (Santiago de Chile, 1948), and the reponse by Julio Jiménez, *La ortodoxia de Maritain: Ante un ataque reciente* (Talca, Chile: Editiones Cervantes, 1948). See also the texts—including a letter by Maritain—compiled in *Una polémica sensacional: Jacques Maritain* (Santiago de Chile, 1944). All this, however, amounts only to a simple repetition of Maritain's ideas and a fruitless discussion of his "orthodoxy." A more personal approach is to be found in Brazil in the work of Tristão de Athayde (Alceu Amoroso Lima), who spread Maritain's thought beginning in the '30s.

9. This was keenly felt by those Latin American Christians who began to awaken to their political commitment. See Juan Luis Segundo, *Función de la Iglesia en la realidad rioplatense* (Montevideo: Barreiro y Ramos, 1962), p. 41.

10. Maritain, *Humanism*, p. 291. This distinction will gain wide acceptance; see for example Alfred de Soras, *Action catholique et action temporelle* (Paris: Spes, 1938).

11. See Maritain, *Humanism*, pp. 264-67. This gave rise to the modern parties of socio-Christian inspiration.

12. In spite of efforts to the contrary, this position still has traces of the ecclesiocentric ideology of which we have made note. For example, Maritain asks how a non-Christian can participate in a political party inspired by Christian principles; but he does not consider the more relevant question in today's world: Under what conditions can a Christian participate in a political party which is alien and perhaps even hostile to a Christian viewpoint?

13. The experiences and thinking of the French Church—source of inspiration for the vanguard in Latin America during recent years—has had a great impact in this regard. (See in this connection, for example, the comments of Hector Borrat,

"¿La Iglesia para qué?," *Cristianismo y Sociedad* no. 22 [1970], pp. 7-29). The distinction of planes was in fact the central point of the more advanced movements of the lay apostolate in Latin America. The works of Congar are most representative of this position; see *Lay People* and the articles in *A Gospel Priesthood*, trans. P.J. Hepburne-Scott (New York: Herder and Herder, 1967) and *Christians Active in the World*, trans. P.J. Hepburne-Scott (New York: Herder and Herder, 1968). See also A. Chavasse et al., *Église et Apostolat*, 2nd ed. (Paris: Casterman, 1955); Gerard Philips, *The Role of the Laity in the Church*, trans. John R. Gilbert and James W. Moudry (Cork: The Mercier Press, Limited, 1956); Jerome Hamer, O.P., *The Church is a Communion* (New York: Sheed and Ward, 1964).

14. See for example *Civilisation et evangelisation: Note Doctrinale du comité théologique de Lyon* (Lyon: Emmanuel Vilte, 1957).

15. This idea appears in writings of the French bishops and is a result of the experience of the specialized apostolic movements. See *Directoire pastoral en matière sociale*, no. 32 (Paris: Bonne Presse, 1954); *Gaudium et spes*, no. 43, echoes this point of view.

16. According to M.D. Chenu, this distinction is a result of French "Social Christianity" ("Misión de la Iglesia en el mundo contemporáneo," *La Iglesia en el mundo de hoy*, ed. Guillermo Barauna [Madrid: Studium, 1967] pp. 390-91).

17. *Christians Active*, p. 71. See also the works mentioned in Note 13. Congar has recently reaffirmed his opinion regarding the existence of these two missions of the Church in "Le rôle de l'Église dans le monde de ce temps," *L'Église dans le monde de ce temps*, 2:305.

18. P.A. Liégé distinguishes between temporal Christian institutions that are "power-bearing" *(potestatives)* and those that are "educational" *(educatives)* in "La mission contre les institutions chrétiennes?" in *Parole et Mission* 4, no. 15 (October 15, 1961): 501-02. The same author distinguishes between "heavy" institutions *(lourdes)*, which endow the Church with power, and "light" ones *(légères)*, which "come under the heading of service," in "La pauvreté, compagne de la mission," in *Église et Pauvreté*, pp. 167-68.

19. See the well-known and pertinent comments of Emmanuel Mounier, for example, "Feu la Chrétienté," *Oeuvres de Mounier*, 4 vols. (Paris: Éditions du Seuil, 1961-63), 3:686-714.

20. See the famous Chapter 3 on "Kingdom, Church and World," and "Hierarchy and Faithful People" in *Lay People*.

21. This is the position taken by Congar, A. Chavasse, G. Philips and others. Karl Rahner, in an article which provoked heated controversy, affirmed that the layman's only concern should be the building up of the world ("L'apostolat des laïcs," *Nouvelle Revue Théologique* 78, no. 1 (January 1956): 3-32. See also Charles Baumgartner, "Formes diverses de l'apostolat des laïcs," *Christus*, no. 13 (January 1957), pp. 9-33, which deals with the same ideas in different terms. Congar explicitly rejected this opinion (*Christians Active*, pp. 78-79). See also the comments of the moderators of the specialized Catholic Action groups for French workers in "A propos de l'apostolat des laïcs," *Masses Ouvrières*, no. 130 (May 1957). pp. 1-29.

22. See for example Chavasse, *Église et apostolat*, p. 18. This work inspired the 1962 pastoral plan of the Chilean bishops, who at that time were at the vanguard of the Latin American Church (The text is reproduced in *Recent Church Documents from Latin America* [Cuernavaca, Mexico: CIF, 1962-63], pp. 1-12).

23. See *Lay People*, Chapter 8, which deals with Catholic Action and the temporal commitment of the laity.

24. See Jourdain Bonduelle, *La révision de vie* (Paris: Les Éditions du Cerf, 1964), and in a more recent perspective C. Perani, *La revisione di vita strumento de evangelizzazione, alla luce del Vaticano II* (Turin, 1968).

25. "Le rôle de l'Église," p. 306.

26. However, this distinction is clearly expressed in the decree on the apostolate of the laity, *Apostolicam actuositatem* (see for example, no. 5).

CHAPTER FIVE

CRISIS OF THE DISTINCTION
OF PLANES MODEL

The acceptance of the New Christendom position entails of course a rejection of previous approaches; it in turn, however, is criticized because of its position on the distinction of planes.

In recent years there has been a questioning of pastoral action and theology based on distinctions which, although they gained ground very slowly, did indeed contribute to the clarification of many problems.[1]

This crisis has become distinctly manifest on two levels: pastoral action and theological reflection.

THE PASTORAL LEVEL

As we have seen, the model which distinguishes faith and temporal realities, Church and world, leads to the perception of two missions in the Church and to a sharp differentiation between the roles of the priest and the layman; this model soon began to lose its vitality and to become a hindrance to pastoral action. Two instances can illustrate this point.

Crisis of the Lay Apostolic Movements

The rise and development of an adult laity has been one of the most important events in the Church in recent decades. Although they foreshadowed a profound ecclesiological and spiritual renewal, the lay apostolic movements as such have nevertheless been experiencing for some time a deep crisis which it would be well to examine and analyze in detail. This crisis, indeed, provides us with a number of lessons and points for reflection.

As we have pointed out, the distinction of planes approach held that the mission of lay apostolic organizations was to evangelize and to inspire the temporal order, without directly intervening. But the life of these movements overflowed this narrow and aseptic conceptual model.

The movements, especially the youth groups, felt called upon to take ever clearer and more committed positions,[2] that is to say, to take on themselves in greater depth the problems of the milieu in which they supposedly assured "a presence of the Church."

Initially this change was presented as deriving from a pedagogical concern: the youth movements could not separate religious formation from political formation.[3] The question, however, went deeper. At stake was the very nature of these organizations: the fact that they took a stand on the temporal plane meant that the Church (especially the bishops) became committed in an area foreign to her, and this was not acceptable. Simultaneously, because of the very dynamics of the movement, the members felt compelled by circumstances to make ever more definite commitments; this necessarily led to a political radicalization incompatible with an *official* position of the Church which postulated a certain asepsis in temporal affairs. Therefore, frictions and even divisions were inevitable.[4]

Crises have occurred and spread.[5] The lay apostolic movements, *such as they are understood in the distinction of planes model*, seem to have burned themselves out.[6]

Growing Awareness of an Alienating Situation

The "social problem" or the "social question" has been discussed in Christian circles for a long time, but it is only in the last few years that people have become clearly aware of the scope of misery and especially of the oppressive and alienating circumstances in which the great majority of mankind exists. This state of affairs is offensive to man and therefore to God. Moreover, today people are more deeply aware both of personal responsibility in this situation and the obstacles these conditions present to the complete fulfillment of all men, exploiters and exploited alike.

People are also more keenly and painfully aware that a large part of the Church is in one way or another linked to those who wield economic and political power in today's world. This applies to its position in the opulent and oppressive countries as well as in the poor countries, as in Latin America, where it is tied to the exploiting classes.

Under these circumstances, can it honestly be said that the Church does not interfere in "the temporal sphere"? Is the Church fulfilling a purely religious role when by its silence or friendly relationships it lends legitimacy to a dictatorial and oppressive government?[7] We discover, then, that the policy of non-intervention in political affairs holds for certain actions which involve ecclesiastical authorities, but not for others. In other words, this principle is not applied when it is a question of maintaining the status quo, but it is wielded when, for example, a lay apostolic movement or a group of priests holds an attitude considered subversive to the established order. Concretely, in Latin America the distinction of planes model has the effect of concealing the real political option of a large sector of the Church—that is, support of the established order. It is interesting to note that when there was no clear understanding of the political role of the Church the distinction of planes model was disapproved of by both civil and ecclesiastical authorities. But when the system—of which the ecclesiastical institution is a central element—began to be rejected, this same model was adopted to dispense the ecclesiastical institution from effectively defending the oppressed and exploited and to enable it to preach a lyrical spiritual unity of all Christians. The dominant groups, who have always used the Church to defend their interests and maintain their privileged position, today—as they see "subversive" tendencies gaining ground in the heart of the Christian community—call for a return to the purely religious and spiritual function of the Church. The distinction of planes banner has changed hands. Until a few years ago it was defended by the vanguard; now it is held aloft by power groups, many of whom are in no way involved with any commitment to the Christian faith. Let us not be deceived, however. Their purposes are very different. Let us not unwittingly aid the opponent.

Further, in the face of the immense misery and injustice, ought not the Church—especially in those areas such as Latin America where it has great social influence—intervene more directly and abandon the field of lyrical pronouncements? In fact, the Church has done so at times, but always clarifying that this was a merely supplementary role.[8] The scope and omnipresence of the problem would seem to render this argument inadequate in our day. More recent options, such as that offered at Medellín, have transcended these limitations and now require another theological foundation.

In short, political options have become radicalized, and the specific commitments which Christians are assuming demonstrate the inadequacies of the theologico-pastoral model of the distinction of planes.

THE LEVEL OF THEOLOGICAL REFLECTION

In a development related to these new pastoral experiences of the Church, contemporary theological reflection has also eroded the model of the distinction of planes. It has done so in two apparently contradictory ways.

An Entirely Worldly World

In all the different responses to the problem we are considering, the world has gradually been acknowledged as existing in its own right. Autonomous with regard to both ecclesiastical authority and the mission of the Church, the world has slowly asserted its secularity. Acknowledgement by the Church of this autonomy manifested itself first with timidity and distrust—hence the expressions "healthy," "just," and "legitimate" autonomy which frequently appear in documents from the magisterium of the Church. But gradually and especially in theological circles, the values and irreversibility of the process to which we now refer as secularization have become more obvious.[9]

Secularization appeared as a breaking away from the tutelage of religion, as a desacralization. This is the most common way of characterizing this process. Harvey Cox writes: "We have defined secularization as the liberation of man from religious and metaphysical tutelage, the turning of his attention away from other worlds and toward this one."[10] This is how the process of secularization has historically been presented. It was an initial attempt to deal with the problem, valid albeit incomplete.

There is a second and more positive approach to this subject, which is already suggested in the final part of the text quoted above. Secularization is, above all, the result of a transformation of the self-understanding of man. From a cosmological vision, man moves to an anthropological vision, due especially to scientific developments.[11] Man perceives himself as a creative subject.[12] Moreover, man becomes aware—as we have noted above—that he is an agent of history, responsible for his own destiny.[13] His mind discovers not only the laws of nature, but also penetrates those of society, history, and psychology. This new self-understanding of man necessarily brings in its wake a different way of conceiving his relationship with God.[14]

In this sense, secularization—and this has been recalled often lately—is a process which not only coincides perfectly with a Christian vision of man, of history, and of the cosmos; it also favors a more complete fulfillment of the Christian life insofar as it offers man the possibility of being more fully human.[15] This realization has engendered efforts to search for the Biblical roots of secularization, efforts at times somewhat "concordist." Biblical faith does indeed affirm the existence of creation as distinct from the Creator; it is the proper sphere of man, whom God himself has proclaimed lord of this creation. *Worldliness*, therefore, is a must, a necessary condition for an authentic relationship between man and nature, of men among themselves, and finally, between man and God.[16]

All this has important ramifications. In the first place, rather than define the world in relation to the religious phenomenon, it would seem that religion should be redefined in relation to the profane. The worldly sphere appears in fact ever more consistent in itself. This is Bonhoeffer's world come of age, *mündig*, the source of his anguished question, "How can we speak about God in this adult world?"[17]

On the other hand—on a very concrete level in which we are particularly interested—if formerly the tendency was to see the world in terms of the Church, today almost the reverse is true: the Church is seen in terms of the world. In the past, the Church used the world for her own ends; today many Christians—and

non-Christians—ask themselves if they should, for example, use
the influence of the Church to accelerate the process of transformation of social structures.

Secularization poses a serious challenge to the Christian community. In the future it will have to live and celebrate its faith
in a *nonreligious* world, which the faith itself has helped create.
It becomes ever more urgent that it redefine the formulation
of its faith, its insertion in the dynamics of history, its morality,
its life-style, the language of its preaching, and its worship. The
secularization process is reaching Latin America insofar as the
history of humanity becomes unified and global. It is true that
some features, and especially some interpretations, are once
again only a simple reflection of the European scene, the fruit
of a kind of *demonstration effect*. However, this should not mis-
lead us. There is a deep-rooted movement; its characteristics
have been poorly studied; because it is peculiar to Latin America,
this makes it no less real. The Latin American, by participating
in his own liberation, gradually is taking hold of the reins of
his historical initiative and perceiving himself as master of his
own destiny. Moreover, in the revolutionary struggle he is freeing himself in one way or another from the tutelage of an alienating religion which tends to support the status quo.[18]

But the problem is complex. It is not a matter of achieving
the same end by other means. Latin America is not purely and
simply passing through "less developed" stages of the secularization experienced in Europe. It could rather be said, if we may
borrow an expression from another discipline, that in Latin
America we are witnessing a secularization process which is
"uneven and combined."[19] A rhythm different from Europe's,
coexistence with other ways of living religion and of experiencing
its relation to the world, the possibility of effectively concretizing
the potentialities of the Gospel and the Churches in order to
contribute to the liberation of Latin American man—all these
factors suggest an original process which defies any simplistic
conceptualization and all extrapolation. A consideration of this
process helps explain many attitudes and crises of people who
might not be fully aware of their root causes. The challenge
of redefinition with regard to an ever more adult world also
faces the Latin American Church, but has very peculiar characteristics.[20]

One Call to Salvation

The temporal-spiritual and profane-sacred antitheses are based on the natural-supernatural distinction. But the theological evolution of this last term has tended to stress the unity which eliminates all dualism. We will recall briefly the high points of this process.

Concern for preserving the gratuitous quality of the supernatural order led to the formulation of the doctrine of *pure nature*. This completely separated human nature from divine grace; it attributed to human nature not a strong orientation toward grace, but rather a bare "lack of repugnance" for it.[21] There was no interior desire for commmunion with God, but rather simple passivity. The supernatural was fundamentally alien to man, a perfection which was superimposed upon him. This viewpoint—which goes back to Cajetan, a less-than-faithful interpreter of Thomas Aquinas[22]—dominated Western Catholic theology for a long period. Not foreign to it are an attitude of distrust of the world and ecclesiocentrism (that is, a view of the Church as exclusive repository of grace), which since the sixteenth century until a short time ago were both found among Catholics.

The inadequacies of this position produced impasses which necessitated searching for other answers. The move forward was towards a distinction, not a separation, between the natural and supernatural orders, based on the *infinite openness* of the human spirit to God. In this view there is in man something more than a "lack of repugnance" for entering into communion with God; it is a real desire. Some were fearful, however, of not being able sufficiently to assert the gratuitous character of this encounter. And so there were timid references to an "eventual and contingent" natural desire mediated through the orientation of human intelligence to being in general (*ens in communi*). According to this position, this desire only proves that the vision of God is a simple possibility; its contingent realization does not affect human nature in any significant way.[23]

The polemical dialogue between these two positions deepened the reflection and issued in a fruitful return to the original thought of Thomas Aquinas. Now there was mention of the presence in man of an *innate desire* to see God. This is at the other extreme from "lack of repugnance." Indeed, the orientation towards God is viewed here as a constitutive element of the human spirit: every act of knowing implicitly contains the desire to know God. This desire defines man's intellectual dynamism.[24] The grace of the vision of God thus culminates a profound aspiration of the human spirit. Man fulfills himself completely only in this communion, dependent upon God's free initiative. The natural and supernatural orders are therefore intimately unified.

The tendency in this development we are describing is to stress unity beyond all distinctions. But this is still to consider it on a metaphysical, abstract, and essentialist level, involving moreover complicated and ultimately fruitless academic arguments. Once the way was cleared, however, for the elimination of dualism, the problem took a sudden new turn; a significant stage was introduced with the recovery of the *historical and existential* viewpoint. In the concrete situation there is but one vocation: communion with God through grace. In reality there is no pure nature and there never has been; there is no one who is not invited to communion with the Lord, no one who is not affected by grace.

This point of view was first supported by Yves de Montcheuil[25] and Henri de Lubac.[26] The novelty of this view (although thoroughly "traditional") and certain ambiguities in language provoked strong reactions. Rahner continued thinking along these lines, and in order to avoid the difficulties encountered by the authors mentioned above proposed the idea of a "supernatural existential," that is, the universal salvific will of God creates in man a deep affinity which becomes a gratuitous ontologico-real determinant of his nature. This is "the central and enduring existential condition of man in the concrete."[27] Blondel, whose influence de Montcheuil and de Lubac have explicitly acknowledged, had attempted something similar. He characterized the state of man as "transnatural." Devoid of supernatural life, man is nevertheless oriented to it by necessity. He is "highly stimulated in relation to this vocation; after the loss of the initial gift, he does not fall back into an undifferentiated nature. Rather he retains the mark of the point of insertion ready and as it were in potency to receive the restitution it needs to attain his real and obligatory destiny."[28]

This perspective, which transcends scholastic argumentation

and expression, is now generally accepted: historically and concretely we know man only as actually called to meet God. All considerations not based on this fact are speculations devoid of any real content. But an even more precise formulation has been sought in an effort to be faithful both to the gratuitous quality of God's gift as well as to its unified and all-embracing character.[29]

With certain important qualifications, this actually had been the line of theological thinking until the rise of the doctrine of pure nature in the sixteenth century. Today this perspective is being revived, due at least in part to a different philosophical and theological context which places more value on what is historical and concrete. The initial and fundamental issue, however, is the unity of the divine vocation and therefore of the destiny of man, of all men. The historical point of view allows us to break out of a narrow, individualistic viewpoint and see with more Biblical eyes that men are called to meet the Lord insofar as they constitute a community, a people. It is a question not so much of a vocation to salvation as a convocation.

The rediscovery of this single convocation to salvation has caused the crumbling of barriers erected diligently but artificially by a certain kind of theology. It reaffirms the possibility of the presence of grace—that is, of the acceptance of a personal relationship with the Lord—in all people, be they conscious of it or not. This in turn has led to the consideration of an anonymous Christianity,[30] in other words, of a Christianity beyond the visible frontiers of the Church.[31] The advent of a "Christendom without the name" has been proclaimed.[32] These expressions are equivocal and the choice of words poor.[33] It will be necessary to refine them so that they will point with greater precision to a reality which is itself indisputable: all men are in Christ efficaciously called to communion with God. To accept the historical viewpoint of the meaning of human existence is to rediscover the Pauline theme of the universal lordship of Christ,[34] in whom all things exist and have been saved.[35]

These developments have manifested themselves in the gradual forsaking of such expressions as *supernatural end*, *supernatural vocation*, and *supernatural order* [36] and in the ever-increasing use of the term *integral*. Martelet rightly observes regarding *Gaudium et spes*, "This term *integral* is perhaps one of the key words of this constitution. In any case, this is how the Council constantly characterizes its way of approaching the vocation of all men and of the whole man."[37] *Integral vocation* (for example in *Gaudium et spes*, no. 57; see also nos. 10, 11, 59, 61, 63, 64, 75, 91 and *Ad gentes*, no. 8) and *integral development (Populorum progressio*, no. 14) are expressions which tend to stress the unity of the call to salvation.[38]

The most immediate consequence of this viewpoint is that the frontiers between the life of faith and temporal works, between Church and world, become more fluid. In the words of Schillebeeckx: "The boundaries between the Church and mankind are fluid not merely in the Church's direction, but also, it may be said, in the direction of mankind and the world."[39] Some even ask if they are really two different things: "Is not the Church also world? ... " Metz asks. "The Church is of the world: in a certain sense the Church is the world: the Church is not Non-World."[40]

But there is another important consequence. This affirmation of the single vocation to salvation, beyond all distinctions, gives religious value in a completely new way to the action of man in history, Christian and non-Christian alike. The building of a just society has worth in terms of the Kingdom,[41] or in more current phraseology, to participate in the process of liberation is already, in a certain sense, a salvific work.[42]

We are faced on the one hand with the affirmation of an ever more autonomous world, not religious, or in more positive terms, a world come of age. On the other hand we are also faced with this single vocation to salvation which values human history in Christian terms, although in a different way than in the past.[43] Caught in this pincer-like movement, which was not exempt from misinterpretation and sloppy expression,[44] the distinction of planes appears as a burnt-out model with nothing to say to the advances in theological thinking.

Both on the level of the concrete commitments of Christians in the world and on that of contemporary theological thought, the distinction of planes model was thus inadequate. If at a given moment this theology stimulated and supported the presence of Christians in the building up of the world, today it is rigid, lacking in dynamism in the face of the new questions being posed, and therefore no longer viable. Whatever was valid in those distinctions can be maintained only within a radical change of perspective.

NOTES

1. André Manaranche recalls and criticizes these distinctions in "Foi d'aujourd'hui et distinctions d'hier," *Projet* 16 (June 1967): 641-56.

2. Regarding one of the first manifestations of this crisis, see *Association catholique de la jeunesse française: Signification d'une crise, Analyse et documents* (Paris: Éditions de l'Epi, 1964).

3. "It is an illusion to believe that young people can be given a living spiritual formation detached from temporal problems . . . . A religious and human education is supposed to enable the militants in our movement to work out in the light of the Gospel a concrete solution to the problems they face in life. They cannot do this except within the movements" (Reports of a leader in the French *Jeunesse Étudiantine Chrétienne* [JEC] in 1950, *ibid.*, p. 59).

4. On the current state of the French JEC see Louis de Vaucelles's article "Les mutations de la J.E.C.," *Études* 333 (August-September 1970): 278-86. The author's "Critical Reflection" seems somewhat harsh to us. Below in Chapter 7 we will treat this question with respect to the Latin American Church.

5. See José A. Díaz, *La crisis permanente de la acción católica* (Barcelona: Nova Terra, 1966). In Latin America, particularly in Brazil, this problem has taken on serious proportions. See Chapter 7 below.

6. Joseph Comblin was already asking some time ago, *Échec de l'action catholique?* (Paris: Éditions Universitaires, 1961). But the solution he proposed seemed to be in direct opposition to the movement which had provoked the crisis.

7. Hugo Assmann analyzes well "La función legitimadora de la religión para la dictadura brasilera," *Perspectivas para el Diálogo* (Montevideo), no. 46 (August 1970), pp. 171-81.

8. See for example *Las tareas de la Iglesia en América Latina* (Bogota: FERES, 1964), and François Houtart and Emile Pin, *The Church in the Latin American Revolution*, trans. Gilbert Barth (New York: Sheed and Ward, 1965), pp. 222-23.

9. *Secularization* is a term which has actually been in circulation for a long time. At first it referred to a return to the world of something which had acquired a certain sacred character, for example Church property. For a history of this idea see Hermann Lübbe, *Säkularisierung. Geschichte eines ideenpolitischen Begriffs* (Freiburg: Alber, 1965). Regarding the different meanings of the term, see Thomas E. Clarke, S.J., "What is Secular Christianity?" in *Proceedings of the Twenty-first Convention of the Catholic Theological Society of America, Providence, Rhode Island, June 20-23, 1966* (Yonkers, New York, 1967), pp. 201-21.

10. *The Secular City* (New York: The Macmillan Company, 1965), p. 17.

11. See Antoine Vergote, "Il realismo della fede di fronte alla desacralizzazione del mondo," in the anthology *Il cristianesimo nella società di domani*, ed. Pietro Prini (Rome: Abete, 1968), pp. 101-13. The author suggests renewing the theology of creation by means of anthropology (pp. 108-12).

12. Carlos Alvarez Calderón in *Pastoral y liberación humana* (Quito: Colección IPLA; Lima: Centro de Estudios y Publicaciones, 1970) shows the consequences for pastoral action of this shift in perspective.

13. See Chapter 2 above.

14. See the excellent comments by Schillebeeckx on "the new image of God" in a secularized world in "La vie religieuse dans un monde sécularisé," *Approches théologiques IV, La mission de l'Église* (Brussels: Éditions du CEP, 1969), pp. 285-89.

15. The first person to point out the potential meaning of secularization for the faith was Friedrich Gogarten in his *Verhängnis und Hoffnung der Neuzeit. Die Säkularisierung als theologisches Problem* (Stuttgart: Friedrich Vorwerk Verlag, 1953), pp. 11ff. English version: *Despair and Hope for Our Time*, trans. Thomas Wieser (Philadelphia: Pilgrim, 1970). See also Juan Ochagavía, "El proceso de secularización: luces y sombras," *Teología y Vida* (Santiago de Chile) 8, no. 4 (1967): 275-90; Heinz Robert Schlette, "Valutazione teologica della secolarizzazione" in *Processo alla religione* (Rome: IDOC Documenti Nuovi, 1968), pp. 39-61; and Karl Rahner, "Theological Reflections on the Problem of Secularization" in L. K. Shook, ed., *Theology of Renewal* (New York: Herder and Herder, 1968), 1:346-357. For a confrontation, handled with an open and understanding attitude, of the idea of secularization with the texts of Vatican II, see Buenaventura Kloppenburg, O.F.M., *El cristiano secularizado* (Bogota: Instituo de Liturgia de Medellín, Ediciones Paulinas, and Indo-American Press Service, 1971). Regarding the relationship between the theology of secularization and acceptance of the norms of industrialized society, see the critical analyses in the anthology *Les deux visages de la théologie de la secularisation* (Tournai: Casterman, 1970), especially the article of Marcel Xhaufflaire, "La théologie après la théologie de la sécularisation" (pp. 85-105).

16. It might be well to recall at this point the distinction initially made by Gogarten between secularization and secularism. The former refers to the historical process itself, which we have described; the latter to an ideology which tends to contain this process within a framework which excludes all religious values (*Vërhangnis*).

17. See *Letters and Papers from Prison*, ed. Eberhard Bethge, trans. Reginald H. Fuller (London: SCM Press, 1953).

18. César Aguiar accurately refers to "Latin American forms of secularization: the revolutionary ideology, the political radicalization—but certainly not science, technique and modern world that Europeans talk of so much, and above all not the urban civilization and social mobility that Cox sees as constitutive of the secular city" ("Currents and Tendencies in Contemporary Latin American Catholicism," *IDOC-NA*, no. 13 [November 14, 1970], p. 61).

19. Leon Trotsky proclaimed the laws of "uneven" and "combined" development, referring to a complex situation in which there coexisted different types of economies, different social and juridical structures, and different rhythms of growth and evolution; this enabled him to explain why the revolution of the proletariat had occurred in Russia, although this country had not attained the unilineal capitalist development of the major Western countries. The idea of an uneven and combined development emphasized the mutual influences among countries. In other words the situation in one country—and its revolutionary potential—must be seen from an international perspective. This notion will be the foundation of the theory of "permanent revolution" (See Trotsky's *The History of the Russian Revolution*, trans. Max Eastman, 3 vols. [New York: Simon and Schuster, 1934], especially 1:5-6; see also the same author's *The Permanent Revolution and Results and Prospects* [London: New Park Publications, 1962]). This expression is now common in the social sciences and is applied to the so-called underdeveloped countries.

20. The precise form this redefinition should take is a controversial point and its being studied. The relationship between evangelization and popular religiosity is beginning to appear in a different light. See for example Segundo Galilea, *Introducción a la religiosidad latinoamericana*, pamphlet (Mexico, D.F., 1967), and

"La religiosidad popular latinoamericana" in the same author's *Para una pastoral latinoamericana* (Mexico D.F.: Ediciones Paulinas, S.A., 1968), pp. 94-146; José Comblin, "Reflexões sôbre a Condição Concreta de Evangelização Hoje," *Revista Brasileira* 27, no. 3 (September 1967): 590-97; Aldo J. Büntig, "Interpretación motivacional del catolicismo popular," *Víspera* (Montevideo), no. 10 (May 1969), pp. 13-20; Felipe Berryman, "Conscientización y religiosidad popular," *Víspera* no. 12 (September 1969), pp. 8-10; in English see Berryman's "Popular Catholicism in Latin America," *Cross Currents* 21, no. 3 (Summer 1971): 284-301; Lucio Gera and Guiermo Rodríguez Melgarejo, "Apuntes para una interpretación de la Iglesia argentina," *Víspera*, no. 15 (February 1970), pp. 59-88; and the critical comments on this last article by M. Kaplún, "Pueblo, fe y alienación" *Perspectivas para el Diálogo*, nos. 44-45 (June-July 1970), pp. 129-35.

21. The doctrine of pure nature has been completely abandoned in contemporary theology. See in this regard an attempt to place it in its context in the history of theology as well as a review of the most recent criticisms it has undergone in Henri de Lubac, *The Mystery of the Supernatural*, trans. Rosemary Sheed (New York: Herder and Herder, 1967), pp. 1-24.

22. In a solid historical work Juan Alfaro delineates the development of theology from Thomas Aquinas to Cajetan: *Lo natural y lo sobrenatural: Estudio histórico desde Santo Tomás hasta Cayetano (1274-1534)* (Madrid: Consejo Superior de Investigaciones Científicas, 1952). See also de Lubac, *Mystery of Supernatural*.

23. See for example M.-D. Roland-Gosselin, O.P., "Béatitude et désir naturel d'après S. Thomas d'Aquin," *Revue des Sciences Philosophiques et Théologiques* 18 (1929): 193-222; and A.-R. Motte, O.P., "Désir naturel et béatitude surnaturelle," *Bulletin Thomiste* 3, nos. 3-4 (July-December 1932): 651-76.

24. See for example Joseph Maréchal, "De Naturali Perfectae Beatitudinis Desiderio," in *Mélanges Joseph Maréchal* (Paris: Desclée de Brouwer, 1950), 1:323-38. J. Alfaro, "Transcendencia e inmanencia de lo sobrenatural," *Gregorianum* 38, no. 1 (1957): 5-50.

25. "Introduction" in Maurice Blondel, *Pages Religieuses* (Paris: Aubier, Éditions Montaigne, 1945).

26. *Surnaturel* (Paris: Aubier, 1946).

27. Karl Rahner, "Concerning the Relationship between Nature and Grace," *Theological Investigations*, vol. 1 (Baltimore: Helicon, 1961), pp. 297-317. See also some later comments in "Nature and Grace," *Theological Investigations*, vol. 4 (Baltimore: Helicon, 1966), pp. 165-188.

28. Albert Valensin, S.J., in *Dictionnaire d'Apologetique de la Foi Catholique*, s.v. "Immanence." See also Maurice Blondel's *History and Dogma* included in *The Letter on Apologetics and History and Dogma*, ed. and trans. Alexander Dru and Illtyd Trethowan (New York: Holt, Rinehart and Winston, 1965). For an integrated view of the discussions brought about by these ideas see the classic article by L. Malevez, "La gratuité du surnaturel," *Nouvelle Revue Théologique* 75, no. 6 (June 1953): 561-86 and 75, no. 7 (July-August 1953): 673-89.

29. This line of thinking appears discreetly in Vatican II. See for example *Gaudium et spes*, nos. 22, 24, and 29. See also Chapter 9 below.

30. See Anita Röper, *The Anonymous Christian*, trans. Joseph Doncel, S.J. (New York: Sheed and Ward, 1963), and the afterword of the same work by Klaus Riesenhuber, S.J., "The Anonymous Christian According to Karl Rahner."

31. Edward Schillebeeckx, *World and Church*, trans. N.D. Smith (New York: Sheed and Ward, 1971), pp. 115-39.

32. See Karl Rahner, *The Christian of the Future* (New York: Herder and Herder, 1967).

33. Misuse of both the term and the idea of anonymous Christianity has recently provoked numerous criticisms. See for example Michel de Certeau, "Apologie de la différence," *Études* 328 (January 1968): 99-101; Maurice Bellet, *Les sens actuel du christianisme: Un exercice initial* (Paris: Desclée deBrouwer, 1969), p. 59; André Manaranche, *Quel salut?* (Paris: Éditions du Seuil, 1969), p. 197. Also regarding implicit faith see P.-A. Liégé, "La foi implicite en procès," *Parole et Mission* 11, no. 41 (April 15, 1968): 203-13. Karl Rahner has answered these criticisms by distinguishing between the problem of terminology—which in the last resort "has no importance at all"—and content—"the thing intended by the terminology." For him the reality itself is indisputable if one wishes to be logical in asserting the universal will of salvation. "Anonymous Christianity and the Missionary Task of the Church," *IDOC-NA*, no. 1 (April 4, 1970), pp. 70-96.

34. See Manuel Ossa's study "Cristianismo y sentido de la historia," *Mensaje* 15, no. 153 (October 1966): 539-51.

35. The writings of Teilhard de Chardin, among others, have greatly influenced the trend toward reaffirmation of Christ as Lord of history and the cosmos. This influence has not always been openly acknowledged; this is so, for example, in the conclusions of the first part of *Gaudium et spes*.

36. The term *supernatural*—which appeared late in theology—is scarcely used by Vatican II and is found almost exclusively in minor documents. It is not used in *Gaudium et spes* or in *Dei verbum; Lumen gentium* contains only two allusions.

37. Gustave Martelet, *Les idées Maîtresses de Vatican II* (Paris: Desclée deBrouwer, 1966), p. 137, n. 1.

38. We do not mean to imply that these terms express a totally coherent teaching of the ecclesiastical magisterium. There are ambiguities even in *Gaudium et spes*. Juan Luis Segundo has pointed them out in "Hacia una exégesis dinámica,"*Víspera*, no. 3 (October 1967), pp. 77-84. "The great difficulty is that Vatican II juxtaposes assertions without working out a perfectly coherent position—but could it have done otherwise?" (Manaranche, "Foi d'aujourd'hui," p. 654).

39. "The Church and Mankind," *The Church and Mankind*, ed. Edward Schillebeeckx, Concilium 1 (Glen Rock, N.J.: Paulist Press, 1965), p. 90. Karl Rahner had included all humanity in the notion of "the People of God" years before; see his "Membership of the Church According to the Teaching of Pius XII's Encyclical 'Mystici Corporis Christi,' " *Theological Investigations*, vol. 2 (Baltimore: Helicon Press, 1963), pp. 1-88.

40. *Theology of the World*, p. 93. From a more eschatological viewpoint, the author later assets that "the decisive relationship between the Church and the world is not spatial but temporal" (*ibid.*, p. 94).

41. Chavasse supported a similar viewpoint when he asserted that the work of civilization is an "indirect apostolate of the Church" (*Église et Apostolate*, pp. 155-57). This idea was rejected by the more orthodox supporters of the distinction of planes model (See the comments of the French *Action Catholique Ouvrière* already mentioned).

42. See Chapter 9 below.

43. See Karl Rahner, "History of the World and Salvation-History," *Theological Investigations*, vol. 5 (Baltimore: Helicon Press, 1966), pp. 97-114. See also Heinz Robert Schlette, *Epiphanie als Geschichte* (Munich: Kösel, 1966).

44. Hans Urs von Balthasar comments ironically but perceptively, "Nowadays,

in the same breath of conviction, we hear it announced that the world has been finally demythologized and has become purely secular; and yet that it must be perceived as a total eucharistic mystery, as the evolving mystical body of Christ: a mythologization and 'divinization' of the cosmos far beyond anything that the medieval realists provided for in their Christian philosophy of the universe. But (in these naïve syntheses) the creation is—in its evolutionary aspect as well—conceived of directly as a theological and sacramental mystery; and, in spite of their previous demythologization, all secular and worldly processes are immediately transformed into spiritual processes. To all intents and purposes, this implies no more than that the processes of the world are subject only to man's technical mind and his way of perceiving them: the world that has been demythologized to the point of atheism is, as such, also the world made sacred to the point of divinizing it. But these are just empty phrases: a noisy chatter with which Christians deceive themselves in the contemporary world—a world which can get along very well without them while, in all innocence, they're doing no more than chucking sand in their own eyes. It you've already secretly cancelled the distinctions, it's absolutely pointless to pretend you can still maintain them; it's ludicrous to think you're saying something deeply meaningful in any Christian sense, when you call the secular 'spiritual,' and the spiritual 'secular' " (*Who is a Christian?* trans. John Cumming [New York: Newman Press, 1968], pp. 48-49; for a similar viewpoint see Manaranche, *Quel Salut?*).

PART 3

THE OPTION BEFORE
THE LATIN AMERICAN CHURCH

We have seen that one of the most fruitful functions of theology—and one in which we are particularly interested in this work—is critical reflection, the fruit of a confrontation between the Word accepted in faith and historical praxis.

Historical developments can help us to discover unsuspected facets of revelation as well as to understand the nature of the Church in greater depth, express it better, and adjust it more successfully to our times (*Gaudium et spes*, no. 44). For this reason the commitment of Christians in history constitutes a true *locus theologicus*.

In this connection it is useful to recall, at least in broad outline, the new awareness of the reality of the continent which Latin Americans have acquired as well as the way in which they understand their own liberation. We will also look at the options which important sectors of the Church are making here in the only predominantly Christian continent among those inhabited by oppressed peoples. The Latin American Church indeed faces peculiar and acute problems related to the process of liberation.

CHAPTER SIX

THE PROCESS OF LIBERATION
IN LATIN AMERICA

Dependence and *liberation* are correlative terms. An analysis
of the situation of dependence leads one to attempt to escape
from it. But at the same time participation in the process of
liberation allows one to acquire a more concrete living awareness
of this situation of domination, to perceive its intensity, and
to want to understand better its mechanisms. This participation
likewise highlights the profound aspirations which play a part
in the struggle for a more just society.

A NEW AWARENESS
OF THE LATIN AMERICAN REALITY

After a long period of real ignorance of its own reality (except
for a brief period of optimism induced by vested interests) Latin
America is now progressing from a partial and anecdotal understanding of its situation to a more complete and structural one.

The most important change in the understanding of the Latin
American reality lies, first, in going beyond a simple, tearful
description with an attendant accumulation of data and statis-
tics, and, second, in having no false hopes regarding the possibility of advancing smoothly and by preestablished steps towards
a more developed society. The new approach consists in paying
special attention to the root causes of the situation and considering them from a historical perspective. This is the point of view

which Latin Americans are beginning to adopt in the face of the challenge of an ever more difficult and contradictory situation.

The Decade of Developmentalism

Latin America in the '50s was characterized by great optimism regarding the possibility of achieving self-sustained economic development. To do this it was necessary to end the stage of *foreign-oriented growth* (exportation of primary products and importation of manufactured products), which made the Latin American countries dependent exclusively upon foreign trade. The more developed countries in the area had already begun to do this. There would then begin an *inward development*. By means of the substitution of imports, expansion of the internal market, and full industrialization, this would lead to an independent society. Fernando Henrique Cardoso and Enzo Faletto wrote that "it could not be denied that at the beginning of the decade of the '50s some of the necessary preconditions were present for this new stage in the Latin American economy, at least in countries such as Argentina, Mexico, Chile, Colombia and Brazil."[1] This approach was based on a favorable set of historical circumstances and was theoretically formulated in serious economic studies.[2] In the political sphere, it was adopted by the populist movements which at different times and with varying influence arose in Latin America.

The developmentalist policies current at that time were supported by international organizations.[3] From their point of view—characterized by structural-functionalist categories—to develop meant to be oriented towards a model abstracted from the more developed societies in the contemporary world. This model was considered to be "modern society" or "industrial society." In achieving this goal, social, political, and cultural obstacles originating from the archaic political structures proper to underdeveloped countries—also referred to as "traditional societies" or "transitional societies"—had to be overcome. The underdeveloped countries thus were considered backward, having reached a lower level than the developed countries. They were obligated, therefore, to repeat more or less faithfully the historical experience of the developed countries in their journey towards modern society. For those located in the heart of the

Empire, this modern society was characterized by high mass consumption.[4]

Underdevelopment and development constituted a *continuum*. Dysfunctional groups would arise within the social system of traditional societies, leading to the creation of social forces opposed to the existing order. "At first, the accumulated pressures would produce partial changes and later the modificiation of society as a whole. According to this model, social systems were regarded as unstable and their transformation would result from the cumulative effect of tension between opposing forces."[5] With the inevitable qualifications and variations, this theory yielded a model and an ideology of modernization which explained the transition of Latin American societies from traditionalism to modernism, from underdevelopment to development.

This point of view sanctioned timid and in the long run deceitful efforts which tended to achieve an ever-greater efficiency. Not only have they failed to eliminate the prevailing economic system, however; they have contributed to its consolidation.[6] Developmentalist policies did not yield the expected results. One of their proponents acknowledged that "after more than half of the decade of the '60s has passed, the *gap* between the two worlds is growing bigger, rather than slowly decreasing as was expected .... While from 1960 to 1970 the developed nations will have increased their wealth by 50 percent, the developing countries, two-thirds of the world's population, will continue to struggle in poverty and frustration."[7] The developmentalist approach has proven to be unsound and incapable of interpreting the economic, social, and political evolution of the Latin American continent. According to Cardoso and Faletto, "One gets the initial impression that the interpretative model and the prognoses—which in the light of purely economic factors could be formulated towards the end of the 1940s—were not sufficient to explain the later course of events."[8]

A change of attitude occured in the '60s. A pessimistic diagnosis of economic, social, and political realities replaced the preceding optimism.[9] Today it is evident that the developmentalist model suffered from grave problems of perspective. It did not sufficiently take into account political factors,[10] and worse, stayed on an abstract and ahistorical level. Underdeveloped, backward societies were statically juxtaposed to modern, developed societies. But, as Theotonio Dos Santos has pointed out, "There is no historical possibility that they will become societies reaching the same stage of development as the developed ones. Historical time is not unilinear. There is no possibility that a contemporary society could evolve to levels achieved earlier by existing societies. All peoples move concurrently and in a parallel fashion towards a new society."[11]

The developmentalist and modernizing approach made it impossible to appreciate both the complexity of the problem and the inevitable conflictual aspects of the process taken as a whole.

The Theory of Dependence

For some time now, another point of view has been gaining ground in Latin America. It has become ever clearer that underdevelopment is the end result of a process. Therefore, it must be studied from a historical perspective, that is, in relationship to the development and expansion of the great capitalist countries. The underdevelopment of the poor countries, as an overall social fact, appears in its true light: as the historical by-product of the development of other countries.[12] The dynamics of the capitalist economy lead to the establishment of a center and a periphery, simultaneously generating progress and growing wealth for the few and social imbalances, political tensions, and poverty for the many.

Latin America was born and developed in this context. "Latin American societies entered into the history of the development of the universal system of interdependence as dependent societies due to Iberian colonization. Their history can be traced to a large extent as the history of the successive modifications of their condition of dependence. The different societies of the region have reached different positions without having been able, up to this time, to break away from the general framework."[13] This initial situation of dependence is the basis for a correct understanding of underdevelopment in Latin America.[14] The Latin American countries are "from the beginning and constitutively dependent."[15] For this reason their social structure is very different from that of the center countries. It is necessary to determine carefully the differences between these two societies and to reformulate the concept which will allow us to analyze the situation and even the internal social structure of the peripheral countries. In regard to the peripheral countries there is reference to development that is "uneven and combined." (This is in opposition to the unilinear process of the developed countries.) The study of the dynamics proper to dependence, their current modalities, and their consequences, is undoubtedly the greatest challenge the social sciences face in Latin America.

The notion of dependence emerges therefore as a key element in the interpretation of the Latin America reality. Cardoso defines it thus: "The relationships of dependence presuppose the insertion of specifically unequal structures. The growth of the world market created relationships of dependence (and domination) among nations. Differences were thus established within the unity comprised by the international capitalist system."[16] But we are not dealing with a purely external factor: "The system of *external* domination, from one country to another, cuts through the dependent structure and interpenetrates it. To the extent that it does, the external structure is experienced as internal."[17] During the past few years we have witnessed in Latin America an acceleration of the process which Cardoso and Faletto call "internationalization of the internal market"[18] and which José Nun refers to as "internalization of dependence."[19] The old forms of imperialistic presence by means of the enclave economy (mining centers and plantations), simple prolongations of the central economies, still exist.[20] But currently foreign investment is gravitating towards the modern sector of the economy, that is to say, towards the more dynamic elements of budding native industry, binding it ever more closely to international capitalism. In this way a new kind of dependence arises, less apparent, but no less real.[21]

This new form of dependence not only does not necessitate defending the status quo. It even includes fostering change in the social situation of the Latin American countries, especially the most backward ones. Modernization and the introduction of greater rationality into the economies is required by the vested interests of new economic groups.[22] These groups are increasingly less tied to any one country and are gradually acquiring the character of great multinational corporations.[23]

It is necessary, therefore, to place in a single perspective the expansion of the developed nations. We must follow the new modalities very closely. These points were originally treated by authors such as Hobson and from another point of view by Rosa

Luxemburg, Lenin, and Bukharin, who formulated the theory of imperialism and colonialism.[24] But despite occasional references (especially in Lenin), their point of view was fundamentally that of the capitalist countries. Franz Hinkelammert writes, "These are authors who live in the centers of the capitalist world and who deal with the problem of imperialism from the point of view of these centers. They experience the expansive strength of capitalism in these centers; they experience the economic crises of the centers and the ramifications which these phenomena have on the dependent periphery which is exploited by the centers . . . . But what happens in the underdeveloped world itself is not analyzed beyond determining the effects of the exploitation of such countries."[25] Latin American social scientists are determined to study the problem from the point of view of the dominated countries, which will allow them to illuminate and to deepen the theory of dependence. This perspective has been overlooked until now; it should lead to a reformulation of the theory of imperialism.[26]

The imbalance between developed and underdeveloped countries—caused by the relationships of dependence—becomes more acute if the cultural point of view is taken into consideration. The poor, dominated nations keep falling behind; the gap continues to grow. The underdeveloped countries, in relative terms, are always farther away from the cultural level of the center countries; for some it is difficult ever to recover the lost ground. Should things continue as they are, we will soon be able to speak of two human groups, two kinds of people: "Not only sociologists, economists, and political theorists, but also psychologists and biologists have pointed with alarm to the fact that the incessant widening of the distance between the developed and the underdeveloped countries is producing a marked separation of two human groups; this implies the appearance, in a short time, of a true anthropological differentiation . . . . At each level of progress and each stage of development, the industrialized countries advance and accumulate strength which allows them to reach new collective goals of a number and degree much higher than those attainable by the underdeveloped countries."[27]

These new insights must not cause us to forget, however, how much needs to be done in working out an adequate theory of dependence. The Latin American social sciences work under the pressure of concern for immediate political action. This pressure is at the same time their strength and their weakness.[28] It provides a solid starting point, a permanent stimulus to reflection, and the guarantee that this reflection will contribute effectively to social change. But this pressure, which contains intuitive and ideological elements, can also endanger the efforts of the social sciences to acquire a sufficiently scientific character and thus provide an authentic framework—broad and detailed at the same time—for interpreting reality. There is urgent need for a purification to eliminate the less scientific approaches, for a clarification of terms used, for an application of the general categories to ever more complex and constantly evolving realities. "A systematic analysis of the forms dependence has taken in Latin America is still to be made," writes Cardoso, "an analysis which will have to consider, on the one hand, the connection among the particular ways in which Latin American economies are tied to the world market, and on the other, the political structures of domination, both internal and external. Without this analysis and without specifying the kinds of dependence, the use of the term can camouflage new equivocations. For one can have recourse to the idea of dependence as a way of 'explaining' internal processes of the dependent societies by a purely 'external' variable—not readily identifiable but omnipresent—which is regarded as a cause. The importance of analyzing the problems of the peripheral countries in terms of dependence, as we understand it, requires an effort to avoid new reifications, which transform concepts into real factors without any precise identification of their real nature."[29] This task is imperative if we wish to make fertile theses effective and avoid pseudo-interpretations and facile solutions.[30]

But only a class analysis will enable us to see what is really involved in the opposition between oppressed countries and dominant peoples. To take into account only the confrontation between nations misrepresents and in the last analysis waters down the real situation. Thus the theory of dependence will take the wrong path and lead to deception if the analysis is not put within the framework of the worldwide class struggle.

The perception of the fact of dependence and its consequences has made possible a new awareness of the Latin American reality. It is now seen clearly that in addition to economic factors, it is also necessary to take into consideration political factors. Development theory must now take into account the situation of dependence and the possibility of becoming free from it. Only in this context can the theory make any sense and have any possibility of being implemented. Studies made along these lines lead one to conclude that autonomous Latin American development is not viable within the framework of the international capitalist system.[31]

The Liberation Movement

To characterize Latin America as a dominated and oppressed continent naturally leads one to speak of liberation and above all to participate in the process. Indeed, *liberation* is a term which expresses a new posture of Latin Americans.

The failure of reformist efforts has strengthened this attitude. Among more alert groups today, what we have called a new awareness of Latin American reality is making headway. They believe that there can be authentic development for Latin America only if there is liberation from the domination exercised by the great capitalist countries, and especially by the most powerful, the United States of America.[32] This liberation also implies a confrontation with these groups' natural allies, their compatriots who control the national power structure. It is becoming more evident that the Latin American peoples will not emerge from their present status except by means of a profound transformation, *a social revolution*, which will radically and qualitatively change the conditions in which they now live. The oppressed sectors within each country are becoming aware—slowly, it is true—of their class interests and of the painful road which must be followed to accomplish the breakup of the status quo. Even more slowly they are becoming aware of all that the building of a new society implies.

Because of urbanization and increased industrialization, the Latin American popular movement grew from 1930 on, demanding greater participation in the economic and political life of its respective countries. Political parties of a populist bent capitalized on this basically urban movement. But the crisis of developmentalist policies to which we have referred, the rise of multinational businesses and their growing control of the economy of Latin America, and the appearance of militant peasant masses on the political scene—all these were responsible for the loss of political leadership, at different times in different countries, which the different forms of populism held up to that point. After a period of disorientation, an intense process of political radicalization began. [33] In this regard, the Cuban revolution has played a catalytic role. With certain qualifications, this revolution serves as a dividing point for the recent political history of Latin America.[34] One final factor in all this is the Sino-Soviet split, which among other things has accelerated the internal breakup of the classical Communist parties and precipitated the birth of new and more radical revolutionary groups.

Guerrilla groups appeared, intending quickly to mobilize the masses: they did this by urging them to follow a radical line more than through an organization really representing their interests. Military defeats followed each other. The political lessons are nevertheless important.[35] Revolutionary political action has diversified in recent years. It has gone from outbreaks of a leftist nationalism in search of definite options—under the pressure of radicalized groups and the masses—through in-depth connections with the popular masses and even the much-discussed "electoral path," to subversion under new forms of armed struggled. Moreover, it is becoming more obvious that the revolutionary process ought to embrace the whole continent. There is little chance of success for attempts limited to a national scope.

This radicalization has brought about a reaction—both domestically and overseas—on the part of the defenders of the established order. This has in turn frequently led to working outside existing institutions and legal norms and to clandestine, even violent political activity. The reaction becomes even more belligerent and in may cases resorts to severe and brutal forms of repression.[36] The effect is what Dom Helder Camara refers to graphically as "the spiral of violence."[37]

In Latin America we are in the midst of a full-blown process of revolutionary ferment. This is a complex and changing situation which resists schematic interpretations and demands a continuous revision of the postures adopted. Be that as it may, the untenable circumstances of poverty, alienation, and exploitation in which the greater part of the people of Latin America live urgently demand that we find a path toward economic, social, and political liberation. This is the first step towards a new society.

These groups and individuals who have raised the banner of

Latin American liberation are most frequently of socialist inspiration; socialism, moreover, represents the most fruitful and far-reaching approach. There is, however, no monolithic orientation. A theoretical and practical diversity is emerging. Strategies and tactics are different and in many cases even contrary. Theoretical approaches also vary. This can be a result both of different interpretations of reality and of conscious or unconscious imitation of others' approaches. Indeed, cultural dependence has a role to play even here. Nevertheless, the search for indigenous socialist paths continues. In this field the outstanding figure of José Carlos Mariátegui, despite the inconclusiveness of his work, continues to chart the course. "We certainly do not wish," he wrote in an often-quoted text, "for socialism in America to be an exact copy of others' socialism. It must be a heroic creation. We must bring Indo-American socialism to life with our own reality, in our own language. This is a mission worthy of a new generation."[38] According to Mariátegui, Marxism is not "a body of principles which can be rigidly applied the same way in all historical climates and all social latitudes .... Marxism, in each country, for each people, works and acts oᵤ the situation, on the milieu, without overlooking any of its modalities."[39] For Mariátegui as for many today in Latin America, historical materialism is above all "a method for the historical interpretation of society."[40] All his work, thought, and action—although not exempt from understandable limitations—was characterized by these concerns. His socialism was creative because it was fashioned in loyalty.[41] He was loyal to his sources, that is, to the central intuitions of Marx, yet was beyond all dogmatism; he was simultaneously loyal to a unique historical reality.[42]

However—and Mariátegui predicted this—only a sufficiently broad, rich, and intense revolutionary praxis, with the participation of people of different viewpoints, can create the conditions for fruitful theory. These conditions are beginning to appear. Without any loss of militancy or radicalness in the theory, they will undoubtedly lead to greater modifications than envisioned by those who sought refuge in easy solutions or in the excommunication of those who did not accept their pat answers, schematizations, and uncritical attitudes toward the historical expressions of socialism. One of the great dangers which threaten the building of socialism in Latin America—pressed as it is by immediate concerns—is the lack of its own solid theory. And this theory must be Latin American, not to satisfy a desire for originality, but for the sake of elementary historical realism.[43]

There is also present in this process of liberation, explicitly or implicitly, a further ramification which it is well to keep in mind. The liberation of our continent means more than overcoming economic, social, and political dependence. It means, in a deeper sense, to see the becoming of mankind as a process of the emancipation of man in history. It is to see man in search of a qualitatively different society in which he will be free from all servitude, in which he will be the artisan of his own destiny.[44] It is to seek the building up of *a new man*. Ernesto Che Guevara wrote, "We revolutionaries often lack the knowledge and the intellectual audacity to face the task of the development of a new human being by methods different from the conventional ones, and the conventional methods suffer from the influence of the society that created them."[45]

This vision is what in the last instance sustains the liberation efforts of Latin Americans. But in order for this liberation to be authentic and complete, it has to be undertaken by the oppressed people themselves and so must stem from the values proper to these people. Only in this context can a true cultural revolution come about.

From this point of view, one of the most creative and fruitful efforts which has been implemented in Latin America is the experimental work of Paulo Freire, who has sought to establish a "pedagogy of the oppressed."[46] By means of an unalienating and liberating "cultural action," which links theory with praxis, the oppressed person perceives—and modifies—his relationship with the world and with other people. He thus makes the transfer from a "naive awareness"—which does not deal with problems, gives too much value to the past, tends to accept mythical explanations, and tends toward debate—to a "critical awareness"—which delves into problems, is open to new ideas, replaces magical explanations with real causes, and tends to dialogue. In this process, which Freire calls "conscientization," the oppressed person rejects the oppressive consciousness which dwells in him, becomes aware of his situation, and finds his own language. He becomes, by himself, less dependent and freer, as he commits himself to the transformation and building up of society.[47] Let us specify, also, that this critical awareness is not a state reached once and for all, but rather a permanent effort of man who seeks to situate himself in time and space, to exercise his creative potential, and to assume his responsibilities. Awareness is, therefore, relative to each historical stage of a people and of mankind in general.

Freire's ideas and methods continue to be developed. All the potentialities of conscientization are slowly unfolding, as well as its limitations. It is a process which can be deepened, modified, reorientated, and extended. This is the task in which in the first place the founder of this movement, as well as many of those who in one way or another have participated in it, are involved.[48]

NOTES

1. *Dependencia y desarrollo en América Latina* (first published in mimeo, Santiago de Chile: ILPES, 1967; republished in Mexico, D.F.: Siglo Veintiuno, 1969), p. 4.

2. The Economic Commission for Latin America (ECLA), an organ of the United Nations, has played a prominent role in this. See the texts which appear in *América Latina: El pensamiento de la CEPAL* (Santiago de Chile: Tiempo Latinoamericano, 1969).

3. United Nations, Organization of American States (OAS), International Monetary Fund (IMF), Inter-american Development Bank (IDB), Agency for International Development (AID), Alliance for Progress.

4. See Rostow, *Stages of Economic Growth*, Chapter 6. For a critique of this work see Fernando Henrique Cardoso, *Cuestiones de sociología del desarrollo en América Latina* (Santiago de Chile: Universitaria, 1968), pp. 10-16, and Antonio García, "La estructura social y el desarollo latinoamerica : Réplica a la teoría del nuevo contrato social de W. W. Rostow," *El Trimestre Económico* (Mexico, D.F.), no. 129 (January-March 1966), pp. 3-42.

5. Fernando Henrique Cardoso, "Desarrollo y dependencia: Perspectivas en el análisis sociológico," in the anthology *Sociología del desarrollo* (Buenos Aires, 1970), pp. 19-20. See also Fernando Henrique Cardoso and Francisco Weffort, "Consideraciones generales sobre el desarrollo," in *Ensayos de interpretación sociológico-política* (Santiago de Chile: Tiempo Latinoamericano, 1970), pp. 14-33.

6. See Cardoso and Faletto, *Dependencia y desarrollo*, and Theotonio Dos Santos, "La crisis de la teoría del desarrollo y las relaciones de dependencia en América Latina" in *La dependencia político-económica de América Latina* (Mexico, D.F.: Siglo Veintiuno, 1969); initially published in *Boletín* (Santiago de Chile), CESO, no. 3, October 1968. On the same subject André Gunder Frank speaks of a "development of underdevelopment"; see his "The Development of Underdevelopment" in *Latin America: Underdevelopment or Revolution* (New York: Monthly Review Press, 1969).

7. Felipe Herrera, "Viabilidad de una comunidad latinoamericano," *Estudios*

Internacionales (Santiago de Chile), no. 1 (April 1967). Along the same lines is the testimony of another important name during the decade of development, the economist Raúl Prebisch, *Hacia una dinámica del desarrollo latinoamericano* (Mexico D.F.: Fondo de Cultura Económica, 1963). See also ECLA's *Economic Study of Latin America, 1966,* especially the texts quoted from the Spanish version in Dos Santos, "Crisis," pp. 164-65. See also Celso Furtado, *Obstacles to Development in Latin America,* trans. Charles Ekker (Garden City, N.Y.: Anchor Books, 1970).

8. Cardoso and Faletto, *Dependencia y desarrollo,* p. 8.

9. Gonzalo Arroyo, S.J., offers a good synthesis of this new situation with ample bibliographical references up to 1968 in "Pensamiento latinoamericano sobre subdesarrollo y dependencia externa," *Mensaje* 17, no. 173 (October 1968): 516-20. This article has been revised and enlarged by the author in "Le sousdéveloppement et la dépendence externe au miroir de la littérature latinoaméricaine," *Cultures et Développement* 2, no. 1 (1969-70): 121-41.

10. "The exclusively economic explanations predominant in developmentalist ideologies slowly gave way to strictly political concerns" (Cardoso, "Desarrollo y dependencia," p. 22).

11. Dos Santos, "Crisis," p. 153.

12. Osvaldo Sunkel has studied the historical genesis of this in *El marco histórico del proceso de desarrollo y subdesarrollo* (Santiago de Chile: ILPES, 1967); this study has been republished in Osvaldo Sunkel and Pedro Paz, *El subdesarrollo latinoamericano y la teoría del desarrollo* (Mexico D.F.: Siglo Veintiuno, 1970). See also the anthology *La dominación de América Latina* (Lima: Moncloa, 1968); Jorge Bravo Bresani, *Desarrollo y subdesarrollo* (Lima: Moncloa, 1967); and Celso Furtado, *Economic Development of Latin America: A Survey from Colonial Times to the Cuban Revolution* (New York: Cambridge University Press, 1970).

13. Anibal Quijano, *El proceso de urbanización en Latinoamérica,* mimeo (Santiago de Chile: CEPAL, 1966), p. 14. See also the same author's *Dependencia, cambio social y urbanización de Latinoamérica,* mimeo (Santiago de Chile: CEPAL, 1967).

14. André Gunder Frank does not accept the traditional thesis concerning the feudalism of Latin American societies. He holds that Latin America has been capitalist (that is, subject to mercantilist capitalism) since its earliest days, or, even earlier, since its conception (*Capitalism and Underdevelopment in Latin America: Historical Studies of Chile and Brazil* (New York and London: Monthly Review Press, 1967). This thesis had already been upheld by Sergio Bagú, *Economía de la sociedad colonial: Ensayo de la historia comparada de América Latina* (Buenos Aires: El Ateneo, 1949). See also the criticism of Dos Santos regarding the methodology and conclusions of Frank; Dos Santos prefers to speak of "precapitalist" means of production in "Capitalismo colonial según A.G. Frank," *Monthly Review* (selected texts in Spanish), November 1968, pp. 17-27. Frank responds to this criticism in *Lumpenburguesía: Lumpendesarrollo* (Bogota: Oveja Negra, 1970).

15. Francisco C. Weffort, *Clases populares e desenvolvimento social,* mimeo (Santiago de Chile: ILPES, 1968), p. 26.

16. "Desarrollo y dependencia," p. 24. Dos Santos proposes the following definition of dependence: "It is a situation in which the economy of one group of countries is conditioned by the development and expansion of another economy. The relationship of interdependence between two or more economies and between certain economies and world trade assumes the form of dependence when some countries (the dominant ones) are able to develop themselves while others (the dependent ones) can only reflect that expansion, which can have a positive or negative effect

upon their immediate development. In any case the basic relationship of dependence leads to a world-wide situation which characterizes the dependent countries as backward and exploited by the dominant countries" ("Crisis," p. 180).

17. Cardoso, "Desarrollo y dependencia," p. 24. "It is not possible in our times to consider the influence of the United States as an external variable which affects the national economic structure merely by means of foreign trade and financing. On the contrary, our dependence is much deeper and more complex; it affects the very roots of the economic and social structure, forming—in the words of Bettelheim—a 'net' from which the backward countries must escape if they intend to actualize their potential. Imperialism must be thought of as structural, active in the core of our national structures, shaping the roots of an economic, technological, political, and cultural dependence.

"One of the elements basic to an understanding of this structural penetration is its relationship with the different social classes in Latin American countries . . . . Imperialism is then no longer a factor operating from 'outside' the dependent countries; it is a force active from 'inside', tied to the national structures. Imperialism becomes 'nationalized' (not because of the interests it defends, but because of its geographic and social ties), while the ruling classes become 'denationalized' (insofar as they foreswear autonomous development—which was still possible up to a certain point—and commit themselves to the defense of imperialist interests, whose profits they share)" (Juan Pablo Franco, *La influencia de los Estados Unidos en América Latina* [Montevideo: Ediciones Tauro, 1967]).

18. *Dependencia y desarrollo*, pp. 130-50.

19. José Nun, *Misión Rockefeller: ¿Porqué y para qué?*, mimeo, 1970, p. 3

20. Regarding the idea of an enclave, see Cardoso and Faletto, *Dependencia y desarrollo*, pp. 48-53.

21. See in this regard, Theotonio Dos Santos, *El nuevo carácter de la dependencia* (Santiago de Chile: CESO, 1968). This work contains data regarding the areas affected by foreign investment, especially in Brazil. See also Nun, *Misión Rockefeller*.

22. "The image of foreign interests is even more offensive. They are imagined to be linked exclusively to an agricultural-export economy and opposed to industrialization. Moreover, the struggle for industrialization is depicted as anti-imperialistic and revolutionary. Despite the fact that in some countries this image may make some sense, for the developing countries it is completely anachronistic. In these countries industrialization and foreign capital join together and progressively become a single reality" (Dos Santos, *Nuevo carácter*, p. 9). Anibal Quijano believes that "the redefinition of the modalities of imperialistic domination in Latin America" provides a general framework within which to understand certain political changes occurring in Latin America (*Carácter y perspectiva del actual régimen militar en el Perú*, mimeo [Santiago de Chile: CESO, 1970]). His framework here is very broad and must be refined by taking into consideration specific national peculiarities.

23. Celso Furtado analyzes the concentration of economic power in large corporations in *La concentración del poder económico en los Estados Unidos y sus reflejos en América Latina* (Buenos Aires: Centro Editor de América Latina, 1969). On multinational corporations see also the study by Harry Magdoff and Paul M. Sweezy, "Notes on the Multinational Corporation," *Monthly Review* 21, no. 5 (October 1969):1-13 and 21, no. 6 (November 1969): 1-13.

24. For a quick overall view of these authors' thought, see Piero Santi, "Il dibat-

tito sull'imperialismo nei classici marxismo, *Crítica Marxista* (Rome), 3rd year, no. 3 (May-June 1965), pp. 84-134; and Charles Pailloux, "La question de l'imperialisme chez V.I. Lenine et Rose Luxemburg," *L'Homme et la Société*, no. 15 (January-March 1970), pp. 103-108.

25. "La teoría clásica del imperialismo, el subdesarrollo y la acumulación socialista," *Cuadernos de la realidad nacional* (Santiago de Chile), no. 4 (June 1970), pp. 137-60.

26. See the studies published in *Imperialismo y dependencia externa* (Santiago de Chile: CESO, 1968). Franz J. Hinkelammert has an interesting essay on this subject in this work. According to him the classical theory of imperialism presupposes "capitalist society is essentially developmentalist and industrializing." Capitalism, the theory says, if left to itself, would unleash totally new productive forces (p. 138); should this not happen, it would be due to obstacles which a bourgeois revolution is called upon to eliminate. Hinkelammert holds, on the other hand, that even if this was the case in the countries which developed first, in the underdeveloped countries—which are the other side of the coin of their progress—capitalism, under any of its forms, produces only stagnation. The only true solution would be then a socialist accumulation—from the beginning. See also Orlando Caputo and Roberto Pizzarro, *Imperialismo, dependencia y relaciones internacionales*, mimeo (Santiago de Chile: CESO, 1970).

27. Augusto Salazar Bondy, "La cultura de la dominación in *Perú problema* (Lima: Moncloa 1968), p. 75. From another ideological context, two Argentine intellectuals, J. Sabato and Natalio Botana, hold, however, that because the scientific-technological revolution is in full swing, Latin America still has the potential to participate and "attain technical-scientific capabilities of its own by making science and technology an integral part of the process of development." The authors refer to the combination of these elements as an "innovation" and outline the strategy for accomplishing it ("La ciencia y la técnica en el desarrollo futuro de América Latina," mimeo, position paper presented at the World Order Models Conference, 1968 (Lima: Instituto de Estudios Peruanos, 1970). See also the comments made by Manuel Sadosky, vice-dean of the School of Science of the University of Buenos Aires, who proposes an "inexpensive science . . . based on national needs . . . at the highest level . . . and allied to an aware and liberating political commitment" ("Construir nuestra ciencia," *Víspera*, no. 18 (August 1970), pp. 16-17. See also the recent work of Orlando Fals Borda, *Ciencia propia y colonialismo intelectual* (Mexico D.F.: Editorial Nuestro Tiempo, 1970).

28. See in this regard the interesting comments of Pablo Gónzalez Casanova in "La sociología y la crisis de América Latina," *CIDOC*, no. 98 (Cuernavaca, Mexico: CIDOC, 1968), pp. 1-9. The author holds that "the new sociology has to face a moral reality. This fact poses a twofold problem: to use its tools both persuasively and also analytically so that popular movements in Latin America will succeed with the maximum of psychological security and the minimum of mistakes"; to this end "the first objective would be to express discoveries in clear and emphatic language to persuade others of the validity of the conclusions"; second, research "cannot follow the same pattern as in recent years, which was believed to be the scientific ideal; but neither can it be like the previous sociology, which was intuitive and rhetorical" (p. 5).

29. Cardoso, "Desarrollo y dependencia," p. 25. The author postulates, moreover, the need for "a kind of preliminary phenomenology of dependence to describe the relationship among the structures implied in the concepts *dependent* and *dominant*" (p. 24).

30. Regarding the factors which should be considered in a theory of dependence and in particular the tasks it is expected to perform, see Arroyo, "Pensamiento latinoamericano" and "Sousdéveloppement." Besides those mentioned by this author, an important task would be to differentiate in greater detail the position of the countries which were already on the road to economic development around 1930 and those which reached this level twenty or more years later. The differences create social and political circumstances which cannot be encompassed by the same categories.

31. The theory of dependence met a new pitfall a short time ago: the danger of being accepted—nominally at least—by representatives of the prevailing system. It is the old policy of domesticating terms and ideas, weakening them, and causing them to lose their subversive character with regard to the status quo. Nun comments that "it is indeed significant that in the past few years dependence has become a habitual topic for discussion in organizations, conferences, and documents approved by the system. This phenomenon can be explained in several ways. The first is tactical. In the face of such a massive and open penetration, it is advisable to reassure public opinion by acknowledging part of the problem and thus silencing the critics. Meanwhile nothing really effective is done to change the situation. Moreover, as in the case of agrarian reform, the purpose is to do away with certain forms of external domination, proper to the classical stage of the agricultural-export cycle, while at the same time restricting the eventual penetration of the area by other competitive powers" (*Misión Rockefeller*, p. 7). We have here the same subtle defense mechanisms employed by the dominant societies which have turned rebellion and protest into successful consumer items; see in this regard Hélan Jaworski, "The Integrated Structures of Dependence and Domination in the Americas," *Freedom and Unfreedom in the Americas: Toward a Theology of Liberation*, ed. Thomas E. Quigley (New York: IDOC, 1971) pp. 16-27.

32. According to his students' notes, Hegel asserted more than 140 years ago that "America is therefore the land of the future where in years to come world history will be forged *perhaps by the antagonism between North and South America* (*La raison dans l'histoire* [Paris: Union Générale D'Éditions, 1965], p. 242; the italics are ours).

33. The bibliography on this subject is extensive. We mention only a few works: James Petras and Maurice Zeitlan, ed., *Latin America: Reform or Revolution?* (New York: Fawcett Publications, Inc., 1968); Orlando Fals Borda, *Las revoluciones inconclusas en América Latina, 1809-1968* (Mexico, D.F.: Siglo Veintiuno, 1968); and an interesting analysis of the present situation by Theotonio Dos Santos, "Dependencia económica y alternativas de cambio en América Latina, in *Lucha de clases y dependencia en América Latina* (Bogota: Oveja Negra, 1970), pp. 239-305. For a critical study of the position of Dos Santos, see Ayton Fausto, "La nueva situación de dependencia y el análisis socio-politico de Theotonio Dos Santos," *Revista Latinoamericana de Ciencias Sociales*, no. 1 (June-December 1971), pp. 198-211.

34. It is common knowledge that the relationship of the current Cuban regime with certain Latin American revolutionary groups has become very complex in the last few years.

35. For a bibliography on this subject, see Richard Gott, *Guerrilla Movements in Latin America* (Garden City, New York: Doubleday & Company, Inc., 1971), pp. 555-69. See also the summary presented by the same author in "La guerrilla en América Latina," *Mensaje* 17, no. 174 (November 1968): 557-66; see also the

documents reproduced in *Primera Conferencia de la Organización Latinoamericana de Solidaridad* (Montevideo: Nativa Libros, 1967); Regis Debray, *Strategy for Revolution*, ed. Robin Blackburn (New York: Monthly Review Press, 1970); *Regis Debray and the Latin American Revolution*, ed. Leo Huberman and Paul M. Sweezy (New York: Monthly Review Press, 1968); and the studies collected together with a reply by Debray, in *Debray y la revolución latinoamericana* (Mexico, D.F.: Nuestro Tiempo, 1969). See also two works with different viewpoints: Alberto Methol Ferré, "La Revolución verde oliva: Debray y la OLAS," *Víspera*, no. 3 (October 1967), pp. 17-39; and Edgar Rodríguez, "La crise du mouvement revolutionnaire latino-americain et l'experience du Venezuela," *Les Temps Modernes* (Paris), July 1970, pp. 74-99. See also Héctor Béjar, *Perú 1965: Apuntes sobre una experiencia guerrillera* (Lima: Campodónico Ediciones, 1969); and Roque Dalton, *¿Revolución en la revolución? y la crítica de derecha* (Havana, 1969). For an evaluation and explanation of the working hypothesis of the numerous studies on these questions being made in the United States, see Pablo González Casanova, "La violence latinoamericaine dans les enquétes empiriques nord-americaines," *L'Homme et la Société*, no. 15 (January-March 1970), pp. 159-81.

36. Among recent examples of this reaction especially notorious is the current Brazilian regime. The torture of political prisoners has been denounced internationally. See the facts, eye-witness accounts, and condemnations in *Torturas en Brasil* (Lima: CEP, 1970).

37. *Spirale de la violence* (Paris: Desclée, deBrouwer, 1970). Dom Helder supports "a liberating moral pressure" to destroy the oppressive and unjust structures which prevail in Latin America. However, there are many who hold that this liberation will sooner or later take some form of counterviolence in response to the legalized violence. For an analysis of certain aspects of revolutionary violence, see the articles published in *Paz e Terra* (Rio de Janeiro), no. 7 (1968); and Francisco León, "La violencia revolucionaria," *Mensaje* 17, no. 175 (December 1968): 621-29.

38. "Aniversario y balance," in *Ideología y política* (Lima: Empresa Editora Amauta, 1969), p. 249.

39. "Mensaje al congreso obrero (1927)" in *ibid.*, p. 112.

40. *Defensa del marxismo* (Lima: Empresa Editora Amauta, 1959), p. 36. He also deals with the "canon of Marx." See also p. 63 and p. 105. Mariátequi borrowed this idea from Benedeto Croce for whom "historical materialism, so-called, *is* not a philosophy of history," but "simply a canon of interpretation" (*Materialismo storico ed economia marxista* [1900] [Bari: Laterza, 1968], pp. 2, xii; English version: *Historical Materialism and the Economics of Karl Marx* [New York: Russell & Russell, 1966]). In another context the current vogue of interpreting Marxism in Latin America according to Althusser has spread the idea of historical materialism as a "science of history" which tries to free itself from all ideological elements. See the studies of two Latin American authors regarding Althusser: Jose A. Giannotti, "Contra Althusser," *Teoria e Pratica* (Sao Paulo), no. 3 (1968), pp. 66-82; and Saúl Karsz, "Lectura de Althusser" in *Lectura de Althusser* (Buenos Aires: Galerna, 1970), pp. 13-230. The former is critical, the latter favorable. We hope to present soon a study of certain questions concerning the ambiguities in the use of the term *materialism* and the various interpretations of Marxism as a total conception of life or a science of history. We hope therefore to situate the vision of man and atheistic ideology in Marxism.

41. "True revolutionaries," wrote Mariátegui, "never act as if history began with them" (*Peruanicemos al Perú*, p. 117).

42. There still has not appeared a deep, critical, and comprehensive study of Mariátegui. See the work of Francisco Posada, *Los orígenes del pensamiento marxista en Latinoamérica* (Madrid: Editorial Ciencia Nueva, 1968); Augusto Salazar Bondy, "El pensamiento de Mariátegui y la filosofía marxista" in *Historia de las ideas en el Perú contemporáneo* (Lima: Moncloa, 1959), 2:311-42; Manfred Kossok, "J.C. Mariátegui y el desarrollo del pensamiento marxista en el Perú," in *Documentos políticos* (Bogota), no. 37 (1964). Antonio Melis, "Mariátegui: Primo marxista dell'America," *Crítica Marxista* (Rome) 5, no. 2 (March-April 1967): 732-57; Robert Paris, "El pensamiento de Mariátegui," *Aportes* (July 1970), pp. 6-30; and the recent well-documented study of Yerko Moretic, *José Carlos Mariátegui* (Santiago de Chile: Universidad Técnica del Estado, 1970).

43. Fidel Castro has repeatedly called for support for this posture. In January 1968 he said, "Our country will deepen its revolutionary ideas and will carry its banners foward as far as it can; our country will maintain its distinctive character, a product of its experience and history; ideologically, its criterion is absolute independence, its own course, determined by our people and our experience"; and some months later, "We do not pretend to be the most perfect revolutionaries, ... but we do have our own way of interpreting socialism. Marxist-Leninism, and communism" (Quoted by Aldo Büntig, "La Iglesia en Cuba, Hacia una nueva frontera," *Revista del CIAS* (Buenos Aires), no. 193 (June 1970), p. 24.

44. See above Chapter 2.

45. "Man and Socialism in Cuba," in *Venceremos! The Speeches and Writings of Ernesto Che Guevara*, ed. John Gerassi (New York: The Macmillan Company, 1968), p. 396. "Let me say, with the risk of appearing ridiculous, that the true revolutionary is guided by strong feelings of love. It is impossible to think of an authentic revolutionary without this quality .... In these conditions the revolutionary leaders must have a large dose of humanity, a large dose of a sense of justice and truth, to avoid falling into dogmatic extremes, into cold scholasticism, into isolation from the masses. They must struggle every day so that their love of living humanity is transformed into concrete deeds, into acts that will serve as an example, as a mobilizing factor" (*ibid.*, p. 398). See also the writings of the young Bolivian Nestor Paz: "I believe that the fight for liberation is rooted in the prophetic line of Salvation-History .... The oft-betrayed whip of justice will fall on the exploiter, that false Christian who forgets that the force of his love ought to drive him to liberate his neighbor from sin, that is to say, from every lack of love. We believe in a 'new man,' made free by the blood and resurrection of Jesus. We believe in a New Earth, where love will be the fundamental law. This will only come about, however, by breaking the old patterns based on egoism" ("Revolutionary Proclamation of Nestor Paz on Leaving to Join the Guerrilla Band of Teoponte" in "Nestor Paz: Mystic, Christian, Guerrilla," *IDOC-NA*, no. 23 (April 10, 1971), p. 45.

46. See Paulo Freire, *Pedagogy for the Oppressed* (New York: Herder and Herder 1970).

47. See Paulo Freire, *La educación como práctica de la libertad* (Montevideo: Tierra Nueva, 1969), and the articles which appeared in *Contribución al proceso de concientización en América Latina*, a special supplement of *Cristianismo y Sociedad* (Montevideo: Junta Latinoamericana de Iglesia y Sociedad, 1968). See also Luis Alberto Gomes de Souza, "Problemática de la educación en América Latina," *Educación Latinoamericana* (Bogota), no. 2 (October 1967), pp. 54-64; the

contributions of Hiber Conteris, Julio Barreiro, Julio de Santa Ana, Ricardo Cetrulo, and Vincent Gilbert in the anthology *Conciencia y Revolución*, (Montevideo: Tierra Nueva, 1969); and Ernani Fiori, "Education and Conscientization," *Conscientization for Liberation*, ed. Louis M. Colonnese (Washington, D.C.: Division for Latin America—USCC, 1971), pp. 123-44.

48. See the comments by Noel Olaya and Germán Zabala, "En la ruta de Golconda," *Víspera*, nos. 13-14 (November-December 1969), pp. 36-39.

CHAPTER SEVEN

THE CHURCH
IN THE PROCESS OF LIBERATION

The Latin American Church has lived and to a large extent continues to live as a ghetto church. The Latin American Christian community came into being during the Counter-Reformation and has always been characterized by its defensive attitude as regards the faith. This posture was reinforced in some cases by the hostility of the liberal and anticlerical movements of the nineteenth century and, more recently, by strong criticism from those struggling to transform the society to which the Church is so tightly linked.

This hostility led the Church to seek the support of the established order and economically powerful groups in order to face its adversaries and assure for itself what it believed to be an opportunity to preach the Gospel peacefully.

But for some time now, we have been witnessing a great effort by the Church to rise out of this ghetto power and mentality and to shake off the ambiguous protection provided by the beneficiaries of the unjust order which prevails on the continent.[1] Individual Christians, small communities, and the Church as a whole are becoming more politically aware and are acquiring a greater knowledge of the current Latin American reality, especially in its root causes. The Christian community is beginning, in fact, to read *politically* the signs of the times in Latin America. Moreover, we have witnessed the taking of positions which could even be characterized as daring, especially compared with previous behavior. We have seen a commitment to liberation which has provoked resistance and mistrust.

All this has required a task of reflection on the questions posed by this new attitude; hence the new theological thinking now occurring in Latin America comes more from the Christian groups committed to the liberation of their people than from the traditional centers for the teaching of theology. The fruitfulness of reflection will depend on the quality of these commitments.

The process is complex and things are changing before our very eyes. Here we focus our attention on participation in the process of liberation and thus do not concern ourselves with other aspects of the life of the Church. It will be helpful to point out some of the highlights which characterize the new situation now being created.[2]

THE COMMITMENT OF CHRISTIANS

The different sectors of the People of God are gradually committing themselves in different ways to the process of liberation. They are becoming aware that this liberation implies a break with the status quo, that it calls for a social revolution. In relation to the entire Latin American Christian community it must be acknowledged that the number of persons involved is small. But the numbers are growing and active and every day they are acquiring a larger hearing both inside and outside the Church.

Laymen

What we have referred to as the pastoral approach of "New Christendom" brought about, among large groups of Christians, a political commitment to the creation of a more just society. In the past, the lay apostolate movements, especially among youth, have given a considerable number of their better leaders to the political parties of socio-Christian inspiration.[3] The "distinction of planes" stage allowed for purification of the motivation of these commitments as well as for the discovery of new perspectives for the action of Christians in the world, in collaboration with people of different points of view.[4] Today, apostolic youth movements have radicalized their political options. It has been true for some time now that in most Latin American countries young militants do not share the orientation of moderate renewal groups.[5]

The ever more revolutionary political options of Christian groups—especially students, workers, and peasants—have frequently been responsible for conflicts between the lay apostolic movements and the hierarchy. These options have likewise caused the movement members to question their place in the Church and have been responsible for the severe crises experienced by some of them.[6]

Moreover, many have discovered in these movements evangelical demands for an ever more resolute commitment to the oppressed peoples of this exploited continent. But the inadequacy of the theologico-pastoral plans which until recently were considered viable by these movements, the perception of the close ties which unite the Church to the very social order which the movements wish to change, the urgent albeit ambiguous demands of political action, the impression of dealing with the "concrete" in the revolutionary struggle—all these factors have caused many gradually to substitute working for the Kingdom with working for the social revolution[7]—or, more precisely perhaps, the lines betwen the two have become blurred.

In the concrete, all this has often meant a commitment to revolutionary political groups.[8] The political situation in Latin America together with the subversion of the status quo advocated by these groups force them to become at least partially clandestine. Moreover, as awareness of existing legalized violence grows, the problem of counterviolence is no longer an abstract ethical concern. It now becomes very important on the level of political efficacy. Perhaps more accurately, it is on this latter level that the question of man himself is concretely considered.[9] Under these conditions, the political activity of Christians takes on new dimensions which have caught by surprise not only the ecclesial structures but also the most advanced pedagogical methods of the lay apostolic movements. It is clear, for example, that the kind of apostolic movement represented by the Catholic Action groups among the French workers—that is, communities of Christians with different political options who meet for a *revision de vie* in the light of the faith—is, as such, not viable. Among other reasons, this is so because political radicalization tends to lead to united—and impassioned—positions and because the kind of activity which develops does not allow for entirely free expression of ideas. The model of the Workers' Catholic Action is valid in a more or less stable society where political commitments can be lived out publicly. This model presupposes and facilitates, moreover, a theoretical dialogue with Marxism in a way which holds little interest for Latin America. On this continent, the oppressed and those who seek to identify with them face ever more resolutely a common adversary, and therefore, the relationship between Marxists and Christians takes on characteristics different from those in other places.[10]

On the other hand, meetings between Christians of different confessions but of the same political option are becoming more frequent. This gives rise to ecumenical groups, often marginal to their respective ecclesiastical authorities, in which Christians share their faith and struggle to create a more just society. The common struggle makes the *traditional* ecumenical programs seem obsolete (a "marriage between senior citizens" as someone has said) and impels them to look for new paths toward unity.[11]

A profound renewal or renaissance of various lay apostolic movements is nevertheless apparent. After the initial impact of a radical *politicization* for which they were inadequately prepared theologically, pedagogically, and spiritually, everything seems to indicate that they are beginning to find new approaches.[12] There are also arising new kinds of groups[13] as well as close collaboration among existing movements. These go beyond any particular specialization, yet recognize the need for specialized pedagogies and are oriented toward a specific social milieu; the "cement" holding them together is their particular posture within the Church and within the Latin American political process. A clear option in favor of the oppressed and their liberation leads to basic changes in outlook; there emerges a new vision of the fruitfulness and originality of Christianity and the Christian community's role in this liberation. This is not a matter merely of a reaffirmation of a choice but also of concrete experiences of how to witness to the Gospel in Latin America today. But many questions remain unanswered. The new vitality that can be foreseen does not have before it a completely clear path.

Priests and Religious

A clearer perception of the tragic realities of the continent, the clear options which political polarization demand, the climate of more active participation in the life of the Church created by Vatican II, and the impulse provided by the Latin American Bishops' Conference at Medellín—all these factors have made priests and religious today one of the most dynamic and restless groups in the Latin American Church.[14] Priests and religious in ever increasing proportions seek to participate more actively in the pastoral decisions of the Church. But, above all, they want the Church to break its ties with an unjust order, and they want it—with renewed fidelity to the Lord who calls it and to the Gospel which it preaches—to cast its lot with those who suffer from misery and deprivation.

In a considerable number of countries, we observe the creation of groups of priests—with characteristics not foreseen by canon law!—who have organized to channel and reinforce their growing concern.[15] These groups are characterized by their determination to commit themselves to the process of liberation and by their desire for radical change both in the present internal structures of the Latin American Church as well as in the manner in which the Church is present and active on this continent of revolution.

These concerns, as well as other factors, have led in many cases to friction with local bishops and apostolic nuncios.[16] We can say that unless deep changes take place this conflictual situation will spread and become more serious in the immediate future.

Moreover, there are many priests who consider it a duty to adopt clear and committed personal positions in the political arena. Some participate actively in politics,[17] often in connection with revolutionary groups. As a matter of fact, this participation is not essentially something new. In many ways the clergy have played and still play a direct participation in political life (barely veiled in some cases under pretexts of a religious nature). The new dimension is that many priests clearly admit the need and obligation to make such a commitment and above all that their options in one way or another place them in a relationship of subversion regarding the existing social order.

There are other factors: for example, the effects of a certain weariness caused by the intensity of the resistance that must be overcome within the Church; and then there is the disenchantment caused by the apparent futility of work regarded as purely "religious," which has little contact with the reality and social demands of the continent. We are facing an "identity crisis."

For some this means a reassessment of the current life-style of the clergy; and for others it means even a reevaluation of the meaning of the priesthood itself. On the other hand, the numbers are growing of those who have found a renewed meaning for their priesthood or religious life in the commitment to the oppressed and their struggle for liberation. For them, the Gospel, the Word of the Lord, the message of love, is a liberating force which attacks the roots of all injustice. This leads them to put in second place the questions now being debated—with different priorities in other parts of the world—regarding the priestly or religious life.[18]

Frequently in Latin America today certain priests are considered "subversive." Many are under surveillance or are being sought by the police. Others are in prison, have been expelled from their country (Brazil, Bolivia, Colombia, and the Dominican Republic are significant examples), or have been murdered by terrorist anti-communist groups.[19] For the defenders of the status quo, "priestly subversion" is surprising. They are not used to it. The political activity of some leftist groups, we might say, is—within certain limits—assimilated and tolerated by the system and is even useful to it to justify some of its repressive measures; the dissidence of priests and religious, however, appears as particularly dangerous, especially if we consider the role which they have traditionally played.[20]

Bishops

The new and serious problems which face the Latin American Church and which shape the conflictual and changing reality find many bishops ill-prepared for their function. There is among them, nevertheless, an awakening to the social dimension of the presence of the Church and a corresponding rediscovery of its prophetic mission.

The bishops of the most poverty-stricken and exploited areas are the ones who have denounced most energetically the injustices they witness.[21] But in exposing the deep causes of these injustices, they have had to confront the great economic and political forces of their countries.[22] They naturally leave themselves open to being accused of meddling in affairs outside their competence and even of being friendly to Marxist ideas. Often this accusation is made, and vigorously, in conservative sectors, both Catholic and non-Catholic. Some of these bishops have become almost political personalities in their respective countries. The consequence has been tightened police vigilance and in some cases death threats on the part of groups of the extreme right.

But it is not just a question of isolated personalities. It is often entire conferences of bishops who openly take a position in this arena.[23] We should also mention the efforts of many bishops to make changes—of varying degrees of radicalness—in Church structures. The results are still much below what is desired and necessary. The first steps do appear to have been taken, but the danger of retreat has not been eliminated, and, above all, there is much yet to be done.

In the majority of cases, options at the episcopal level regarding social transformation have been expressed in written statements, but there have also been cases in which these declarations have been accompanied by very concrete actions: direct intervention in workers' strikes, participation in public demonstrations, etc.[24]

STATEMENTS AND ATTEMPTS AT REFLECTION

From these commitments on which we have commented briefly, there have emerged statements explaining them and outlining a theologico-pastoral reflection upon them.[25]

During the past three years there has appeared a great number of public statements by lay movements, groups of priests and bishops, or national conferences of bishops. As regards doctrinal authority and impact, the most important text we will mention is, of course, that of the Episcopal Conference at Medellín (1968). To a certain extent, the others can be ordered around it. But without these others, it would not be possible to grasp accurately the process which led to Medellín or the repercussions flowing from it. These other statements go beyond Medellín. Their options are clearer and less easily neutralized by the system. They are also closer to concrete commitments. Moreover, these statements express the sentiments of large sectors of the People of God. It is a somewhat muffled voice which still does not actually arise from the oppressed—condemned as they have been to a long silence—except through many filters. It is, however, a first attempt at speaking out.

From the point of view of the issues being discussed here, we can classify these texts into two necessarily related themes: the transformation of the Latin American reality and the search for new forms of the Church's presence on the contemporary scene.

Towards a Transformation
of the Latin American Reality

One unifying theme which is present throughout these documents and which reflects a general attitude of the Church is the acknowledgement of the *solidarity of the Church* with the Latin American reality. The Church avoids placing itself above this reality, but rather attempts to assume its responsibility for the injustice which it has supported both by its links with the established order as well as by its silence regarding the evils this order implies. "We recognize that we Christians for want of fidelity to the Gospel have contributed to the present unjust situation through our words and attitudes, our silence and inaction," claim the Peruvian bishops.[26] More than 200 laymen, priests, and bishops of El Salvador assert that "our Church has not been effective in liberating and bettering Salvadorian man. This failure is due in part to the above-mentioned incomplete concept of the salvation of man and the mission of the Church and in part to the fear of losing privileges or suffering persecution."[27]

As for the bishops' vision of reality, they describe the misery and the exploitation of man by man in Latin America as "a situation of injustice that can be called institutionalized violence";[28] it is responsible for the death of thousands of innocent victims.[29] This view allows for a study of the complex problems of counterviolence without falling into the pitfalls of a double standard which assumes that violence is acceptable when the oppressor uses it to maintain "order" and is bad when the oppressed invoke it to change this "order." Institutionalized violence violates fundamental rights so patently that the Latin American bishops warn that "one should not abuse the patience of a people that for years has borne a situation that would not be acceptable to any one with any degree of awareness of human rights."[30] An important part of the Latin American clergy request, moreover, that "in considering the problem of violence in Latin America, let us by all means avoid equating the *unjust violence* of the oppressors (who maintain this despicable system) with the *just violence* of the oppressed (who feel obliged to use it to achieve their liberation)."[31] Theologically, this situation of injustice and oppression is characterized as a "sinful situation" because "where this social peace does not exist, there we will find social, political, economic, and cultural inequalities, there we will find the rejection of the peace of the Lord, and a rejection of the Lord Himself."[32] With this in mind, an important group of priests declared, "We feel we have a right and a duty to condemn unfair wages, exploitation, and starvation tactics as clear indications of sin and evil."[33]

The reality so described is perceived ever more clearly as resulting from a situation of dependence, in which the centers of decision are to be found outside the continent; it follows that the Latin American countries are being kept in a condition of neo-colonialism.[34] It has been asserted that underdevelopment "can be only understood in terms of the *dependency relationship* with the developed world that it results from. In large measure the underdevelopment of Latin America is a *byproduct* of capitalist development in the West."[35] The interpretation of Latin American reality in terms of dependency is adopted and considered valid "insofar as it allows us to seek a causal explanation, to denounce domination, and to struggle to overcome it with a commitment to liberation which will produce a new society."[36] This perspective is also clearly adopted by a seminar on the problems of youth sponsored by the Education Department of the Latin American Episcopal Council. It stresses that "Latin American dependency is not only economic and political but also cultural."[37]

Indeed, in texts of the Latin American Church of varying origins and degrees of authority, in the last few years there has been a significant although perhaps not completely coherent replacement of the theme of *development*[38] by the theme of *liberation*.[39] Both the term and the idea express the aspirations to be free from a situation of dependence; the "Message of the Bishops of the Third World" states that "an irresistible impulse drives these people on to better themselves and to free themselves from the forces of oppression."[40] In the words of 120 Bolivian priests: "We observe in our people a desire for liberation and a movement of struggle for justice, not only to obtain a better standard of living, but also to be able to participate in the socio-economic resources and the decision-making process of the country."[41] The deeper meaning of these expressions is the insistence on the need for the oppressed peoples of Latin America to control their own destiny. Quoting *Populorum progressio* Medellín advocates therefore, a "liberating education." The bishops see this as "the key instrument for liberating the masses from all servitude and for causing them to ascend 'from less human to more human conditions,' bearing in mind that man is responsible for and 'the principle author of his success or failure.' "[42] Moreover, liberation from this servitude is considered in an important passage of Medellín as a manifestation of liberation from sin made possible by Christ: "It is the same God who, in the fullness of time, sends his Son in the flesh so that He might come to liberate all men from the slavery to which sin has subjected them: hunger, misery, oppression and ignorance, in a word, that injustice and hatred which have their origin in human selfishness."[43]

The Church wishes to share in this aspiration of the Latin American peoples; the bishops at Medellín think of themselves as belonging to a people who are "beginning to discover their proper self-awareness and their task in the consort of nations."[44] "We are vitally aware of the social revolution now in progress. We identify with it."[45] Argentinian priests and laymen also declare their total commitment to the process of liberation: "We wish to express our total commitment to the liberation of the oppressed and the working class and to the search for a social order radically different from the present one, an order seeking to achieve more adequately justice and evangelical solidarity."[46]

Faced with the urgency of the Latin American situation, the Church denounces as insufficient those partial and limited measures which amount only to palliatives and in the long run actually consolidate an exploitative system. Those projects are therefore criticized which by their superficiality create mirages and cause setbacks.[47] At a deeper level, considering that the problems are rooted in the structures of capitalist society which produce a situation of dependency, it is stated "that it is necessary to change the very bases of the system,"[48] since "a true solution to these problems can only come about within the context of a far-reaching transformation of existent structures."[49] Hence the criticism of "developmentalism," which advocates the capitalist model as a solution,[50] and the calls for a radicalization of reforms which would otherwise "in the long run ... serve to consolidate new forms of the capitalist system, bringing with them a new dependence less evident but not less real."[51] Hence also the term *social revolution* appears more frequently and opposition to it is less.[52]

For some, participation in this process of liberation means not allowing themselves to be intimidated by the accusation of being "communist."[53] On the positive side it can even mean taking the path of *socialism*. A group of Colombian priests affirmed, "We forthrightly denounce neo-colonial capitalism, since it is incapable of solving the acute problems that confront our people. We are led to direct our efforts and actions toward the building of a Socialist type of society that would allow us to eliminate all forms of man's exploitation of his fellow man, and that fits in with the historical tendencies of our time and the distinctive character of Colombians."[54] According to the Argentinian Priests for the Third World, this socialism will be a "Latin American socialism that will promote the advent of the New Man."[55]

In a speech which has been bitterly debated and attacked, one of the most influential figures of the Mexican Church, Don Sergio Méndez Arceo, asserted: "Only socialism can enable Latin America to achieve true development .... I believe that a socialist system is more in accord with the Christian principles of true brotherhood, justice, and peace .... I do not know what kind of socialism, but this is the direction Latin America should go. For myself, I believe it should be a democratic socialism."[56] Old prejudices, inevitable ideological elements, and also the ambivalence of the term *socialism* require the use of cautious language and careful distinctions. There is always the risk that statements in this regard may be interpreted differently by different people.[57] It is therefore important to link this subject to another which enables us at least under one aspect to clarify what we mean. We refer to the progressive radicalization of the debate concerning private property. The subordination of private property to the social good has been stressed often.[58] But difficulties in reconciling justice and private ownership have led many to the conviction that "private ownership of capital leads to the dichotomy of capital and labor, to the superiority of the capitalist over the laborer, to the exploitation of man by man .... The history of the private ownership of the means of production makes evident the necessity of its reduction or suppression for the welfare of society. We must hence *opt for social ownership of the means of production.*"[59]

The case of Chile is particularly interesting. The electoral victory of a socialist government poses a decisive and potentially very fruitful challenge to Chilean Christians. The first reactions are already being felt, but it is well to remember that they come out of a long tradition of participation by various groups in the struggle for liberation of the oppressed sectors. A group of priests attached to the university parish in Santiago writes, "The capitalist system exhibits a number of elements which are against man. . . . Socialism, although it does not deliver man from injustices caused by personal attitudes nor from the ambiguity inherent in all systems, does offer a fundamental equality of opportunity. Through a change in the relationships of production, it dignifies labor so that the worker, while humanizing nature, becomes more of a person. It offers a possibility for the even development of the country for the benefit of all, especially the most neglected. It asserts that the motivation of morality and social solidarity is of higher value than that of individual interest, etc." The transformation of man emerges as a simultaneous task: "All this can be implemented if together with the transformation of the economic structure, the transformation of man is undertaken with equal enthusiasm. We do not believe man will automatically become less selfish, but we do maintain that where a socio-economic foundation for equality has been established, it is more possible to work realistically toward human solidarity than it is in a society torn asunder by inequity." The attitude of Christians is based on the understanding that the coming of the Kingdom implies the building of a just society. "If our country engages in an all-out struggle against misery, the Christian, who should participate fully in it, will interpret whatever progress is achieved as a first implementation of the Kingdom proclaimed by Jesus. In other words, today the Gospel of Christ implies (and is incarnated in) man's multiple efforts to obtain justice."[60] The MOAC (Workers' Catholic Action Movement) has this to say regarding the victory of the new Chilean regime: "This fact embodies a great hope and a great responsibility for *all* workers and their organizations: active and watchful collaboration to bring about a more just society which will permit the integral liberation of those oppressed by an inhuman and anti-Christian system such as capitalism."[61]

More recently, a large group of priests has taken a clear stand in favor of the socialist process occurring in Chile: "Socialism, characterized by the social appropriation of the means of production, opens the path to a new economy. This economy makes possible an autonomous and more rapid development as well as an overcoming of the division of a society into antagonistic classes. Nevertheless socialism is not only a new economy. It should also generate new values which make possible the emergence of a society of greater solidarity and brotherhood in which the worker assumes with dignity the role which is his. We feel commited to this process already underway and wish to contribute to its success." Further they state, "The profound reason for this commitment is our faith in Jesus Christ, which is deepened, renewed, and takes on flesh according to historical circumstances. To be a Christian is to be in solidarity. To be in solidarity at this time in Chile is to participate in the historical task which the people has set for itself."[62] In a document directed to the bishops' synod in Rome, the Peruvian bishops stated: "When governments arise which are trying to implant more just and human societies in their countries, we propose that the Church commit itself to giving them its backing; contributing to the elimination of prejudice; recognizing the aspirations they hold; and encouraging the search for their own road toward a socialist society."[63]

Finally, the process of liberation requires the *active participation of the oppressed*; this certainly is one of the most important themes running through the writings of the Latin American Church. Based on the evidence of the usually frustrated aspirations of the popular classes to participate in decisions which affect all of society,[64] the realization emerges that it is the poor who must be the protagonists of their own liberation: "It is primarily up to the poor nations and the poor of the other nations to effect their own betterment."[65] Rejecting every kind of paternalism, the ONIS priests say, "We believe that social transformation is not simply a revolution for the people, but that the people themselves especially farmers and working men, exploited and unjustly kept in the background, must take part in their own liberation."[66] The participation of the oppressed presupposes an awareness on their part of their unjust situation. "Justice, and therefore peace," say the Latin American bishops, "conquer by means of a dynamic action of awakening (*concientización*) and organization of the popular sectors which are capable of pressing public officials who are often impotent in their social projects without popular support."[67]

However, existing structures block popular participation and marginate the great majorities, depriving them of channels for expression of their demands.[68] Consequently, the Church feels compelled to address itself directly to the oppressed—instead of appealing to the oppressors—calling on them to assume control of their own destiny, committing itself to support their demands, giving them an opportunity to express these demands, and even articulating them itself.[69] At Medellín a pastoral approach was approved which encourages and favors "the efforts of the people to create and develop their own grass-roots organizations for the redress and consolidation of their rights and the search for true justice."[70]

A New Presence of the Church in Latin America

A call to struggle against oppressive structures and to construct a more just society would have very little impact, however, if the whole Church did not rise to the level of these demands by means of a profound revision of its presence in Latin America.

a) The first evidence of this revision which can be culled from the texts mentioned is that, having acknowledged the Church's responsibility in the current situation, they strongly insist that the Church and in particular the bishops fulfill a role of *prophetic denunciation* of these grave injustices rampant in Latin America, which have already been characterized as "sinful situations." The bishops at Medellín asserted, "To us, the Pastors of the Church, belongs the duty ... to denounce everything which, opposing justice, destroys peace."[71] They are moved to make this denunciation by the "duty of solidarity with the poor, to which charity leads us. This solidarity means that we make ours their problems and their struggles, that we know how to speak with them. This has to be concretized in criticism of injustice and oppression, in the struggle against the intolerable situation which a poor person has to tolerate."[72] Even further, the bishops are asked to go "beyond statements about situations ..., to concentrate on concrete events, and ... to take positions regarding them."[73] The Peruvian bishops commit themselves to denounce injustice, supporting these denunciations, if necessary, "by concrete gestures of solidarity with the poor and the oppressed."[74] Aware of the difficulties which this solidarity with the poor may bring to those who practice it, the bishops assembled in Medellín declared: "We express our desire to be very close always to those who work in the self-denying apostolate with the poor in order that they will always feel our encouragement and know that we will not listen to parties interested in distorting their work."[75] There is likewise an awareness of the political implications of these actions and of the criticisms which arise from certain sectors: "No one should allow himself to be intimidated," say the Mexican bishops, "by those who—apparently zealous to preserve the 'purity' and 'dignity' of priestly and religious activity—characterize this intervention of the Church as 'political.' Frequently this false zeal veils the desire to impose a law of silence when the real need is to lend a voice to those who suffer injustice and to develop the social and political responsibility of the People of God."[76]

The denunciation of social injustices is certainly the prevailing theme in the texts of the Latin American Church. This denunciation is a manner of expressing the intention of becoming disassociated from the existing unjust order. "When a system ceases to promote the common good and favors special interests, the Church must not only denounce injustice but also break with the evil system."[77] The denunciation of injustice implies the rejection of the use of Christianity to legitimize the established order.[78] It likewise implies, in fact, that the Church has entered into conflict with those who wield power.[79] And finally it leads to acknowledging the need for the separation of Church and state because "this is of primary importance in liberating the Church from temporal ties and from the image projected by its bonds with the powerful. This separation will free the Church from compromising commitments and make it more able to speak out. It will show that in order to fulfill its mission, the Church relies more on the strength of the Lord than on the strength of Power. And the Church will be able to establish ... the only earthly ties which it should have: communion with the disinherited of our country, with their concerns and struggles."[80]

The prophetic task of the Church is both constructive and critical and is exercised in the midst of a process of change: "The prophetic task of justice demands, on the one hand, that the Church point out those elements within a revolutionary process which are truly humanizing and encourage the determined, dynamic, and creative participation of its members in this process. On the other hand, the Church must point out the dehumanizing elements also to be found in a process of change. But this function is not appropriate if the creative participation of the Christian community within the society has not already occurred. The Cuban Church is called to this twofold task within our revolution."[81]

b) A second thematic line in the texts we have examined is the urgent need for a *conscienticizing evangelization.* "To us, the Pastors of the Church, belongs the duty to educate the Christian conscience, to inspire, stimulate, and help orient all of the initiatives that contribute to the formation of man," asserted the bishops at Medellín.[82] This awareness of being oppressed but nevertheless of being masters of their own destiny is nothing other than a consequence of a well-understood evangelization: "As we see it, a perhaps faulty presentation of the Christian message may have given the impression that religion is indeed the opiate of the people. And we would be guilty of betraying the cause of Peru's development, if we did not stress the fact that the doctrinal riches of the Gospel contain a revolutionary thrust."[83] Indeed, "the God whom we know in the Bible is a liberating God, a God who destroys myths and alienations, a God who intervenes in history in order to break down the structures of injustice and who raises up prophets in order to point out the way of justice and mercy. He is the God who liberates slaves (Exodus), who causes empires to fall and raises up the oppressed."[84] The whole climate of the Gospel is a continual demand for the right of the poor to make themselves heard, to be considered preferentially by society, a demand to subordinate economic needs to those of the deprived. Was not Christ's first preaching to "proclaim the liberation of the oppressed?"[85] The content of the message itself, the process of liberation in Latin America, and the demands for participation on the part of the people, all determine "the priority of a conscienticizing evangelization. This evangelization will free, humanize, and better man ... and will be nourished by the recovery of a living faith committed to human society."[86] The same idea appears in another important text: "In Latin America today evangelization in the context of the youth movements is closely linked to conscientization—insofar as this is understood as an analysis

of reality which has Christ as its center and which seeks the
liberation of the person."[87] At Medellín the bishops have resolved
"to be certain that our preaching, liturgy, and catechesis take
into account the social and community dimension of Christianity,
forming men committed to world peace."[88] Others point out that
this conscienticizing evangelization is a form of "service and
commitment to the poorest; evangelizing action ought to be
directed preferentially to this group, not only because of the
need to understand their life, but also to help them become aware
of their own mission, by cooperating in their liberation and
development"[89] It is then to the oppressed that the Church
should address itself and not so much to the oppressors; furthermore, this action will give true meaning to the Church's witness
to poverty. "Poverty in the Church will only be truly achieved
when the Church focuses on the evangelization of the oppressed
as its primary duty."[90]

c) *Poverty* is, indeed, one of the most frequent and pressing
demands placed on the Latin American Church. Vatican II
asserts that the Church ought to carry out its mission as Christ
did "in poverty and under oppression" (*Lumen gentium*, no. 8.).
This is not the image given by the Latin American Christian
community as a whole.[91] Rather, poverty is an area in which
countersigns are rampant: "Instead of talking about the Church
of the poor, we must be a poor Church. And we flaunt this commitment with our real estate, our rectories and other buildings,
and our whole style of life."[92] At Medellín it was made clear
that poverty expresses solidarity with the oppressed and a protest against oppression. Suggested ways of implementing this
poverty in the Church are the evangelization of the poor, the
denunciation of injustice, a simple life-style, a spirit of service,
and freedom from temporal ties, intrigue, or ambiguous prestige.[93]

d) The demands placed on the Church by prophetic denunciation, by the conscienticizing evangelization of the oppressed,
and by poverty sharply reveal the *inadequacy of the structures
of the Church* for the world in which it lives. These structures
appear obsolete and lacking in dynamism before the new and
serious challenges. "The very structures in which we operate,"
says a group of Bolivian priests, "often prevent us from acting
in a manner that accords with the Gospel. This, too, deeply concerns us; for we see that it greatly complicates the chances of

bringing the Gospel to the people. The Church cannot be a
prophet in our day if she herself is not turned to Christ. She
does not have the right to talk against others when she herself
is a cause of scandal in her interpersonal relations and her internal structures."[94] There arises, therefore, the urgent need for
a profound renewal of the present ecclesial structures. It is the
opinion of lay movement representatives that "pastoral structures are insufficient and inadequate. The overall pastoral structure must be reworked if it is to be adequate to the sociological
situation in which it is to be carried out."[95] This has been the
sense of the seminal effort at Medellín; its implementation is
urgent.[96]

e) "The profound changes in Latin America today necessarily
affect the priest in his ministry and in his life-style," assert
the Latin American bishops.[97] The need to change the current
life-style of the clergy[98] is to be considered in this light, especially
regarding their commitment to the creation of a new society.
Although the denunciation of injustice has political overtones,
it is first of all a fundamental demand of the Gospel, since it
concerns, according to a group of Argentinian priests, "the great
option of man for his rights, his freedom, and his personal dignity
as a son of God. Moreover, we feel that if we did not denounce
injustice we would be responsible for and accessory to the injustices being committed. The exercise of our ministry inevitably
leads us to commitment and solidarity."[99] There is need for
change also with regard to ways of earning a living: "New ways
must be found to support the clergy. Those who do not wish
to live on stipends or from teaching religion should be allowed
to experiment . . . . A secular job could be very healthy: they
would find themselves in the real world of men *(Presbyterorum
ordinis*, no. 8); it would lessen the temptation to servility on
the part of those who depend totally on the clerical institution;
it would likewise diminish the financial problems of the institutional Church. It would give a great deal more independence
from the government and the armed forces; and finally it would
contribute in many of us to the development of a strong apostolic
vocation disengaged from all unhealthy ties."[100] Changes are
also urged regarding greater participation of lay people, religious, and priests in the pastoral decisions of the Church.[101]

The documents produced by various sectors of the Latin American Church over the last several years are especially abundant

and worthy of a more complete and detailed technical analysis.[102]
We have recorded here only the most representative texts which
fall within the scope of this work. The issues discussed are mark-
edly different from those being dealt with up to a short time
ago.[103] Moreover, in the approach to the problems there is apparent a *growing radicalization*. Although there is still a long road
ahead, positions are being taken which are no longer so ambiguous or naive. There is a new attitude—ever more lucid and
demanding—suggestive of a qualitatively different society and
of basically new forms of the Church's presence in it.

NOTES

1. Ivan Vallier accurately points to the beginnings of this separation in
"Religious Elites: Differentiations and Developments in Roman Catholicism," in
Elites in Latin America, Seymour Martin Lipset and Aldo Solari, eds. (New York:
Oxford University Press, 1967), pp. 190-232. I have some reservations about the
typology he proposes, however.

2. Among the most recent projects, see for the Church in Argentina the excellent
analysis by Luis Gera and Guillermo Rodríguez, "Apuntes para una interpretación
de la Iglesia Argentina" in *Víspera*, no. 15 (February 1970), pp. 59-88. Regarding
certain aspects of the Peruvian Church, see the study by Carlos Alberto Astiz,
"The Catholic Church in Politics: the Peruvian Case" (position paper presented
at the Eighth World Congress of the International Political Science Association,
Munich, August 31-September 5, 1970). The Cuban Church is now living through
a totally new experience, which can provide many lessons for all of Latin America.
See on this point, Aldo Büntig, "Iglesia en Cuba," who traces the evolution of
the posture of the Church toward the present Cuban regime and examines the
situation. Regarding recent developments in the Brazilian Church, see the account
by Henri Fresquet, "L'Église catholique au Bresil" in *Le Monde* (Paris), September
8-10, 1970. Regarding the Bolivian Church see the interesting report by Lorenzo
Pérez, "Bolivia: la Iglesia y la política," *Spes*, no. 11 (October 1970), pp. 1-9. See
also Jordan Bishop, "Christianisme et révolution en Amérique Latine," *Ésprit*
39, no. 1 (January 1971): 16-30; in English see Bishop's "The Church in Latin
America," in *Shaping a New World: An Orientation to Latin America*, ed. Edward
L. Cleary, O.P. (Maryknoll, New York: Orbis Books [1971]). Regarding other aspects
of the life of the Latin Ameican Church, see René Laurentin, *L'Amérique latine
à l'heure de l'enfantement* (Paris: Éditions du Seuil, 1969); Hector Borrat "Le heurt
de l'Église et des pouvoirs publics en Amérique Latine," *Terre Entière*, nos. 42-43
(July-October 1970), pp. 35-67. For another point of view, it might be interesting
to see also the report commissioned by the U.S. State Department: Luigi Einaudi,
Richard Maullin, Alfred Sepan, and Michael Fleet, *Latin American Institutional
Development: The Changing Catholic Church* (Santa Monica, California: The Rand
Corporation, 1969).

3. The Chilean instance was perhaps the most typical and also the most lasting. See G. Wayland-Smith, *The Christian Democratic Party in Chile*, Cuernavaca, Mexico, CIDOC Sondeo, no. 39.

4. This period began around 1960-62 among university movements of various South American countries; see, for example, the change from the "historical ideal," reminiscent of Maritain (see JUC *Boletim Nacional*, no. 4, 1960, Rio de Janeiro) to "historical awareness," obviously influenced by Henrique de Lima Vaz (see Equipo Nacional, "Reflexões sôbre o sentido do movimento" in JUC, *Boletim Nacional*, no. 1, 1963). See also Gustavo Gutiérrez, *Misión de la Iglesia y apostolado universitario*, pamphlet (Lima: UNEC, 1960); and Patricio Rodó, *Promoción del laicado*, pamphlet (Montevideo, 1963).

5. See for example the role of lay apostolic movements in the Brazilian revolutionary Left. In this regard see Candido Mendes, *Memento dos vivos* (Rio de Janeiro: Tempo Brasileiro,1966), and Marcio Moeira Alves, *O Cristo do povo* (Rio de Janeiro: Ed. Sabía, 1968).

6. Literature on this problem is abundant but not easily accessible. See, however, a good panoramic view of university apostolic movements in Gilberto Giménez, *Introducnión a una pedagogía de la pastoral universitaria*, MIEC-JECI, Servicio de Documentación (Montevideo), series 1, doc. 19, 1968. See also the report presented to Pope Paul VI by the Department of University Pastoral Planning of CELAM: "La realidad universitaria y sus implicaciones pastorales" in *Educación Latinoamericana* (Bogota), October 1968. The problem is particularly acute in the Brazilian Church; see in this regard Michael Schooyans, *O desafío de secularização*, (São Paulo: Ed. Herder, 1968).

7. Roqueplo has considered this problem well although in a slightly different context (*Expérience du monde*, pp. 41-44). "One of the reasons," he writes, "why I am writing this book is the experience of these crises and the lack of reflection there has been on them" (p. 42, n. 19). See also Alfonso Alvarez Bolado's excellent observations, within the framework of the Spanish situation, in "Compromiso terrestre y crisis de fe" in *Vida cristiana y compromiso terrestre* (Bilbao: Editorial Mensajero, 1970), pp. 151-218. This was partially published in *Víspera*, no. 22 (April 1971), pp. 9-17.

8. In this connection, Enrique López Oliva has published *Los católicos y la revolución latinoamericana* (Havana: Instituto del Libro, 1969). Its publication in Montevideo has been announced; see *Pensamiento Crítico* (Havana), no. 31 [August 1969], p. 190). Regarding collaboration and dialogue with Marxist groups, see Arturo Gaete, "El largo camino del diálogo cristiano-marxista," *Mensaje* 17, no. 169 (June 1968): 209-19; see also by the same author, "Socialismo y comunismo: historia de una problemática condenación," *Mensaje* 20, no. 200 (July 1971): 290-302.

9. Regarding attitudes in Christian circles, see Aguiar, "Currents and Tendencies."

10. Fidel Castro's statement regarding Camilo Torres is interesting in this regard: "Camilo Torres is the case of a priest who went to die for those struggling to liberate their people. This is why he has become a symbol of the revolutionary unity of the people of Latin America" (Speech delivered January 4, 1969, quoted in Büntig, "Iglesia en Cuba," p. 40).

11. In Evangelical churches, just as in some sectors of the Catholic Church, ties with the current unjust order are being rejected: "Our churches are not only an integral part of these structures which perpetuate the oppression, but they even reinforce this state of human alienation by claiming to operate 'by divine

THE CHURCH IN THE PROCESS OF LIBERATION   121

right,' if we may use this expression" (Christian Lalive D'Épinay, "La Iglesia evangélica y la revolución latinoamericana," in *CIDOC*, no. 78, 1968, p. 6). See also Waldo A. Cesar, Richard Shaull, Orlando Fals Borda, Beatriz Muniz de Souza, *Protestantismo e imperialismo na América Latina* (Petropolis, Brazil: Vozes, 1968). ISAL (Iglesia y Sociedad para América Latina) is an important experiment in cooperation among Christians of different denominations who have made a clear option for liberation. See the statements made by Julio de Santa Ana, "ISAL: un movimiento anti-imperialista y antioligárquico," in *NADOC*, no. 95, October 15, 1969. See also the lucid analaysis of Rubem Alves, "El protestantismo como una forma de colonialismo," *Perspectivas para el Diálogo*, no. 38 (November 1968), pp. 242-48.

12. This new emphasis is just beginning to be treated in writing. See for example, at the level of peasant movements, Silvio Sant'Anna's *Una experiencia de concientización: Con MIJARC en el Cono Sur*, MIEC-JECI, series 2, doc. 7, 1969. Regarding labor, see the conclusions of the Latin American Meeting of Coordinating Teams of JOC, held in Lima in 1970. The experiences and reflections of Buenaventura Pelegrí deal with university movements: *Introducción a la metodologia de los movimientos apostolicos universitarios*, MIEC-JECI, series 1, doc. 17-18, 1969, and *Pedagogia de la explicitación de la fe*, MIEC-JECI, series 1, doc. 20-21, 1970.

13. The symposia on the theology of liberation provide an interesting example. See Gustavo Pérez Ramírez, "Palabras introductorias" in *Aportes para la liberación* (Bogota: Editorial Presencia, 1970), pp. 1-4; in English see "Theology of Liberation: Bogota, 1970" in *IDOC-NA*, no. 14 (November 28, 1970), pp. 66-78.

14. For a good synoptic view see Michel de Certeau, "Problèmes actuels du sacerdoce en Amérique Latine," *Recherches de Sciences Religieuses* 56, no. 4 (October-December 1968): 591-601; also J. Comblin, "Problèmes sacerdotaux d'Amérique Latine," *La Vie Spirituelle* 118, no. 547 (March 1968): 319-43. Regarding Brazilian problems, see the results of a recent study by José Marins, "Pesquisa sobre o clero do Brasil," in *Revista Eclesiástica Brasileira* 29, no. 1 (March 1969): 121-38. As regards religious, one ought to mention the active and interesting work carried on by the Latin American Conference for Religious (CLAR), as a result of its commitment to the process of liberation.

15. "Sacerdotes para el Tercer Mundo" (Argentina) and "Movimiento Sacerdotal ONIS (Oficina Nacional de Investigación Social"; Peru) are at this point perhaps the most active and best organized. Until recently, although it moves within a different perspective, the "Golconda" group (Colombia) also qualified; this group has had a deep impact. Similar groups exist in Ecuador (Comisión Nacional de Presbíteros), Chile ("Los Ochenta"), Guatemala (Confederación de Sacerdotes de Guatemala [CODESGUA]), and Mexico (Movimiento de Sacerdotes para el Pueblo). The "Declaración de la comisión permanente del episcopado argentino" is very critical of some of the theses of the "Sacerdotes para el Tercer Mundo" movement (see *NADOC*, no. 164, September 1970); see also in this regard the letter addressed by Bishop Jerónimo Podestá to the Argentinian Episcopal Conference (*NADOC*, no. 183, January 1971) and especially the extensive and well-documented reply of the Priests for the Third World: *Nuestra reflexión: Carta a los obispos argentinos* (Buenos Aires, 1970); for selected texts in English in this connection see "Argentina: Priests for the Third World," *IDOC-NA*, no. 15 (December 12, 1970), pp. 58-96. Concerning these groups, see also the short study of Gonzalo Arroyo, "Católicos de izquierda en América Latina, *Mensaje* 19, no. 191 (August 1970): 369-72.

16. These clashes have taken place in almost all Latin American countries, the most serious being perhaps in Brazil, Argentina, and Guatemala. In this regard see the documents reproduced by SEDOC (Petropolis, Brazil), CIDOC (Cuernavaca, Mexico), and NADOC (Lima, Peru).

17. The instance of Camilo Torres is well known. See his collected works in *Camilo Torres por el P. Camilo Torres, 1956-1965.* (Cuernavaca, Mexico: CIDOC, 1966); English version: *Camilo Torres, Revolutionary Writings* (New York: Herder and Herder, 1969); in English see also *Revolutionary Priest: The Complete Writings & Messages of Camilo Torres,* ed. John Gerassi (New York: Vintage Books, 1971); see also *Camilo Torres: liberacion o muerte* (Havana: Instituto del Libro, 1967); and the most complete edition, *Camilo Torres, cristianismo y revolucion* (Mexico, D.F.: Era, 1970). See also Germán Guzmán, *Camilo Torres,* trans. John D. Ring (New York: Sheed and Ward, 1969). This is a well-documented work, but some of its opinions are debatable; see the comments of Oscar Maldonado, "El Camilo Torres de Germán Guzmán," *CIDOC,* no. 48, 1967. See also José María González Ruiz, "Camilo Torres o el buen samaritano," *Perspectivas para el Diálogo,* no. 25 (July 1968), pp. 139-41; see also an essay which situates Camilo Torres in Colombian political history: Orlando Fals Borda, *Subversion and Social Change in Colombia,* trans. Jacqueline D. Skiles (New York: Columbia University Press, 1969), pp. 160-69. See also Horacio Bogorje and others, *Retrato de Camilo Torres* (Mexico: D.F.: Grijalbo, 1969). On some of the repercussions of Camilo Torres, see Enrique López Oliva, *El camilismo en la América Latina* (Havana: Casa de las Américas, 1970); according to this author the impact of Torres demonstrates that the "Latin American revolutionary front" is gaining ground (p. 11). Torres is not at all a unique case. Political commitment is found in differing degrees among many priests in Latin America.

18. After recognizing certain similarities between the movements, Jorge Vernazza, in the name of the Permanent Secretariat of the "Sacerdotes para el Tercer Mundo" movement wrote as follows to a representative of the "Exchanges et Dialogue" movement in France: "However, we believe that our focus is fundamentally different. Our main objective is not 'to put an end to our status as clergy,' but rather to commit ourselves as priests to the Latin American revolutionary process. Undoubtedly our social and ecclesiastical conditioning is very different: Latin America demands above all a salvation which is verified in liberation from widespread injustice and oppression. It is the Church that must proclaim and support this liberation, and the Church is in the eyes of the people permanently linked to the image and function of the priest. It is for this reason that—although our actions and words may cause, in fact have already caused, opposition and suspicion on the part of much of the 'official' Church—we are concerned that we do not appear to be separate from it. We do not want to detract from the efficacy of our action and we believe that the Church has a great conscienticizing impact upon the people . . . . It seems to us that for many sociological and historical reasons we Latin Americans regard the 'clerical status' differently than you. Perhaps less formality and efficiency and also more relaxed and 'democratic' social relationships in our ecclesiastical government have led us to feel less oppressed by it . . . . Therefore, we believe that our very commitments to man and the revolutionary process impel us to continue as clerics" (Letter dated December 10, 1969, which appeared in *Enlace,* the bulletin of the Priests for the Third World movement [Buenos Aires], no. 10 [1970], pp. 22-23).

And in an open letter to the Dutch clergy regarding the problem of celibacy, the same group of Argentinian priests says: "Celibate or married, the important thing is that you make present in today's world the salvation of Jesus Christ. But this salvation in 1970 demands an end of the 'imperialism of money....' You, priests of Holland, you are witnesses of Jesus Christ and his salvation in a rich, imperialistic, and exploitative country. Allow us to address this call to you: While you were celibate you did not know how or were not able to be the voice of the exploited countries, those suffering the consequences of the unjust economic policy of the leaders of your countries. We hope that once you are married you can do this better. Indeed, if marriage does not help you to be more open to the world in general and especially to those who are being exploited by the 'laws' of international trade, you will have accomplished nothing more than becoming more bourgeois. Remember that while you seek the right to establish a home, many poor people in the Third World are renouncing theirs to give themselves completely to the liberation of their brother" (in *Liberación* [Mexico, D.F.], March 1970).

19. A recent example of this is Henrique Pereira, a priest in Recife, Brazil. See the documentation reproduced in *SEDOC*, August 1969, pp. 143-49; also, "Ante el asesinato del P. Henrique Pereira," *Spes*, no. 1, September 1969. See also in this connection the thoughts of Buenaventura Pelegrí, "Meditación ante el cadáver del Padre Henrique," *Víspera*, no. 12 (September 1969) pp. 3-7.

20. In this regard, after affirming that "Marxism needs to develop, to become less rigid, to interpret today's realities objectively and scientifically. to behave as a revolutionary force and not as a pseudo-revolutionary Church," Fidel Castro adds, "these are the paradoxes of history. When we see that sectors of the clergy are becoming revolutionary forces, how can we resign ourselves to sectors of Marxists becoming ecclesiastical forces?" (Speech delivered at the concluding session of the Congress of Intellectuals, January 12, 1968, quoted in Fidel Castro, *Révolution Cubaine* [Paris: Maspero, 1969], 2:253).

21. See for example the writings of Dom Helder Camara published in several volumes in *Pronunciamientos de Dom Helder*, Nordeste II, Secretariado Regional, CNBB, Recife, Brazil; *Revolution Through Peace*, ed. Ruth N. Anshen, trans. Amparo McLean (New York: Harper and Row, 1971); see also his *Church and Colonialism: The Betrayal of the Third World*, trans. William McSweeney (Denville, New Jersey: Dimension Books, 1969), and José de Broucker, *Dom Helder Camara: The Violence of a Peacemaker*, trans. Herma Briffault (Maryknoll, New York: Orbis Books, 1970); see also A.B. Fragoso, *Évangile et révolution sociale* (Paris: Les Éditions du Cerf, 1969).

22. See the outspoken analysis of the situation in Brazil presented by Dom Cándido Padim as a working paper for the Ninth General Assembly of the National Conference of Brazilian Bishops in 1968, "La doctrina de la seguridad nacional a la luz de la doctrina de la Iglesia" in Roberto Magni and Lirio Zanotti, *America Latina: La Chiesa si contesta* (Rome: Editori Riuniti, 1969), pp. 240-67. For an overview and the recent position of the Brazilian bishops in their difficult situation see Charles Antoine, "L'episcopat brasilien face au pouvoir (1962-1969)," in *Études* 333 (July 1970): 84-103. The author ends his study asserting that "the year 1969 ends with the official position of the Brazilian bishops being considerably weaker. Undoubtedly their assertions are clearly stated, perhaps even aggressively so, but their impact is greatly reduced by the context." See also Charles Antoine, *L'Église et le pouvoir au Brésil: Naissance du militarisme* (Paris: Desclée DeBrouwer, 1971), to be published in English by Orbis Books.

23. A well known instance is the excommunication of three high officials of the Paraguayan government (a minister and two police chiefs) by the bishops of Paraguay. Excommunication is an unusual procedure today. But it is even more unusual that it should be used against persons in power who claim to defend "Western and Christian" civilization (see "Los sucesos de octubre en Asunción," *Spes*, no. 3 [November, 1969], pp. 6-9; and *Paraguay: conflicto Iglesia-estado, Informe especial*, mimeo [Montevideo: Centro de Documentación MIEC-JECI, 1969]).

24. Norman Gall recounts some of these instances in "La reforma católica," in *Mundo Nuevo*, June 1970, pp. 20-43; see also Norman Gall, "Latin America: The Church Militant," *Commentary*, April 1970, pp. 25-37.

25. Many of these texts have been published in *Between Honesty and Hope: Documents from and about the Church in Latin America, Issued at Lima by the Peruvian Bishops' Commission for Social Action*, trans. John Drury (Maryknoll, New York: Maryknoll Publications, 1970). See also the documents published in *Medellín, La Iglesia nueva* (Montevideo: Cuadernos de Marcha, 1968); and a more recent publication, *Iglesia latinoamericana,¿ protesta o profecía?* (Avellaneda, Argentina: Ediciones Búsqueda, 1969); and also *Los católicos postconciliares en la Argentina* (Buenos Aires: Galerna, 1970). We will cite the texts only of the last three years.

26. "Closing Statement of the Thirty-sixth Peruvian Episcopal Conference," 1969, in *Between Honesty and Hope*, p. 230. The same idea is found in "Message to the People of Latin America," *The Church in the Present-Day Transformation of Latin America in the Light of the Council*, Documents of the Second General Conference of Latin American Bishops, Medellín, Colombia, August-September 1968, vol. 2, *Conclusions* (Bogota: General Secretariat of CELAM, 1970), p. 39; hereafter this work is cited as *Medellín;* and also Dom Helder Camara's speech at the tenth convention of CELAM, 1966, in *Between Honesty and Hope*, pp. 30-31. See also "Los cristianos y el poder," a statement of lay people and priests from Sante Fe, Argentina, 1968, in *Iglesia latinoamericana*, pp. 121-22; "Carta de sacerdotes tucumanos al arzobispo de Buenos Aires," 1969, *ibid.*, p. 137; "La Iglesia en el proceso de transformación," a statement from a meeting of laymen, priests, religious, and bishops in Cochabamba, Bolivia, 1968, *ibid.*, p. 154; *Carta pastoral del episcopado mexicano sobre el desarrollo e integración del país*, Mexico D.F., 1968, pp. 9, 12.

27. Conclusions of the first week of joint pastoral planning in El Salvador, June 1970, in *NADOC*, no. 174, p. 2. "The first thing that the Church must do is confess publicly its sin" (General Statement of the "Encuentro sobre el hombre nuevo" of the Cuban Christian Student Movement in *Spes*, no. 4 [December 1969], p. 3).

28. "Peace," no. 16, in *Medellín*. We must emphasize that this is not merely a phrase mentioned in passing; the whole document is constructed around this focus. See also "A Letter to the Peoples of the Third World," a message signed by eighteen Third World bishops in *Between Honesty and Hope*, pp. 10-11. In the "Declaración del II seminario de sacerdotes latinoamericanos," organized by ILADES in 1970, there is a denunciation of the fact that injustice "has put law and order at its service" (*NADOC*, no. 122, p. 3). "Let us recall the great amount of violence that this situation entails for those who suffer under it, especially if we consider that while their rights are theoretically recognized, in practice they are denied within the present economic and social order" ("Carta pastoral de Adviento de Monseñor Parteli y su presbíterio," Montevideo, 1967, p. 11). For a commentary on the Medellín text concerning institutionalized violence, see Gon-

zalo Arroyo, "Violencia institucionalizada en América Latina," *Mensaje* 17, no. 175 (December 1968): 534-44. See also Pierre Bigo, "Ensenanza de la Iglesia sobre la violencia," *Mensaje* 17, no. 174 (November 1968):574-78.

29. In "Carta al Presidente del Brasil," 1965, the bishop of San Andrés and his clergy denounce, among other things, the fact that unemployment "threatens with death, with slaughter, thousands of workers" (*Iglesia latinoamericana*, p. 174). See especially "Latin America: A Continent of Violence," a document signed by more than 900 Latin American priests, 1968, in *Between Honesty and Hope*, pp. 81-84. The same idea is expressed by an episcopate which is considered moderate, *Carta del episcopado mexicano*, pp. 10-21.

30. "Peace," no. 16, in *Medellín*.

31. "Continent of Violence," in *Between Honesty and Hope*, p. 84.

32. "Peace," no. 14, in *Medellín*; see also no. 1, "Justice," no. 2, and Dom Helder Camara, in *Between Honesty and Hope*, p. 32; "Opresión social y silencio de los cristianos," a statement of priests of San Juan, Argentina, 1969, in *Iglesia latinoamericana*, p. 141.

33. "Brazilian Realities and the Church," a statement of 300 Brazilian priests, 1967, in *Between Honesty and Hope*, p. 138. See also "Carta de 120 sacerdotes de Bolivia a su conferencia episcopal," 1970, in *NADOC*, no. 148, p. 2. Concerning the rejection of God implied in injustice, see *Nordeste, Desenvolvimento sem justica* (Recife, Brazil: Ação católica operária, Secretariado Regional do Nordeste, 1967), especially p. 78.

34. "Peace," nos. 2-10, in *Medellín*.

35. "Presence of the Church in Latin American Development," a document drawn up by presiding officers of various episcopal commissions for social action at Itapoán, Brazil, in May 1968, in *Between Honesty and Hope*, p. 21. See also *Populorum progressio* and Latin American Realities," a communiqué issued by participants in the first seminar for priests sponsored by the Social Department of CELAM in Chile, 1967, and signed by 38 priests, *ibid.*, p. 71; "A Lay Critique of the Medellín Draft," a statement of leaders of various Latin American lay organizations, 1968, in *Between Honesty and Hope*, p. 194; "Underdevelopment in Colombia," a document issued by the priests who met at Golconda, Colombia, in 1968, in *Between Honesty and Hope*, p. 85-86; "Los cristianos y el imperialismo," a statement of Bolivian Protestants and Catholics, 1969, in *Iglesia latinoamericana*, p. 167; "II Seminario de ILADES," pp. 2-3; "Conclusiones de la Comisión Ecuatoriana de Justicia y Paz," December 1970, in *NADOC*, no. 191.

36. "Orientaciones del Encuentro Regional Andino de Justicia y Paz" (Peru), 1970, in *NADOC*, no. 147, p. 2. (The whole document is of interest.) The political situation in Cuba is very different from that of the other Latin American countries. It is of interest to note what the Cuban bishops say in this area after several years of silence. Regarding difficulties for development, they assert, "There are internal difficulties stemming from the newness of the problems and technical complexity as well as from the deficiencies and sins of men. No less serious, however, are the external difficulties, which are connected to the complicated contemporary structures of relationships among nations. These structures are unjustly disadvantageous to the weak, small, and underdeveloped countries. Is this not the case of the economic blockade to which our country has been subjected, a blockade whose automatic prolongation has caused severe hardships to our country?" (Communiqué of the Cuban Episcopal Conference, April 10, 1969, in *SEDOC*, September 1969, p. 350).

37. *Juventud y cristianismo en América Latina*, document of the Department of Education of CELAM (Bogota: Indo-American Press Service, 1969), p. 23.

38. *Presencia activa de la Iglesia en el desarrollo y la integración de América Latina*, Conclusions of the Episcopal Conference of CELAM, Mar de Plata, 1966, Documentos CELAM, no. 1 (Bogota: CELAM, 1967).

39. This substitution has been very well treated by Héctor Borrat in "El gran impulso," *Víspera*, no. 7 (October 1968), p. 9

40. "Letter to Peoples of the Third World," in *Between Honesty and Hope*, p. 3.

41. "Carta de 120 sacerdotes de Bolivia a su Conferencia Episcopal," 1970, in *NADOC*, no. 148, p. 2. "For some time now, however, a new element has been taking shape in this panorama of poverty and injustice. It is the rapid and growing self-awareness of the exploited peoples, who see a real possibility for their own liberation. For many this liberation is impossible without a fundamental change in the socioeconomic structures of our continent. More than a few feel that the time is already past for accomplishing this by purely nonviolent means"("Continent of Violence," in *Between Honesty and Hope*, p. 83).

42. "Education," no. 8, in *Medellín*.

43. "Justice," no. 3, in *Medellín*. The notion of liberation is found frequently in other documents from Medellín as well ("Message of the People of Latin America," "Introduction to the Final Documents," "Pastoral concern for the Elites," "Poverty of the Church," etc.). See also "Statement of Peruvian Episcopal Conference," in *Between Honesty and Hope*, pp. 228-34; "*Populorum progressio* and Latin American Realities," *ibid.*, pp. 70-73; "Underdevelopment in Colombia," *ibid.*, pp. 85-92; and the ONIS statement of October 4, 1969, in *IDOC-NA*, no. 4 (May 23, 1970), pp. 37-41 (the original Spanish version is "Conclusiones del II Encuentro Nacional de ONIS" in *Movimiento Sacerdotal ONIS, Declaraciones* [Lima: Centro de Estudios y Publicaciones, 1970]). This idea is a constant theme in the documents of ONIS.

44. Cardinal Landázuri Ricketts, "Closing Address at Medellín Episcopal Conference," in *Between Honesty and Hope*, p. 223.

45. Cardinal Landázuri Ricketts "Servants to Society," baccalaureate address at the University of Notre Dame, 1966, in *Between Honesty and Hope*, p. 60.

46. "Cristianos y poder," in *Iglesia latinoamericana*, p. 120; see also "The Socioeconomic Structures of Peru," a declaration by a group of priests in Peru, 1968, in *Between Honesty and Hope*, p. 79.

47. "Encuentro Regional Andino," p. 5.

48. "El presente de la transformación nacional," in *ONIS Declaraciones*, p. 42. See this entire document as well as the ONIS statement of January 22, 1970, in *IDOC-NA*, no. 4, pp. 41-43. (Original version: "Declaración ante problemas laborales," in *ONIS Declaraciones*, p. 36). Regarding the rejection of capitalism, see also "Carta pastoral de Adviento," pp. 7-8.

49. ONIS statement in *IDOC-NA*, no. 4, p. 43. See also "Evangelio y explotación," a statement of priests and lay people of Chaco, Argentina, 1968, in *Iglesia lationamericana*, p. 126; "Hacia una sociedad mas justa," a statement of lay people and priests of Corrientes, Argentina, 1968, *ibid.*, p. 116; "ISAL en Bolivia, Pronunciamiento ante las guerrillas de Teoponte," 1970, in *NADOC*, no. 157, pp. 6-7. See also "Manifesto of the Executive Committee, ISAL, Bolivia," in *IDOC-NA*, no. 17 (January 16, 1971), pp. 27-32.

50. "If the economic and social policies followed in the last fifteen years have not allowed for the resolution of the problem of poverty in Latin America, this

is because of the very conception of development which has inspired them. The objective has been for each of the countries of this continent to pass from a kind of preindustrial society to a kind of modern capitalist society. But this limits the problem simply to its technical aspects. The human dimension is disregarded; the deep sources of injustice remain intact" (P. Muñoz Vega, Archbishop of Quito, "Hora del cambio de estructuras y justicia social," September 1970, in *NADOC*,no. 171, p. 5). See also "II Seminario de ILADES," p. 5

51. "Against a Reconstruction of Injustice," statement of ONIS in *IDOC-NA*, no. 16 (December 26, 1970), p. 93 (Originally appearing in *Expreso* [Lima], July 27, 1970, p. 8). The document refers to the tenacity of domination and its recourse to modernization to preserve itself.

52. Landázuri Ricketts, in *Between Honesty and Hope*, p. 61; "Letter to Peoples of the Third World," *ibid.*, p. 4; "Socioeconomic Structures of Peru," *ibid.*, p. 78; "The Church in Bolivia," letter of eighty Bolivian priests to their bishops, in *Between Honesty and Hope*, p. 141. "Clearly this situation cannot be overcome without real revolution, one that will displace the present ruling classes in our country through whom foreign domination is exercised" ("Underdevelopment in Colombia," in *Between Honesty and Hope*, p. 86; see also the ONIS statement in *IDOC-NA*, no. 4, pp. 37-41).

53. "It is easy to hurl the charge of communism at all those who, lacking any ties with the party or the ideology, dare to point out the materialistic roots of capitalism; at all those who dare to point out that, strictly speaking, we do not yet have one uniform socialism or capitalism, but a variety of socialisms and capitalisms" (Helder Camara, in *Between Honesty and Hope*, p. 35). "In certain circles there arises the fear, the suspicion, or the accusation of 'communism.' It seems to us that this is no time for the luxury of fearing communism in Peru. Indeed, when social consciousness, or authentic national consciousness, is the patrimony of only a few, and when economic inequality, cultural disintegration, and exploitation affect the great majority, it is naive or immoral to accuse of communism certain efforts, certain achievements, or certain concurrences" ("El presente de la transformación nacional," in *ONIS Declaraciones*, p. 42; see this entire document).

54. "Underdevelopment in Colombia," in *Between Honesty and Hope, p. 90.*

55. "Coincidencias básicas," in *Sacerdotes para el Tercer Mundo* (Buenos Aires: Ed. del Movimiento, 1970), p. 69. This is also the option of ISAL in Bolivia; see *NADOC*, no. 147, pp. 5-8; and "Presentación de ISAL al ampliado de la COB," mimeo, May 1970, p. 1. "A new man and a new society cannot be reached by capitalistic paths because the moving force of every type of a capitalism is private profit and private ownership for profit. The oppressed will not be liberated by becoming capitalist. A new man and a new society will not be possible unless labor comes to be understood as the only effective human principle, when the fundamental stimulus of the economic antivity of man is social interest, when capital is subordinated to the work, and the me..ns of production come under social ownership" ("Private Property and the New Society,") a statement of ONIS in *IDOC-NA*, no. 16 (December, 26, 1970), p. 96. See also "Letter to Peoples of the Third World," in *Between Honesty and Hope*, pp. 6-7. "The truly new man is he who feels himself called to the daily activity of creating a better present and future, who struggles for the elimination of poverty, injustice, discrimination, exploitation, and every act of oppression constituted by the elements characteristic of capitalist society" (statement of the Cuban MEC in *Spes*).

56. "Proyección y transformación de la Iglesia en Latinoamérica," an address

delivered July 17, 1970, in "Confrontación de dos obispos mexicanos," *CIP Documenta* (Cuernavaca, Mexico), no. 7 (September 1970), p. 4. This same issue includes the reaction of the Archbishop of Puebla and the controversy caused by the address of the Bishop of Cuernavaca. See also the statements of Bishop Gerardo Valencia to CENOS (Mexico, D.F.), February 10, 1970: "With my companions of Golconda I definitively proclaim myself to be a revolutionary and a socialist, because we cannot remain indifferent before the capitalist structure which is leading the people of Colombia and Latin America into injustice and the greatest of frustrations."

57. In this regard see the position—which is qualified, but which opens the possibility of an interesting dialogue—of Jorge Manrique, Archbishop of La Paz, in "El socialismo y la Iglesia en Bolivia," a pastoral exhortation of October 1970, in *NADOC*, no. 175 (English text in *IDOC-NA*, no. 16 [December 26, 1970], pp. 54-64). In the conclusions of their third national meeting, ISAL-Bolivia clarifies what it understands by socialism and concludes, "There are not, therefore, any third paths to socialism which are not of the socialist government of the people" (February 23, 1971). It is well known that Paul VI has initiated a new attitude of openness orientated toward a better understanding of socialism. He distinguishes among "the various levels of expression of socialism: a generous aspiration and a seeking for a more just society, historical movements with a political organization and aim, and an ideology which claims to give a complete and self-sufficient picture of man" (*Octogesima adveniens*, no. 31).

58. See, for example, "Letter to Peoples of the Third World," in *Between Honesty and Hope*, pp. 6-7. The Archbishop of La Paz advocates a new Christian ethic which ought to "recognize that work is more important than property in the use of material goods . . . . Thus every system of property ought to be evaluated according to its ability to humanize life and the labor of the working man." ("Enfoque de la nueva ética cristiana," pastoral letter, in *CIDOC*, no. 224, 1970, p. 4).

59. "Private Property," statement of ONIS, *IDOC-NA*, no. 16, pp. 94-95. See also the ONIS statement "La Iglesia ante la reforma agraria," in *Iglesia latinoamericana*, pp. 335-36; "Coincidencias," in *Sacerdotes para el Tercer Mundo*, p. 70. All this recasts the interpretation of the so-called social doctrine of the Church. See *Carta del episcopado mexicano*, p. 21. Regarding the meaning that the social doctrine might have today, see Manaranche, *Y a-t-il une éthique social-chrétienne?* and Luis Velaochaga, "La doctrina social de la Iglesia," in *Expreso* (Lima), August 16, 1970.

60. *El presente de Chile y el Evangelio*, mimeo (Santiago de Chile, 1970).

61. *CIDOC*, no. 254, 1970. See also the statement of Jorge Hourton, the Bishop of Puerto Montt, regarding the result of the presidential election in *CIDOC*, no. 251, 1970, and the communiqué of the Rural Catholic Action in *CIDOC*, no. 255, 1970.

62. "Comunicado a la prensa de los sacerdotes participantes en las jornadas 'Participación de los cristianos en la construcción del socialismo en Chile,' " in *El Mercurio* (Santiago de Chile), April 17, 1971.

63. *Justicia en el Mundo*, Lima, August 14, 1971; English translation in *IDOC-NA*, no. 37 (December 11, 1971), p. 9. See also the articles by Ricardo Antoncich in the daily *Expreso* (Lima), September-October 1971.

64. See "Presence of the Church," in *Between Honesty and Hope*, p. 28.

65. "Letter to Peoples of the Third World," *ibid.*, p. 9. "They must count on themselves and their own initiatives more than on the help of the rich" (*ibid.*);

they must unite and defend their right to life (*ibid.*, p. 11). See also "Statement of Peruvian Episcopal Conference," *ibid.*, p. 257; "Declaración de ISAL," in *NADOC*, no. 147, p. 7; "Chile, voluntad de ser," Permanent Committee of the Chilean Bishops, 1968, p. 11c.

66. *IDOC-NA*, no. 4, p. 38. See also *ONIS Declaraciones*, p. 24, regarding the participation of the peasant in agrarian reform and the ONIS statement in *IDOC-NA*, no. 16, pp. 91-94. See also *Carta del episcopado mexicano*, pp. 22, 37, 49-50.

67. "Peace," no. 18, in *Medellín*; see also no. 7 and *ONIS Declaraciones*, pp. 29-37.

68. "Statement of Peruvian Episcopal Conference," in *Between Honesty and Hope*, pp. 229-30 and also p. 231; see for example "*Populorum progressio* and Latin American Realities," in *Between Honesty and Hope*, p. 71; and "Cristianos y poder," in *Iglesia latinoamericana*, p. 121. "The fact that they had to have recourse to such measures as the occupation of churches is also a reflection on the press and the other media of communication, property of those in economic power and hence the voice of their interests. These media play down the masses as of little importance, turn a deaf ear to their just claims, gloss over or make no mention of petitions, labor disputes and other events which are a true echo of the life of these sectors of the population" (ONIS statement in *IDOC-NA*, no. 4, p. 42). See also *Carta del episcopado mexicano*, pp. 12-14, 25. Paternalism and margination of the poor have also been present in the Church; see the statement of the Argentinian lay people, 1968, in *Iglesia latinoamericana*, p. 109.

69. "Hopefully the Church will now address herself as well to those who are the victims of the unjust structures and to the organizations that represent them" ("The Church's Shortcomings," a statement by Peruvian laymen, in *Between Honesty and Hope*, p. 157). "To our brother peasants and workers we say that we will do all in our power to 'encourage and support all the efforts of the people ... ' " ("Statement of Peruvian Episcopal Conference," *ibid.*, p. 231).

70. "Peace," no. 27, in *Medellín*.

71. *Ibid.*, no. 20. See also "Lay Critique," in *Between Honesty and Hope*, p. 200.

72. "Poverty of the Church," no. 10, in *Medellín*.

73. "Carta del clero peruano a la Asamblea episcopal," in *Iglesia latinoamericana*, p. 321.

74. "Statement of Peruvian Episcopal Conference," in *Between Honesty and Hope*, p. 231.

75. "Poverty of the Church," no. 11, in *Medellín*.

76. *Carta del episcopado mexicano*, pp. 28-29.

77. "Letter to Peoples of the Third World," in *Between Honesty and Hope*, p. 5.

78. See, for example, the statement of the Argentinian Priests for the Third World on the consecration of Argentina to the Immaculate Heart of Mary by General Juan Carlos Onganía, president of the country, in 1969 (*NADOC*, no. 115, and *IDOC-NA*, no. 15, pp. 75-78); the document rejects both the utilization of religious sentiment to endorse an unjust situation as well as the attempt to make the Church seem to be in agreement with the existing policy.

79. See "Carta de los obispos paraguayos," 1969, addressed to the congress of the country, "in the face of the grave threat to the moral conscience and the dignity of the nation represented by the new bill on the 'Defense of Democracy and the Political and Social Order of the State' ... "; the Paraguayan Church vigorously rejected the bill (*NADOC*, no. 89, pp. 1-3). See also the "Carta pastoral de Monseñor de Jerónimo Pechillo, Prelado de Coronel Oviedo," Paraguay, 1970,

which states that conflicts exist between the Church and the state because "the Church in Paraguay cannot remain blind and deaf to the continuous violation of the rights which God has given to man" (*NADOC*, no. 129, pp. 3-4).

80. "Clero peruano a la Asamblea episcopal," in *Iglesia latinoamerica*, pp. 314-15. "One of the clearest signs of the evangelical independence and liberty that our church is meant to give would be the relinquishing of every economic tie with political power and the renouncing of every type of legal protection and privilege, including all the various rights acquired in the course of our history" (ONIS statement in *IDOC-NA*, no. 4, p. 39); "The Church as institution must break off every concrete tie to any kind of public economic or social power, even at the risk of being persecuted and criticized or of losing economic resources or possibilities of support; it must do this in order to be always, like Christ, at the service of those who suffer, the poorest and most needy, and to witness to the poverty that all men need in the service of justice and love" ("Carta pastoral de Adviento," p. 19).

81. Statement of the Cuban MEC in *Spes*.

82. "Peace," no. 20, in *Medellín*.

83. "Socioeconomic Structures of Peru," in *Between Honesty and Hope*, p. 74. "The absence of authentic evangelization often leads to a situation where the religious attitudes of our people act as a brake on personal initiative and integral development. So we must present the faith as a factor promoting change and a more just society" ("Underdevelopment in Colombia," in *Between Honesty and Hope*, p. 91); see also *Carta del episcopado mexicano*, pp. 16-17.

84. "Manifiesto de la Iglesia metodista de Bolivia," 1970, in *NADOC*, no. 140, p. 3; English version in *IDOC-NA*, no. 7, pp. 39-48. This same document points out the need for an effort at conscientization: "The formation of a critical awareness in the Bolivian people ... is part of the mission which God has entrusted to us" (*ibid.*, p. 6). Within the process of liberation there are possibilities for an authentic ecumenism: "We believe that the Christian churches are able to give a common message in these decisive moments, thus indicating the love which comes from God to all men, the dignity of the human being, as well as offering an invitation to join the struggle for a more just Peru" ("Llamado a las Iglesias," of the Ecumenical Committee of Churches of Lima, 1969, in *NADOC*, no. 59).

85. "Evangelio y subversión," manifesto of 21 priests from Buenos Aires, 1967, in *Iglesia latinoamericana*, p. 106.

86. Statement of the Pastoral Conference of the Diocese of Salto, Uruguay, 1968, in *Iglesia latinoamericana*, p. 373. "The Commission ought to contribute to awakening in the whole people of God an awareness of the seriousness and the urgency of the process of liberation in such a way that the action of the Church is orientated toward this change and their active participation in it" ("Encuentro Regional Andino," in *NADOC*, no. 147, p. 4).

87. *Juventud y cristianismo*, p. 35. See also *Pastoral indigenista en México*, the final document of the first pastoral meeting on the mission of the Church in the aboriginal cultures (Bogota: Department of Missons of CELAM, 1970), pp. 40-42.

88. "Peace, no. 24, in *Medellín*.

89. "Pastoral Conference," Salto, Uruguay, in *Iglesia latinoamerica*, p. 374.

90. *Ibid.*, p. 377. See also "Poverty," no. 9, in *Medellín*.

91. There are few serious studies regarding the wealth of the Church in Latin America. Some bishops are beginning to be concerned with the problem. See, for example, "Statement of Peruvian Episcopal Conference," in *Between Honesty and*

Hope, p. 232; and "Resoluciones de la conferencia episcopal ecuatoriana," June 1969, in *NADOC*, no. 73

92. "Church in Bolivia," in *Between Honesty and Hope*, p. 142; see also "Brazilian Realities," regarding commercialized faith and Church property, *ibid.*, pp. 135-36. See also the clear, extensive statement of the Conferencia Latinoamericana de Religiosas (CLAR), *Pobreza y vida religiosa en América Latina* (Bogota, 1970).

93. "Poverty of the Church," nos. 8-18, in *Medellín*.

94. "Church in Bolivia," in *Between Honesty and Hope*, pp. 141-42. See also "Formation of the Clergy," no. 1, in *Medellín*; "Joint Pastoral Planning," no. 5, *ibid.*, "Presence of the Church in Latin American Development," in *Between Honesty and Hope*, pp. 22-23; "Underdevelopment in Colombia,"*ibid.*, pp. 89-90; "Church's Shortcomings," *ibid.*, pp. 156-57; the statement of the Argentinian lay people in *Iglesia latinoamericana*, pp. 108-10.

95. "Lay Critique," in *Between Honesty and Hope*, p. 22. See also *Carta del episcopado mexicano*, p. 54. "What we propose is the rejuvenation of the structures of the Church. We consider this to be its greatest need so that they might capacitate it for its present task, to commit itself to society in the construction of the new man" (statement of the Cuban MEC, in *Spes*).

96. See "Declaración de Sacerdotes para el Tercer Mundo," 1970, in *NADOC*, no. 147, p. 9. Regarding education in particular, see the controversial case of the closing of an important school in Mexico by the Jesuits in "Motivos principales de nuestra decisión sobre el Instituto Patria," in *NADOC*, no. 194.

97. "Priests," no. 1, in *Medellín*.

98. See for example *La pastoral en las misiones de América Latina* (Bogota: Departamento de Misiones del CELAM, 1968), pp. 38-39.

99. "Carta de Sacerdotes tucumanos," in *Iglesia latinoamericana*, p. 137; see also "Sacerdotes bonaerenses responden a su obispo," 1969, *ibid.*, pp. 130-31; "Underdevelopment in Colombia," in *Between Honesty and Hope*, pp. 87-89; "Socioeconomic Structures of Peru," *ibid.*, p. 79.

100. "Clero peruano," in *Iglesia latinoamericana*, p. 318; see also ONIS statement, *IDOC-NA* no. 4, pp. 37-41. After recalling that in general priests make their living from religious services, the Ecuadorian priests assert that "today this situation has become intolerable, not only in the eyes of society, but also in the eyes of the priest himself, both because of the impression of exploitation it gives as well as the necessity of depending on alms. It is for this reason that priests are thinking about taking up professions that will provide them with the income necessary to earn a living" ("Conclusiones de la primera convención nacional de presbíteros del Ecuador," January 1970, in *NADOC*, no. 141, p. 13).

101. See, for example, "Por qué los sacerdotes recurrimos a la opinión pública," letter of 57 priests to the Archbishop of Quito, December 1968, in *NADOC*, no. 30.

102. See the essay of Ricardo Cetrulo on the "level of depth" of these texts in "Conclusiones críticas," in *Iglesia latinoamericana*, pp. 403-24.

103. The change of tone—and origin—can be easily seen by consulting, for example, *Recent Church Documents from Latin America*, CIF Monograph (Cuernavaca, Mexico: CIF, 1963), where episcopal documents of 1962-63 are reproduced.

CHAPTER EIGHT

STATEMENT OF THE QUESTIONS

Although until recently the Church was closely linked to the established order, it is beginning to take a different attitude regarding the exploitation, oppression, and alienation which prevails in Latin America.[1] This has caused concern among the beneficiaries and defenders of capitalist society, who no longer can depend on what used to be—whether consciously or unconsciously—one of their mainstays. This concern is reflected, for example, in the *Rockefeller Report*. After asserting that the Church has become a "force dedicated to change—revolutionary change if necessary," it notes apprehensively and patronizingly that the Church "may be somewhat in the same situation as the young—with a profound idealism, but as a result, in some cases, vulnerable to subversive penetration; ready to undertake a revolution if necessary to end injustice, but not clear either as to the ultimate nature of the revolution itself or as to the governmental system by which the justice it seeks can be realized."[2] Certain groups within the Church, as we have noted above, are beginning to be regarded as subversive and are even being harshly repressed. All this creates for the Latin American Church a completely new situation and forces it to face problems for which the Church—and especially ecclesiastical authority—is poorly prepared. "The daily events in the life of the Church," writes César Aguiar, "go far beyond the expectations of the ordinary Christian. Five years ago who would have thought that in our continent priests would be murdered, Christians persecuted, priests deported, the Catholic press silenced and attacked, ecclesiastical premises searched, etc.? Probably nobody. Five years ago even the most radical Christians viewed events through utopian lenses and did not grasp their dramatic historical implications."[3]

During the last three years, written statements (more moderate than the concrete commitments of many Christians) have multiplied. Many of them are endowed with great doctrinal authority. There is, however, a dangerous disproportion between what is asserted and called for in these documents and the attitudes of the greater part of the Latin American Church. This is particularly serious for a Church which claims to live according to "a truth which is done."[4]

Nevertheless, the commitments of Christians in Latin America and the texts which attempt to explicate them are gradually fashioning an authentic "political" option of the Church on this continent. Many of these actions are ambiguous, romantic, or careless, but this must not distract us from their fundamental direction. It is true that this option is not that of the majority of the Latin American Christian community; it is, however, the option of its most dynamic sectors, which have a growing influence and a promising future. As a whole the Church in the past has reflected—and indeed still reflects —the ideology of the dominant groups in Latin America. This is what has begun to change.

In this context we must include the Medellín Conference as a major event. At Medellín, the Latin American Church, despite the climate created by the Eucharistic Congress held in Bogota immediately before it, realistically perceived the world in which it was and clearly saw its place in that world. In short, it began to be aware of its own coming of age and to take the reins of its own destiny.[5] Vatican II speaks of the underdevelopment of peoples, of the developed countries and what they can and should do about this underdevelopment; Medellín tries to deal with the problem from the standpoint of the poor countries, characterizing them as subjected to a new kind of colonialism. Vatican II talks about a Church in the world and describes the relationship in a way which tends to neutralize the conflicts; Medellín demonstrates that the world in which the Latin American Church ought to be present is in full revolution. Vatican II sketches a general outline for Church renewal; Medellín provides guidelines for a transformation of the Church in terms of its presence on a continent of misery and injustice.

Medellín, despite its imperfections and lacunae, legitimates newly-created phenomena in the Latin American Church; efforts at renewal now therefore enjoy unexpected support. Above all, Medellín provides an impulse for new commitments. But the Christian community in Latin American is now living in a post-Medellín period, which (like the postconciliar era) is characterized by dwelling on many of the old questions; there is, however, a new and sharper awareness of these questions. In the post-Medellín period (like in the postconciliar one) some groups would like the surprising consequences of positions they took to be forgotten or mitigated. They cannot contradict the letter of what was said, so they try to declare it inapplicable, valid only for special and carefully defined situations. This effort attempts to devalue not only the authority of Medellín but the spirit which it engendered. It is a useless exercise. If and when it should be accomplished, the Medellín texts will be obsolete. We will be facing a completely new situation. Rather than desperately try to protect these statements from erroneous or deliberately exaggerated interpretations, therefore, it is important to work out their exegesis in concrete reality. Their validity will be confirmed in the *praxis* of the Christian community. Only in this way will they have Gospel freshness and permanent historical validity.

Here we shall gather under various headings the more important theologico-pastoral questions posed by this new situation. They will be the basis for the rest of the book.

a) The options which Christians in Latin America are taking have brought a fundamental question to the fore: What is the *meaning of the faith* in a life committed to the struggle against injustice and alienation? How do we relate the work of building a just society to the absolute value of the Kingdom? For many the participation in the process of liberation causes a wearying, anguished, long, and unbearable dichotomy between their life of faith and their revolutionary commitment. What is called for is not to accuse them of confusing the Kingdom with revolution, only because they take the latter seriously and because they believe that the Kingdom is incompatible with the present unjust situation and that in Latin America the coming of the Kingdom presupposes the breaking up of this state of affairs; these accusations often come from those who are comfortably established in a very safe "religious" life. Rather, what is called for is to search out theological responses to the problems which arise in the life of a Christian who has chosen for the oppressed and against the oppressors. Moreover, the close collaboration with people of different spiritual outlooks which this option provides leads one to ponder the contribution proper to the faith. This question must be carefully considered in order to avoid the petty ambition of "having more."

b) The problem, however, is not only to find a new theological framework. The *personal and community prayer* of many Christians committed to the process of liberation is undergoing a serious crisis. This could purify prayer life of childish attitudes, routine, and escapes. But it will not do this if new paths are not broken and new spiritual experiences are not lived. For example, without "contemplative life," to use a traditional term, there is no authentic Christian life; yet what this contemplative life will be is still unknown. There is great need for a spirituality of liberation; yet in Latin America those who have opted to participate in the process of liberation as we have outlined it above, comprise, in a manner of speaking, a first Christian generation. In many areas of their life they are without a theological and spiritual tradition. They are creating their own.

(c) The Latin American reality, *the historical moment* which Latin America is experiencing, is *deeply conflictual.* One of Medellín's great merits is to have been rooted in this reality and to have expressed it in terms surprisingly clear and accessible for an ecclesiastical document. Medellín marks the beginning of a new relationship between theological and pastoral language on the one hand and the social sciences which seek to interpret this reality on the other.[6] This relationship gives rise to statements which are to a large extent contingent and provisional; this is the price one must pay for being incisive and contemporary and for expressing the Word *today* in our everyday words. But this language is only a reflection of a deeper process, a new awareness. The commitments and statements referred to in the two preceding chapters are placing us face to face with a new social experience of Latin Americans and with new directions that the Christian community is beginning to take. It is important to be aware of the newness of this phenomenon. It implies a different, very concrete way of looking at the historical process, that is, of perceiving the presence of the Lord in history, who encourages us to be artisans of this process. Moreover, because of close contact with those who see historical development from a Marxist viewpoint, we are led to review and revitalize the eschatological values of Christianity, which stress not only the provisional nature of historical accomplishments, but above all their openness towards the total communion of all men with God. We Christians, however, are not used to thinking in conflictual and historical terms. We prefer peaceful conciliation to antagonism and an evasive eternity to a provisional arrangement. We must learn to live and think of peace in conflict and of what is definitive in what is historical. Very important in this regard are collaboration and dialogue with those who from different vantage points are also struggling for the liberation of oppressed peoples. At stake is the meaning of Christians' participation in this liberation.

d) The Latin American Church is sharply *divided* with regard to the process of liberation. Living in a capitalist society in which one class confronts another, the Church, in the measure that its presence increases, cannot escape—nor try to ignore any longer—the profound division among its members. Active participation in the liberation process is far from being a uniform position of the Latin American Christian community. The majority of the Church continues to be linked in many different ways to the established order. And what is worse, among Latin American Christians there are not only different political options within a framework of free interplay of ideas; the polarization of these options and the extreme seriousness of the situation have even placed some Christians among the oppressed and persecuted and others among the oppressors and persecutors, some among the tortured and others among the torturers or those who condone torture. This gives rise to a serious and radical confrontation between Christians who suffer from injustice and exploitation and those who benefit from the established order. Under such circumstances, life in the contemporary Christian community becomes particularly difficult and conflictual. Participation in the Eucharist, for example, as it is celebrated today, appears to many to be an action which, for want of the support of an authentic community, becomes an exercise in make-believe.[7]

From now on it is impossible not to face the problems which arise from this division between Christians, which has reached such dramatic proportions. Clarion calls to Christian unity which do not take into account the deep causes of present condi-

138   A THEOLOGY OF LIBERATION

tions and the real prerequisites for building a just society are
merely escapist. We are moving towards a new idea of unity
and communion in the Church. Unity is not an event accomplished once and for all, but something which is always in the
process of becoming, something which is achieved with courage
and freedom of spirit, sometimes at the price of painful, heart-
rending decisions. Latin America must brace itself for such
experiences.

e) In Latin America, the Church must place itself squarely
within the process of revolution, amid the violence which is present in different ways. The Church's *mission* is defined practically and theoretically, pastorally and theologically in relation
to this revolutionary process. That is, its mission is defined more
by the political context than by intraecclesiastical problems. Its
greatest "o-mission" would be to turn in upon itself. Because
of the options which, with the qualifications we have indicated,
the Christian community is making, it is faced ever more clearly
with the dilemma now confronting the whole continent: to be
for or against the system, or more subtly, to be for reform or
revolution. Many Christians have resolutely decided for the difficult path which leads to the latter. Confronted with this polarization, can ecclesiastical authority remain on the level of general statements? On the other hand, can it go beyond them and
still remain within what is traditionally considered to be its
specific mission?

For the Latin American Church, it is becoming increasingly
clearer that to be in the world without being of the world means
concretely to be in the system without being of the system. It
is evident that only a break with the unjust order and a frank
commitment to a new society can make the message of love
which the Christian community bears credible to Latin Americans. These demands should lead the Church to a profound revision of its manner of preaching the Word and of living and cele-
brating its faith.

f) Closely connected with this problem is another very controversial question: Should *the Church put its social weight*
behind social transformation in Latin America? Some are wor-
ried that it would be a mistake for the Church to attempt to
achieve the necessary and urgent changes.[8] The fear is that
the Church will become linked to the future established order,
albeit a more just one. There is also a fear that an effort in

this direction will end in a noisy failure: the Latin American bishops are not all of one mind and do not have the necessary means at their disposal to orientate Christians as a whole toward social progress.[9]

The relevance of these fears cannot be denied. There is indeed great risk. But the social influence of the Church is a fact. Not to exercise this influence in favor of the oppressed of Latin America is really to exercise it against them, and it is difficult to determine beforehand the consequences of this action. Not to speak is in fact to become another kind of Church of silence, silence in the face of the despoliation and exploitation of the weak by the powerful. On the other hand, would not the best way for the Church to break its links with the existing order—and in the process lose its ambiguous social prestige—be precisely to denounce the fundamental injustice upon which this order is based? Often the Church alone is in a position publicly to raise its voice and its protest. When some churches have attempted to do this, they have been harassed by the dominant groups and repressed by the political power.[10] In order to reflect on what action the Latin American Church should take and to act accordingly, it is necessary to consider its historical and social coordinates, its here and now. To neglect doing this is to remain on an abstract and ahistorical theological level; or, perhaps more subtly, it is to remain on the level of a theology more concerned with avoiding past errors than with discovering the originality of the present situation and committing itself to tomorrow.

g) The Latin American Christian community lives on a poor continent, but the image it projects is not, as a whole, that of a *poor Church*. The *Conclusions* of Medellín accurately acknowledge this fact, which can be verified by anyone who takes the time to get to know the impression of the average Latin American. Prejudices and generalizations undoubtedly distort the image, but no one can deny its fundamental validity. The majority of the Church has covertly or openly been an accomplice of the external and internal dependency of our peoples. It has sided with the dominant groups, and in the name of "efficacy" has dedicated its best efforts to them. It has identified with these sectors and adopted their style of life. We often confuse the possession of basic necessities with a comfortable position in the world, freedom to preach the Gospel with protection by powerful groups, instruments of service with the means of power. It is nevertheless important to clarify exactly what the witness of poverty involves.

Despite the hopes aroused by the options we have mentioned, many Christians in Latin America regard them very skeptically. They think that these choices have opened up too late and that real changes in the Church will result only from the social transformations which the whole continent is undergoing. Many even fear—as do many non-Christians—that the efforts of the Latin American Church will only make it the Latin American version of di Lampedusa's "Leopard."

This danger is real and we must be aware of it. In any case, by confronting the problems facing it—with all their peculiar characteristics—the Latin American Church ought to be gradually asserting its *own personality*. The situation of dependency which pervades the continent is also present in the ecclesiastical realm. The Latin American Church was born dependent and still remains in circumstances which have prevented it from developing its peculiar gifts.[11] Like on the socio-economic and political levels, this dependency is not only an external factor; it molds the structures, life and thought of the Latin American Church, which has been more a Church-reflection than a Church-source.[12]

This is another of the constant complaints of laymen, priests, religious, and bishops in Latin America.[13] Overcoming the colonial mentality is one of the important tasks of the Christian community. In this way, it will be able to make a genuine contribution to the enrichment of the universal Church; it will be able to face its real problems and to sink deep roots into a continent in revolution.[14]

NOTES

1. Thomas G. Sanders asserts, "The Roman Catholic Church has long been criticized for helping to maintain an anachronistic social system and economic underdevelopment.... Yet today no institution in Latin America is changing more rapidly than the Catholic Church" ("The Church in Latin America," *Foreign Affairs* 48, no. 2 [January 1970]: 285).

2. *The Rockefeller Report on the Americas* (Chicago: Quadrangle Books, 1969), p. 31. "Today the most ancient monarchy seated on the rock of the first bishop of Rome is faced with a subversion of its sacred values. And it is not the silent

and scandalized laity, but rather the clergy who are breaking through the rigid boundaries of their evangelical service to become on not a few occasions standard bearers for an openness to Marxism—with all the ferocity and incontinence in which converts traditionally have gloried" (Alberto Lleras Camargo, *Visión*, May 9, 1969, p. 17).

3. "La Iglesia perseguida: desafío latinoamericano," *Perspectivas para el Diálogo*, no. 35 (July 1969), p. 148.

4. In this regard see the observations of Michel de Certeau, "L'articulation du *dire* et du *faire*," *Études Théologiques et Religieuses* (Montpellier), 45, no. 1 (1970): 25–44.

5. In the process which has led to this posture, the Latin American Episcopal Council (CELAM) has played a decisive role. Even though when it began in 1955 it was something new among ecclesiastical structures of that time, its activity was confined to traditional models. The change occurred in 1963 under the orientation of Don Manuel Larraín, the Bishop of Talca, Chile. During his presidency there were created the various departments of CELAM, which assumed different pastoral areas. In these departments bishops and experts collaborated closely. Beginning in 1966, while Dom Avelar Brandão was president, meetings were organized which produced statements—at times quite surprising. These meetings likewise manifested an initial effort at reflection and commitment. They were also an effective preparation for Medellín: Vocations (Lima, 1966); Education (on Catholic universities; Buga, 1967); Missions (Melgar, 1968); Social Action (Itapoán, 1968); and the Diaconate (Buenos Aires, 1968).

6. See the alarmed observations concerning the bishops' conference at Medellín which this caused: Alberto Lleras Camargo, "La Iglesia militante," *Visión*, September 29, 1968.

7. This is why there is now talk of the gradual creation of "two Churches." Regarding the Evangelical Churches Christian Lalive d'Epinay writes, "Between these two forms of Churches there exists a qualitative break which makes any reformist transition impossible. The transformation of Latin American Protestantism implies a radical challenge to the first form. It implies creating breaches in that petrified structure so that it destructuralizes. Only in this way will a new restructuring be possible. Here—as in the socio-political field in Latin America—the reformist path is no longer feasible. And only radical challenge will enable the opening of new paths" (*CIDOC*, no. 78, p. 12).

8. See the perceptive analyses of Juan Luis Segundo, "¿Hacia una Iglesia de Izquierda?" *Perspectivas para el Diálogo*, no. 32 (April 1969), pp. 35–39 and Ricardo Cetrulo, "Utilización política de la Iglesia" *ibid.*, pp. 40–44.

9. Hector Borrat observes that the hopes awakened for the role of the Church-institution by Medellín are beginning to turn into frustration and uneasiness ("La Iglesia ¿para qué?" p. 14).

10. César Aguiar speaks of the emergence in Latin America of a different kind of "Underground Church," underground in relation to the political establishment and not to ecclesiastical power (as is the case of the churches of the affluent countries). He also foresees the need to develop a theology of persecution, which might enable a rediscovery of the meaning of the cross, "which we had forgotten for some time" ("Currents and Tendencies," *IDOC–NA*, no. 13, p. 63). But this will not come simply from the radicalness of the commitment. Borrat points out perceptively and satirically that "the Church is going to pay a very heavy price for the revolutionary novitiate of some of its members. . . . It is easy to foresee

that during the '70s no other social group will be as vulnerable as the Church to the mechanisms of repression. There are few so naively stubborn as certain groups of the vanguard within the Church. They publicize their 'subversion,' they profess their violence before exercising it, they hand themselves over freely to their political adversaries" ("La Iglesia ¿para qué?," p. 12).

11. See Gustavo Gutiérrez, "De la Iglesia colonial a Medellín," *Víspera*, no. 16 (April 1970), pp. 3–8.

12. See Henrique de Lima Vaz, "Igreja-reflexo vs. Igreja-fonte," *Cadernos Brasileiros*, March–April 1968. What Hegel has already pointed out is indeed still valid: "Whatever happens in America is only the echo of the old world and the expression of a foreign life." He further asserted that "America should separate itself from the soil on which universal history has developed until now" (*Raison dans l'histoire*, p. 242).

13. Regarding theological reflection, it has been stated that "there is an urgent need for the Latin American hierarchy to urge its theologians to work up new aspects of theology that are in line with local needs. They cannot rest content with a theology that was elaborated, in large measure, by theologians living in other regions and under different historical conditions" ("Presence of the Church in Latin American Development," in *Between Honesty and Hope*, p. 22); see also "Working Draft of the Medellín Conference," *ibid.*, pp. 191–92. "This is a critical moment . . . ," stated Cardinal Landázuri Ricketts in his closing address at the Medellín Episcopal Conference. "It marks the end of several things: a stage of religious dependence, a long period of imitating alien ideologies and postures. We now propose to seek solutions from within our real situation and potential" (*Between Honesty and Hope*, p. 224).

14. Regarding the role of "Christian consciousness" in the growth of Latin American consciousness, see the fine study of Enrique Düssel, *América latina y conciencia cristiana* (Quito: IPLA, 1970).

PART 4

PERSPECTIVES

It would be well at this point to summarize the questions discussed in the preceding pages and to outline, from a theological point of view, some of the ideas they suggest, or more precisely, to indicate the basic directions of the work to be done in this field.

Attempting to be true to the method suggested in the first part of this study, we will use as our point of departure the questions posed by the social praxis in the process of liberation as well as by the participation of the Christian community in this process within the Latin American context. The Latin American experience holds special interest for us. But it is clear that the commitment to the process of liberation occurs also in churches in other places of the world in different forms and with varying degrees of intensity. Any recourse to the Word of the Lord as well as all references to contemporary theology will be made with reference to this praxis.[1]

The most important point seems to be the following: the scope and gravity of the process of liberation is such that to ponder its significance is really to examine the meaning of Christianity itself and the mission of the Church in the world. These questions are posed, explicitly or implicitly, by the commitments which Christians are making in the struggle against an unjust and alienated society. This serious self-examination is occurring in the very midst of the Church. J. B. Metz correctly comments on this point: "Today it is more the person of faith who lives within the Church than he who lives outside it to whom the faith must be justified."[2] The exhortation of Leo the Great,

143

"Christian, know your dignity," is not easily understood and accepted by today's Christian.

Only this approach fully reveals the import of the questions we are considering and allows us to consider in a new way the meaning of the process of liberation in the light of faith.

NOTES

1. To avoid repetition we will not explicitly mention the experiences—and the texts which outline a reflection on them—which we have already cited in the third part of this work. But it is clear that the reflections which follow do not add to these commitments to the process of liberation which is underway in Latin America. On the contrary, these commitments substantially and permanently nourish these reflections; moreover, they constitute their arena of verification.

2. *Risposta dei teologi*, p. 68.

SECTION ONE

FAITH AND THE NEW MAN

It is not our purpose to deal with all the complex questions which this heading suggests, but only to consider briefly some of the aspects of the subject which concern us.

From the viewpoint of faith, the motive which in the last instance moves Christians to participate in the liberation of oppressed peoples and exploited social classes is the conviction of the radical incompatibility of evangelical demands with an unjust and alienating society. They feel keenly that they cannot claim to be Christians without a commitment to liberation. But the articulation of the way in which this action for a more just world is related to a life of faith belongs to the level of intuition and groping—at times in anguish.

If theology is a critical reflection—in the light of the Word accepted in faith—on historical praxis and therefore on the presence of Christians in the world, it should help us to establish this relationship. Theological reflection should attempt to discern the positive and negative values in this presence. It should make explicit the values of faith, hope, and charity contained in it. And it should contribute to correcting possible aberrations as well as the neglect of other aspects of Christian life, pitfalls into which the demands of immediate political action, regardless of how generous it is, sometimes allow us to fall. This too is the task of critical reflection, which by definition should not be simply a Christian justification a posteriori.[1] Basically this reflection should contribute in one way or another to a more evangelical, more authentic, more concrete, and more efficacious commitment to liberation.

145

It is important to keep in mind that beyond—or rather, through—the struggle against misery, injustice, and exploitation the goal is the *creation of a new man*. Vatican II has declared, "We are witnesses of the birth of a new humanism, one in which man is defined first of all by his responsibility toward his brothers and toward history" (*Gaudium et spes*, no. 55). This aspiration to create a new man is the deepest motivation in the struggle which many have undertaken in Latin America.[2] The fulfillment of this dream (if it can ever be completely fulfilled) can be only vaguely perceived by this generation, but this aspiration even now inspires their commitment.[3]

This quest poses questions and challenges to the Christian faith. What the faith says about itself will demonstrate its relationship to this goal of the people who are struggling for the emancipation of others and of themselves. Indeed, an awareness of the need for self-liberation is essential to a correct understanding of the liberation process. It is not a matter of "struggling for others," which suggests paternalism and reformist objectives, but rather of becoming aware of oneself as not completely fulfilled and as living in an alienated society. And thus one can identify radically and militantly with those—the people and the social class—who bear the brunt of oppression.

In the light of faith, charity, and hope, what then is the meaning of this struggle, this *creation*? What does this option mean to *man*? What is the significance of *novelty* in history and of an orientation towards the future? These are three pertinent questions,[4] three indicators which contemporary theology haltingly pursues; but above all, they are three tasks to be undertaken.

NOTES

1. Karl Rahner speaks of the not too distant possibility that the Church give an "univocal no" to certain tendencies or interpretations of Christianity (*Risposta dei teologi*, p. 71).

2. See above Chapter 6.

3. What Karl Marx wrote more than a hundred years ago is still valid: "The present generation is like the Jews whom Moses led through the desert. Not only does it have to conquer a new world, it also has to perish to give room to the men who are to live in the new world" (*Les luttes sociales en France 1848–1850* [Paris: Éditions Sociales, 1952], p. 90; English translation: *The Class Struggles in France (1848–50)* [New York: International Publishers, 1934]).

4. These recall in a certain way the celebrated programmatic questions of Kant: "What can I *know*? What ought I to *do*? What may I *hope*?" ("The Critique of Pure Reason," in *Kant*, Great Books of the Western World, Vol. 42, p. 236; the italics are ours). Regarding the meaning and evolution of these questions, see Jean Louis Bruch, *La philosophie religieuse de Kant* (Paris: Aubier, Éditions Montaigne, 1968), pp. 21–30.

CHAPTER NINE

LIBERATION AND SALVATION

What is the relationship between salvation and the process of the liberation of man throughout history? Or more precisely, what is the meaning of the struggle against an unjust society and the creation of a new man in the light of the Word? A response to these questions presupposes an attempt to define what is meant by salvation, a concept central to the Christian mystery. This is a complex and difficult task which leads to reflection on the meaning of the saving action of the Lord in history. The salvation of the whole man is centered upon Christ the Liberator.

SALVATION: CENTRAL THEME OF THE CHRISTIAN MYSTERY

One of the great deficiencies of contemporary theology is the absence of a profound and lucid reflection on the theme of salvation.[1] On a superficial level this might seem surprising, but actually it is what often happens with difficult matters: people are afraid to tackle them. It is taken for granted that they are understood. Meanwhile, new edifices are raised on old foundations established in the past on untested assumptions and vague generalities. The moment comes, however, when the whole building totters; this is the time to look again to the foundations. This hour has arrived for the notion of salvation.[2] Recently various works have appeared attempting to revise and deepen our understanding of this idea.[3] These are only a beginning.

We will not attempt to study this criticism in detail, but will only note that a consideration of this question has revealed two

focal points; one follows the other in the manner of two closely
linked stages.

From the Quantitative ...

The questions raised by the notion of salvation have for a
long time been considered under and limited by the classical
question of the "salvation of the pagans." This is the quantitative, extensive aspect of salvation; it is the problem of the number of persons saved, the possibility of being saved, and the role
which the Church plays in this process. The terms of the problem
are, on the one hand, the universality of salvation, and on the
other, the visible Church as the mediator of salvation.

The evolution of the question has been complex and fati-
guing.[4] Today we can say that in a way this evolution has ended.
The idea of the universality of the salvific will of God, clearly
enunciated by Paul in his letter to Timothy, has been established. It has overcome the difficulties posed by various ways
of understanding the mission of the Church and has attained
definite acceptance.[5] All that is left to do is to consider the
ramifications, which are many.[6]

Here we will briefly consider one important point and leave
for later a treatment of the repercussions of this idea on
ecclesiological matters. The notion of salvation implied in this
point of view has two very well-defined characteristics: it is a
cure for sin in this life; and this cure is in virtue of a salvation
to be attained beyond this life. What is important, therefore,
is to know how a man outside the normal pale of grace, which
resides in the institutional Church, can attain salvation. Multiple explanations have attempted to show the extraordinary
ways by which a person could be assured of salvation, understood above all as life beyond this one. The present life is considered to be a test: one's actions are judged and assessed in relation to the transcendent end. The perspective here is moralistic,
and the spirituality is one of flight from this world. Normally,
only contact with the channels of grace instituted by God can
eliminate sin, the obstacle which stands in the way of reaching
that life beyond. This approach is very understandable if we
remember that the question of "the salvation of the pagans"
was raised at the time of the discovery of people belonging to

other religions and living in areas far from those where the
Church had been traditionally rooted.

... to the Qualitative.

As the idea of the universality of salvation and the possibility
of reaching it gained ground in the Christian consciousness and
as the quantitative question was resolved and decreased in
interest, the whole problem of salvation made a qualitative leap
and began to be perceived differently. Indeed, there is more to
the idea of the universality of salvation than simply asserting
the possibility of reaching it while outside the visible frontiers
of the Church. The very heart of the question was touched in
the search for a means to widen the scope of the possibility of
salvation: man is saved if he opens himself to God and to others,
even if he is not clearly aware that he is doing so. This is valid
for Christians and non-Christians alike—for all people. To speak
about the presence of grace—whether accepted or rejected—in
all people implies, on the other hand, to value from a Christian
standpoint the very roots of human activity. We can no longer
speak properly of a profane world.[7] A *qualitative and intensive*
approach replaces a *quantitative and extensive* one. Human existence, in the last instance, is nothing but a yes or a no to
the Lord: "Men already partly accept communion with God,
although they do not explicitly confess Christ as their Lord,
insofar as they are moved by grace (*Lumen gentium*, no. 16),
sometimes secretly (*Gaudium et spes*, nos. 3, 22), renounce their
selfishness, and seek to create an authentic brotherhood among
men. They reject union with God insofar as they turn away from
the building up of this world, do not open themselves to others,
and culpably withdraw into themselves (Mt. 25:31–46)."[8]
From this point of view the notion of salvation appears differently than it did before. Salvation is not something other-
worldly, in regard to which the present life is merely a test.
Salvation—the communion of men with God and the communion
of men among themselves—is something which embraces all
human reality, transforms it, and leads it to its fullness in
Christ: "Thus the center of God's salvific design is Jesus Christ,
who by his death and resurrection transforms the universe and
makes it possible for man to reach fulfillment as a human being.
This fulfillment embraces every aspect of humanity: body and

spirit, individual and society, person and cosmos, time and eternity. Christ, the image of the Father and the perfect God-Man, takes on all the dimensions of human existence."[9]

Therefore, sin is not only an impediment to salvation in the afterlife. Insofar as it constitutes a break with God, sin is a historical reality, it is a breach of the communion of men with each other, it is a turning in of man on himself which manifests itself in a multifaceted withdrawal from others. And because sin is a personal and social intrahistorical reality, a part of the daily events of human life, it is also, and above all, an obstacle to life's reaching the fullness we call salvation.

The idea of a universal salvation, which was accepted only with great difficulty and was based on the desire to expand the possibilities of achieving salvation, leads to the question of the intensity of the presence of the Lord and therefore of the religious significance of man's action in history. One looks then to this world, and now sees in the world beyond not the "true life," but rather the transformation and fulfillment of the present life. The absolute value of salvation—far from devaluing this world—gives it its authentic meaning and its own autonomy, because salvation is already latently there. To express the idea in terms of Biblical theology: the prophetic perspective (in which the Kingdom takes on the present life, transforming it) is vindicated before the sapiential outlook (which stresses the life beyond).[10]

This qualitative, intensive approach has undoubtedly been influenced by the factor which marked the last push toward the unequivocal assertion of the universality of salvation, that is, the appearance of atheism, especially in the heart of Christian countries. The nonbeliever is not interested in an other-worldly salvation, as are believers in other religions; rather he considers it an evasion of the only question he wishes to deal with: the value of earthly existence. The qualitative approach to the notion of salvation attempts to respond to this problem.[11]

The developments which we have reviewed here have allowed us definitively to recover an essential element of the notion of salvation which had been overshadowed for a long time by the question of the possibility of reaching it. We have recovered the idea that salvation is an intrahistorical reality. Furthermore, salvation—the communion of men with God and the communion of men among themselves—orients, transforms, and guides history to its fulfillment.

HISTORY IS ONE

What we have recalled in the preceding paragraph leads us to affirm that, in fact, there are not two histories, one profane and one sacred, "juxtaposed" or "closely linked." Rather there is only one human destiny, irreversibly assumed by Christ, the Lord of history. His redemptive work embraces all the dimensions of existence and brings them to their fullness. The history of salvation is the very heart of human history. The Christian consciousness arrived at this unified view after an evolution parallel to that experienced regarding the notion of salvation. The conclusions converge. From an abstract, essentialist approach we moved to an existential, historical, and concrete view which holds that the only man we know has been efficaciously called to a gratuitous communion with God. All reflection, any distinctions which one wishes to treat, must be based on this fact: the salvific action of God underlies all human existence.[12] The historical destiny of humanity must be placed definitively in the salvific horizon. Only thus will its true dimensions emerge and its deepest meaning be apparent. It seems, however, that contemporary theology has not yet fashioned the categories which would allow us to think through and express adequately this unified approach to history.[13] We work, on the one hand, under the fear of falling back again into the old dualities, and, on the other, under the permanent suspicion of not sufficiently safeguarding divine gratuitousness or the unique dimension of Christianity. Although there may be different approaches to understanding it, however, the fundamental affirmation is clear: there is only one history[14]—a "Christofinalized" history.

The study of two great Biblical themes will allow us to illustrate this point of view and to understand better its scope. The themes are the relationship between creation and salvation and the eschatological promises.

Creation and Salvation

The Bible establishes a close link between creation and salvation. But the link is based on the historical and liberating experience of the Exodus. To forget this perspective is to run the risk of merely juxtaposing these two ideas and therefore losing the

rich meaning which this relationship has for understanding the
recapitulating work of Christ.

Creation: the First Salvific Act

The Bible does not deal with creation in order to satisfy
philosophic concerns regarding the origin of the world. Its point
of view is quite another.

Biblical faith is, above all, faith in a God who reveals himself
through historical events, a God who saves in history. Creation
is presented in the Bible, not as a stage previous to salvation,
but as a part of the salvific process: "Praise be to God the Father
of our Lord Jesus Christ. ... In Christ he chose us before the
world was founded, to be dedicated, to be without blemish in
his sight, to be full of love; and he destined us—such was his
will and pleasure—to be accepted as his sons through Jesus
Christ" (Eph. 1:3–5).[15] God did not create only in the beginning;
he also had an end in mind. God creates all men to be his children.[16] Moreover, creation appears as the first salvific act:
"Creation," writes Von Rad, "is regarded as a work of Yahweh
in history, a work within time. This means that there is a real
and true opening up of historical prospect. No doubt, Creation
as the first of Yahweh's works stands at the very remotest
beginnings—only, it does not stand alone, other works are to
follow."[17] The creation of the world initiates history,[18] the
human struggle, and the salvific adventure of Yahweh. Faith
in creation does away with its mythical and supernatural
character. It is the work of a God who saves and acts in history;
since man is the center of creation, it is integrated into the history which is being built by man's efforts.

Second Isaiah—"the best theologian among Old Testament
writers"[19]—is an excellent witness in this respect. His texts are
frequently cited as one of the richest and clearest expressions
of the faith of Israel in creation. The stress, however, is on the
saving action of Yahweh; the work of creation is regarded and
understood only in this context: "But now this is the word of
the Lord, the word of your creator, O Jacob, of him who
fashioned you, Israel: Have no fear; for I have paid your ransom;
I have called you by name and you are my own" (43:1; cf. 42:5–6).
The assertion is centered on the redemption (or the Covenant).
Yahweh is at one and the same time Creator and Redeemer:
"For your husband is your maker, whose name is the Lord of

Hosts; your ransomer is the Holy One of Israel who is called God of all the earth" (54:5). Numerous psalms sing praise to Yahweh simultaneously as Creator and Savior (cf. Pss. 74, 89, 93, 95, 135, 136). But this is because creation itself is a saving action: "Thus says the Lord, your ransomer, who fashioned you from birth: I am the Lord who made all things, by myself I stretched out the skies, alone I hammered out the floor of the earth" (Isa. 44:24; cf. also Amos 4:12 ff.; 5:8 ff.; Jer. 33:25 ff.; 10:16; 27:5; 32:17; Mal. 2:10). Creation is the work of the Redeemer. Rendtorff says: "A more complete fusion between faith in creation and salvific faith is unimaginable."[20]

Political Liberation: Self-Creation of Man

The liberation from Egypt—both a historical fact and at the same time a fertile Biblical theme—enriches this vision and is moreover its true source.[21] The creative act is linked, almost identified with, the act which freed Israel from slavery in Egypt. Second Isaiah, who writes in exile, is likewise the best witness to this idea: "Awake, awake, put on your strength, O arm of the Lord, awake as you did long ago, in days gone by. Was it not you who hacked the Rahab in pieces and ran the dragon through? Was it not you who dried up the sea, the waters of the great abyss, and made the ocean depths a path for the ransomed?" (51:9–10) The words and images refer simultaneously to two events: creation and liberation from Egypt. Rahab, which for Isaiah symbolizes Egypt (cf. 30:7; cf. also Ps. 87:4), likewise symbolizes the chaos Yahweh had to overcome to create the world (cf. Pss. 74:14; 89:11).[22] The "waters of the great abyss" are those which enveloped the world and from which creation arose, but they are also the Red Sea which the Jews crossed to begin the Exodus. Creation and liberation from Egypt are but one salvific act. It is significant, furthermore, that the technical term *bara*, designating the original creation, was used for the first time by Second Isaiah (43:1, 15; cf. Deut. 32:6) to refer to the creation of Israel. Yahweh's historical actions on behalf of his people are considered creative (41:20; 43:7; 45:8; 48:7).[23] The God who frees Israel is the Creator of the world.

The liberation of Israel is a political action. It is the breaking away from a situation of despoliation and misery and the beginning of the construction of a just and fraternal society. It is the suppression of disorder and the creation of a new order.

The initial chapters of Exodus describe the oppression in which the Jewish people lived in Egypt, in that "land of slavery" (13:3; 20:2; Deut. 5:6): repression (1:10–11), alienated work (5:6–14), humiliations (1:13–14), enforced birth control policy (1:15–22). Yahweh then awakens the vocation of a liberator: Moses. "I have indeed seen the misery of my people in Egypt. I have heard their outcry against their slave-masters. I have taken heed of their sufferings, and have come down to rescue them from the power of Egypt. ... I have seen the brutality of the Egyptians towards them. Come now; I will send you to Pharaoh and you shall bring my people Israel out of Egypt" (3:7–10).

Sent by Yahweh, Moses began a long, hard struggle for the liberation of his people. The alienation of the children of Israel was such that at first "they did not listen to him; they had become impatient because of their cruel slavery" (6:9). And even after they had left Egypt, when they were threatened by Pharaoh's armies, they complained to Moses: "Were there no graves in Egypt, that you should have brought us here to die in the wilderness? See what you have done to us by bringing us out of Egypt! Is not this just what we meant when we said in Egypt, 'Leave us alone; let us be slaves to the Egyptians'? We would rather be slaves to the Egyptians than die here in the wilderness" (14:11–12). And in the midst of the desert, faced with the first difficulties, they told him that they preferred the security of slavery—whose cruelty they were beginning to forget—to the uncertainties of a liberation in process: "If only we had died at the Lord's hand in Egypt, where we sat round the fleshpots and had plenty of bread to eat!" (16:3). A gradual pedagogy of successes and failures would be necessary for the Jewish people to become aware of the roots of their oppression, to struggle against it, and to perceive the profound sense of the liberation to which they were called. The Creator of the world is the Creator and Liberator of Israel, to whom he entrusts the mission of establishing justice: "Thus speaks the Lord who is God, he who created the skies, ... who fashioned the earth. ... I, the Lord, have called you with righteous purpose and taken you by the hand; I have formed you, and appointed you ... to open eyes that are blind, to bring captives out of prison, out of the dungeons where they lie in darkness" (Isa. 42:5–7).

Creation, as we have mentioned above, is regarded in terms of the Exodus, a historical-salvific fact which structures the

faith of Israel.[24] And this fact is a political liberation through
which Yahweh expresses his love for his people and the gift
of total liberation is received.

Salvation: Re-Creation and Complete Fulfillment

Yahweh summons Israel not only to leave Egypt but also and
above all to "bring them up out of that country into a fine, broad
land; it is a land flowing with milk and honey" (3:8). The Exodus
is the long march towards the promised land in which Israel
can establish a society free from misery and alienation.
Throughout the whole process, the religious event is not set
apart. It is placed in the context of the entire narrative, or more
precisely, it is its deepest meaning. It is the root of the situation.
In the last instance, it is in this event that the dislocation
introduced by sin is resolved and justice and injustice, oppression and liberation, are determined. Yahweh liberates the Jewish people politically in order to make them a holy nation: "You
have seen with your own eyes what I did to Egypt. ... If only
you will now listen to me and keep my covenant, then out of
all peoples you shall become my special possession; for the whole
earth is mine. You shall be my kingdom of priests, my holy
nation" (19:4-6). The God of Exodus is the God of history and
of political liberation more than he is the God of nature. Yahweh
is the Liberator, the *goel* of Israel (Isa. 43:14; 47:4; Jer. 50:34).
The Covenant gives full meaning to the liberation from Egypt;
one makes no sense without the other: "The Covenant was a
historical event," asserts Gelin, "which occurred in a moment
of disruption, in an atmosphere of liberation; the revolutionary
climate still prevailed: an intense spiritual impulse would arise
from it, as often happens in history."[25] The Covenant and the
liberation from Egypt were different aspects of the same
movement,[26] a movement which led to encounter with God. The
eschatological horizon is present in the heart of the Exodus.
Casalis rightly notes that "the heart of the Old Testament is
the Exodus from the servitude of Egypt and the journey
towards the promised land. ... The hope of the people of God
is not to return to the mythological primitive garden, to regain
paradise lost, but to march forward towards a new city, a human
and brotherly city whose heart is Christ."[27]

Yahweh will be remembered throughout the history of Israel
by this act which inaugurates its history, a history which is

a re-creation. The God who makes the cosmos from chaos is the same God who leads Israel from alienation to liberation. This is what is celebrated in the Jewish passover. André Neher writes: "The first thing that is expressed in the Jewish passover is the certainty of freedom. With the Exodus a new age has struck for humanity: redemption from misery. If the Exodus had not taken place, marked as it was by the twofold sign of the overriding will of God and the free and conscious assent of men, the historical destiny of humanity would have followed another course. This course would have been radically different, as the redemption, the *geulah* of the Exodus from Egypt, would not have been its foundation.... All constraint is accidental; all misery is only provisional. The breath of freedom which has blown over the world since the Exodus can dispel them this very day."[28] The memory of the Exodus pervades the pages of the Bible and inspires one to reread often the Old as well as the New Testaments.

The work of Christ forms a part of this movement and brings it to complete fulfillment. The redemptive action of Christ, the foundation of all that exists, is also conceived as a re-creation and presented in a context of creation (cf. Col. 1:15–20; 1 Cor. 8:6; Heb. 1:2; Eph. 1:1–22).[29] This idea is particularly clear in the prologue to the Gospel of St. John.[30] According to some exegetes it constitutes the foundation of this whole Gospel.[31]

The work of Christ is a new creation. In this sense, Paul speaks of a "new creation" in Christ (Gal. 6:15; 2 Cor. 5:17). Moreover, it is through this "new creation," that is to say, through the salvation which Christ affords, that creation acquires its full meaning (cf. Rom. 8). But the work of Christ is presented simultaneously as a liberation from sin and from all its consequences: despoliation, injustice, hatred. This liberation fulfills in an unexpected way the promises of the prophets and creates a new chosen people, which this time includes all humanity. Creation and salvation therefore have, in the first place, a Christological sense: all things have been created in Christ, all things have been saved in him (cf. Col. 1:15–20).[32]

Man is the crown and center of the work of creation and is called to continue it through his labor (cf. Gen. 1:28). And not only through his labor. The liberation from Egypt, linked to and even coinciding with creation, adds an element of capital importance: the need and the place for man's active participation in the building of society. If faith "desacralizes" creation, making it the area proper for the work of man, the Exodus from Egypt, the home of a sacred monarchy, reinforces this idea: it is the "desacralization" of social praxis, which from that time on will be the work of man.[33] By working, transforming the world, breaking out of servitude, building a just society, and assuming his destiny in history, man forges himself. In Egypt, work is alienated and, far from building a just society, contributes rather to increasing injustice and to widening the gap between exploiters and exploited.

To dominate the earth as Genesis prescribed, to continue creation, is worth nothing if it is not done for the good of man, if it does not contribute to his liberation, in solidarity with all, in history. The liberating initiative of Yahweh responds to this need by stirring up Moses' vocation. Only the *mediation of this self-creation*—first revealed by the liberation from Egypt—allows us to rise above poetic expressions and general categories and to understand in a profound and synthesizing way the relationship between creation and salvation so vigorously proclaimed by the Bible.

The Exodus experience is paradigmatic. It remains vital and contemporary due to similar historical experiences which the People of God undergo. As Neher writes, it is characterized "by the twofold sign of the overriding will of God and the free and conscious consent of men." And it structures our faith in the gift of the Father's love. In Christ and through the Spirit, men are becoming one in the very heart of history, as they confront and struggle against all that divides and opposes them. But the true agents of this quest for unity are those who today are oppressed (economically, politically, culturally) and struggle to become free.[34] Salvation—totally and freely given by God, the communion of men with God and among themselves—is the inner force and the fullness of this movement of man's self-generation which was initiated by the work of creation.

Consequently, when we assert that man fulfills himself by continuing the work of creation by means of his labor, we are saying that he places himself, by this very fact, within an all-embracing salvific process. To work, to transform this world, is to become a man and to build the human community; it is also to save. Likewise, to struggle against misery and exploitation and to build a just society is already to be part of the saving action, which is moving towards its complete fulfillment. All this means

that building the temporal city is not simply a stage of "humanization" or "pre-evangelization" as was held in theology up until
a few years ago. Rather it is to become part of a saving process
which embraces the whole of man and all human history. Any
theological reflection on human work and social praxis ought
to be rooted in this fundamental affirmation.

Eschatological Promises

A second important Biblical theme leads to converging conclusions. We refer to the eschatological promises. It is not an
isolated theme, but rather, as the former one, it appears
throughout the Bible. It is vitally present in the history of Israel
and consequently claims its place among the People of God
today.

Heirs According to the Promise

The Bible is the book of the Promise, the Promise made by
God to men which is the efficacious revelation of his love and
his self-communication; simultaneously it reveals man to himself. The Greek word which the New Testament uses to designate the Promise is *epangelía*, which also means "word pledged,"
"announcement," and "notification"; it is related to *evangelion*.[35] This Promise, which is at the same time revelation and
Good News, is the heart of the Bible. Albert Gelin says that
"this Promise lies behind the whole Bible, and it makes it the
book of hope, the slight hope stronger than experience, as Peguy
said, which persists through all trials and is reborn to greater
strength after every setback."[36] The Promise is revealed, ap-
peals to man, and is fulfilled throughout history. The Promise
orients all history towards the future and thus puts revelation
in an eschatological perspective.[37] Human history is in truth
nothing but the history of the slow, uncertain, and surprising
fulfillment of the Promise.

The Promise is a gift accepted in faith. This makes Abraham
the father of believers. The Promise was first made to him (cf.
Gen. 12:1–3; 15:1–16) that he and his posterity would be, as St.
Paul says in a vigorous and fertile expression, "the heirs of the
world" (Rom. 4:13).[38] For this reason Jesus, John the Baptist
(Luke 3:8; 13:16; 16:22; 19:9), and Paul (Gal. 3:16–29; Rom. 4;
Heb. 11), place Abraham at the beginning of the work of sal-
vation.[39] This Promise is "given to those who have such faith"

in Jesus Christ (Gal. 3:22). The Promise is fulfilled in Christ, the Lord of history and of the cosmos. In him we are "the 'issue' of Abraham, and so heirs by promise" (Gal. 3:29). This is the mystery which remained hidden until "the fullness of time."

But the *Promise* unfolds—becoming richer and more definite—in the *promises* made by God throughout history. "The first expression and realization of the Promise was the Covenant."[40] The kingdom of Israel was another concrete manifestation. And when the infidelities of the Jewish people rendered the Old Covenant invalid, the Promise was incarnated both in the proclamation of a New Covenant, which was awaited and sustained by the "remnant," as well as in the promises which prepared and accompanied its advent. The Promise enters upon "the last days" with the proclamation in the New Testament of the gift of the Kingdom of God.[41]

The Promise is not exhausted by these promises nor by their fulfillment; it goes beyond them, explains them, and gives them their ultimate meaning. But at the same time, the Promise is announced and is partially and progressively fulfilled in them. There exists a dialectical relationship between the Promise and its partial fulfillments. The resurrection itself is the fulfillment of something promised and likewise the anticipation of a future (cf. Acts 13:23); with it the work of Christ is "not yet completed, not yet concluded"; the resurrected Christ "is still future to himself."[42] The Promise is gradually revealed in all its universality and concrete expression: it is *already* fulfilled in historical events, but *not yet* completely; it incessantly projects itself into the future, creating a permanent historical mobility. The Promise is inexhaustible and dominates history, because it is the self-communication of God. With the Incarnation of the Son and the sending of the Spirit of Promise this self-communication has entered into a decisive stage (Gal. 3:14; Eph. 1:13; Acts 2: 38–39; Luke 24:29). But by the same token, the Promise illuminates and fructifies the future of humanity and leads it through incipient realizations towards its fullness.[43] Both the present and future aspects are indispensable for tracing the relationships between Promise and history.

Eschatology: The Future and the Historical Present

In recent years the eschatological dimension of revelation—and consequently of Christian existence—has been rediscovered.

According to traditional dogmatic theology, the treatise on the "last things" (death, judgment, heaven, hell, the end of the world, the resurrection of the dead) was a kind of appendix not too closely related to the central themes. This treatise began to be referred to as eschatology.[44] Its etymology suggested its appropriateness: *éscatos* 'last' and *logos* 'treatise.'[45]

Toward the end of the nineteenth century, the eschatological theme appeared in liberal Protestant theological studies (Johannes Weiss, Albert Schweitzer) on the message of Jesus and the faith of the primitive Christian community. Moltmann points out the impact of the rise of this line of thinking, but recalls also the pointlessness of these first efforts.[46] "Dialectical theology" came onto this scene from another vantage point and made eschatology the center of its thinking. The "first" Barth is its best representative. Under the influence of Kant, Barthian eschatology is what Urs von Balthasar calls "transcendental eschatology": eternity is the form of true being; time is nothing but appearance and shadow; the ultimate realities are the first principle of everything[47] and therefore the limit of all time.[48] It was this viewpoint, according to Moltmann, "which prevented the break-through of eschatological dimensions in dogmatics."[49]

But the eschatological theme has continued to gain in importance.[50] The term is controversial;[51] the notion much debated.[52] One idea, however, has emerged: the Bible presents eschatology as the driving force of salvific history radically oriented toward the future. Eschatology is thus not just one more element of Christianity, but the very key to understanding the Christian faith.

Basing his study on a rigorous exegesis of the Old Testament, Von Rad has completed an important attempt at clarification in this area. He believes it is inaccurate to think of the eschatological sphere as a "consistent body of ideas, made up of complex cosmic and mythological expectations about the future, from which the prophets drew what they wanted."[53] To reserve the term *eschatological* to designate the end of time, the fulfillment of history, that is to say, extrahistorical events, he thinks is not enough.[54] For Von Rad, the prophets have "eschatologized" Israel's conceptions of time and history. However, what is characteristic of the prophets is, on the one hand, their orientation toward the *future* and, on the other, their concern with the *present*.

It is due to their posture toward the *future* that the prophets are the typical representatives of the Yahwist religion. What is characteristic of the prophets' message is that the situation they announce "cannot be understood as the continuation of what went before."[55] Their starting point is an awareness of a break with the past; the sins of Israel have rendered it unacceptable; the guarantees given by Yahweh are no longer in force. Salvation can come only from a new historical action of Yahweh which will renew in unknown ways his earlier interventions in favor of his people; the signs announcing this action come to be dimly seen by the prophets rereading those earlier events. The Exodus is a favorite theme of the prophets; what they retain of it is fundamentally the break with the past and the projection toward the future.[56] This causes Von Rad to conclude that "the message of the prophets has to be termed eschatological whenever it regards the old historical bases of salvation as null and void," and he notes that "we ought then to go on and limit the term. It should not be applied to cases where Israel gave a general expression of her faith in the future, or ... in the future of one of her sacred institutions." Von Rad ends by saying that "the prophetic teaching is only eschatological when the prophets expelled Israel from the safety of the old saving actions and suddenly shifted the basis of salvation to a future action of God."[57] The core of eschatological thought is in this tension towards that which is to come, towards a new action of God. Hope in new acts of God is based on Yahweh's "fidelity," on the strength of his love for his people which was manifested in the past initiatives on their behalf. These new actions lead to and are nourished by an act to take place at the end of history.[58]

But there is another facet of the prophetic message which we have already considered and which will help us—despite its apparent opposition to the orientation toward the future which we have just mentioned—to pinpoint the notion of eschatology. We refer to the prophets' concern for the present, for the historical vicissitudes which they witness. Because of this concern the object of their hope is very proximate. But, this "closeness" does not exclude an action of Yahweh at the end of history. Indeed, the prophetic message proclaims and is realized in a proximate historical event; at the same time, it is projected beyond this event. This has been perceptively and clearly explained by Steinmann with respect to messianism in his comments on

Isaiah's oracle of the "soul." The author distinguishes two meanings in this prophecy: the first, the only one comprehensible to his contemporaries, points to something "immediately offered by Yahweh to remedy the tragic situation created in Jerusalem by the onslaught of the Syro-Ephraimitic League";[59] this is the birth of a new heir to the crown. The second sense is but dimly perceived by the prophet: "It is through the gift of a child that Yahweh will save the world."[60] The eschatological prophecy refers, therefore, to a concrete event, and *in* it to another fuller and more comprehensive one to which history must be open.[61] What is especially important for an accurate understanding of eschatology is the relationship between these events. The relationship is found in the projection towards the future included in the present event. From a similar point of view, Von Rad interprets Deuteronomy, the book which contains the theology of the Covenant: "It is certain, literally, that Deuteronomy comes from the time after the conquest, for it speaks of the people on Mt. Horeb; thus it functions as fiction; because they had been living on the land for a long time. But here we see a clearly eschatological feature which permeates the whole. All the salvific benefits which it mentions, including a life of 'rest,' are proposed to the community again, now that it is called to decide for Yahweh. We are faced with one of the most interesting problems of Old Testament theology: the promises which have already been realized historically are not invalidated, but continue to be true in a new context and somewhat different form. The promise of the land was preached again without interruption as a future good, even after it had been achieved."[62] This interpretation allows him to speak of the eschatological scope of Deuteronomy, an opening to the future which is not only not suppressed by the implementations in the present, but is rather affirmed and dynamized by them.

The historical implementations of promises in the *present* are—insofar as they are ordered toward what is to come—as characteristic of eschatology as the opening to the *future*. More precisely, this tension toward the future lends meaning to and is expressed in the present, while simultaneously being nourished by it. It is thus that the attraction of "what is to come" is the driving force of history. The action of Yahweh in history and his action at the end of history are inseparable. It has been said often in recent years that the expression used

in Exod. 3:14 *('Ehyeh asher 'ehyeh)* is correctly translated not
as "I am who am," which can be interpreted within our
categories in the sense of a vigorous but static assertion of God's
transcendence, but rather as "I will be who will be." A new
kind of transcendence is emphasized: God reveals himself as
a force in our future and not as an ahistorical being.[63] Grammat-
ically both translations are valid. It would be better perhaps,
to use an expression which emphasizes the characteristic of per-
manence: "I am he who is being." But the use of similar expressions (thirty-one times throughout the Bible) and the context
of the Covenant in which the above passage is found, lead us
rather to stress the active sense of the terminology employed.
"To be" in Hebrew means "to become," "to be present," "to
occupy a place." "I am" would mean "I am with you," "I am
here ready to act" ("When I put forth my power against the
Egyptians and bring the Israelites out from them, then Egypt
will know that I am the Lord" [Exod. 7:5]). "I am the Lord, I
will release you. ... I will rescue you. ... I will adopt you as
my people. ... I will lead you to the land. ... I will give it to
you for your possession" (Exod. 6:6–9; cf. also 3:10, 17; 8:18).[64]

The full significance of God's action in history is understood
only when it is put in its eschatological perspective; similarly,
the revelation of the final meaning of history gives value to
the present. The self-communication of God points towards the
future, and at the same time this Promise and Good News reveal
man to himself and widen the perspective of his historical commitment here and now.

Eschatological Promises: Historical Promises

What has been said will help us to frame better a classic question regarding the interpretation of Old Testament texts. We
refer to the so-called "spiritualizing influence" which the New
Testament has on them.[65]

According to this hypothesis, what the Old Testament
announces and promises on the "temporal" and "earthly" level
has to be translated to a "spiritual" level. A "carnal" viewpoint
kept the Jewish people from seeing the hidden, figurative sense
of these announcements and promises, which is revealed clearly
only in the New Testament. This hermeneutical principle is
strongly held in Christian circles. And it is not new. A famous
text of Pascal's echoes this ancient tradition: "The prophecies

have a hidden and spiritual meaning to which this people were hostile, under the carnal meaning which they loved. If the spiritual meaning had been revealed, they would not have loved it."[66]

Let us take as a recent and representative example of this line of interpretation the opinion of a well-known exegete. Regarding the prophetic promises, Grelot asserts with his usual precision that there is a fundamental misunderstanding of the object of these promises. "On the one hand," he writes, "they seem to refer to the *temporal* redemption of Israel, freed from secular oppression and reestablished in its past status in such a way that all nations participate in its privileges and enjoy with it the earthly goods promised at the time of the first Covenant. But on the other hand, they also seem to refer to the *spiritual* redemption of all men, as can be inferred from some of the brightest pages, not the longest but the purest."[67] In order to clarify this ambiguity, it is necessary to argue from the principle that the true object of the promises is veiled by the figurative language used by the prophets. The problem at hand, therefore, is to discover "what has to be taken literally and what is to be understood figuratively."[68] The answer is clear: the object of these promises is the "permanent *spiritual* drama of humanity which touches directly on the mystery of sin, suffering, and salvation, which constitutes the substance of its destiny"; the texts which transmit these promises to us, however, have only an "accidental relationship with *political* history."[69] The true sense is therefore the "spiritual" one. The New Testament will make this sense perfectly clear.[70]

But is this really a true dilemma: either spiritual redemption or temporal redemption? Is not there in all this an "excessive spiritualization" which Congar advises us to distrust?[71] All indications seem to point in this direction. But there is, perhaps, something deeper and more difficult to overcome. The impression does indeed exist that in this statement of the problem there is an assumption which should be brought to the surface, namely a certain idea of the spiritual characterized by a kind of Western dualistic thought (matter-spirit), foreign to the Biblical mentality.[72] And it is becoming more foreign also to the contemporary mentality.[73] This is a disincarnate "spiritual," scornfully superior to all earthly realities. The proper way to pose the question does not seem to us to be in terms of "temporal

promise or spiritual promise." Rather, as we have mentioned
above, it is a matter of partial fulfillments through liberating
historical events, which are in turn new promises marking the
road towards total fulfillment. Christ does not "spiritualize" the
eschatological promises; he gives them meaning and fulfillment
today (cf Luke 4:21);[74] but at the same time he opens new perspectives by catapulting history forward, forward towards total
reconciliation.[75] The hidden sense is not the "spiritual" one,
which devalues and even eliminates temporal and earthly
realities as obstacles; rather it is the sense of a fullness which
takes on and transforms historical reality.[76] Moreover, it is only
in the temporal, earthly, historical event that we can open up
to the future of complete fulfillment.

It is not sufficient, therefore, to acknowledge that eschatology
is valid in the future as well as in the present. Indeed, this can
be asserted even on the level of "spiritual" realities, present
and future. We can say that eschatology does not lessen the
value of the present life and yet express this in words which
might be misleading. If by "present life" one understands only
"present *spiritual* life," one does not have an accurate understanding of eschatology. Its presence is an intrahistorical reality. The grace-sin conflict, the coming of the Kingdom, and the
expectation of the parousia are also necessarily and inevitably
historical, temporal, earthly, social, and material realities.

The prophets announce a kingdom of peace. But peace presupposes the establishment of justice: "Righteousness shall yield
peace and its fruit [shall] be quietness and confidence forever"
(Isa. 32:17; cf. also Ps. 85).[77] It presupposes the defense of the
rights of the poor, punishment of the oppressors, a life free from
the fear of being enslaved by others, the liberation of the
oppressed. Peace, justice, love, and freedom are not private
realities; they are not only internal attitudes. They are social
realities, implying a historical liberation. A poorly understood
spiritualization has often made us forget the human consequences of the eschatological promises and the power to transform unjust social structures which they imply. The elimination
of misery and exploitation is a sign of the coming of the Kingdom. It will become a reality, according to the Book of Isaiah,
when there is happiness and rejoicing among the people because
"men shall build houses and live to inhabit them, plant vine-
yards and eat their fruit; they shall not build for others to
inhabit nor plant for others to eat.... My chosen shall enjoy

the fruit of their labor" (65:21–22) because the fruit of their labor will not be taken from them. The struggle for a just world in which there is no oppression, servitude, or alienated work will signify the coming of the Kingdom. The Kingdom and social injustice are incompatible (cf. Isa. 29:18–19 and Matt. 11:5; Lev. 25:10 ff. and Luke 4:16–21). "The struggle for justice," rightly asserts Dom Antonio Fragoso, "is also the struggle for the Kingdom of God."[78]

The eschatological promises are being fulfilled throughout history, but this does not mean that they can be identified clearly and completely with one or another social reality; their liberating effect goes far beyond the foreseeable and opens up new and unsuspected possibilities. The complete encounter with the Lord will mark an end to history, but it will take place in history. Thus we must acknowledge historical events in all their concreteness and significance, but we are also led to a permanent detachment. The encounter is present even now, dynamizing humanity's process of becoming and projecting it beyond man's hopes (1 Cor. 2:6–9); it will not be planned or predesigned.[79] This "ignorance" accounts for the active and committed hope for the gift: Christ is "the Yes pronounced upon God's promises, every one of them" (2 Cor. 1:20).

CHRIST AND COMPLETE LIBERATION

The conclusion to be drawn from all the above is clear: salvation embraces all men and the whole man; the liberating action of Christ—made man in this history and not in a history marginal to the real life of man—is at the heart of the historical current of humanity; the struggle for a just society is in its own right very much a part of salvation history.

It is fitting, nevertheless, to reconsider the question, reviewing how it has been posed and examining other aspects of it. This will allow us, furthermore, to summarize the ideas presented in this chapter.

Temporal Progress and the Growth of the Kingdom

Chapter 3 of the first part of *Gaudium et spes* begins by asking about the meaning and value of human activity (no. 33) and ends by recalling, in an often-quoted text that "earthly progress must be carefully distinguished from the growth of Christ's kingdom. Nevertheless, to the extent that the former can contribute to the better ordering of human society, it is of vital concern to the kingdom of God" (no. 39). The terms used are intentionally general, making different interpretations possible. The history of this text can help both our exegetical efforts and—what is of special interest to us—to clarify the question which it poses.

The so-called Schema 13 became the most awaited document of the Council, after the interventions of Cardinals Montini and Suenens towards the end of the first session of the Council. Its principal task was to show the attitude of the Church towards the world.[80] A preliminary text, the so-called "Schema of Zurich," was presented at the third session of the Council; it was heavily attacked both inside and outside the conciliar chambers due to what was considered a "dualistic" approach to the natural and supernatural orders.[81] Its recasting produced what became known as the "Schema of Ariccia," which formed the basis for the present Constitution.

The tone of the Schema of Ariccia was very different from the former document. It vigorously stresses the unity of the vocation of man (see Part 1, Chapter 4) and recalls what its principal drafter calls "this elemental but very forgotten truth that redemption embraces the totality of creation." And he adds, "This profound unity of the divine plan for man, creation, and the Kingdom is a leitmotiv of Schema 13."[82] Indeed, the Schema asserts that "man's history and the history of salvation are closely implicated with each other; in the present, definitive economy of salvation the order of redemption includes the order of creation" (no. 50).[83] Two consequences flow from this statement. The first concerns the mission of the Church: "Since redemption includes the order of creation, the ministry of the Church necessarily encompasses—from its particular point of view—the whole complexus of human realities and problems" (no. 51). The phrase "from its particular point of view" seeks to establish the angle from which the scope of the mission of the Church ought to be considered. But this restriction does not detract from the strength and even the boldness of the text. The second consequence also results from "the inclusion of all creation in the order of redemption"; it refers to the unity of the Christian life: "All human activities, even the most humble, must be vivified for Christians by the Spirit of God and ordered to the Kingdom of God" (no. 52).[84] The text is based on the attitude of the prophets who "saw in injustice not a social disorder or an offense to the poor, but a violation of the divine law and an insult to the holiness of God." It emphasizes the fact that Christ not only did "not soften this doctrine; he perfected it" (no. 52). In this connection it refers to 1 John 3:14 and Matt. 25:31-46, texts which emphasize the oneness of man's attitude toward God and his neighbor; these texts have disappeared from the final version of the Constitution.

These texts make it very clear that the Schema of Ariccia adopts the "one history" approach. It defines, helps us to understand, and even corrects the formulation of the distinction which constitutes the immediate antecedent of no. 39 of *Gaudium et spes:* "It is clear that the perfection of the social state is of an order completely different from that of the growth of the Kingdom of God, and they cannot be identified" (no. 43). The text continues, "In all, the form of organization and government adopted by society has a great impact on the human and moral behavior of its citizens, making their entrance into the Kingdom easier or more difficult." Despite the intentions, the choice of words here is unfortunate and gives the impression of a static, extrinsicist, and even moralistic treatment of the question. In comparison, the present text, despite its general character, is better, but it lacks the context of the unified vision which the Schema of Ariccia presented.

The Schema of Ariccia was discussed at the beginning of the fourth session of the Council. At this time it was asked that the distinction between the natural and supernatural orders be clarified and that the confusion between temporal progress and salvation be avoided. This was supported, both by the "minority" as well as some representatives of the conciliar "majority" (Cardinals Doepfner and Frings). There was also objection to an excessive optimism. It was asked that more stress be laid on the meaning of sin and it was feared that the autonomy of the temporal sphere was not sufficiently emphasized. The text was watered down. The present Chapter 4 of the first part of *Gaudium et spes* does not emphasize as strongly as did the Schema of Ariccia the concrete and historical unity of these two orders.[85] With this background, the distinction established in *Gaudium et spes*, no. 39, can be seen in a different light.[86]

The Council refrained from delving into debatable theological questions. It did not oppose the position adopted in the Schema of Ariccia, but fell back on only those assertions which enjoyed a large consensus. This approach had been the intention of the drafters at Ariccia when they presented the text. Because these were "extremely serious questions deeply affecting the spirit of our contemporaries and at the same time referring to very difficult and unclarified problems of Christian revelation," the Mixed Commission did "not wish to espouse specific opinions; rather it preferred to limit itself to transmitting the common doctrine of the Church."[87] However, in the judgment of many persons the Ariccia text went beyond this moderate and prudent approach, and therefore its expressions had to be softened. The final text is limited to two general affirmations: there is a close relationship between temporal progress and the growth of the Kingdom, but these two processes are distinct. Those engaged in the latter not only cannot be indifferent to the former; they must show a genuine interest in and value it. However, the growth of the Kingdom goes beyond temporal progress. In short, there is close relationship but no identification. The conciliar text does not go beyond this. The field is open, within this framework, for different theological postures.[88] The dialogue among them will allow a penetration of this question and will gradually lead to a new consensus, as has happened so often in the history of the Church.

Populorum progressio goes a step further. Integral development is regarded as the change from less human to more human living conditions: "Less human conditions first affect those who are so poor as to lack the minimum essentials for life; ... then they affect those who are oppressed by social structures which have been created by abuses of ownership or by abuses of power, by the exploitation of the workers or by unfair business deals." This subhuman condition is characterized by sin and injustice. It is necessary to rise gradually from this position toward a more human state of things: "More human conditions of life clearly imply passage from want to the possession of necessities, overcoming social evils, increase of knowledge and acquisition of culture. Other more human conditions are increased esteem for the dignity of others, a turning toward the spirit of poverty, cooperation for the common good, and the will for peace. Then comes the acknowledgment by man of supreme values and of God, their source and finality." Then comes the most important text, expressed in new terms: "Finally, and above all, are faith, a gift of God accepted by man's good-will, and unity in the charity of Christ, who calls us all to share as sons in the life of the living God, the Father of all men" (no. 21). "More human ... finally, and above all,"—not superhuman or supernatural. This is a fuller idea of what is human, the reaffirmation of the single vocaton to the grace of communion with God. This is why there is no solution based on a continuity between what is "natural" and grace; rather there is a profound integration and an ordering toward the fullness of all that is human in the free gift of the self-communication of God. This text is rich in implications and has a freshness absent from other parts of the encyclical dealing with social and economic questions. These ideas are not, however, treated in depth nor outlined with great detail and their ramifications are not elaborated. That is a task which still would have to be undertaken.

The Horizon of Political Liberation

The texts of the magisterium of the Church to which we have referred (with the exception of some points in *Populorum progressio)* are typical of the way contemporary theology treats this question. The approach seems to preclude the question regarding the ultimate meaning of man's action in history or, to express it in the terms of *Gaudium et spes*, of the relationship between temporal progress and the growth of the Kingdom. Temporal progress is seen preferably in the dominion of nature by science and technology and in some of the repercussions on the development of human society; there is no radical challenge to the unjust system on which it is based. The conflictual aspects of the political sphere are absent; or rather they have been avoided.

Theologically, therefore, we will consider temporal progress as a continuation of the work of creation and explore its connection with redemptive action. Redemption implies a direct relation to sin, and sin—the breach of friendship with God and others—is a human, social, and historical reality which originates in a socially and historically situated freedom.

"Creation," the cosmos, suffers from the consequences of sin. To cite Rom. 8 in this regard is interesting and does broaden our perspective, but this passage is not directly related to the question at hand. The immediate relationship between creation and redemption easily leads to a juxtaposition or to an artificial inclusion of the former into the latter, in which creation is granted autonomy and yet struggles to escape from the strait-jacket it is thus put into. It will be necessary to look at the question from a greater distance, or in other terms, to penetrate it more deeply, in order to capture in a single view or to establish on a single principle the creation-redemption relationship. In the way the problem has previously been stated, there is a curious omission of the liberating and protagonistic role of man, the lord of creation and coparticipant in his own salvation.[89] As we have already pointed out in this chapter, only the concept of the mediation of man's self-creation in history can lead us to an accurate and fruitful understanding of the relationship between creation and redemption. This line of interpretation is suggested by the outstanding fact of the Exodus; because of it, creation is regarded as the first salvific act and salvation as a new creation. Without the perspective of political liberation we cannot go beyond a relationship between two separate "orders," that of creation and that of redemption.[90] The liberation approach subverts also the very "order" involved in the posing of the question.

The work of man, the transformation of nature, continues creation only if it is a human act, that is to say, if it is not alienated by unjust socio-economic structures. A whole theology of work, despite its evident insights, appears naive from a political point of view. Teilhard de Chardin is among those who contributed most to a search for a unity between faith and the "religion of the world," but he does so from a scientific point of view. He values the dominion over nature man has achieved and speaks of it as the penetration point of evolution, enabling man to control it. Politically his vision is, on the whole, neutral.[91] This focus has had a definite impact, as could be expected, on the views of theologians of the developed world. The faith-science conflict and the application of science to the transformation of the world have sapped most of their energy. This is why concern for human society is translated into terms of development and progress.[92] In other areas the problems are different.

The concerns of the so-called Third World countries revolve around the social injustice-justice axis, or, in concrete terms, the oppression-liberation axis.[93] Thus there is a great challenge to the faith of Christians in these countries. In contradistinction to a pessimistic approach to this world which is so frequent in traditional Christian groups and which encourages escapism, there is proposed in these other countries an optimistic vision which seeks to reconcile faith and the world and to facilitate commitment. But this optimism must be based on facts. Otherwise, this posture can be deceitful and treacherous and can even lead to a justification of the present order of things. In the underdeveloped countries one starts with a rejection of the existing situation, considered as fundamentally unjust and dehumanizing. Although this is a negative vision, it is nevertheless the only one which allows us to go to the root of the problems and to create without compromises a new social order, based on justice and brotherhood. This rejection does not produce an escapist attitude, but rather a will to revolution.

The concept of political liberation—with economic roots— recalls the conflictual aspects of the historical current of humanity. In this current there is not only an effort to know and dominate nature. There is also a situation—which both affects and is affected by this current—of misery and despoliation of the fruit of man's work, the result of the exploitation of man by man; there is a confrontation between social classes and, therefore, a struggle for liberation from oppressive structures which hinder man from living with dignity and assuming his own destiny. This struggle is the human activity whose ultimate goal must in the first place be enlightened by faith. Once this has been achieved, other facets will likewise be illuminated. The horizon of political liberation allows for a new approach to the problem, it throws new light on it, and it enables us to see aspects which had been but dimly perceived; it permits us also to get away from an alleged apolitical science and provides a different context for the crucial role of scientific knowledge in the historical praxis of man. Other religions think in terms of cosmos and nature; Christianity, rooted in Biblical sources, thinks in terms of history. And in this history, injustice and oppression, divisions and confrontations exist. But the hope of liberation is also present.

Christ the Liberator

The approach we have been considering opens up for us—and
this is of utmost importance—unforeseen vistas on the problem
of sin. An unjust situation does not happen by chance; it is not
something branded by a fatal destiny: there is human responsibility behind it. The prophets said it clearly and energetically
and we are rediscovering their words now. This is the reason
why the Medellín Conference refers to the state of things in
Latin America as a "sinful situation," as a "rejection of the
Lord."[94] This characterization, in all its breadth and depth, not
only criticizes the individual abuses on the part of those who
enjoy great power in this social order; it challenges all their
practices, that is to say, it is a repudiation of the whole existing
system—to which the Church itself belongs.

In this approach we are far, therefore, from that naive optimism which denies the role of sin in the historical development
of humanity. This was the criticism, one will remember, of the
Schema of Ariccia and it is frequently made in connection with
Teilhard de Chardin and all those theologies enthusiastic about
human progress. But in the liberation approach sin is not considered as an individual, private, or merely interior reality—asserted just enough to necessitate a "spiritual" redemption
which does not challenge the order in which we live. Sin is
regarded as a social, historical fact, the absence of brotherhood
and love in relationships among men, the breach of friendship
with God and with other men, and, therefore, an interior, personal fracture. When it is considered in this way, the collective
dimensions of sin are rediscovered. This is the Biblical notion
that José María González Ruiz calls the "hamartiosphere," the
sphere of sin: "a kind of parameter or structure which objectively conditions the progress of human history itself."[95]
Moreover, sin does not appear as an afterthought, something
which one has to mention so as not to stray from tradition or
leave oneself open to attack. Nor is this a matter of escape into
a fleshless spiritualism. Sin is evident in oppressive structures,
in the exploitation of man by man, in the domination and slavery
of peoples, races, and social classes. Sin appears, therefore, as
the fundamental alienation, the root of a situation of injustice
and exploitation.[96] It cannot be encountered in itself, but only

in concrete instances, in particular alienations.[97] It is impossible
to understand the concrete manifestations without understanding the underlying basis and vice versa. Sin demands a radical
liberation, which in turn necessarily implies a political
liberation.[98] Only by participating in the historical process of
liberation will it be possible to show the fundamental alienation
present in every partial alienation.

This radical liberation is the gift which Christ offers us. By
his death and resurrection he redeems man from sin and all
its consequences, as has been well said in a text we quote again:
"It is the same God who, in the fullness of time, sends his Son
in the flesh, so that He might come to liberate all men from
all slavery to which sin has subjected them: hunger, misery,
oppression, and ignorance, in a word, that injustice and hatred
which have their origin in human selfishness."[99] This is why
the Christian life is a passover, a transition from sin to grace,
from death to life, from injustice to justice, from the subhuman
to the human. Christ introduces us by the gift of his Spirit into
communion with God and with all men. More precisely, it is
because he introduces us into this communion, into a continuous
search for its fullness, that he conquers sin—which is the negation of love—and all its consequences.

In dealing with the notion of liberation in Chapter 2, we distinguished three levels of meaning: political liberation, the liberation of man throughout history, liberation from sin and
admission to communion with God. In the light of the present
chapter, we can now study this question again. These three
levels mutually effect each other, but they are not the same.
One is not present without the others, but they are distinct:
they are all part of a single, all-encompassing salvific process,
but they are to be found at different levels.[100] Not only is the
growth of the Kingdom not reduced to temporal progress;
because of the Word accepted in faith, we see that the fundamental obstacle to the Kingdom, which is sin, is also the root
of all misery and injustice; we see that the very meaning of
the growth of the Kingdom is also the ultimate precondition
for a just society and a new man. One reaches this root and
this ultimate precondition only through the acceptance of the
liberating gift of Christ, which surpasses all expectations. But,
inversely, all struggle against exploitation and alienation, in
a history which is fundamentally one, is an attempt to vanquish

selfishness, the negation of love. This is the reason why any effort to build a just society is liberating. And it has an indirect but effective impact on the fundamental alienation. It is a salvific work, although it is not all of salvation. As a human work it is not exempt from ambiguities, any more than what is considered to be strictly "religious" work. But this does not weaken its basic orientation nor its objective results.

Temporal progress—or, to avoid this aseptic term, the liberation of man—and the growth of the Kingdom both are directed toward complete communion of men with God and of men among themselves. They have the same goal, but they do not follow parallel roads, not even convergent ones. The growth of the Kingdom is a process which occurs historically *in* liberation, insofar as liberation means a greater fulfillment of man. Liberation is a precondition for the new society, but this is not all it is. While liberation is implemented in liberating historical events, it also denounces their limitations and ambiguities, proclaims their fulfillment, and impels them effectively towards total communion. This is not an identification. Without liberating historical events, there would be no growth of the Kingdom. But the process of liberation will not have conquered the very roots of oppression and the exploitation of man by man without the coming of the Kingdom, which is above all a gift. Moreover, we can say that the historical, political liberating event *is* the growth of the Kingdom and *is* a salvific event; but it is not *the* coming of the Kingdom, not *all* of salvation. It is the historical realization of the Kingdom and, therefore, it also proclaims its fullness. This is where the difference lies. It is a distinction made from a dynamic viewpoint, which has nothing to do with the one which holds for the existence of two juxtaposed "orders," closely connected or convergent, but deep down different from each other.

The very radicalness and totality of the salvific process require this relationship. Nothing escapes this process, nothing is outside the pale of the action of Christ and the gift of the Spirit. This gives human history its profound unity. Those who reduce the work of salvation are indeed those who limit it to the strictly "religious" sphere and are not aware of the universality of the process. It is those who think that the work of Christ touches the social order in which we live only indirectly or tangentially, and not in its roots and basic structure. It is those who in order to protect salvation (or to protect their interests) lift salvation from the midst of history, where men and social classes struggle to liberate themselves from the slavery and oppression to which other men and social classes have subjected them. It is those who refuse to see that the salvation of Christ is a radical liberation from all misery, all despoliation, all alienation. It is those who by trying to "save" the work of Christ will "lose" it.

In Christ the all-comprehensiveness of the liberating process reaches its fullest sense. His work encompasses the three levels of meaning which we mentioned above. A Latin American text on the missions seems to us to summarize this assertion accurately: "All the dynamism of the cosmos and of human history, the movement towards the creation of a more just and fraternal world, the overcoming of social inequalities among men, the efforts, so urgently needed on our continent, to liberate man from all that depersonalizes him—physical and moral misery, ignorance, and hunger—as well as the awareness of human dignity (*Gaudium et spes*, no. 22), all these originate, are transformed, and reach their perfection in the saving work of Christ. In him and through him salvation is present at the heart of man's history, and there is no human act which, in the last instance, is not defined in terms of it."[101]

NOTES

1. This is clearly indicated by Piet Smulders, "La Iglesia como sacramento de la salvación," in *La Iglesia del Vaticano II*, ed. Guillermo Baraúna (Madrid: Juan Flors, 1966), 1:379; French version: "L'Église sacrement du salut," *L'Église de Vatican II* (Paris: Les Éditions du Cerf, 1966), 2:313–38. More recently Yves Congar has written, "There is a question on which very little has been written: What does it mean, for the world and for man, to be saved? In what does salvation consist?" (*Situation et tâches*, p. 80; see also p. 68); and in another place he writes, "It is necessary to ask ourselves again very seriously about our idea of salvation. There is hardly any other theological notion implying immediate consequences—very concrete and very important—which has been left so vague and which calls in a most urgent way for an adequate elaboration" ("Christianisme et libération de l'homme," *Masses Ouvrières*, no. 258 [December 1969], p. 8).

2. Even including the very term *salvation;* with its connotation of evasion it would seem more and more inadequate to express the reality in question.

3. See Juan Luis Segundo, "Intelecto y salvación," *Salvación y construcción del mundo*, pp. 47–91; Manaranche, *Quel salut?*; Christian Duquoc, "Qu'est-ce que le salut?" in *L'Eglise vers l'avenir*, ed. M. D. Chenu (Paris: Les Éditions du Cerf,

1969), pp. 99–102; and the interesting posing of the question in the recent article of Jean-Pierre Jossua, "L'enjeu de la recherche théologique actuelle sur le salut," *Revue des Sciences Philosophiques et Théologiques* 54, no. 1 (January 1970): 24–25. The old book of Congar, *The Wide World My Parish: Salvation and its Problems*, trans. Donald Attwater (Baltimore: Helicon Press, 1961) gathered together different studies on the notion of salvation and opened new paths which are still relevant. Moreover, we cannot forget in this regard the concerns and intuitions of Teilhard de Chardin.

4. For a historical study of this point, see the classic work of Louis Capéran, *Le problème du salut des infidèles*, 2 vols. (Toulouse: Grand Séminaire, 1934); see also Angel Santos Hernández, *Salvación y paganismo* (Santander: Editorial Sal Terrae, 1960).

5. See the solid study of Hendrik Nys, *Le salut sans l'Évangile* (Paris: Les Éditions du Cerf, 1966); see also the article of Joseph Ratzinger, "Salus extra ecclesiam nulla est," in *Naturaleza salvífica de la Iglesia* (Barcelona: do-c, 1964); English mimeo published by do-c (Rome), research paper no. 88.

6. In the first place, for a theology of the Church (see below Chapter 12) and therefore for a theology of missionary activity, see the study done by the missionary periodical *Spiritus*, no. 24 (August–September 1965), and the position papers of the Thirty-fifth Missiology Week gathered in *Repenser la mission* (Louvain: Desclée deBrouwer, 1965); these are revealing examples of the crisis caused by this revision which has led to the clear and simple affirmation of the universality of salvation. See the state of the question of this revision in Boniface Willems, "Who Belongs to the Church?" in Concilium 1, pp. 131–51.

7. "For the orthodox tradition, the profane does not exist, only the profaned" (Olivier Clement, "Un ensayo de lectura ortodoxa de la constitución," in *La Iglesia en el mundo de hoy* (Madrid: Studium, 1967), p. 673. The same idea is found in Charles Moeller, "Renewal of the Doctrine of Man," *Theology of Renewal* (Montreal: Palm, 1968), p. 458.

8. *La pastoral en las misiones de América Latina*, conclusions of the meeting at Melgar organized by the Department of Missions of CELAM (Bogota, 1968), pp. 16–17. The same idea is found in another text which also presents an interesting theological reflection: "Men respond of their own free will to this salvation that is offered to them in Christ. They can respond to it somehow, even when they do not know Jesus Christ explicitly; they do so when, under the influence of grace, they try to move out of their egotism, to take on the task of constructing the world, and to enter into communion with their fellow men. . . . They fail to respond when they refuse to recognize this task of building the world and serving others in fellowship, thus committing sin" ("Working Draft of the Medellín Conference," in *Between Honesty and Hope*, p. 189).

9. *Ibid.*, pp. 187–88.

10. Regarding the interpretation of the Beatitudes in Luke from this viewpoint, see below Chapter 13. In the interesting essay on the notion of salvation which we have already mentioned, Juan Luis Segundo notes a difference in focus between the thinking of Paul and the other authors of the New Testament, a difference parallel to the one we have just pointed out; Segundo concludes, "We can say then that Christianity, although like the religions of extraterrestrial salvation because of its absolute salvation, differs from them because it introduced this absolute value into the midst of the historical and apparently profane reality of the existence of man" ("Intelecto y salvación," p. 87).

11. Some years ago Christian Duquoc compared these two positions from another viewpoint: "What mattered then to the theologian was the way man worked in relation to his transcendent end; what matters to him today is what man does" ("Eschatologie et réalités terrestres," *Lumière et Vie* 9, no. 50 [November–December 1960]:5).

12. See above Chapter 5.

13. In this regard see the effort of Jossua, "L'enjeu."

14. We will cite the testimony of two theologians considered rather moderate in their views. From a Biblical perspective, Pierre Grelot writes, "Profane history and sacred history are not two separate realities.... They are intertwined in each other. Concretely there is *only one* human history which develops *at the same time* on these two levels. The grace of redemption, whose mysterious itinerary constitutes sacred history, is at work in the very heart of profane history.... Sacred history integrates all of profane history, on which it confers, in the last instance, its intelligible meaning." Having said this, the author adds, "In the midst of profane history, which runs down through the centuries, sacred history has its points of emergence which enable us to establish its reality and know its essential aspects" (*Sens chrétien de l'Ancien Testament* [Tournai: Desclée & Cie, Éditeurs, 1962], p. 111). Nevertheless, the notion of "points of emergence" does not seem very clear. Do these have their own history in the midst of the general history of humanity? Are they necessary to establish the reality of sacred history? Or are they nothing more than the interpretation of history in the light of the Word of God?

For his part, Emile Rideau believes that "if the vocation of the world and of man is supernatural, there does not exist, in fact and in the deepest sense, anything but a supernatural reality. The profane world is nothing but an abstraction in relation to the supernatural world of faith" ("Y a-t-il un monde profane?" *Nouvelle Revue Théologique* 88, no. 10 [December 1966]:1080). This does not weaken for him the consistency of the temporal sphere, because we are before "a lively dialectic of the relationship between, on the one hand, a world that is not profane only because it is not perceived as divine and, on the other, a supernatural reality which seeks to assume it, to ransom it, to consecrate it, to divinize it" (*ibid.*, p. 1082).

The position of Karl Rahner, on the other hand, seems more ambiguous; see "History of the World and Salvation-history," in *Theological Investigations*, 5:97–114. See also Ovidio Pérez Morales, who clearly affirms the existence of a single history: *Fe y desarrollo* (Caracas: Ediciones Paulinas, 1971), p. 49.

15. See the comments of Heinrich Schlier, *Der Briefe an die Epheser* (Dusseldorf: Patmos-Verlag, 1958), pp. 37–48.

16. See the reflections of Piet Schoonenberg concerning the mutual implications of creation and the Covenant in *Covenant and Creation* (London: Sheed and Ward, 1968). pp. 141–49.

17. Gerhard Von Rad, *Old Testament Theology*, trans. D. M. G. Stalker (New York: Harper and Brothers, 1962), 1:139; see also Von Rad's, *Genesis*, trans. John H. Marks (London: SCM Press Ltd, 1961).

18. "With the creation of the world (the six-day schema) the dimension of history opens up. Only by referring history to the creation of the world could the saving action within Israel be brought into its appropriate theological frame of reference, because creation is part of Israel's etiology" (Von Rad, *Old Testament Theology* [New York: Harper & Row, Publishers, 1965], 2:341–42).

19. A. Jacob, *Théologie de l'Ancien Testament* (Neuchatel: Delachaux et Niestlé,

1953), p. 43. Regarding the message of Deutero-Isaiah, see the excellent article of A. Gamper, "Der Verkündigungsauftrag Israels nach Deutero-Jesaja," *Zeitschrift für Katholische Theologie* 91 (1969): 411–29.

20. "Die theologische Stellung des Schöpfungsglaubens bei Deuterojesaias," *Zietschrift für Theologie und Kirche* 51 (1954):10, cited by Walter Kern, "La creación como presupuesto de la Alianza," in *Mysterium Salutis* (Madrid: Cristiandad, 1969), 1:503; original German: *Mysterium Salutis* (Einsiedeln, Zurich, Cologne: Benziger Verlag, 1967).

21. As is well known the accounts of the creation are strongly marked by the experience of the Exodus and the Covenant. This is the case especially in the so-called *Yahwistic* narrative; Gen. 2:4–16 follows the outline of the Covenant pact.

22. See Jean Steinmann, *Le prophète Isaïe* (Paris: Les Éditions du Cerf, 1950), p. 221.

23. See Kern, "Creación como presupuesto."

24. In this regard see Rubem Alves, *A Theology of Human Hope* (Washington, D.C.: Corpus Books, 1969), p. 129. See Also Arnaldo Zenteno, *Liberación social y Cristo* (Mexico, D.F.: Secretariado Social Mexicano, 1971).

25. Albert Gelin, "Moise dans l'Ancien Testament," in *Moïse, L'homme de l'Alliance* (Paris: Desclée & Cie, Éditeurs, 1955), p. 39.

26. Regarding the central characteristic of the theme of the Covenant, see the short but interesting note of Beltrán Villegas, "El tema de la Alianza y el vocabulario teológico del A. T.," *Teología y Vida* 2, no. 3 (July–September 1961):178–82; and in a recent exegetical perspective, see the analysis of Paul Beauchamp, "Propositions sur l'Alliance de l'Ancien Testament comme structure centrale," *Recherches de Science Religieuse* 58, no. 2 (April–June 1970):161–93.

27. Cited by Congar in "Christianisme et liberation," p. 8.

28. *Moses and the Vocation of the Jewish People*, trans. Irene Marinoff (New York: Harper Torchbooks, 1959), pp. 136–37.

29. See the commentary on some of these texts in Franz Mussner, "Creación en Cristo," in *Mysterium Salutis*, 1:506–11.

30. See Charles Harold Dodd, *The Interpretation of the Fourth Gospel* (Cambridge [Eng.]: University Press, 1953), p. 269; Charles Kingsley Barrett, *The Gospel According to St. John* (London: S.P.C.K., 1955), pp. 125–32; and A. Feuillet, "Prologue du quatrième Évangile," *Supplément au Dictionnaire de la Bible*, fasc. 44, 1969, col. 623–88.

31. "With a little arrangement," writes M. E. Boismard, "we might say that St. John meant to divide Christ's life into seven periods of seven days, in seven weeks. We should do wrong to see in this a mere puerile game on the part of the evangelist, or even a convenient or artificial frame in which to enclose the life of Christ. This structural scheme corresponds to the plan already indicated in the Prologue: to draw a parallel between the work of creation and the work of the Messias: the seven times seven days of Messianic ministry correspond to the seven days of creation" (*St. John's Prologue*, trans. Carisbrooke Dominicans [Westminster, Md.: Newman Press, 1957], p. 107).

32. See Severino Croatto, "La creación en la Kerygmática actual," in *Salvación y construcción del mundo*, pp. 95–104; A. Feuillet, *Le Christ sagesse de Dieu d'après les Épitres pauliennes* (Paris: J. Gabalda et Cie, 1966); regarding this work and this theme in general, see the perceptive observations of Juan Alfaro, *Hacia una teología del progreso humano* (Barcelona: Herder, 1969), p. 22, no. 22.

33. This was pointed out very clearly by Harvey Cox in *The Secular City*. But it should be clarified that this "desacralization" refers to something different from

the "sacred": it is not what is untouchable and separated from profane life, but rather something present and active in the heart of human history.

34. Frantz Fanon put it quite emphatically: "To educate the masses politically ... means ... to try, relentlessly and passionately, to teach the masses that everything depends on them; that if we stagnate it is their responsibility, and that if we go forward it is due to them too, that there is no such thing as a demiurge, that there is no famous man who will take the responsibility for everything, but that the demiurge is the people themselves and the magic hands are finally only the hands of the people" (*The Wretched of the Earth*, pp. 157–58).

35. In Hebrew there is no special term to signify *promise*. A combination of terms and expressions designate it: blessing, oath, inheritance, promised land. See Julius Schniewind and Gerhard Friedrich, "Epangelia," in *Theological Dictionary of the New Testament*, 2:576 ff.

36. *The Key Concepts of the Old Testament*, trans. George Lamb (New York: Sheed and Ward, 1955), pp. 36–37.

37. Jürgen Moltmann, *Theology of Hope*, pp. 139 ff.

38. Joseph Huby observes that "the object of the promise, 'to inherit the world,' is not found in this form in the passage from Genesis (15:1–7) to which Paul refers. 'This land' which God promised to Abraham was the land of Canaan. But in other texts (Gen. 12:3; 22:17–18) the promise was extended by the proclamation of blessings that would include all the families and nations of the earth. Therefore Jewish thought, according to certain of its representatives, was led to extend the boundaries of the land promised to Abraham until they were coterminous with the boundaries of the world" (*Saint Paul, Épître aux Romains* [Paris: Beauchesne et ses Fils, 1957], p. 173).

39. In reality this is not an innovation. In the Old Testament the oath of God to the patriarchs is often recalled; see Deut. 1:8; 6:10, 18; 7:8; Ecclus. 44:19–23; Jer. 11:5; Mic. 7:20; Ps. 105:6–9.

40. Gelin, *Key Concepts*, p. 37.

41. "What we call the New Testament is the realization of the promise, and the actual taking possession of the inheritance" (L. Cerfaux, *The Church in the Theology of St. Paul*, trans. Geoffrey Webb and Adrian Walker [New York: Herder and Herder, 1959], p. 35). Incipiently we should say, to be exact. But what we are saying concerning the historical fulfillment of the promise should not make us forget the lesson of Exodus: the significance of the self-generation of man in the historical political struggle. On this point we are far from the position of Jurgen Moltmann (*Theology of Hope*) criticized perceptively by Rubem Alves (*Theology of Human Hope*, pp. 55–68); Moltmann would give the impression that he does not keep sufficiently in the mind the participation of man in his own liberation.

42. Karl Barth, *Kirchliche Dogmatik* 4/3, pp. 385 and 387, quoted by Moltmann, *Theology of Hope*, p. 87.

43. "The reason," Moltmann asserts, "for the overplus of promise and for the fact that it constantly overspills history lies in the inexhaustibility of the God of promise, who never exhausts himself in any historic reality but comes 'to rest' only in a reality that wholly corresponds to him" (*Theology of Hope*, p. 106).

44. The term is not very old. In 1924, E. Mangenot said that *eschatology* had been "used, for some years now, especially in Germany and England, to designate the part of systematic theology which treats ultimate ends." He noted that this term "has still not received general acceptance in French theology" (*Dictionnaire de Théologie Catholique*, s.v., "Eschatologie").

45. In Ecclesiasticus the term *escata* is used to speak of death and judgment after this life (7:36; 28:6; 38:20).

46. *Theology of Hope*, pp. 37–39.

47. "In the Biblical sense, to speak of the last things is to speak of an end understood so radically, of a reality so transcendent to all things, that the existence of these things would be solely and integrally rooted in that reality, of an end, therefore, that in truth is also their source" (Karl Barth, *Die Auferstehung der Toten* [Zurich: Evangelischer Verlag, 1953], p. 61; the first edition is 1924; English translation: *The Resurrection of the Dead*, trans. H. J. Stenning [New York: Fleming H. Revell Co., 1933]).

48. "To speak of final history, of the last time, would be to speak only of an end so radically understood, of a reality so elevated over every event and temporality, that to refer to the end of history and time would really be to refer to that which establishes all time and everything that occurs in it. Final history would signify the same thing as original history. The limit of time would be the limit of all time, that is the origin of time" (*ibid.*, p. 59); these texts are cited by Raúl Gabás Pallas, *Escatología protestante en la actualidad* (Vitoria: Editorial Eset, 1964), pp. 67–68; the author presents the thinking on the question of the most important contemporary Protestant theologians.

49. Moltmann, *Theology of Hope*, p. 40.

50. Karl Rahner describes well the evolution of the term *eschatology* in *Sacramentum Mundi* (New York: Herder and Herder, 1968), 2:242–46. See also Rahner's, "The Hermeneutics of Eschatological Assertions," in *Theological Investigations*, 4:323–46.

51. Moltmann notes that "the term 'eschato-*logy*' is wrong. There can be no 'doctrine' of the last things, if by 'doctrine' we mean a collection of theses which can be understood on the basis of experiences that constantly recur and are open to anyone" (*Theology of Hope*, p. 17).

52. See Von Rad, *Old Testament Theology*, 2:112 ff.

53. *Ibid.*, p. 113.

54. *Ibid.*, p. 114.

55. *Ibid.*, p. 115.

56. Rudolf Bultmann says that "radical openness for the future" is the characteristic and definitive trait of existence according to the Bible *(Primitive Christianity in its Contemporary Setting*, trans. R. H. Fuller [New York: Meridian Books, 1956], pp. 180 ff.).

57. Von Rad, *Old Testament Theology*, 2:118. See also Norbert Lohfink "Escatología en el Antiguo Testamento," *Exégesis bíblica y teología* (Salamanca: Ediciones Sígueme, 1969), pp. 163–87.

58. John A. T. Robinson notes that *parousia* is a term with no plural. The presence (or coming) of Christ is a unique event and is not repeated *(Jesus and His Coming* [New York: Abingdon Press, 1957], p. 185).

59. *Le prophète Isaïe*, p. 89.

60. *Ibid.*, p. 92. An objection to this interpretation is posed in terms of this dilemma: Is Emmanuel the Messiah or is Ezequiel? Steinmann rightly answers, "Emmanuel is the Messiah in Ezekiel." He clarifies his position saying, "Emmanuel is incarnated in the time of Isaias, but the promises of which he is the object transcend him (like those made to Abraham) and refer to Christ, the definitive Anointed One. Ezequiel has exercised his role of Savior without exhausting it" (*ibid.*, p. 377).

61. This is why Gelin speaks of a "bivalence" of the concept of eschatology in the Old Testament: "It designates either the end of the world or an important event in human history like the beginning of a new era" (*Supplément au Dictionnaire de la Bible*, s.v. "Messianisme").

62. Cited in Lohfink, *Exégesis bíblica*, pp. 169–70.

63. See Wolfhart Pannenberg, "The God of Hope," in *Basic Questions in Theology*, trans. George H. Kehm (Philadelphia: Fortress Press, 1971), 2:235–49.

64. See George T. Montague, *The Biblical Theology of the Secular* (Milwaukee: Bruce Publishing Company, 1968); Georges Auzou, *De la servidumbre al servicio* (Madrid: Ediciones FAX, 1969), pp. 114–26; French edition, *De la servitude au service* (Paris: Édition de l'Orante, 1961); and Michel Allard, "Note sur la formule ''Ehyeh aser 'ehyeh,'" in *Recherches de Science Religieuse* 45, no. 1 (January–March 1957):79–86. "The shade of meaning expressed by the verb *'ehyeh* is not so much the possession of being. Rather it should be understood as referring to a presence, an openness toward another subject" (*ibid.*, p. 85).

65. This question is but a part of a broader one: the relationship between the two Testaments. As is well known the hiatus which Bultmann believed existed between the two contributed to a devaluation of the Old Testament texts. Today the attitude is changing. The present concerns of Christian life and theology are leading us—at times with a certain simplistic approach—to a recovery of the Old Testament. Von Rad, who dedicates several lucid pages to this point, believes that this is a "still debated question" in which there are two aspects: "that the Old Testament is to be understood in the light of Christ" and "that we also need the Old Testament to understand Christ." Regarding the first point it seems to him that we can speak of a general consensus. This is not so regarding the second point (*Old Testament Theology*, 2:386). To illuminate this second proposition, to clarify certain interpretative criteria, would avoid the impression of opportunism which at times is given by recourse to Old Testament texts. For this illumination there were perhaps necessary certain conditions which are beginning to be met: a critical attitude, for example, regarding our "Western" categories concerning time and history, or spirit and matter.

66. "Pensées," no. 571, in *Pascal*, Vol. 33 of Great Books of the Western World, p. 274.

67. *Le sens chrétien de l'Ancien Testament*, p. 392.

68. *Ibid.*, p. 395.

69. *Ibid.*, p. 396. In the quoted texts the italics are the author's.

70. *Ibid.*, pp. 397–98. "The promises of temporal goods are substituted by purely spiritual ones" (M. García Cordero, "Promesas," in *Enciclopedia de la Biblia* (Barcelona: Ediciones Garriga, 1963), 5:1291. From a similar perspective see Leon Roy, "Libération, Liberté," *Vocabulaire de théologie biblique*, 2nd ed. (Paris: Les Éditions du Cerf, 1970), p. 661.

71. "Christianisme et libération," p. 7.

72. As has often been recalled, in the Bible the spiritual realm is not opposed to the corporal nor to the material, but rather to the carnal—understood as a selfish turning in upon oneself. This is why Paul does not hesitate to speak of a "spiritual body" (1 Cor. 15:44) and of a "carnal mind" (Col. 2:18). In this regard see Beltrán Villegas, "El Evangelio: una noticia siempre increíble," *Mensaje* 20, no. 196 (January–February 1971):27, n. 7. See also the classic study of John A. T. Robinson, *The Body: A Study in Pauline Theology* (London: SCM Press, 1952).

73. On this point see the brief observations of Lohfink, *Exégesis bíblica*, p. 184.

74. Yves Congar, "Mystère de Jésus et Église des pauvres," in *L'Église aujourd'hui* (Paris: Desclée et Cie., 1967), p. 55.

75. "Christ wants the liberation of man and his total liberation, ... and this is not limited to his spiritual liberation" (Antonio Fragoso, *Évangile et révolution sociale* [Paris: Les Éditions du Cerf, 1969], p. 15).

76. To support his interpretation of the hidden and veiled meaning of the prophecies, Grelot asserts that we can speak of "a *spiritual* meaning hidden under the *letter* of the prophecies." The author immediately recognizes that the Pauline distinction between letter and spirit initially was applied to the Law, but he adds, "Its transposition to the problem of the prophecies is not therefore any less legitimate" (*Sens chrétien de l'Ancien Testament*, p. 394, n. 1). But is it just a question of a transposition from the Law to prophecy? Does the transposition not carry with it a transformation of the very sense of the distinction? The *letter* is not opposed to the spirit as the *terrestrial* is to the spiritual. Paul's distinction belongs to another order of ideas. Thomas Aquinas put it very well: "The letter denotes any writing that is external to man, even that of the moral precepts such as are contained in the Gospel" (*Summa Theologica*, I-II, q. 106, art. 2).

77. This text of Isaiah (added after the promulgation of the Constitution) is legitimately interpreted in *Gaudium et spes* (no. 78) as referring to social justice.

78. *Évangile et révolution social*, p. 15. The text continues, "It is impossible that the Gospel should not strike the conscience of Christians and stimulate an understanding among all men of good will regarding the liberation of all, especially the poorest and most abandoned." "To struggle to establish justice among men," wrote the Peruvian bishops, "is to begin to be just before the Lord" ("Justice in the World," in *IDOC-NA*, no. 37 [December 11, 1971], p. 5).

79. "The mystery of the 'when' and 'where,' " comments Rudolf Schnackenburg, "is reserved to the knowledge and decision of God. This fact gives us an important key to the understanding of Jesus' preaching about the future. The eschaton is reserved to the wisdom and command of God." Thus Jesus' "sayings do not emphasize the doctrine but rather the challenge and admonition. The prophetic style and form in which Jesus presents his preaching about the future manifests forcefully and solemnly that Jesus is concerned with the proper teaching of the eschatological disposition" (*Present and Future* [Notre Dame: University of Notre Dame Press, 1966], pp. 10, 16–17). "What a theologian," writes Karl Rahner, "must state in the first place regarding this future is, it seems to me, that it remains unknown not only for reasons of fact, but also for reasons of right" ("L'avenir de la théologie," *Nouvelle Revue Théologique* 93, no. 1 [January 1971]:4).

80. See the excellent history of the text in Philippe Delhaye, "Histoire des textes de la Constitution pastorale," *L'Église dans le monde de ce temps*, 1:215–77.

81. See the summary of the statements made in this regard in the Council in *Relationes particulares*, "Schema of Ariccia," p. 98. See also the address "Church and World" by Edward Schillebeeckx in September 1964 in the do-c Center in Rome and reproduced in his *Le monde et l'Église* (Brussels: Éditions du CEP, 1967), pp. 149–67; English version in mimeo as a do-c research paper, series 2, papers dealing with Schema 13.

82. Pierre Hauptmann, "La schema de la Constitution Pastorale, De ecclesia in mundo huius temporis," *Études et documents*, publication of the conciliar secretariat of the French episcopate, August 25, 1965, p. 9.

83. The basis of this affirmation is the Incarnation. "The Word of the Father assumed through the Incarnation the entire man, body and soul; in him he sanc-

tified all nature created by God, not excluding matter; thus everything that exists acclaims the Redeemer in its own way" (*ibid.*).

84 This number is the basis for *Gaudium et spes*, no. 43.

85. The relationship which Ariccia (no. 50) establishes between creation and redemption gave rise at this initial stage to a text modified in this way: "Although in the present economy the order of redemption includes in itself the order of creation, and the history of men is profoundly implicated in the history of salvation, this inclusion, nevertheless, in no way destroys the order of creation; rather it elevates it and preserves it in its dignity." After much reworking, there resulted the final version: "Though the same God is Savior and Creator, Lord of human history as well as of salvation history, in the divine arrangement itself the rightful autonomy of the creature, and particularly of man, is not withdrawn. Rather it is reestablished in its own dignity and strengthened in it" (*Gaudium et spes*, no. 41). Because of this same effort at moderation regarding the mission of the Church, the first lines of no. 51 of the Schema of Ariccia—already quoted—are reduced, or rather transformed, into "The union of the human family is greatly fortified and fulfilled by the unity, founded on Christ, of the family of God's sons" (*Gaudium et spes*, no. 42).

86. Thirty-seven bishops were opposed to the final version of no. 39. According to them it is impossible to distinguish adequately in the concrete between temporal progress and the growth of the Kingdom, for charity unites the two processes. They believed, moreover, that to assert that the first was of "importance" to the second is a very vague formula which says nothing ("Expensio modorum" in Chapter 3, Part 1, pp. 225–26). Schillebeeckx believes that this opposition was well founded ("Foi chrétienne et attente terrestre," *L'Eglise dans le monde de ce temps* [Tours: Mame, 1967], p. 135, no. 5.

87. Statement of G. Garrone, September 21, 1965, regarding Chapter 3 of the first part in "Relationes circa schema Constitutionis Pastoralis de Ecclesia in mundo huius temporis," p. 8.

88. In an excellent article, Juan Luis Segundo examines three possible interpretations of *Gaudium et spes*, no. 39: "The ends of temporal progress and those of the Kingdom are different"; "the ends of temporal progress and the ends of the progress of the Kingdom are the same" the difference being that the Christians "know"; the third is distinguished from the second only in the affirmation that the Church also contributes to history "the content of revelation" ("Evangelización y humanización," *Perspectivas para el Diálogo*, no. 41 [March 1970], pp. 9–17).

89. According to the famous text of St. Augustine of Hippo, quoted in the Schema of Ariccia but not found in the final version, "He who made you without you does not justify you without you. He created you without your knowing it: he will justify you if you will it."

90. The text of Ariccia does not escape these reproaches. In it there is a tendency to oversimplify by identifying the "order" of creation with the natural order and redemption with the supernatural order.

91. The well documented work of P. L. Mathieu, *La pensée politique et économique de Teilhard de Chardin* (Paris: Éditions du Seuil, 1969), gathers and synthesizes the thinking of Teilhard in this regard. In spite of the effort of the author, the impression that one gets from this work is clear: the questions of social justice, of the exploitation of man by man, do not occupy an important place in the concerns of the illustrious Jesuit.

92. This is the basis for certain works like the theologies of development, prog-

ress, etc. It is not a matter merely of the title, but also, especially, of the fashion of posing and resolving the question. The greater part of these authors recognize the influence of Teilhard in the posing of the problem.

93. As André Gunder Frank correctly points out, the term *dependence* is definitely nothing more than a euphemism for oppression, injustice, and alienation (*Lumpenburgesía*, p. 18).

94. See "Peace," nos. 1 and 14, in *Medellín*.

95. *Pobreza evangélica y promoción humana*, p. 29.

96. The religious resonances of Hegel's use of the term *alienation (Entäusserung et Entfremdong)* are well known. See George Cottier, *L'athéisme du jeune Marx* (Paris: Librairie Philosophique J. Vrin, 1959), pp. 34–43; and Albert Chapelle, *Hegel et la religion, Annexes, Les textes théologiques de Hegel* (Paris: Éditions Universitaires, 1967), pp. 99–125.

97. See Christian Duquoc, "Qu'est-ce que le salut?," pp. 101–2.

98. Without overestimating its importance, it is interesting to recall here the comparison that Marx establishes between sin and private ownership of the means of production. Because of this private ownership the worker is separated, alienated, from the fruit of his work: "This primitive accumulation plays in political economy about the same part as original sin in theology. Adam bit the apple, and thereupon sin fell on the human race" ("Capital," Part 8, Chapter 26, in *Marx*, Great Books of the Western World, 50:354).

99. "Justice," no. 3, in *Medellín*. The italics are ours. See also the interesting reflections of Eduardo Pironio, *La Iglesia que nace entre nosotros* (Bogota: Indo-American Press Service, 1970).

100. This is what was implied, partially and in other terms, in the text of *Populorum progressio* which we have already quoted.

101. *La pastoral en las misiones de América Latina*, p. 16.

CHAPTER TEN

ENCOUNTERING GOD IN HISTORY

As was mentioned above, the purpose of those who participate in the process of liberation is to "create a new man." We have attempted to answer our first question, namely, what is the meaning of this struggle, this creation, in the light of the Word accepted in faith? We can now ask ourselves what does this option mean for *man*?

In their political commitments, people today are particularly sensitive to the fact that the vast majority of mankind is not able to satisfy its most elementary needs; often they seek to make the service of those who suffer from oppression or injustice the guiding principle of their lives. Moreover, even Christians evaluate "religious" things in terms of their meaning for man. This approach is not without ambiguities, but many prefer, in the words of José María González Ruiz, "to err on the side of man."

We mentioned earlier that theology is tending more and more to reflect on the anthropological aspects of revelation.[1] But the Word is not only a Word about God and *about* man: the Word is *made* man. If all that is human is illuminated by the Word, it is precisely because the Word reaches us through human history; Von Rad comments that "it is in history that God reveals the secret of his person."[2] Human history, then, is the location of our encounter with him, in Christ.[3] Recalling the evolution of the revelation regarding the presence of God in the midst of his people will aid us in clarifying the form this encounter in history takes. Both his presence and our encounter with him lead humanity forward, but we celebrate them in the present in eschatological joy.

HUMANITY: TEMPLE OF GOD

The Biblical God is close to man; he is a God of communion with and commitment to man. The active presence of God in the midst of his people is a part of the oldest and most enduring Biblical promises. In connection with the first Covenant, God said: "I shall dwell in the midst of the Israelites, I shall become their God, and by my dwelling among them they will know that I am the Lord their God who brought them out of Egypt. I am the Lord their God" (Exod. 29:45–46; cf. 26:11–12). And in the proclamation of the new Covenant, God said: "They shall live under the shelter of my dwelling; I will become their God, and they shall become my people. The nations shall know that I the Lord am keeping Israel, sacred to myself, because my sanctuary is in the midst of them forever" (Ezek. 37:27–28). This presence, often with the connotation of a dwelling, that is to say, a presence in a particular place *(Shekinah)*,[4] characterizes the type of relationship established between God and man. Thus, Congar can write: "The story of God's relations with his creation and especially with man is none other than the story of his ever more generous, ever deeper Presence among his creatures."[5]

The promise of that presence was fulfilled in different ways throughout history until it reached its fullness in a manner which surpassed all expectations: God became man. Henceforth God's presence became both more universal and more complete.

At the outset of the history of the chosen people, God revealed himself especially on the *mountain*. Sinai was a privileged place for meeting God and for his manifestations (Exod. 19). Yahweh ordered Moses, "Come up to me on the mountain" (Exod. 24:12; Deut. 10:1), because on the mountain rested the glory of the Lord (Exod. 24:16–17). The God of Israel was known for a long time as "a god of the hills and not a god of the valleys" (1 Kings 20:28). The presence of Yahweh came closer when it was linked to the *tent* which accompanied the Israelites in their pilgrimage through the desert. This was a place of encounter with Yahweh which Moses placed outside the camp and here spoke with Yahweh whenever Israel needed detailed instructions (Exod. 33:7–11; Num. 11:16, 24–26; Deut. 31:14).[6] The same was true of the *Ark of the Covenant*, which also in a sense implied a dwelling place of Yahweh;[7] in it Moses spoke with Yahweh (Num. 1:1). The idea of a dwelling was stressed to the point that there was even a curious identification between Yahweh and the Ark: "Whenever the Ark began to move, Moses said, 'Up, Lord and may thy enemies be scattered and those that hate thee flee before thee.' When it halted, he said, 'Rest, Lord of the countless thousands of Israel'" (Num. 10:35–36; cf. also Josh. 4:5, 13; 1 Sam. 4:17).

The tent, the Ark (and even the mountain) underscore the mobility of the presence of the Lord, who shared the historical vicissitudes of his people (2 Sam. 7:6–7). In a certain way, they precluded any precise, physical location. The situation changed with the temple.[8] The land of Canaan was initially designated as Yahweh's dwelling place. It was the land promised by him, and he was not to be found outside of it. David feared exile because he did not wish to be far from Yahweh (1 Sam. 26:19–20). After the prophet Elisha cured his leprosy, Naaman took a handful of the soil of Canaan to be able to offer sacrifices beyond its borders (2 Kings 5:15–19). Certain places in the land of Canaan were privileged: these were the sanctuaries, generally located in high places. But very soon, especially after the Deuteronomic reform, there was but one official sanctuary in Jerusalem: Solomon's temple. The different traditions converged there: the obscurity of the Holy of Holies recalled the darkness through which Moses climbed Mt. Sinai; the Ark was placed in the temple; the temple is the heart of Jerusalem, and Jerusalem is the center of the land of Canaan—hence the importance of the temple in the life of the Israelites.[9] The connotation of house, dwelling, was greater than in the previous cases (2 Sam. 7:5; 1 Kings 3:1–3; Amos 1:2; and Isa. 2:2; 37:14; Ps. 27:4).

But at the same time—and to keep the balance—it was proclaimed that no temple could contain Yahweh. This idea was expressed forcefully in the famous prophecy of Nathan, motivated by David's desire to erect a temple for Yahweh (2 Sam. 7).[10] Moreover, at the very moment that the temple was consecrated, Solomon admitted that heaven is Yahweh's dwelling place: "Hear the supplication of thy servant and of thy people Israel when they pray towards this place. Hear thou in heaven thy dwelling and, when thou hearest, forgive" (1 Kings 8:30). The theme of the dwelling place of God in the heavens was old (cf. Gen. 11:5; 18:21; 28:12; Exod. 19:11; Deut. 4:36; Ps. 2:4), but it emerged clearly—and with the full strength of its transcendence and universality—at the very moment when man erected a dwelling, a fixed place, for the privileged encounter with Yahweh. The idea of a heavenly abode gathered strength gradually, especially after the exile. In the temple itself, the Holy of Holies was an empty space: God dwells everywhere.[11]

While these notions of transcendence and universality were taking shape and becoming established, the prophets were harsh in their criticism of purely external worship. Their censure extended to places of worship; God's presence is not bound to a material structure, to a building of stone and gold. "Men shall speak no more of the Ark of the Covenant of the Lord," writes Jeremiah. "They shall not think of it nor remember it nor resort to it; it will be needed no more" (Jer. 3:16). And regarding the temple: "These are the words of the Lord: heaven is my throne and earth my footstool. Where will you build a house for me, where shall my resting place be? All these are of my own making and these are mine.... The man I will look to is a man downtrodden and is humble and distressed, one who reveres my words" (Isa. 66:1–2). The last line indicates the essence of the criticism: Yahweh's preference is for a profound, interior attitude. To this effect, in proclaiming the new Covenant, Yahweh says: "I will take the heart of stone from your body and give you a heart of flesh. I will put my spirit into you and make you conform to my statutes, keep my laws and live by them" (Ezek. 36:26–27; cf. Jer. 31:33). God will be present in the very heart of every man.

This proclamation was completely fulfilled with the *Incarnation* of the Son of God: "So the Word became flesh; he came to dwell [pitch his tent] among us" (John 1:14). Nathan's prophecy was accomplished in a most unexpected way. Christ not only announces a prayer "in spirit and in truth" which will have no need for a material temple (John 4:21–23), but he presents himself as the temple of God: "Destroy this temple ... and in three days I will raise it again." And John specifies: "The temple he was speaking of was his body" (2:19, 20). And Paul tells us: "It is in Christ that the complete being of the Godhead dwells embodied" (Col. 2:9; cf. Eph. 2:20–22; 1 Pet. 2:4–8). God manifests himself visibly in the humanity of Christ, the God-Man, irreversibly committed to human history.

Christ is the temple of God. This explains Paul's insistence that the Christian community is a temple of living stones, and that each Christian, a member of this community, is a *temple of the Holy Spirit:* "Surely you know that you are God's temple, where the Spirit of God dwells. Anyone who destroys God's temple will himself be destroyed by God, because the temple of God is holy; and that temple you are" (1 Cor. 3:16–17): "Do you not know that your body is a shrine of the indwelling Holy Spirit, and the Spirit is God's gift to you?" (1 Cor. 6:19).[12] The Spirit sent by the Father and the Son to carry the work of salvation to its fulfillment dwells in every man—in men who form part of a very specific fabric of human relationships, in men who are in concrete historical situations.

Furthermore, not only is the Christian a temple of God; every man is. The episode with Cornelius proves that the Jews "were astonished that the gift of the Holy Spirit should have been poured out even on Gentiles." Peter draws the conclusion: "Is anyone prepared to withhold the water for baptism from these persons, who have received the Holy Spirit just as we did ourselves?" (Acts 10:45, 47; cf. 11:16–18 and 15:8). For this reason the words of Christ apply to every man: "Anyone who loves me will heed what I say; then my Father will love him, and we will come to him and make our dwelling with him" (John 14:23). "Many constitute the temple, but invisibly," says Congar referring to the well-known expression of Augustine of Hippo. "Many seem to be within who are in reality without and others seem to be without who are in reality within."[13] In the last instance, only the Lord "knows his own" (2 Tim. 2:19).

What we have here, therefore, is a twofold process. On the one hand, there is a universalization of the presence of God: from being localized and linked to a particular people, it gradually extends to all the peoples of the earth (Amos 9:7; Isa. 41:1–7; 45:20–25; 51:4; and the entire Book of Jonah). On the other hand, there is an internalization, or rather, an integration of this presence: from dwelling in places of worship, this presence is transferred to the heart of human history; it is a presence which embraces the whole man. Christ is the point of convergence of both processes. In him, in his personal uniqueness, the particular is transcended and the universal becomes concrete. In him, in his Incarnation, what is personal and internal becomes visible. Henceforth, this will be true, in one way or another, of every man.

Finally, let us emphasize that here there is no "spiritualization" involved. The God made flesh, the God present in each and every man, is no more "spiritual" than the God present on the mountain and in the temple. He is even more "material."

He is no less involved in human history. On the contrary, he has a greater commitment to the implementation of his peace and justice among men. He is not more "spiritual," but he is closer and, at the same time, more universal; he is more visible and, simultaneously, more internal.

Since God has become man, humanity, every man, history, is the living temple of God. The "pro-fane," that which is located outside the temple, no longer exists.

CONVERSION TO THE NEIGHBOR

The modes of God's presence determine the forms of our encounter with him. If humanity, each man, is the living temple of God, we meet God in our encounter with men; we encounter him in the commitment to the historical process of mankind.

To Know God Is To Do Justice

The Old Testament is clear regarding the close relationship which exists between God and the neighbor. This relationship is a distinguishing characteristic of the God of the Bible. To despise one's neighbor (Prov. 14:21), to exploit the humble and poor worker, and to delay the payment of wages are to offend God: "You shall not keep back the wages of a man who is poor and needy, whether a fellow-countryman or an alien living in your country in one of your settlements. Pay him his wages on the same day before sunset, for he is poor and his heart is set on them: he may appeal to the Lord against you, and you will be guilty of sin" (Deut. 24:14–15; cf. Exod. 22:21–23). This explains why "a man who sneers at the poor insults his maker" (Prov. 17:5).

Inversely, to know, that is to say, to love Yahweh is to do justice to the poor and oppressed. When he proclaimed the New Covenant, after asserting that Yahweh would inscribe his law in the hearts of men, Jeremiah said: "No longer need they teach one another to know the Lord; all of them, high and low alike, shall know me" (31:34). But Jeremiah advises us exactly on what knowing God entails: "Shame on the man who builds his house by unjust means, and completes its roof-chambers by fraud, making his countrymen work without payment, giving them no wage for their labor! Shame on the man who says, 'I will build a spacious house with airy roof-chambers, set windows in it, panel it with cedar, and paint it with vermilion'! If your cedar is more splendid, does that prove you are a king? Think of your father: he ate and drank, dealt justly and fairly; all went well with him. He dispensed justice to the cause of the lowly and poor; did this not show he knew me? says the Lord" (22:13–16). Where there is justice and righteousness, there is knowledge of Yahweh; when these are lacking, it is absent: "There is no good faith or mutual trust, no knowledge of God in the land, oaths are imposed and broken, they kill and rob; there is nothing but adultery and license, one deed of blood after another" (Hos. 4:1–2; cf. Isa. 1). To know Yahweh, which in Biblical language is equivalent to saying to love Yahweh, *is* to establish just relationships among men, it *is* to recognize the rights of the poor. The God of Biblical revelation is known through interhuman justice. When justice does not exist, God is not known; he is absent. "God is everywhere," says the priest to the sacristan in José María Arguedas's novel *Todas las sangres*. And the sacristan, who knows no metaphysics, but is well acquainted with injustice and oppression, replies with accurate Biblical intuition: "Was God in the heart of those who broke the body of the innocent teacher Bellido? Is God in the bodies of the engineers who are killing 'La Esmeralda'? In the official who took the corn fields away from their owners ... ?" Likewise, Medellín asserts: "Where this social peace does not exist there will we find social, political, economic, and cultural inequalities, there will we find the rejection of the peace of the Lord, and a rejection of the Lord himself" ("Peace," no. 14).

On the other hand, if justice is done, if the alien, the orphan, and the widow are not oppressed, "Then I will let you live in this place, in the land which I gave long ago to your forefathers for all time" (Jer. 7:7). This presence of Yahweh is active; he it is who "deals out justice to the oppressed. The Lord feeds the hungry and sets the prisoner free. The Lord restores sight to the blind and straightens backs which are bent; the Lord loves the righteous and watches over the stranger; the Lord gives heart to the orphan and widow but turns the course of the wicked to their ruin." So "the Lord shall reign forever" (Ps. 146:7–10).[14]

This encounter with God in concrete actions towards others, especially the poor, is so profound and enriching that by basing themselves on it the prophets can criticize—always validly—all

purely external worship. This criticism is but another aspect
of the concern for asserting the transcendence and universality
of Yahweh. "Your countless sacrifices, what are they to me?
says the Lord; I am sated with whole offerings of rams.... The
offer of your gifts is useless, the reek of sacrifice is abhorrent
to me.... Though you offer countless prayers, I will not listen.
There is blood on your hands.... Cease to do evil and learn
to do right, pursue justice and champion the oppressed; give
the orphan his rights, plead the widow's cause" (Isa. 1:10–17).
We love God by loving our neighbor: "Is not this what I require
of you as a fast: to loose the fetters of injustice, to untie the
knots of the yoke, to snap every yoke and set free those who
have been crushed? Is it not sharing your food with the hungry,
taking the homeless poor into your house, clothing the naked
when you meet them and never evading a duty to your kins-
folk?" (Isa. 58:6–7). Only then will God be with us, only then
will he hear our prayer and will we be pleasing to him (Isa.
58:9–11). God wants justice, not sacrifices. Emphasizing the
bond between the knowledge of God and interhuman justice,
Hosea tells us that Yahweh wishes knowledge and not
holocausts: "O Ephraim, how shall I deal with you? How shall
I deal with you, Judah? Your loyalty to me is like the morning
mist, like dew that vanishes early. Therefore have I lashed you
through the prophets and torn you to shreds with my words;
loyalty is my desire, not sacrifice, not whole-offerings but the
knowledge of God" (Hos. 6:4–6).

Although it is true that in the texts cited the neighbor is
essentially a member of the Jewish community, the references
to aliens, who together with widows and orphans form a classic
trilogy, indicate an effort to transcend these limitations.[15]
Nevertheless, the bond between the neighbor and God is
changed, deepened, and universalized by the Incarnation of the
Word. The famous text so often quoted in recent years, Matt.
25:31–45, is a very good illustration of this twofold process.

Christ in the Neighbor

The parable of the final judgment,[16] which concludes Matthew's eschatological discourse, seems to many to summarize
the essence of the Gospel message.[17] Exegetes are alarmed by

the way that many theologians use this text and by the consequences which have been deduced for Christian life. Various
recent studies have attempted to deal with these new questions;
they have not, however, delved into the basic problems.[18] There
are many factors involved in the reevaluation of the text. It
is fertile soil for research by exegetes and theologians.

Jean-Claude Ingelaere, author of the most extensive and
detailed of the studies made along these lines, observes that
this pericope poses two fundamental questions: who are the
nations judged by the Son of God and who are "the least of
the brethren" of the Son of Man? In relation to these two questions, Ingelaere distinguishes three lines of interpretation of
this text which have developed to date: some believe that this
is a judgment of all men—Christians and non-Christians —according to their love of neighbor, and particularly of the needy;
others see in this a judgment of Christians with regard to their
behavior towards the disadvantaged members of the Christian
community itself (Origen, Luther); and finally, a minority
believe it refers to the judgment of pagans based on their
attitude towards Christians. The author obviously opts for the
third interpretation. Although the work is thorough and well
documented, it is less than convincing. The two restrictions
involved in this third exegesis—although they do easily resolve
various minor questions (for example, the failure to recognize
Christ implied in the question, "When did we see you hungry,"
etc.)—go against the obvious sense of the text and the context,
which stress the universality of the judgment and the central
and universal character of charity.[19] This is actually an attempt
to revive an old thesis of H. J. Holtzmann,[20] hardly mentioned
by Ingelaere, which M. J. Lagrange, based on Loisy, Wiss, and
Wellhausen, characterized as "strangely illogical."[21] The majority of the exegetes opt for what Ingelaere considers the first
interpretation. The henotheistic expression "all nations" (v. 32)
is considered to have a "clearly universal sense."[22] According
to Mühlen, it includes "not the pagans as distinguished from
the Jews and the Christians, but in fact all men: pagans, Jews,
and Christians."[23] On the other hand, there is also a general
consensus regarding the universality of the content of the
expression: "the least of my brethen" (v. 40). This term designates "all the needy, whoever they may be, and not only Christians."[24]

This is the line of thinking we will follow. The passage is rich
in teachings. Basing our study on it and in line with the subject
which interests us, we wish to emphasize three points: the stress
on communion and brotherhood as the ultimate meaning of
human life; the insistence on a love which is manifested in concrete actions, with "doing" being favored over simple "knowing";[25] and the revelation of the human mediation necessary
to reach the Lord.

Man is destined to total communion with God and to the fullest
brotherhood with all men. "Dear friends, let us love one another,
because love is from God. Everyone who loves is a child of God
and knows God, but the unloving know nothing of God. For God
is love" (1 John 4:7–8). This was Christ's revelation. To be saved
is to reach the fullness of love; it is to enter into the circle of
charity which unites the three Persons of the Trinity; it is to
love as God loves. The way to this fullness of love can be no
other than love itself, the way of participation in this charity,
the way of accepting, explicitly or implicitly, to say with the
Spirit: "Abba, Father" (Gal. 4:6). Acceptance is the foundation
of all brotherhood among men. To sin is to refuse to love, to
reject communion and brotherhood, to reject even now the very
meaning of human existence. Matthew's text is demanding:
"Anything you did not do for one of these, however humble,
you did not do for me" (25:45). To abstain from serving is to
refuse to love; to fail to act for another is as culpable as
expressly refusing to do it. This same idea is found later in John:
"The man who does not love is still in the realm of death" (1
John 3:14). The parable of the Good Samaritan ends with the
famous inversion which Christ makes of the original question.
They asked him, "Who is my neighbor?" and when everything
seemed to point to the wounded man in the ditch on the side
of the road, Christ asked, "Which of these three do you think
was neighbor to the man who fell into the hands of the robbers?"
(Luke 10:29, 36). The neighbor was the Samaritan who
approached the wounded man and *made him his neighbor*. The
neighbor, as has been said, is not he whom I find in my path,
but rather he in whose path I place myself, he whom I approach
and actively seek. The other aspects of the Christian life become
meaningful if they are animated by charity; otherwise, in Paul's
words, they simply are empty actions (cf. 1 Cor. 13). This is why
Matthew's text says we will be definitively judged by our love

for men, by our capacity to create brotherly conditions of life.
From a prophetic viewpoint, the judgment ("crisis") will be
based, according to Matthew, on the new ethic arising from this
universal principle of love.[26]

But this charity exists only in concrete actions (feeding the
hungry, giving drink to the thirsty, etc.);[27] it occurs of necessity
in the fabric of relationships among men. "Faith divorced from
deeds is barren" (James 2:20). To know God is to do justice: "If
you know that he is righteous, you must recognize that every
man who does right is his child" (1 John 2:29). But charity does
not exist alongside or above human loves; it is not "the most
sublime" achievement of man like a grace superimposed upon
human love. Charity is God's love in us and does not exist outside our human capabilities to love and to build a just and
brotherly world, to "establish ties" as Saint-Exupéry says. "But
if a man has enough to live on, and yet when he sees his brother
in need shuts up his heart against him, how can it be said that
the divine love dwells in him? My children, love must not be
a matter of words or talk; it must be genuine and show itself
in action" (1 John 3:17–18). Loving us as a man, Christ reveals
to us the Father's love. Charity, the love of God for men, is found
incarnated in human love—of parents, spouses, children,
friends—and it leads to its fullness. The Samaritan approached
the injured man on the side of the road not because of some
cold religious obligation, but because "his heart was melting"
(this is literally what the verb *splankhnizein* means in Luke
10:33; cf. Luke 1:7, 8; 7:13; 15:20), because his love for that man
was made flesh in him.[28]

Luis Buñuel's film *Nazarín* is an excellent illustration of the
idea we are attempting to convey. A first reading (which generally coincides with a first viewing) invites us to identify with
Nazarín, an evangelical priest, poor and unhappy with the
ecclesiastical establishment. Completely commited to doing
good for the love of God, Nazarín appears gradually to discover
the uselessness and failure of charity. And then he understands:
the love of God is an illusion; only the love of man is important.
The enigmatic final sequence emphasizes this revelation of man
free from deceiving religious mediation. The outline is clear and
so has been cited as an example of the "horizontalist" tendency
of our times.[29] However, a second reading will reveal that, in
fact, Nazarín's charity never existed. He did everything "out
of duty." He never really loved with a human love as a man

of flesh and blood. His heart never melted. He was more
interested in the charitable action *he* was performing than in
the concrete *person* for whom it was done. Buñuel cruelly enjoys
showing the disastrous consequences of these charitable acts
as well as Nazarín's indifference toward them. Nazarín goes
through this world as if he were not in it. (The actor evidences
this attitude by mechanically reciting his lines.) Buñuel subtly
but persistently opposes the "charity" of Nazarín to the vital
human love of other characters and shows that all Nazarín is
capable of doing for the love of God the others can do for the
love of man (for example, the sequence of the town besieged
by cholera). This indifference and this contrast are revealing:
Nazarín's charity is foreign to human love. It is a fleshless charity and, therefore, nonexistent. Does "simple" human love displace God's love? No. Rather, what is discredited is a so-called
charity which really has nothing to do with true love for men.
This is the reason that, whether intentionally or not, Nazarín
is on the right path: he will find the authentic love of God only
by means of a real, concrete approach to men.[30] The painful
complaint of César Vallejo's poem is addressed to the God of
"Christians" like Nazarín: "My God, if you had been a man,
you would know how to be God."[31] The lesson of Buñuel (that
"atheist by the grace of God," as he himself once said) is
paradoxical but fruitful: there is nothing more "horizontalist"
than charity with no color or human flavor.

We turn to the third idea we wished to consider in connection
with this text of Matthew: human mediation to reach God.[32]
It is not enough to say that love of God is inseparable from
the love of one's neighbor. It must be added love for God is
unavoidably expressed *through* love of one's neighbor.[33]
Moreover, God is loved in the neighbor: "But if a man says,
'I love God,' while hating his brother, he is a liar. If he does
not love the brother whom he has seen, it cannot be that he
loves God whom he has not seen" (1 John 4:20). To love one's
brother, to love all men, is a necessary and indispensable mediation of the love of God; it *is* to love God: "You did it for me,
... you did not do it for me." In his perceptive homily at the
closing of the Council, Paul VI commented on Matthew's text
saying that "a knowledge of man is a prerequisite for a knowledge of God"; and he summarized the objective of the Council
as "a pressing and friendly invitation to mankind of today to

rediscover in fraternal love the God 'to turn away from Whom is to fall, to turn to Whom is to rise again, to remain in Whom is to be secure, to return to Whom is to be born again, in Whom to dwell is to live' (St. Augustine, *Solil.* I, i, 3; P. L. 32, 870)."[34]

Ingelaere examines the different explanations regarding the identification of Christ and the neighbor. One of these he characterizes as being of a mystical order and "limited to establishing and contemplating this mysterious link between Christ and the poor" (A. Durand, T. H. Robinson); another sees in the Son of Man the ideal man, the archetype of the new humanity "already present in each individual" (J. Héring); a third says that the Son of Man identifies with men "by an act of substitution" (T. Preiss); another sees in the Son of Man a "collective reality" (T. W. Manson); and finally there are those who believe that they see in this identification simply an expression which dramatizes the "Christological meaning" of love of the neighbor (G. Gross). Ingelaere discards each one of these explanations, and in line with his theory which restricts "the least" to Christians, he considers that the Lord is represented on earth by his followers (cf. Matt. 18:20). "This relationship," concludes the author, "is so intimate that every act directed towards his followers is an act done for the Son of Man present in their midst: this is 'sympathy' in the strongest sense of the word."[35]

But really this conclusion is valid not only for Christians, but for all men who, in one way or another, welcome the Word of the Lord into their heart. God's presence in humanity, in each man, which is expressed, for example, in the idea of the temple mentioned above, seems to us more fruitful and richer in ramifications.[36] It is in the temple that we find God, but in a temple of living stones, of closely related men, who together make history and fashion themselves. God is revealed in history, and it is likewise in history that men encounter his Word made flesh. Christ is not a private individual; the bond which links him to all men gives him a unique historical role.[37] God's temple is human history; the "sacred" transcends the narrow limits of the places of worship.[38] We find the Lord in our encounters with men, especially the poor, marginated, and exploited ones. An act of love towards them is an act of love towards God. This is why Congar speaks of "the sacrament of our neighbor," who as a visible reality reveals to us and allows us to welcome the Lord: "But there is one thing that is privileged to be a paradoxical sign of God, in relation to which men are able to manifest their deepest commitment—our Neighbor. The sacrament of our Neighbor!"[39]

"The lottery vendor who hawks tickets 'for the big one,'" wrote Vallejo in another poem, "somehow deep down represents God."[40] But every man is a lottery vendor who offers us "the big one": our encounter with that God who is deep down in the heart of each man.[41]

Nevertheless, the neighbor is not an occasion, an instrument for becoming closer to God.[42] We are dealing with a real love of man for his own sake and not "for the love of God," as the well-intended but ambiguous and ill-used cliché would have it—ambiguous and ill-used because many seem to interpret it in a sense which forgets that the love for God is expressed in a true love for man himself. This is the only way to have a true encounter with him. That my action towards another is at the same time an action towards God does not detract from its truth and concreteness, but rather gives it even greater meaning and import.

It is also necessary to avoid the pitfalls of an individualistic charity. As it has been insisted in recent years, the neighbor is not only man viewed individually. The term refers also to man considered in the fabric of social relationships, to man situated in his economic, social, cultural, and racial coordinates. It likewise refers to the exploited social class, the dominated people, and the marginated race. The masses are also our neighbor, as Chenu asserts.[43] This point of view leads us far beyond the individualistic language of the I-Thou relationship. Charity is today a "political charity," according to the phrase of Pius XII. Indeed, to offer food or drink in our day is a political action; it means the transformation of a society structured to benefit a few who appropriate to themselves the value of the work of others. This transformation ought to be directed toward a radical change in the foundation of society, that is, the private ownership of the means of production.

Our encounter with the Lord occurs in our encounter with men, especially in the encounter with those whose human features have been disfigured by oppression, despoliation, and alienation and who have "no beauty, no majesty" but are the things "from which men turn away their eyes" (Isa. 53:2–3). These are the marginal groups, who have fashioned a true culture for themselves and whose values one must understand if he wishes to reach them.[44] The salvation of humanity passes through them; they are the bearers of the meaning of history and "inherit the Kingdom" (James 2:5). Our attitude towards them, or rather our commitment to them, will indicate whether or not we are directing our existence in conformity with the will of the Father. This is what Christ reveals to us by identifying himself with the poor in the text of Matthew.[45] A theology of the neighbor, which has yet to be worked out, would have to be structured on this basis.[46]

A SPIRITUALITY OF LIBERATION

To place oneself in the perspective of the Kingdom means to participate in the struggle for the liberation of those oppressed by others. This is what many Christians who have committed themselves to the Latin American revolutionary process have begun to experience. If this option seems to separate them from the Christian community, it is because many Christians, intent on domesticating the Good News, see them as wayward and perhaps even dangerous. If they are not always able to express in appropriate terms the profound reasons for their commitment, it is because the theology in which they were formed—and which they share with other Christians—has not produced the categories necessary to express this option, which seeks to respond creatively to the new demands of the Gospel and of the oppressed and exploited peoples of this continent. But in their commitments, and even in their attempts to explain them, there is a greater understanding of the faith, greater faith, greater fidelity to the Lord than in the "orthodox" doctrine (some prefer to call it by this name) of reputable Christian circles.[47] This doctrine is supported by authority and much publicized because of access to social communications media, but it is so static and devitalized that it is not even strong enough to abandon the Gospel. It is the Gospel which is disowning it.

But theological categories are not enough. We need a vital attitude, all-embracing and synthesizing, informing the totality as well as every detail of our lives; we need a "spirituality."[48] Spirituality, in the strict and profound sense of the word is the dominion of the Spirit. If "the truth will set you free" (John 8:32), the Spirit "will guide you into all the truth" (John 16:13) and will lead us to complete freedom, the freedom from everything that hinders us from fulfilling ourselves as men and sons of God and the freedom to love and to enter into communion with God and with others. It will lead us along the path of liberation because "where the Spirit of the Lord is, there is liberty" (2 Cor. 3:17).

A spirituality is a concrete manner, inspired by the Spirit, of living the Gospel; it is a definite way of living "before the Lord," in solidarity with all men, "with the Lord," and before men. It arises from an intense spiritual experience, which is later explicated and witnessed to. Some Christians are beginning to live this experience as a result of their commitment to the process of liberation. The experiences of previous generations are there to support it, but above all, to remind them that they must discover their own way. Not only is there a contemporary history and a contemporary Gospel; there is also a contemporary spiritual experience which cannot be overlooked. A spirituality means a reordering of the great axes of the Christian life in terms of this contemporary experience. What is new is the synthesis that this reordering brings about, in stimulating a deepened understanding of various ideas, in bringing to the surface unknown or forgotten aspects of the Christian life, and above all, in the way in which these things are converted into life, prayer, commitment, and action.

The truth is that a Christianity lived in commitment to the process of liberation presents its own problems which cannot be ignored and meets obstacles which must be overcome. For many, the encounter with the Lord under these conditions can disappear by giving way to what he himself brings forth and nourishes: love for man. This love, however, does not know the fullness of its potential. This is a real difficulty, but the solution must come from the heart of the problem itself. Otherwise, it would be just one more patchwork remedy, a new impasse. This is the challenge confronting a spirituality of liberation. Where oppression and the liberation of man seem to make God irrelevant—a God filtered by our longtime indifference to these problems—there must blossom faith and hope in him who comes to root out injustice and to offer, in an unforeseen way, total liberation. This is a spirituality which dares to sink roots in the soil of oppression-liberation.

A spirituality of liberation will center on a *conversion* to the neighbor, the oppressed person, the exploited social class, the despised race, the dominated country. Our conversion to the Lord implies this conversion to the neighbor. Evangelical conversion is indeed the touchstone of all spirituality. Conversion means a radical transformation of ourselves; it means thinking, feeling, and living as Christ—present in exploited and alienated man. To be converted is to commit oneself to the process of the liberation of the poor and oppressed, to commit oneself lucidly, realistically, and concretely. It means to commit oneself not only generously, but also with an analysis of the situation and a strategy of action. To be converted is to know and experience the fact that, contrary to the laws of physics, we can stand straight, according to the Gospel, only when our center of gravity is outside ourselves.

Conversion is a permanent process in which very often the obstacles we meet make us lose all we had gained and start anew. The fruitfulness of our conversion depends on our openness to doing this, our spiritual childhood. All conversion implies a break. To wish to accomplish it without conflict is to deceive oneself and others: "No man is worthy of me who cares more for father or mother than for me." But it is not a question of a withdrawn and pious attitude. Our conversion process is affected by the socio-economic, political, cultural, and human environment in which it occurs. Without a change in these structures, there is no authentic conversion. We have to break with our mental categories, with the way we relate to others, with our way of identifying with the Lord, with our cultural milieu, with our social class, in other words, with all that can stand in the way of a real, profound solidarity with those who suffer, in the first place, from misery and injustice. Only thus, and not through purely interior and spiritual attitudes, will the "new man" arise from the ashes of the "old."

The Christian has not done enough in this area of conversion to the neighbor, to social justice, to history. He has not perceived clearly enough yet that to know God *is* to do justice. He still does not live *in one sole action* with both God and all men. He still does not situate himself in Christ without attempting to avoid concrete human history. He has yet to tread the path which will lead him to seek effectively the peace of the Lord in the heart of the social struggle.

A spirituality of liberation must be filled with a living sense of *gratuitousness*. Communion with the Lord and with all men is more than anything else a gift. Hence the universality and the radicalness of the liberation which it affords. This gift, far from being a call to passivity, demands a vigilant attitude. This is one of the most constant Biblical themes: the encounter with the Lord presupposes attention, active disposition, work, fidelity to his will, the good use of talents received. But the knowledge that at the root of our personal and community existence lies the gift of the self-communication of God, the grace of his friendship, fills our life with gratitude. It allows us to see our encounters with men, our loves, everything that happens in our life as a gift. There is a real love only when there is free giving —without conditions or coercion. Only gratuitous love goes to our very roots and elicits true love.

Prayer is an experience of gratuitousness. This "leisure" action, this "wasted" time, reminds us that the Lord is beyond the categories of useful and useless.[49] God is not of this world. The gratuitousness of his gift, creating profound needs, frees us from all religious alienation and, in the last instance, from all alienation. The Christian committed to the Latin American revolutionary process has to find the way to real prayer, not evasion. It cannot be denied that a crisis exists in this area and that we can easily slide into dead ends.[50] There are many who—nostagically and in "exile," recalling earlier years of their life—can say with the psalmist: "As I pour out my soul in distress, I call to mind how I marched in the ranks of the great to the house of God, among exultant shouts of praise, the clamor of the pilgrims" (Ps. 42:4). But the point is not to backtrack; new experiences, new demands have made heretofore familiar and comfortable paths impassable and have made us undertake new itineraries on which we hope it might be possible to say with Job to the Lord, "I knew of thee then only by report, but now I see thee with my own eyes" (42:5). Bonhoeffer was right when he said that the only credible God is the God of the mystics. But this is not a God unrelated to human history. On the contrary, if it is true, as we recalled above, that one must go through man to reach God, it is equally certain that the "passing through" to that gratuitous God strips me, leaves me naked, universalizes my love for others, and make it gratuitous. Both movements need each other dialectically and move toward a synthesis. This synthesis is found in Christ; in the God-Man we encounter God and man. In Christ man gives God a human countenance and God gives man a divine countenance.[51] Only in this perspective will we be able to understand that the "union with the Lord," which all spirituality proclaims, is not a separation from man; to attain this union, I must go through man, and the union, in turn, enables me to encounter man more fully. Our purpose here is not to "balance" what has been said before, but rather to deepen it and see it in all of its meaning.

The conversion to the neighbor, and in him to the Lord, the gratuitousness which allows me to encounter others fully, the unique encounter which is the foundation of communion of men among themselves and of men with God, these are the source of Christian *joy*. This joy is born of the gift already received yet still awaited and is expressed in the present despite the difficulties and tensions of the struggle for the construction of a just society. Every prophetic proclamation of total liberation is accompanied by an invitation to participate in eschatological joy: "I will take delight in Jerusalem and rejoice in my people" (Isa. 65:19). This joy ought to fill our entire existence, making us attentive both to the gift of integral liberation of man and history as well as to the detail of our life and the lives of others. This joy ought not to lessen our commitment to man who lives in an unjust world, nor should it lead us to a facile, low-cost conciliation. On the contrary, our joy is paschal, guaranteed by the Spirit (Gal. 5:22; 1 Tim. 1:6; Rom. 14:17); it passes through the conflict with the great ones of this world and through the cross in order to enter into life. This is why we celebrate our joy in the present by recalling the passover of the Lord. To recall Christ is to believe in him. And this celebration is a feast (Apoc. 19:7),[52] a feast of the Christian community, those who explicitly confess Christ to be the Lord of history, the liberator of the oppressed. This community has been referred to as the small temple in contradistinction to the large temple of human history.[53] Without community support neither the emergence nor the continued existence of a new spirituality is possible.

The Magnificat expresses well this spirituality of liberation. A song of thanksgiving for the gifts of the Lord, it expresses humbly the joy of being loved by him: "Rejoice, my spirit, in God my Savior; so tenderly has he looked upon his servant, humble as she is. . . . So wonderfully has he dealt with me, the Lord, the Mighty One" (Luke 1:47–49). But at the same time it is one of the New Testament texts which contains great implications both as regards liberation and the political sphere. This thanks-

giving and joy are closely linked to the action of God who liberates the oppressed and humbles the powerful. "The hungry he
has satisfied with good things, the rich sent empty away"
(52–53). The future of history belongs to the poor and exploited.
True liberation will be the work of the oppressed themselves;
in them, the Lord saves history. The spirituality of liberation
will have as its basis the spirituality of the *anawim*.[54]

Living witnesses rather than theological speculation will
point out, are already pointing out, the direction of a spirituality
of liberation. This is the task which has been undertaken in
Latin America by those referred to above as a "first Christian
generation."

NOTES

1. See above Chapter 1. See also Christian Duquoc, "Eschatologie et réalités
terrestres," *Lumière et Vie* 9, No. 50 (November–December 1960): 4–22.

2. *Old Testament Theology*, 2:338. "The self-revelation of God in the Biblical
witnesses is not of a direct type in the sense of a theophany, but is indirect and
brought about by means of the historical acts of God" (Wolfhart Pannenburg,
Revelation as History, ed. Wolfhart Pannenburg, trans. David Granskou [New
York: The Macmillan Company, 1968], p. 125).

3. Following Bonhoeffer, André Dumas writes "The space of God is the world;
the secret of the world is the hidden presence of God. Jesus Christ is the structur-
alization of this space and the name of this secret" (*Une théologie de la réalité*
[Geneva: Éditions Labor et Fides, 1968], p. 182; English version: *Dietrich
Bonhoeffer: Theologian of Reality*, trans. R. M. Brown [New York: Macmillan,
1971]).

4. "This Hebrew word *(Shekinah)* should be translated by *indwelling* rather
than by *presence*. It indicates that God takes up his abode in some given place
and dwells there. Whilst the word 'presence' does not imply any place, any attach-
ment, any preference, 'indwelling' presupposes that there has been a choice of
a place in which to remain" (M.-J. Lagrange, *Le judaïsme avant Jésus-Christ* [Paris,
1931], p. 446, quoted in Yves M.-J. Congar, O.P., *The Mystery of the Temple*
[Westminister, Md.: The Newman Press, 1962], p. 18, n. 9).

5. Congar, *Mystery of the Temple*, p. ix.

6. Von Rad points out the difference between the tent on the one hand and
the Arc and its tabernacle on the other (*Old Testament Theology*, 1:234–39).

7. Some exegetes consider the Arc as a throne; see Frank Michaeli, *Dieu a
l'image de l'homme* (Neuchatel: Delachaux & Niestlé S.A., 1950), p. 59.

8. Martin Buber is against the conceptions of God which conceal these localiza-
tions in the Arc and the temple and sees in this "a classic expression of the tensions
between the free God of history and the fettered deity of natural things" (*The
Prophetic Faith* [New York: Harper & Row, Publishers, 1960], p. 83).

9. "Since the Temple had thus exercised an attractive function which led to the crystallization of various traditions, it can be understood that piety was determined by it and became centered in its orbit" (Edmond Jacob, *Theology of the Old Testament*, trans. Arthur W. Heathcote and Philip J. Allcock [London: Hodder & Stoughton, 1958], p. 259.)

10. See the commentary of Congar, *Mystery of the Temple*, pp. 20–53.

11. This has frequently been noted; see for example Montague, *Biblical Theology of the Secular*, p. 15.

12. The "body" *(soma)* in the Jewish apocalypse signifies the whole person insofar as he has a corporeal existence in an historical world of interpersonal relationships. The body is the precondition for the possibility of these relationships. From that time on true worship will be celebrated in this world (see Rom. 12:1). See Anton Grabner-Haider, "Zur Kultkritik im Neuen Testament," *Diakonia* 4 (1969): 138–46; and Heribert Mühlen, *L'Esprit dans l'Église* (Paris: Les Éditions du Cerf, 1969), 1:169–73.

13. Congar, *Mystery of the Temple*, pp. 197–98.

14. On this subject see the excellent study of Sigmund Mowinckel, *Die Erkenntnis Gottes bei den alttestamentlichen Propheten* (Oslo, 1941).

15. See K. Hruby, "L'amour du prochain dans la pensée juive," *Nouvelle Revue Théologique* 91, no. 5 (May 1969): 493–516.

16. We speak of "parable," following the standard usage; but as has been noted, the text in question is difficult to classify. A misunderstanding due especially to the context has resulted in the classification of this eschatological vision as a parable; see Théo Preiss, *Life in Christ*, trans. Harold Knight (Naperville, Ill.: Alec R. Allenson, Inc., 1957), p. 46.

17. According to Roger Mehl for certain theologians "the summary of the Gospel is Matt. 25:31–46" ("La catholicité de l'Église," *Revue d'Histoire et de Philosophie Religieuses* 48, no. 4 [1968]: 369). Indeed this is what an exegete like Wolfgang Trilling believes; he writes, "The passage is ... a summary of the whole teaching of the Gospel and a restatement of its demands in the light of judgment" *(The Gospel According to St. Matthew* [New York: Herder and Herder, 1969], 2:216). The central position that this text holds in the thinking of John A. T. Robinson is well known; see *Honest to God* (Philadelphia: The Westminster Press, 1963), especially p. 61.

18. See J. Winandy, "La scène du Jugément dernier," *Sciences Ecclésiastiques*, 1966, pp. 170–86. Lamar Cope, "Matthew 25:31–46, 'The Sheep and the Goats' Reinterpreted," *Novum Testamentum* 11, Fasc. 1/2 (January–April 1969): 32–44; Jean-Claude Ingelaere, "La 'parabole' du Jugément Dernier (Matthieu 25:31–46)," *Revue d'Histoire et de Philosophie Religieuses* 50, no. 1 (1970): 23–60.

19. Among other things if the interpretation of Ingelaere were exact, the love of which Matthew speaks could be practiced only by pagans in contact with Christians.

20. *Die Synoptiker*, 3rd ed. (Tubingen, 1901).

21. *Évangile selon Saint Matthieu*, 7th ed. (Paris: J. Gabalda et Cie, Éditeurs, 1948), p. 485. The position of Lagrange is rather complicated: the judgment is universal but the teaching is addressed in the first place to Christians: "Everyone appears together at the judgment, but from then on Christ is concerned only with his disciples" *(ibid.)*.

22. Wolfgang Trilling, *Das wahre Israel: Studien zur Theologie des Matthäus evangeliums* (Munich, 1964), p. 26. See also by the same author *Gospel According to St. Matthew*, 2:216.

23. Mühlen, *Esprit dans l'Eglise*, 1:149. See also Josef Schmid, *Das Evangelium des Matthäus* (Ratisbona, 1952), pp. 352 ff., cited in *ibid.*; and Georg Strecker, *Der Weg der Gerechtigkeit: Untersuchung zur Theologie des Matthäus* (Gottingen: Vandenhoeck & Ruprecht, 1962), pp. 218–19.

24. Pierre Bonnard, *L'Évangile selon Saint Matthieu* (Neuchatel: Éditions Delachaux & Niestlé, 1963), p. 367. "The Son of Man has made himself one with all those who objectively need help, whatever be their subjective dispositions. It is not said that these hungry ones, strangers, prisoners, were Christians. The Son of Man sees in any wretch his brother; . . . his love as shepherd of Israel claims to be in solidarity with the whole of human misery in all ranges and ultimate depths" (Preiss, *Life in Christ*, p. 52). See also Joachim Jeremias, *The Parables of Jesus*, trans. S. H. Hooke (London: SCM Press Ltd., 1954), p. 143, and Trilling, *Gospel According to St. Matthew*, 2:219. See also Jacques Dupont, "La iglesia y la pobreza," *La Iglesia del Vaticano II*, p. 427.

25. Preiss has noted that for the verb "to do" (see vv. 40, 44) Jesus must have used the Aramaic *abad* which means both "to do" and "to serve"; quoted by Bonnard, *Matthieu*, p. 366.

26. Hence the expression "ethical prophecy" (Bonnard, *Matthieu*, p. 366). From this "primacy of the ethical demand," Strecker draws certain consequences for ecclesiology: "The elect of all nations are gathered together. No attention is paid to their membership in the community; they are judged only according to their good works." Thus, "the Church and the world are put on the same footing." Both "are presented in this point of time as complex dimensions, embracing both good and bad and presupposing the responsibility of man for his actions." This does not prevent, nevertheless, that "the community of the Lord should be the legitimate and authentic representative of the eschatological challenge in the world" (*Der Weg der Gerechtigkeit*, pp. 218–19).

27. See Isa. 58:7; Job 31:17, 19, 21; Ezek. 18:7, 16.

28. See UNEC, *Caridad y amor humano* (Lima: Tierra Entera, 1966).

29. Congar, *Situation et tâches*, p. 67.

30. Is this the perspective at the beginning of the final sequence? Does the Nazarín—in the middle of the journey carrying in his hands the material proof of an act of human and disinterested love—take up the journey again? Does he begin his life again? It is impossible not to think of the last scene of Fellini's film, *Nights of Cabiria*.

31. "Los dados eternos" in *Heraldos negros*.

32. "This human history is the only way to reach God" (Edward Schillebeeckx, "L'immagine de Dio," *Ricerca*, March 31, 1968, p. 11).

33. See Alfaro, *Teología del progreso humano*, p. 114.

34. Address of Pope Paul VI, December 7, 1965, included in Xavier Rynne, *The Fourth Session* (New York: Farrar, Straus and Giroux, 1965), p. 325. Regarding Mic. 6:8 Albert Gelin writes, "There is no doubt that the expression is orientated toward fraternal love. The Old Testament had already prepared the formula of Gal. 5:14: by loving our brothers we reach God" ("La sainteté de l'homme selon l'Ancien Testament," *Bible et Vie Chrétienne*, no. 19 [September–November 1957], p. 45).

35. "Jugement Dernier," pp. 56–59.

36. Mühlen explains this identification of Christ with the poor by using his idea of the "Great I" (*Grand Moi*). The author uses this expression to refer to what others call the "corporate personality," a notion which seems to be deduced from

the Old Testament. For Mühlen this is the "central notion of the Bible" (*Esprit dans l'Église*, 1:118). It expresses a special relationship of solidarity between the individual and the community. It has three elements: "(a) the primitive I, the source of a community; (b) the community itself; (c) the real unity between the two" (*ibid.*, 1:122). The community "is really recapitulated in the individual I which originates it, and on the other hand the community is the 'irradiation' and the historical 'expansion' of this individual I" (*ibid.*, 1:134). The best expression of this notion of the "Great I" would be the "Son of Man" (Dan. 7:13). Matt. 25:31–45 refers to the Son of Man: Christ is identified with the poor and forms with them "a unity which is difficult to understand outside of the Old Testament conception of the 'Great I'" (*ibid.*, 1:143). Thus there is neither substitution nor representation but rather identification between Christ and the poor.

37. See the comment of Christian Duquoc in *Christologie: Essai dogmatique, L'homme Jesus* (Paris: Les Éditions du Cerf, 1968), pp. 213–61.

38. See Juan Luis Segundo, "Desarrollo y subdesarrollo: polos teológicos," *Perspectivas para el Diálogo*, no. 43. (May 1970), pp. 76–80.

39. *The Wide World My Parish*, p. 124. Congar sees in this the basis for the possibility of universal salvation: "We may call it the realm of 'God in disguise': he is really met, the dialogue is really with him, but he does not call himself God and one does not know that it is he" (*Wide World*, p. 120). Javier Alonso Hernández studies the "sacramental value of history," in *Teología y desarrollo* (Lima: Centro Arquidiocesano de Pastoral, 1969), pp. 184–91.

40. "La de a mil" in *Heraldos negros*.

41. Regarding these subjects see the analyses of Emmanuel Levinas, *Totality and Infinity*, trans. Alphonso Lingis (Pittsburgh: Duquesne University Press, 1969), pp. 194–219.

42. "To love man ... not as a means but as the first step toward the final and transcendent goal which is the basis and cause of every love" (Paul VI, Address of December 7, 1965, in Rynne, *Fourth Session*, p. 325).

43. See also Jean Cardonnel, "Dieu et l'urgence des masses," *Esprit* 36, no. 370 (April 1968): 661–76; Hugo Assmann believes that in a world "that is becoming more and more socialized we are called to recover the Biblical primacy of the people over the individual" ("Fe y promoción humana," *Perspectivas para el Diálogo*, no. 36 [August 1969], p. 181).

44. In this regard for the cases of Mexico and Puerto Rico, see the works of Oscar Lewis, *Five Families: Mexican Case Studies in the Culture of Poverty* (New York: John Wiley, 1962) and *La Vida* (New York: Random, 1966).

45. The poem of León Felipe which Che Guevara liked so much is well known. Because it was found recopied among Guevara's papers, some attribute the poem to him:

Christ I love you
not because you descended from a star
but because you revealed to me
that man has blood
tears
anguish
keys
tools
to open the doors closed to light
Yes! You taught us that man is God ...
a poor God crucified like you
and the one who is at your left on Golgotha
the bad thief
is God too!

46. See José María González Ruiz, *Pobreza evangélica y promoción humana* (Barcelona: Nova Terra, 1966), p. 87.

47. We need only read Camilo Torres or Nestor Paz Zamora—to mention two who have left something in writing—to be convinced of this. It would be a mistake for theologians who might be offended by certain deficiencies of expression to ignore these efforts to penetrate what the Word of the Lord is saying to man in the Latin American context.

48. Arturo Gaete observed a short time ago the need for a "spirituality of liberation" ("Definición e indefinición de la Iglesia en política," *Mensaje* 19, no. 191 [August 1970]: 375). See also the attempt of Arturo Paoli, *Dialogo della liberazione* (Brescia: Morcelliana: 1970), to be published in English by Orbis Books. The poet Ernesto Cardenal offers us a collection of profound "Psalms" which seek and sing liberation in the midst of modern forms of oppression and exploitation of man by man (*Psalms of Struggle and Liberation* [New York: Herder and Herder, 1971]). See also the interesting ideas of Gonzalo Arroyo on the "rebel communities": "Rebeldía cristiana y compromiso comunitario," *Mensaje* 17, no. 167 (March–April 1968): 78–83.

49. See José María González Ruiz, *Dios es gratuito, pero no superfluo* (Madrid: Ediciones Marova, 1970).

50. This has been clearly pointed out in "Pastoral Concern for the Elites," no. 13, in *Medellín*.

51. If Vallejo was correct when he said "My God, if you had been a man, today you would know how to be God," it could also be said, "If you had been God, today you would know how to be man."

52. See the excellent considerations of Harvey Cox in *The Feast of Fools* (Cambridge: Harvard University Press, 1969).

53. Conrad Eggers Lan, *Cristianismo y nueva ideología* (Buenos Aires, 1968), pp. 47–48, quoted by Juan Luis Segundo, "Desarrollo y subdesarrollo: polos teológicos," p. 79.

54. See below Chapter 13. "Christians and their pastors should know how to recognize the hand of the Almighty in those events that occur sporadically—when the powerful are dethroned and the lowly are exalted, when the rich are sent away empty-handed and the needy are filled" ("Letter to Peoples of the Third World," in *Between Honesty and Hope*, p. 6).

CHAPTER ELEVEN

ESCHATOLOGY AND POLITICS

The commitment to the creation of a just society and, ultimately, to a new man, presupposes confidence in the future.
This commitment is an act open to whatever comes. What is
the meaning of this *new* reality in the light of faith?

It has often been noted that a characteristic of contemporary
man is that he lives in terms of tomorrow, oriented towards
the future, fascinated by what does not yet exist. The spiritual
condition of today's man is more and more determined by the
model of the man of tomorrow. Man's awareness of himself is
heavily affected by the knowledge that he is outgrowing his
present condition and entering a new era,[1] a world "to the second power," fashioned by his own hands.[2] We live on the verge
of man's epiphany, his "anthropophany." History is no longer,
as it was for the Greeks, an *anamnesis*, a remembrance. It is
rather a thrust into the future. The contemporary world is full
of latent possibilities and expectations. History seems to have
quickened its pace. The confrontation of the present with the
future makes man impatient.

But are we not painting an idealized picture, valid perhaps
for other places, but not for Latin America? It is, indeed, inaccurate to regard this sketch as a complete description of the contemporary life-experience of this continent. Large numbers of
Latin Americans suffer from a fixation which leads them to
overvalue the past. This problem has been correctly interpreted
by Paulo Freire. It is one of the elements of what he has called
a precritical consciousness, that is, the consciousness of a man
who has not taken hold of the reins of his own destiny. Neverthe-

less, it is necessary to recall that the revolutionary process now under way is generating the kind of man who critically analyzes the present, controls his destiny, and is oriented towards the future. This kind of person, whose actions are directed toward a new society yet to be built, is in Latin America more of a motivating ideal than a reality already realized and generalized. But things are moving in this direction. A profound aspiration for the creation of a new man underlies the process of liberation which the continent is undergoing.[3] This is a difficult creation which will have to overcome conflicts and antagonisms. Rightly does Medellín comment that "we are on the threshold of a new epoch in the history of our continent. It appears to be a time full of zeal for full emancipation, of liberation from every form of servitude, of personal maturity and of collective integration. In these signs we perceive the first indications of the painful birth of a new civilization."[4]

Latin America faces a complex situation which does not allow for a simple acceptance or rejection of this orientation toward the future which we noted as characteristic of contemporary man. But this situation does lead us to recognize the existence of other realities, of a transitional situation, and to specify that this thrust toward the future occurs *above all* when one participates in the building up of a just society, qualitatively different from the one which exists today. Moreover, one gets the impression that many in the developed countries do not have an intense experience, in political matters, of this typical characteristic of today's man, because they are so attached—in both the East and the West—not to the past, but rather to an affluent present which they are prepared to uphold and defend under any circumstances.

Here we have the same two approaches which we have already considered. For some, especially in the developed countries, the openness towards the future is an openness to the control of nature by science and technology with no questioning of the social order in which they live. For others, especially in dependent and dominated areas, the future promises conflicts and confrontations, a struggle to become free from the powers which enslave men and exploit social classes. For these people the development of productive forces, in which scientific and technological advances do indeed play an important part, dialectically demands however that the established order be questioned. Without such a challenge, there is no true thrust into the future.

Be that as it may, the intensification of revolutionary ferment, which is to be found in varying degrees in the modern world, is accentuating and accelerating this thrust towards what is to come.[5] All this creates a complex reality which challenges the Christian faith. The idea of eschatology as the driving force of a future-oriented history attempts to provide a response.[6] But, as we have noted before, this opening of eschatology to the future is inseparably joined with its historical contemporaneity and urgency. This notion of eschatology is diametrically opposed to that which "eschatologist" theologians upheld some twenty years ago in opposition to the "Incarnationalists."[7] For them the eschatological tendency expressed the wish for a disengagement of the Christian faith from the powers of this world; the basis for this was a lack of interest in terrestrial realities and a historical pessimism which discouraged any attempt at great tasks. This school was also easy prey of all kinds of conciliatory juxtapositions.[8]

The current eschatological perspective has overcome these obstacles. Not only is it not an escape from history, but also it has clear and strong implications for the political sphere, for social praxis.[9] This is what recent reflections on hope, on the political impact of the evangelical message, and on the relationship between faith and historical utopia are convincingly demonstrating.

TO ACCOUNT FOR THE HOPE

This new approach to eschatological problems has led to a renewal of the theology of hope. Before, this was very much forgotten or relegated to a modest place in the middle of the treatise "on the virtues," in which the theology of faith enjoyed the lion's share. "Saved in hope" (Rom. 8:24) we have in us the promised Spirit (Gal. 3:14), which makes us "overflow with hope" (Rom. 15:13; Acts 26:6). The Christian is, above all, he who must account for the hope that is in him (1 Pet. 3:15).

Some years ago Gabriel Marcel made a valuable contribution to the rediscovery of the role hope plays in reflecting on the Christian life and on the existence of all men. But his approach was personal and conversational and did not stress the implications that hope has in historical and political reality.[10]

Ernst Bloch's focus is different. His most important work is entitled "The Hope Principle" (*Das Prinzip Hoffnung*). For Bloch man is he who hopes for and dreams of the future; but it is an active hope which subverts the existing order. He accepts Marx's assertion that "philosophers have only *interpreted* the world, in various ways; the point, however, is to *change it*." He uses as his point of departure what Marx himself, in his first thesis on Feuerbach, asserted had been left out of all materialistic theories: "The chief defect of all hitherto existing materialism—that of Feuerbach included—is that the thing [*Gegenstand*], reality, sensuousness, is conceived only in the form of the *object* [*Objekt*] or of *contemplation* [*Anschauung*], but not as *human sensuous activity, practice*, not subjectively."[11] Bloch attempts to clarify in his work the meaning of these aspects of revolutionary activity, that is to say, of the practico-critical activity.[12]

For Bloch there are two kinds of affections: those of society (envy, avarice) and those of expectation (anguish, fear, hope). The latter anticipate the future. Of these hope is the most important as well as the most positive and most liberating. Hope is "the most human of all emotions and only men can experience it. It is related to the broadest and most luminous horizon."[13] Hope is a "daydream" projected into the future; it is the "yet not-conscious" (*Noch-Nicht-Bewusst*), the psychic representation of that which "is not yet" (*Noch-Nicht-Sein*). But this hope seeks to be clear and conscious, a *docta spes*. When that which is "yet not-conscious" becomes a conscious act, it is no longer a state of mind; it assumes a concrete utopic function, mobilizing human action in history. Hope thus emerges as the key to human existence oriented towards the future, because it transforms the present. This ontology of what "is not yet" is dynamic, in contrast to the static ontology of being, which is incapable of planning history.[14] For Bloch what is real is an open-ended process. On one occasion he asserted that the formula "S is not yet P" summarizes his thought.[15] Bloch brings us into the area of the possibilities of potential being; this allows us to plan history in revolutionary terms.

The contemporary theology of hope is passing through the breach unexpectedly opened by Bloch.[16] Moltmann[17] and Pannenberg[18] have found in Bloch's analyses the categories which allow them to think through some of the important Biblical themes: Eschatology, Promise, Hope. In this, they are only following an indication of Bloch himself who said: "Where there is hope, there is also religion."[19]

For Moltmann, the Biblical revelation of God is not, as it was for the Greek mind, the "epiphany of the eternal present," which limits itself to explaining what exists.[20] On the contrary, revelation speaks to us about a God who comes to meet us and whom we can only await "in active hope."[21] The present order of things, that which is, is profoundly challenged by the Promise;[22] because of his hope in the resurrected Christ, man is liberated from the narrow limits of the present and can think and act completely in terms of what is to come. For Moltmann, a theology of hope is simultaneously a theology of resurrection.[23] The resurrected Christ is man's future. The statements of the Promise "do not seek to illuminate the reality which exists, but the reality which is coming,"[24] and therefore establish the conditions for the possibility of "new experiences."[25] Thus there is maintained "a specific *inadaequatio rei et intellectus*" regarding "the existing and given reality,"[26] inaugurating a promising and productive "open stage for history."[27]

But as Alves has noted, for Moltmann the challenge to the present is derived from the Promise. The present is denied because of the Promise and not because of a human, concrete, historical experience. For Moltmann "there is one transcendental hope (because not related to any specific situation) that makes man aware of the pain of his present.... The event of promise, therefore, is the beginning of the criticism of everything that is."[28] God would resemble the Aristotelian *primum movens*, "pulling history to its future, but without being involved in history."[29] Hence the danger of "docetism" which Alves thinks he perceives in Moltmann's thought: "It is not the incarnation which is the mother of the future, but rather the transcendental future which makes man aware of the incarnation."[30]

It cannot be denied that despite all his efforts, Moltmann has difficulty finding a vocabulary both sufficiently rooted in man's concrete historical experience, in his present of oppression and exploitation, and yet abounding in potentialities—a vocabulary rooted in his possibilities of self-liberation.[31] Hence perhaps his

idea of theological concepts mentioned above,[32] which "anticipate future being" and "do not limp after reality." But we are
dealing with a human, historical, concrete, present reality,
which we must do to prevent failure in our encounter with man
—and with the God who is to come. The death and resurrection
of Jesus are our future, because they are our perilous and hope-
ful present. The hope which overcomes death must be rooted
in the heart of historical praxis; if this hope does not take shape
in the present to lead it forward, it will be only an evasion, a
futuristic illusion. One must be extremely careful not to replace
a Christianity of the Beyond with a Christianity of the Future;
if the former tended to forget the world, the latter runs the
risk of neglecting a miserable and unjust present and the
struggle for liberation.[33]

Despite these critical observations, Moltmann's work is
undoubtedly one of the most important in contemporary
theology.[34] It offers a new approach to the theology of hope and
has injected new life into the reflection on various aspects of
Christian existence. Among other things, it helps us overcome
the association between faith and fear of the future which Moltmann rightly considers characteristic of many Christians.[35]

To hope does not mean to know the future, but rather to be
open, in an attitude of spiritual childhood, to accepting it as
a gift. But this gift is accepted in the negation of injustice, in
the protest against trampled human rights, and in the struggle
for peace and brotherhood. Thus hope fulfills a mobilizing and
liberating function in history. Its function is not very obvious,
but it is real and deep. Peguy has written that Little Hope,
which seemed to be led by her two older sisters, Faith and Charity, actually leads them. But this will be true only if hope in
the future seeks roots in the present, if it takes shape in daily
events with their joys to experience but also with their injustices to eliminate and their enslavements from which to be liberated. Camus was right when in another context he said "true
generosity towards the future consists in giving everything to
the present."

The somewhat overwhelming emergence of reflection both on
eschatology and on its implications on the level of social praxis
has put the theology of hope in the forefront. In former years,
one had the impression that a theology centered on the love
of God and neighbor had replaced a theology concerned espe-

cially with faith and the corresponding orthodoxy. The primacy of faith was followed by the "primacy of charity." This permitted the notion of love of neighbor to be recovered as an essential element of Christian life. But paradoxically, at the same time this was also partially responsible for the fact that for some the relationship with God was obscured and became difficult to live out and understand.[36] Today, due partly perhaps to such impasses, the perspective of a new primacy seems to be emerging—that of hope, which liberates history because of its openness to the God who is to come. If faith was reinterpreted by charity, both are now being reevaluated in terms of hope. All this is very sketchily drawn; we are also, of course, confronted here with a question of emphasis. Christian life and theological reflection must integrate these various dimensions into a profound unity. But the history of the Christian community continuously demonstrates how certain aspects of Christian experience are stressed at different times. New syntheses follow. It is possible that the evolution which we have recalled is leading us to one of these syntheses.

Be this as it may, it might be interesting to trace a parallel between this evolution of theology and that which we find in the thought of three very influential men of our times who have had a great impact on theology: Hegel, Feuerbach, and Marx. We will do this briefly, and only suggestively, but with the belief that a deeper study of this parallel would illuminate our theological reflection.

Feuerbach strongly contrasted love with faith: "Faith is the opposite of love."[37] For him faith was a way of opposing man to God. Indeed, the essence of man is the human race and this essence is concretely realized by love, the expression of the need one human being has for another.[38] God for him is this essence projected outside of man, outside reality. "Knowledge of God is self-knowledge."[39] To find himself again, man must abandon faith in this nonexistent being. Human love is "the truth" (in the Hegelian sense of the word) of Christianity. Faith is based on the affirmation of God; love is based on the affirmation of man. Faith separates; love unites. Faith particularizes; love universalizes. Faith divides man within; love unifies him. Faith oppresses; love liberates.[40] For Feuerbach, the Hegelian system was based on faith, hence its strongly Christian character, its rigidity, its authoritarian and repressive characteristics.[41]

Attempting to place himself in opposition to Hegelian thought, Feuerbach seeks to center his doctrine on love, going so far as to formulate it as a "religion of love."[42]

Marx, who accepts many of Feuerbach's criticisms of Hegel—especially those directed against religion—comments ironically on the religion of love of the so-called "true socialists," who find their inspiration in Feuerbach.[43] Moreover, he takes Feuerbach to task for overlooking the need for a revolution, due to his erroneous way of relating theory and praxis. In a well-turned phrase, Marx said: "As far as Feuerbach is a materialist he does not deal with history, and as far as he deals with history he is not a materialist."[44] Marx's idea of praxis is different; it is based on a dialectical conception of history—necessarily advancing, with eyes fixed on the future and with real action in the present, towards a classless society based on new relationships of production.

The theology of hope, on which Marxian thought exercises a certain amount of influence through the work of Bloch, is a response to the "death of God" approach, in which the presence of Feuerbach's thought is evident.[45]

THE POLITICAL DIMENSION OF THE GOSPEL

The relationship between Gospel and politics is an old question; but it has also become very contemporary, having recently taken on a new dimension. The above chapters have touched on this. In this context we will study two ideas which are currently the subject of lively controversy: the so-called "new political theology" and the public character of the witness and message of Jesus.

The "New Political Theology"

The eschatological vision becomes operative, the theology of hope becomes creative, when it comes in contact with the social realities of today's world and gives rise to what has been called "political theology."[46] Following the line of thought proposed by Bloch and Moltmann (and also by Pannenberg), Metz attempts to show the implications of eschatology and hope for political life.[47] He does not mean to suggest the creation of "a new theological discipline"; his intention is "to lay bare ... a basic feature within theological awareness at large."[48] The approach is, therefore, that of fundamental theology.[49]

Political theology is an ambiguous expression. Metz has acknowledged this from the beginning.[50] Because of criticism, he has had to repeat and deepen his reasons for using such a controversial term.[51] This will be better understood if we study the content of his approach.

Metz's point of departure is what he considers a new way of thinking about the *political sphere*. He refers to the process of emancipation and autonomy of the political sphere which reached maturity with the Enlightenment (*Aufklärung*).[52] Since the Enlightenment, the political order is an order of freedom. The political structures are no longer given, previous to man's freedom, but are rather realities based on freedom, taken on and modified by man. Political history is, from that time forward, the history of freedom. This new definition of politics carefully distinguishes between state and society. The distinction, which "has an essentially anti-totalitarian thrust,"[53] allows us to differentiate between the public sphere of the state or the Church (or the combination of them) as powers from the public sphere "in which the interests of all men as a social group are expressed."[54] Because in some cases this distinction was not made, we have had authoritarian and repressive "political theologies" which sought to restore a "Christian State" (Bonald, Donoso Cortés, etc.). Metz's position not only does not "abandon the distinction and the emancipation of politics from the 'religious' order," as some of his critics mistakenly assert, "rather it *presupposes it*."[55] He goes even further and asserts that what is important above all is to perceive the political sphere as the proper area of freedom. Without this focus one cannot understand what Metz means by his approach in political theology. For him all thought (and therefore all theology) which does not take into account the challenge born of the Enlightenment is precritical (or of the first degree); and inversely, all reflection which is aware of it is postcritical (or of the second degree). On this basis, Metz says that his political theology is opposed to "all forms of theology which politicize directly" and conditionally rejects "the mistaken notions of the neo-politicization of the faith or the neo-clericalization of poli-

tics, which seem to be associated with the idea of political theology, due to its historical ballast."[56] This is why he prefers to
call his own approach *"new* political theology."

The shattering of the unity between religious and social life
which began in modern times made the Christian religion
appear as "a particular phenomenon within a pluralistic milieu.
Thus its absolute claim to universality seemed to be historically
conditioned."[57] The Enlightenment, and later Marx, criticized
religion, considering it an ideology emanating from specific
social and historical structures. Theology, according to Metz,
reacted by placing the social dimension of the Christian message
on a secondary and accidental level and insisting upon its essentially private aspect. The life of faith was thus reduced to a
personal option and was abstracted from the social world in
which it lived. This kind of theology "sought to solve its problem,
a problem born of the Enlightenment, by eliminating it. . . .
The religious consciousness formed by this theology attributes
but a shadowy existence to the social and political reality."[58]
This private, interior version of Christianity is proper to tran-
scendentalist, existentialist, and personalist theologies. Faced
with such an attitude which avoids the problem, the first task
of political theology is the *de-privatization* which allows for criticism of "the understanding of the datum of our theology."[59]

The definition of the political sphere will keep the new political
theology from mixing "politics and religion, the way the old
political theology did." But at the same time, the de-
privatization of the message will prevent religion from becoming uninterested in politics "and concerning itself with its
proper sphere, that is, speaking about God, as the critics of the
new political theology recommend."[60] Having rejected this alternative, the new political theology can advance positively
towards the determination of a new kind of relationship
"between religion and society, between Church and societal
'publicness,' between eschatological faith and societal life,"[61]
between *theory and practice.*[62] This determination cannot be
carried out by means of a precritical method condemned to identifying these realities anew, but by means of a reflection of the
second degree, postcritical. The new type of relationship thus
achieved will be based on the "critical, liberating force in regard
to the social world and its historical process"[63] possessed by the
saving message proclaimed by Jesus. This message becomes

present and active because of what Metz calls the *memoria Christi*: "commemorating the advent of the Kingdom of God in the love of Jesus towards marginated men."[64] The proclamation of the saving message is translated into promises of freedom, justice, and peace which make up the "eschatological proviso" and whose role is to stress the "provisional" character of "every historically real status of society."[65]

All this will lead the Church to become an *"institution of social criticism."*[66] Its critical mission will be defined as a service to the history of freedom, or more precisely, as a service to the liberation of man. The Church and not the individual Christian would then be the subject of the praxis of liberation, enlivened by the evangelical message. But in order for this to be true, the Church will have to become a nonrepressive institution, a "second degree institution," critical and liberating. The current situation of the Church, a legacy of its past, seems to negate this possibility. Nevertheless Metz thinks it is possible, because the very existence of the Church as institution is under the sign of the eschatological proviso. The Church does not exist for itself. Preaching hope in the Kingdom of God, she lives "on the proclamation of her own proviso."[67] Metz is aware that this is an ideal concept of the Church and that for the Church to be an institution of freedom a new praxis is needed. Is this new praxis possible? He responds that his political theology lives in the hope that by exercising its critical function toward society the Church will find a new awareness of itself.[68]

The ideas advanced tentatively by Metz created great interest, but they also were severely criticized on various counts. He has been faulted for not taking the political domain seriously enough,[69] for using ambiguous philosophical notions,[70] for simplifying history and not respecting the pluralism of the political options of Christians,[71] for falling into neoclericalism,[72] for not having clearly determined what he means by political theology,[73] for neglecting the area proper to political ethics,[74] for painting too ideal a picture of the role the Church can play as a critical agent,[75] and for limiting the role of the Church to a function of negative criticism.[76]

Metz has tried to respond to these criticisms by expressing his thought more precisely. In formulating these responses he has had to enter into his critics' point of view and so he has perhaps lost some of his initial aggressiveness. In any case, many points need to be clarified and many questions remain open. We will consider only two.

Reading the works of Metz one gets the impression of a certain inadequacy in his analyses of the contemporary political situation. On the one hand, because the climate in which his reflections develop is far from the revolutionary ferment of the Third World countries, he cannot penetrate the situation of dependency, injustice, and exploition in which most of mankind finds itself. His conception of the political sphere lacks what could be acquired both by the experience of the confrontations and conflicts stemming from the rejection of this oppression of some men by others and of some countries by others, as well as by the experience of the aspiration to liberation which emerges from the heart of these conditions.[77] Moreover, as a result there is a need for a critique of certain assumptions in Metz's thought. Indeed, the situation of the dominated countries explains more than one characteristic of the affluent societies, which are the immediate context for the new political theology. This explains the rather abstract level on which the political sphere is at times treated in Metz's writings. The analyses of political theology would have much to gain from the contribution of the social sciences; some of his supporters as well as Metz himself seem now to be turning to them. The analyses would also have much to gain from the contribution of certain aspects of Marxism, which, despite (or because of?) the mediation of Bloch's thought, do not seem to be sufficiently present.

However, Metz reacts, and rightly so, to a theology of secularization which advocates ultimately a peaceful coexistence of (privatized) faith with a secularized world; that is to say, he reacts to a conformist theology, which tends to become an ideology of advanced industrial society. Hence the critical character of Metz's thought when he stresses the public and political dimension of faith. Despite all this, he does not seem to have completely shaken off the theology of secularization. His analyses will have to be continued and deepened. This has been the purpose of Metz himself and of some of his former students who are now working energetically and intelligently in this direction.[78] Moreover, the universal existence of a secularized world and the privatization of the faith seem to have been taken for granted by political theology without further critical examination. Nevertheless, in places like Latin America, things are different.[79] The process here does not have the characteristics it exhibits in Europe. Faith, the Gospel, the Church, have in Latin America a complex public dimension which has played (and still plays) an important role in support of the established order, although currently it seems to be withdrawing its support—with unforeseeable consequences. To speak in this instance of a "privatization" of the faith would be to oversimplify the problem. It is understandable that Metz did not take these realities into account; but it is a serious and dangerous error for those who wish to transplant his ideas without qualification to ignore them. Besides, does not the "privatization" of the faith in fact hide other forms of politicization of the faith and of the Church? It is urgent that these questions be analyzed, but this cannot be done from a purely intraecclesiastical perspective.[80]

The new political theology represents, nevertheless, a fertile effort to think the faith through. It takes into consideration the political dimension of the faith and is indeed aware of the most pervasive and acute problems which today's man encounters. It also represents an original recasting of the question of the function of the Church in the world today. This has been a breath of fresh air for European theology. It has contrasted with other contemporary theological trends more tied to "tradition" but less related to living and urgent issues. But the approach of the new political theology must avoid the pitfalls both of "naiveté" regarding the influences of advanced capitalist society as well as of a narrow ecclesiastical framework, if it wishes to reach the arena where the future of society and the Church is being decided.

Jesus and the Political World

The current concern about the liberation of the oppressed, about the social revolution which is to transform the present order, about the counterviolence opposed to the violence which the existing order produces—and with which it defends itself —have all led many Christians to ask themselves about the attitude of Jesus regarding the political situation of his time. The question may surprise us. If so, it is because we take it for granted that Jesus was not interested in political life: his mission was purely religious. Indeed we have witnessed a process which Comblin terms the "iconization" of the life of Jesus:

"This is a Jesus of hieratic, stereotyped gestures, all representing theological themes. To explain an action of Jesus is to find in it several theological meanings. In this way, the life of Jesus is no longer a human life, submerged in history, but a theological life—an icon. As happens with icons, his actions lose their human context and are stylized, becoming transformed into signs of the transcendent and invisible world."[81] The life of Jesus is thus placed outside history, unrelated to the real forces at play. Jesus and those whom he befriended, or whom he confronted and whose hostility he earned, are deprived of all human content. They are there reciting a script. It is impossible not to experience a sensation of unreality when presented with such a life of Jesus.

To approach the man Jesus of Nazareth, in whom God was made flesh, to penetrate not only in his teaching, but also in his life, what it is that gives his word an immediate, concrete context, is a task which more and more needs to be undertaken. One aspect of this work will be to examine the alleged apolitical attitude of Jesus, which would not coincide with what we mentioned earlier regarding the Biblical message and Jesus' own teaching. Hence, a serious reconsideration of this presupposition is necessary. But it has to be undertaken with a respect for the historical Jesus, not forcing the facts in terms of our current concerns. If we wished to discover in Jesus the least characteristic of a contemporary political militant we would not only misrepresent his life and witness and demonstrate a lack of understanding on our part of politics in the present world; we would also deprive ourselves of what his life and witness have that is deep and universal and, therefore, valid and concrete for today's man.

The more recent studies on the life of Jesus related to the political problems of his time, although they have not reached a consensus on all matters, have highlighted some aspects of the question which had been somewhat neglected until now. We will concentrate on three of them which we consider indisputable: the complex relationship between Jesus and the Zealots, his attitude toward the leaders of the Jewish people, and his death at the hands of the political authorities.

It is becoming clearer that the *Zealot movement* is very important for an understanding of the New Testament and especially of the life and death of Jesus.[82] To situate Jesus in his time implies an examination of his connection with this movement of religious and political resistance to the Roman oppressors. Some of Jesus' close associates were Zealots (from the Greek *zelos* 'zeal'). He exercised a great attraction over these people who loved the Law, who were strong nationalists, who fiercely opposed Roman domination, and who ardently awaited the impending arrival of the Kingdom which was to end this situation. Cullmann has proved that some of the direct disciples of Jesus were Zealots or had some connection with them; he concludes his study with this assertion: "One of the Twelve—Simon the Zealot—*certainly* belonged to the Zealots; others *probably* did, like Judas Iscariot, Peter, and *possibly* the sons of Zebedee."[83] But there is more. We find many points of agreement between the Zealots and the attitudes and teachings of Jesus, for example, his preaching of the coming of the Kingdom and the role he himself plays in its advent, the assertion—which has been variously interpreted—that "the Kingdom of Heaven has been subjected to violence and violent men are seizing it" (Matt. 11:12), his attitude toward the Jews who worked for the Romans, his action of purifying the temple,[84] his power over the people who wanted to make him king.[85] For these reasons, Jesus and his disciples were often related to the Zealots (cf. Acts 5:37; 21:38; cf. also Luke 13:1).[86]

But at the same time, Jesus kept his distance from the Zealot movement. The awareness of the universality of his mission did not conform with the somewhat narrow nationalism of the Zealots. Because they disdainfully rejected the Samaritans and pagans, the Zealots must have objected to the behavior of Jesus towards them. The message of Jesus is addressed to all men. The justice and peace he advocated know no national boundaries.[87] In this he was even more revolutionary than the Zealots, who were fierce defenders of literal obedience to the Law; Jesus taught an attitude of spiritual freedom toward it. Moreover, for Jesus the Kingdom was, in the first place, a gift. Only on this basis can we understand the meaning of the active participation of man in its coming; the Zealots tended to see it rather as the fruit of their own efforts. For Jesus, oppression and injustice were not limited to a specific historical situation; their causes go deeper and cannot be truly eliminated without going to the very roots of the problem: the disintegration of brotherhood and communion among men. Besides, and this will have enormous consequences, Jesus is opposed to all politico-religious messianism which does not respect either the depth of the religious

realm nor the autonomy of political action. Messianism can be
efficacious in the short run but the ambiguities and confusions
which it entails frustrate the ends it attempts to accomplish.
This idea was considered as a temptation by Jesus; as such,
he rejected it.[88] The liberation which Jesus offers is universal
and integral; it transcends national boundaries, attacks the
foundation of injustice and exploitation, and eliminates politico-
religious confusions, without therefore being limited to a purely
"spiritual" plane.

It is not enough, however, to say that Jesus was not a Zealot.
There are those who seek, in good faith but uncritically, to
cleanse Jesus from anything which can give even an inkling
of a political attitude on his part. But Jesus' posture precludes
all oversimplification. To close one's eyes to this complexity
amounts to letting the richness of his testimony on this score
escape.

During all his public life, Jesus confronted the *groups in power*
of the Jewish people. Herod, a man employed by the Roman
oppressor, was called "the Fox" (Luke 13:32). The publicans,
whom the people considered as collaborators with the dominant
political power, were placed among the sinners (Matt. 9:10;
21:31; Luke 5:30; 7:34). The Sadducees were conscious that Jesus
threatened their official and privileged position. Jesus' preaching strongly challenged their skepticism in religious matters;
they were in the majority in the Great Sanhedrin which condemned him. His criticism of a religion made up of purely external laws and observances also brought him into violent confrontation with the Pharisees. Jesus turned to the great prophetic
tradition and taught that worship is authentic only when it is
based on profound personal dispositions, on the creation of true
brotherhood among men, and on real commitment to others,
especially the most needy (cf., for example, Matt. 5:23–24; 25:
31–45). Jesus accompanied this criticism with a head-on opposition to the rich and powerful and a radical option for the poor;
one's attitude towards them determines the validity of all religious behavior; it is above all for them that the Son of Man
has come. The Pharisees rejected Roman domination, but they
had structured a complex world of religious precepts and norms
of behavior which allowed them to live on the margin of that
domination. They certainly accepted coexistence. The Zealots
were well aware of this, thus their opposition to the Pharisees

despite many other points of agreement with them. When Jesus struck against the very foundation of their machinations, he unmasked the falsity of their position and appeared in the eyes of the Pharisees as a dangerous traitor.

Jesus *died at the hands of the political authorities*, the oppressors of the Jewish people. According to the Roman custom, the title on the cross indicated the reason for the sentence; in the case of Jesus this title denoted political guilt: King of the Jews.[89] Cullmann can therefore say that Jesus was executed by the Romans as a Zealot leader;[90] and he finds an additional proof of this affirmation in the episode of Barabbas who was undoubtedly a Zealot: "When he is set alongside Jesus it is quite clear that for the Romans both cases involved the same crime and the same verdict. Jesus, like Barabbas, was condemned by the Romans and not by the Jews, and in fact *as a Zealot*."[91] The Sanhedrin had religious reasons for condemning a man who claimed to be the Son of God, but it also had political reasons: the teachings of Jesus and his influence over the people challenged the privilege and power of the Jewish leaders. These political considerations were related to another which affected the Roman authority itself: the claim to be Messiah and King of the Jews. His trial closely combined these different reasons.[92] Crespy can therefore state: "If we attempt to conclude our investigation we see clearly that the trial of Jesus was a *political* trial and that he was condemned for being a Zealot, although the accusation was not solidly established."[93] From the moment he started preaching, Jesus' fate was sealed: "I have spoken openly to all the world" (John 18:20), he tells the High Priest. For this reason John's Gospel presents the story of Jesus as a case "brought, or intended to be brought, against Jesus by the world, represented by the Jews. This action reached its public, judicial decision before Pontius Pilate, the representative of the Roman state and holder of political power."[94]

What conclusions can we draw from these facts about the life of Jesus? For Cullmann—one of the authors who has studied this problem most seriously and carefully—the key to the behavior of Jesus in political matters is what he calls "eschatological radicalism,"[95] which is based on the hope of an impending advent of the Kingdom. Hence it follows that "for Jesus, all the realities of this world were necessarily *relativized* and that his allegiance, therefore, had to lie beyond the alternatives of 'existing order' or 'revolution.'"[96] Jesus was not uninterested in action in this world, but because he was waiting for an imminent end of history, he "was concerned *only* with the conversion of the individual and was not interested in a reform of the social structures." According to Cullmann, the attitude of Jesus cannot therefore be transposed to our times without qualification. From the moment that the development of history shows us that the end of the world is not imminent, it becomes clear that "more just social structures also promote the individual change of character required by Jesus." Henceforward, "a reciprocal action is therefore required between the conversion of the individual and the reform of the structures."[97]

In interpreting the behavior of Jesus in political matters, Cullmann gives the hope of the imminent end of time a definitive role. What has been called "consequent eschatology," in the perspective opened by Schweitzer, already held that Jesus had erroneously announced and awaited the imminent coming of the Kingdom.[98] This is a difficult and controversial exegetical point.[99] This approach does not provide a sufficiently sound basis for an understanding of the attitude of Jesus regarding political life. The interpretation is based on Jesus' words but tends to diffuse or debilitate the tension between the present and the future which characterizes his preaching on the Kingdom.

Moreover, Cullmann uses this belief of Jesus to support his insistence on personal conversion as opposed, in a certain sense, to the need for the transformation of the structures; the latter would appear only when the waiting draws long. But, in fact, when he preached personal conversion, Jesus pointed to a fundamental, permanent attitude which was primarily opposed not to a concern for social structures, but to purely formal worship, devoid of religious authenticity and human content.[100] In this, Jesus was only turning to the great prophetic line which required "mercy and not sacrifice," "contrite hearts and not holocausts." Now then, for the prophets this demand was inseparable from the denunciation of social injustice and from the vigorous assertion that God is known only by doing justice.[101] To neglect this aspect is to separate the call to personal conversion from its social, vital, and concrete context. To attribute the concern for social structures—except with the qualifications operative today—to the prolongation of the waiting period impoverishes and definitely distorts this dimension.

What then are we to think of Jesus' attitude in these matters?[102] The facts we have recalled vigorously ratify what we know of the universality and totality of his work. This universality and totality touch the very heart of political behavior, giving it its true dimension and depth. Misery and social injustice reveal "a sinful situation," a disintegration of brotherhood and communion; by freeing us from sin, Jesus attacks the roots of an unjust order. For Jesus, the liberation of the Jewish people was only one aspect of a universal, permanent revolution. Far from showing no interest in this liberation, Jesus rather placed it on a deeper level, with far reaching consequences.

The Zealots were not mistaken in feeling that Jesus was simultaneously near and far away. Neither were the leaders of the Jewish people mistaken in thinking that their position was imperiled by the preaching of Jesus, nor the oppressive political authorities when they sentenced him to die as a traitor. They were mistaken (and their followers have continued to be mistaken) only in thinking that it was all accidental and transitory, in thinking that with the death of Jesus the matter was closed, in supposing that no one would remember it. The deep human impact and the social transformation that the Gospel entails is permanent and essential because it transcends the narrow limits of specific historical situations and goes to the very root of human existence: the relationship with God in solidarity with other men. The Gospel does not get its political dimension from one or another particular option, but from the very nucleus of its message. If this message is subversive, it is because it takes on Israel's hope: the Kingdom as "the end of domination of man over man; it is a Kingdom of contradiction to the established powers and on behalf of man."[103] And the Gospel gives Israel's hope its deepest meaning; indeed it calls for a "new creation."[104] The life and preaching of Jesus postulate the unceasing search for a new kind of man in a qualitatively different society. Although the Kingdom must not be confused with the establishment of a just society, this does not mean that it is indifferent to this society. Nor does it mean that this just society constitutes a "necessary condition" for the arrival of the Kingdom nor that they are closely linked, nor that they converge. More profoundly, the announcement of the Kingdom reveals to society itself the aspiration for a just society and leads it to discover

unsuspected dimensions and unexplored paths. The Kingdom
is realized in a society of brotherhood and justice; and, in turn,
this realization opens up the promise and hope of complete communion of all men with God. The political is grafted into the
eternal.

This does not detract from the Gospel news; rather it enriches
the political sphere. Moreover, the life and death of Jesus are
no less evangelical because of their political connotations. His
testimony and his message acquire this political dimension precisely because of the radicalness of their salvific character: to
preach the universal love of the Father is inevitably to go
against all injustice, privilege, oppression, or narrow nationalism.

FAITH, UTOPIA, AND POLITICAL ACTION

The term *utopia* has been revived within the last few decades
to refer to a historical plan for a qualitatively different society
and to express the aspiration to establish new social relations
among men.[105] Numerous studies have been and continue to be
made on utopian thought as a dynamic element in the historical
becoming of humanity. We must not forget, however, that what
really makes this utopian thought viable and highlights its
wealth of possibilities is the revolutionary experience of our
times. Without the support of the life—and death—of many
people who, rejecting an unjust and alienating social order,
throw themselves into the struggle for a new society, the idea
of a utopia would never have left the realm of academic discussion.

The guidelines for utopian thought were essentially established by Thomas More's famous *Utopia*. Later, the term
degenerated until it became in common language synonymous
with illusion, lack of realism, irrationality.[106] But because today
there is emerging a profound aspiration for liberation—or at
least there is a clearer consciousness of it—the original meaning
of the expression is again gaining currency.[107] Utopian thought
is taking on, in line with the initial intention, its quality of being
subversive to and a driving force of history. Three elements
characterize the notion of utopia as we shall develop it in the
following pages: its relationship to historical reality, its verification in praxis, and its rational nature.

Utopia, contrary to what current usage suggests, is characterized by its *relationship to present historical reality*. The literary style and fine sarcasm exhibited by More have deceived some and distracted others toward accidentals, but it has been demonstrated that the background of his work was the England of his time. The fiction of a Utopia in which the common good prevails, where there is no private property, no money or privileges, was the opposite of his own country, in whose politics he was involved. More's Utopia is a city of the future, something to be achieved, not a return to a lost paradise.[108] This is the characteristic feature of utopian thought in the perspective from which we are speaking here. But this relationship to historical reality is neither simple nor static. It appears under two aspects which are mutually necessary and make for a complex and dynamic relationship. These two aspects, in Freire's words, are denunciation and annunciation.[109]

Utopia necessarily means a denunciation of the existing order. Its deficiencies are to a large extent the reason for the emergence of a utopia. The repudiation of a dehumanizing situation is an unavoidable aspect of utopia. It is a matter of a complete rejection which attempts to strike at the roots of the evil. This is why utopia is revolutionary and not reformist. As Eric Weil says, "Revolutions erupt when man is discontent with his discontent" (discontent with his reformism?). This denunciation of an intolerable state of affairs is what Marcuse has called—in the context of the affluent societies in which his thought moves—the "Great Refusal."[110] This is the retrospective character of utopia.

But utopia is also an annunciation, an annunciation of what is not yet, but will be; it is the forecast of a different order of things, a new society.[111] It is the field of creative imagination which proposes the alternative values to those rejected.[112] The denunciation is to a large extent made with regard to the annunciation. But the annunciation, in its turn, presupposes this rejection, which clearly delimits it retrospectively. It defines what is not desired. Otherwise, although it might seem to be an advancement, this utopia could be a subtle retrogression. Utopia moves forward; it is a pro-jection into the future, a dynamic and mobilizing factor in history. This is the prospective character of utopia.

According to Freire, between the denunciation and the annunciation is the time for building, the historical *praxis*. Moreover, denunciation and annunciation can be achieved only *in* the praxis. This is what we mean when we talk about a utopia which is the driving force of history and subversive of the existing order. If utopia does not lead to action in the present, it is an evasion of reality. The utopian thesis, writes Ricoeur, is efficacious only "in the measure in which it gradually transforms historical experience," and he asserts, "Utopia is deceiving when it is not concretely related to the possibilities offered to each era."[113] A rejection will be authentic and profound only if it is made within the very act of creating more human living conditions—with the risks that this commitment implies today, particularly for dominated peoples. Utopia must necessarily lead to a commitment to support the emergence of a new social consciousness and new relationships among people. Otherwise, the denunciation will remain at a purely verbal level and the annunciation will be only an illusion. Authentic utopian thought postulates, enriches, and supplies new goals for political action, while at the same time it is verified by this action. Its fruitfulness depends upon this relationship.

In the third place, utopia, as we understand it, belongs to the *rational* order. This viewpoint has been vigorously defended by Blanquart, who notes perceptively that utopia "is not irrational except as it relates to a transcended state of reason (the reason of conservatives), since in reality it takes the place of true reason."[114] Utopias emerge with renewed energy at times of transition and crisis, when science has reached its limits in its explanation of social reality, and when new paths open up for historical praxis.[115] Utopia, so understood, is neither opposed to nor outside of science. On the contrary, it constitutes the essence of its creativity and dynamism. It is the prelude of science, its annunciation. The theoretical construct which allows us to know social reality and which makes political action efficacious demands the mediation of the creative imagination: "The transition from the empirical to the theoretical presupposes a jump, a break: the intervention of the imagination."[116] And Blanquart points out that imagination in politics is called utopia.[117]

This is the difference between utopia and ideology. The term *ideology* has a long and varied history and has been understood

in very different ways.[118] But we can basically agree that
ideology does not offer adequate and scientific knowledge of
reality; rather, it masks it. Ideology does not rise above the
empirical, irrational level.[119] Therefore, it spontaneously fulfills
a function of preservation of the established order. Therefore,
also, ideology tends to dogmatize all that has not succeeded in
separating itself from it or has fallen under its influence. Political action, science, and faith do not escape this danger. Utopia,
however, leads to an authentic and scientific knowledge of reality and to a praxis which transforms what exists.[120] Utopia is
different from science but does not thereby stop being its
dynamic, internal element.[121]

Because of its relationship to reality, its implications for
praxis, and its rational character, utopia is a factor of historical
dynamism and radical transformation. Utopia, indeed, is on the
level of the cultural revolution which attempts to forge a new
kind of man. Freire is right when he says that in today's world
only the oppressed person, only the oppressed class, only the
oppressed peoples can denounce and announce.[122] Only they are
capable of working out revolutionary utopias and not conservative or reformist ideologies. The oppressive system's only future
is to maintain its present of affluence.

The relationship between faith and political action could,
perhaps, be clarified by recalling the comments we have made
above regarding the historical plan designated by the term
utopia. When we discussed the notion of liberation, we said that
we were dealing with a single process; but it is a complex, differentiated unity, which has within itself various levels of meaning which are not to be confused: economic, social, and political
liberation; liberation which leads to the creation of a new man
in a new society of solidarity; and liberation from sin and entrance into communion with God and with all men.[123] The first
corresponds to the level of scientific rationality which supports
real and effective transforming political action; the second
stands at the level of utopia, of historical projections, with the
characteristics we have just considered; the third is on the level
of faith. These different levels are profoundly linked; one does
not occur without the others. On the basis of the clarifications
we have just made, we can perhaps go one step further towards
understanding the bond which unites them. It is not our inten-

tion to reduce to an oversimplified schematization what we have said regarding the complex relationship which exists between the Kingdom and historical events, between eschatology and politics. However, to shed light on the subject from another point of view may be helpful.

To assert that there is a direct, immediate relationship between faith and political action encourages one to seek from faith norms and criteria for particular political options. To be really effective, these options ought to be based on rational analyses of reality. Thus confusions are created which can result in a dangerous politico-religious messianism which does not sufficiently respect either the autonomy of the political arena or that which belongs to an authentic faith, liberated from religious baggage. As Blanquart has pointed out, politico-religious messianism is a backward-looking reaction to a new situation which the messianists are not capable of confronting with the appropriate attitude and means. This is an "infrapolitical movement" which "is not in accord with the Christian faith either."[124]

On the other hand, to assert that faith and political action have nothing to say to each other is to imply that they move on juxtaposed and unrelated planes. If one accepts this assertion, either he will have to engage in verbal gymnastics to show—without succeeding—how faith should express itself in a commitment to a more just society; or the result is that faith comes to coexist, in a most opportunistic manner, with any political option.

Faith and political action will not enter into a correct and fruitful relationship except through the effort to create a new type of person in a different society, that is, except through utopia, to use the term we have attempted to clarify in the preceding paragraphs.[125] This plan provides the basis for the struggle for better living conditions. Political liberation appears as a path toward the utopia of a freer, more human man, the protagonist of his own history.[126] Che Guevara has said: "Socialism currently, in this stage of the construction of socialism and communism, has not as its only purpose to have shining factories; it is intended to help the whole man; man must be transformed as production increases, and we would not be doing our job well if we produced only things and not at the same time men." It follows that for him the important thing for the building up of a new society is simultaneously "a daily increase in both productivity and awareness."[127]

Utopia so understood, far from making the political struggler a dreamer, radicalizes his commitment and helps him keep his work from betraying his purpose—which is to achieve a real encounter among men in the midst of a free society without social inequalities. "Only utopia," comments Ricoeur, "can give economic, social, and political action a human focus."[128] The loss of utopia is responsible for man's falling into bureaucratism and sectarianism, into new structures which oppress men. The process, apart from understandable ups and downs and deficiencies, is not liberating if the plan for a new man in a freer society is not held to and concretized. This plan is not for later, when political liberation will have been attained. It ought to go side by side with the struggle for a more just society at all times. Without this critical and rational element of historical dynamism and creative imagination, science and political action see a changing reality slip out of their hands and easily fall into dogmatism. And political dogmatism is as worthless as religious dogmatism; both represent a step backward towards ideology. But for utopia validly to fulfill this role, it must be verified in social praxis; it must become effective commitment, without intellectual purisms, without inordinate claims; it must be revised and concretized constantly.

The historical plan, the utopia of liberation as the creation of a new social consciousness and as a social appropriation not only of the means of production, but also of the political process, and, definitively, of freedom, is the proper arena for the cultural revolution. That is to say, it is the arena of the permanent creation of a new man in a different society characterized by solidarity. Therefore, that creation is the place of encounter between political liberation and the communion of all men with God. This communion implies liberation from sin, the ultimate root of all injustice, all exploitation, all dissidence among men. Faith proclaims that the brotherhood which is sought through the abolition of the exploitation of man by man is something possible, that efforts to bring it about are not in vain, that God calls us to it and assures us of its complete fulfillment, and that the definitive reality is being built on what is transitory. Faith reveals to us the deep meaning of the history which we fashion with our own hands: it teaches us that every human act which is oriented towards the construction of a more just society has value in terms of communion with God—in terms of salvation; inversely it teaches that all injustice is a breach with him.

In human love there is a depth which man does not suspect: it is through it that man encounters God. If utopia humanizes economic, social, and political liberation, this humanness—in the light of the Gospel—reveals God. If doing justice leads us to a knowledge of God, to find him is in turn a necessary consequence. The mediation of the historical task of the creation of a new man assures that liberation from sin and communion with God in solidarity with all men—manifested in political liberation and enriched by its contributions—does not fall into idealism and evasion. But, at the same time, this mediation prevents these manifestations from becoming translated into any kind of Christian ideology of political action or a politico-religious messianism. Christian hope opens us, in an attitude of spiritual childhood, to the gift of the future promised by God. It keeps us from any confusion of the Kingdom with any one historical stage, from any idolatry toward unavoidably ambiguous human achievement, from any absolutizing of revolution. In this way hope makes us radically free to commit ourselves to social praxis, motivated by a liberating utopia and with the means which the scientific analysis of reality provides for us. And our hope not only frees us for this commitment; it simultaneously demands and judges it.

The Gospel does not provide a utopia for us; this is a human work.[129] The Word is a free gift of the Lord. But the Gospel is not alien to the historical plan; on the contrary, the human plan and the gift of God imply each other. The Word is the foundation and the meaning of all human existence; this foundation is attested to and this meaning is concretized through human actions. For whoever lives by them, faith, charity, and hope are a radical factor in spiritual freedom and historical creativity and initiative.

In this way, the claim that "the victory which has conquered death is our faith" will be lived, inescapably, at the very heart of history, in the midst of a single process of liberation which leads that history to its fulfillment in the definitive encounter with God. To hope in Christ is at the same time to believe in the adventure of history, which opens infinite vistas to the love and action of the Christian.

NOTES

1. See the excellent article of some years ago by Karl Rahner, "Unterwegs zum neuen Menschen," *Wort und Wahrheit* 16 (1961): 807–19, and reproduced as "Christianity and the 'New Man'" in *Theological Investigations,* 5:135–53; and more recently Harvey Cox, *On Not Leaving it to the Snake,* pp. 91–150.

2. Karl Rahner, "La nouvelle terre," *Écrits théologiques* (Bruges: Desclée deBrouwer, 1970), 10:113.

3. See above Chapter 6.

4. "Introduction," no. 4, in *Medellín.*

5. Jürgen Moltmann, "Gott in der Revolution," in *Diskussion zur "Theologie der Revolution,"* pp. 65–68. In English see "God in Revolution," in Moltmann's *Religion, Revolution and the Future,* trans. M. Douglas Meeks (New York: Charles Scribner's Sons, 1969).

6. Regarding this new situation of contemporary man, see Edward Schillebeeckx "The Interpretation of Eschatology," in *The Problem of Eschatology,* ed. Edward Schillebeeckx and Boniface Willems, Concilium 41 (New York: Paulist Press, 1969), pp. 42–56.

7. See the famous article of Léopold Malevez, "Deux théologies catholiques de l'histoire," in *Bijdragen* (1949), pp. 225–40. See also Gustave Thils, *Christian Attitudes* (Dublin: Scepter, 1959).

8. The focus of this tendency was the periodical *Dieu Vivant,* published between 1945 and 1955 and dedicated from its first issue to presenting "an eschatological conception of Christianity." In this regard see the study of Bernard Besret, *Incarnation ou eschatologie, Contribution à l'histoire du vocabulaire religieux contemporain 1935–1955* (Paris: Les Éditions du Cerf, 1964), pp. 122–44. Roger Aubert stated ironically and perceptively on this subject, "Incarnation or eschatology? Immanence or transcendence? Immanence *and* transcendence has been the answer. And this is very correct. But it is easier to change a conjunction and get rid of a question mark than it is to build a balanced system in which all the elements are in their proper places. Theologians today are still busy in the construction of this system, but ... it is easy to see that the quarries are still open" (*La théologie catholique au milieu du XXe siècle* [Tournai-Paris: Casterman, 1954], pp. 69–70). And they still are.

9. See above Chapter 9. See also C. Dumont, "De trois dimensions retrouvées en théologie: eschatologie-orthopraxie-hermeneutique," *Nouvelle Revue Théologique* 92, no. 6 (June–July 1970): 570. One of the first efforts to bring out the relationship between eschatology and political commitment is Georges Didier, "Eschatologie et engagement chrétien," *Nouvelle Revue Théologique,* 75, no. 1 (January 1953): 3–14; the categories used say little to us today, however.

10. See "Sketch of a Phenomenology and a Metaphysic of Hope," in *Homo Viator,* trans. Emma Crauford (New York: Harper and Row, Publishers, Harper Torchbook, 1962), pp. 29–67.

11. "Theses on Feuerbach," nos. 11 and 1, in Karl Marx and Friedrich Engels,

On Religion (New York: Schocken Books, 1964), pp. 72 and 69; italics in the original.

12. With Lukacs and Korsch, Bloch belongs to what some have called "esoteric Marxism," and to what Bloch himself prefers to call "the warm current of Marxism"—concerned with achieving the real through what today is only potential. On the Marxism of Bloch see Werner Maihofer, "Ernst Blochs Evolution des Marxismus, in *Über Ernst Bloch* (Frankfurt: Suhrkamp, 1968), pp. 112–29.

13. *Das Prinzip Hoffnung*, p. 82.

14. See Ernst Bloch, *Philosophische Grundfragen. Zur Ontologie des Noch-Nicht-Seins* (Frankfurt: Suhrkamp, 1961).

15. Quoted in Harvey Cox's prologue to a collection of Bloch's works, *Man on his Own*, trans. E. B. Ashton (New York: Herder and Herder, 1970), p. 9.

16. Bloch is concerned with the relationship between atheism and Christianity; see his last work *Atheismus im Christentum* (Frankfurt: Suhrkamp, 1968). In it he maintains that "only an atheist can be a good Christian and only a Christian can be a good atheist." The second part of this sentence is a reply of Moltmann used by Bloch (see Moltmann's introduction to *Über Ernst Bloch*, p. 28). For him the Bible is a profoundly revolutionary book, for it brings the good news of the limitless possibilities of man. The fundamental affirmation of the Bible is what is said in Genesis, "You will be like gods." This is expressed in historical figures throughout the Old Testament, it is revealed clearly in the key event of the Exodus, and it finds its categorical realization with Christ. Nevertheless, for Bloch all this cannot be understood in its true significance except by an "atheistic interpretation" of the Bible. Therefore "only an atheist can be a good Christian." At the same time, however, Bloch opposes a dogmatic and positivistic atheism and advocates a "nonconformist atheist movement." Thus "only a Christian can be a good atheist." Although his position is fundamentally different from the Bible, it must be said that Bloch offers us a stimulating and perceptive reading of it.

17. "It is difficult to imagine a philosophy other than that of *The Hope Principle* which could be more useful in helping us to renew and elaborate the Christian doctrine of hope" (Jürgen Moltmann, "Die Kategorie Novum in der christlichen Theologie," in *Ernst Bloch zu ehren*, ed. S. Unseld [Frankfurt: Suhrkamp, 1965], p. 243; in English see " 'Behold, I make all things new': The Category of the New in Christian Theology," in *The Future as the Presence of Shared Hope*, ed. Maryellen Muckenhirn [New York: Sheed and Ward, 1968]).

18. "Perhaps Christian theology will one day have to thank Ernst Bloch's philosophy of hope for giving it the courage to recover in the full sense its central category of eschatology. . . . Bloch has taught us about the overwhelming power of the still-open future and of the hope that reaches out to it in anticipation for not only the life and thought of man but in addition for the ontological uniqueness of everything in reality" (Wolfhart Pannenberg, *Basic Questions in Theology*, 2:237–38).

19. *Das Prinzip Hoffnung*, p. 1404.

20. Moltmann, *Theology of Hope*, p. 84.

21. *Ibid.*, p. 16

22. *Ibid.*, pp. 18 and 86.

23. And a "theology of universal history," Pannenberg would add, which seeks to reinterpret Christianity on the basis of history taken in its totality. On the thinking of Pannenberg, see the fine article of Claude Geffré, "La théologie de l'histoire comme problème herméneutique: W. Pannenberg," *Études Théologiques et Religieuses* 46, no. 1 (1971): 13–27; and Ignace Berten, *Histoire, révélation et*

foi, Dialogue avec W. Pannenberg (Brussels: Éditions du CEP, 1969). These authors differ, however, in their way of conceiving the role of the resurrection of Jesus in history. For Pannenberg, "With the resurrection of Jesus, the end of history has already occurred" (*Revelation as History*, p. 142). Moltmann replies that the resurrection of Christ is "the source of the risen life of all believers" and that therefore "believers find their future *in him* and not merely *like* him. Hence they wait for their future by waiting for his future" (*Theology of Hope*, p. 83; see also pp. 76–84).

24. Moltmann, *Theology of Hope*, p. 18.

25. *Ibid.*

26. *Ibid.*, p. 85.

27. *Ibid.*, p. 86.

28. *Theology of Human Hope*, pp. 59–60. See also Hugo Assmann, *Teología de la liberación*, MIEC-JECI, series 1, doc. 23–24, 1970, pp. 37–38.

29. *Theology of Human Hope*, p. 59.

30. *Ibid.*, p. 67.

31. See above Chapter 9.

32. See above Chapter 1.

33. Moltmann is aware of the danger of ignoring the present life (*Theology of Hope*, pp. 26–32), but in the terms in which this concern is expressed it does not seem to transcend the limitations which we have just indicated. His more recent works, however, show an interesting evolution and a fruitful opening to the historical struggle of man today; see the two articles we have already mentioned, "Gott in der Revolution" and "Toward a Political Hermeneutic of the Gospel," as well as "The Christian Theology of Hope and its Bearing on Development," in *In Search of a Theology of Development* (Geneva: SODEPAX, 1970), pp. 93–100. In this last work Moltmann establishes a rich distinction between on the one hand that which becomes, the foreseeable, the calculable, the object of futurology, which he proposes to call *future*, and on the other hand that which comes, the desirable, that which cannot be calculated but only anticipated, which can be designated by the term *avenir* (in German *Zu-kunft*, which translates the Latin *adventus*, the equivalent of *parousia;* pp. 97–98). Cf. similar ideas proposed by Karl Rahner, "Autour du concept de l'avenir," *Écrits théologiques*, 10:95–103.

34. See a collection of reactions to this work, Wolf-Dieter Marsch, ed., *Diskussion über die "Theologie der Hoffnung" von Jürgen Moltmann* (Munich: Chr. Kaiser Verlag, 1967).

35. "Gott in der Revolution," p. 69.

36. See the observations of Pablo Fontaine regarding the questions which revolutionary political commitment poses to the life of faith in *El revolucionario cristiano y la fe*, MIEC-JECI, series 1, doc. 25, 1970.

37. Ludwig Feuerbach, *The Essence of Christianity*, trans. George Eliot (New York: Harper & Row, Publishers, 1957), p. 257.

38. *Ibid.*, pp. 1–12. "If human nature is the highest nature to man, then practically also the highest and first law must be the love of man to man" (*ibid.*, p. 271).

39. *Ibid.*, p. 12.

40. *Ibid.*, pp. 247–69.

41. Feuerbach was not aware of the writings of Hegel's youth. In them love occupies an outstanding position. "Religion," wrote Hegel, "is identical to love" ("Amour et religion" [Fragment of 1798] in *L'Ésprit du christianisme et son destin*

[Paris: J. Vrin, 1967], p. 146). Commenting on this and other similar fragments, Paul Asveld concludes, "Through love man rises to the level of the Absolute. In Hegel's Frankfurt writings love corresponds to the intellectual intuition of Schelling" (*La pensée religieuse du jeune Hegel* [Louvain: Publications Universitaires de Louvain, 1953], pp. 166–67). In the works of his maturity love does not seem to play the same role as in the texts of his youth (See A. Chapelle, *Hegel et la religion*, 2:62–64). Hegel speaks nevertheless of love as "the substantial bond of the world" in his *Leçons sur la philosophie de la religion*, trans. J. Gibelin (Paris: J. Vrin, 1954), part 3, p. 216; in English see *Lectures on the Philosophy of Religion*, 3 vols., trans. E. B. Speirs and J. Burdon Sanderson (New York: Humanities Press Inc., 1962).

42. See Feuerbach, *Manifestes philosophiques, textes choisis (1839–1845)* (Paris: Presses Universitaires de France, 1960), p. 200. The final lines of *The Essence of Christianity* are well known: "It needs only that the ordinary course of things be interrupted in order to vindicate to common things an uncommon significance, *to life, as such, a religious import*. Therefore let bread be sacred for us, let wine be sacred, and also let water be sacred! Amen" (p. 278; italics in the original). J. P. Osier is thus correct when he asserts that "Feuerbach is not irreligious but atheistic" (Preface to *L'essence du christianisme* [Paris: Maspero, 1968], p. 65). See the excellent study by Marcel Xhaufflaire, *Feuerbach et la théologie de la sécularisation* (Paris: Les Éditions du Cerf, 1970).

43. See Karl Marx, "Circular contra Kriege (1846)" in Karl Marx and Friedrich Engels, *Marx-Engles Werke, Ergänzungsband, Schriften Bis 1944* (Berlin, 1968). 4:12–16. H. Kriege was a "sentimental communist," an emigrant to the United States, a friend of W. Weitling, and one of the heads of "true socialism." Regarding this current see the harsh words dedicated to it in "The Communist Manifesto" (*Capital, The Communist Manifesto and other Writings* [New York: The Modern Library, 1932], pp. 349–51). When he criticizes this tendency Marx is in reality criticizing Feuerbach: " 'True socialism' with its different ramifications appears as the most authentic creation of Feuerbachian thought" (Henri Arvon, *Ludwig Feuerbach ou la trasformation du sacré*[Paris: Presses Universitaires de France, 1957], p. 114; see also Xhaufflaire, *Feuerbach*, pp. 189–211).

44. "German Ideology," in *Writings of the Young Karl Marx on Philosophy and Society*, trans. and ed. Loyd D. Easton and Kurt H. Guddat (Garden City, New York: Doubleday and Co., 1967), p. 419. As Xhaufflaire correctly points out, the restoration of the "new religion" is according to Feuerbach the "praxis" which will transform the world; for him it is necessary "to change mentalities before restructuring the world" (*Feuerbach*, p. 209).

45. See Thomas J. J. Altizer and William Hamilton, *Radical Theology and the Death of God* (Indianapolis: Bobbs Merrill, 1966). See also Thomas W. Ogletree, *The Death of God Controversy* (Nashville: Abingdon, 1966). Thus it is that the so-called "Theology of the death of God"—which some mistakenly believe to be the inevitable final phase of the process of secularization—has certain characteristics which we might dare to call "pre-Marxist."

46. The most important work of Johannes B. Metz on this subject is the address given at the International Congress of Theology at Toronto, August 20–24, 1967, "The Church and the World in the Light of a 'Political Theology.' " It is included in Metz's *Theology of the World*, pp. 107–140.

47. Metz speaks of political theology as "eschatological theology" ("Politische Theologie in der Diskussion," in Helmut Peukert, ed., *Diskussion zur "politische*

Theologie" [Mainz, Munich: Grunewald-Kaiser, 1969], p. 280; see also *Theology of the World*, p. 91).

48. "The Church's Social Function in the Light of a 'Political Theology,'" *Faith and the World of Politics*, ed. Johannes B. Metz, Concilium 36 (New York: Paulist Press, 1968), p. 9.

49. Claude Geffré has pointed this out very well, putting political theology in the context of fundamental theology in "Recent Developments in Fundamental Theology: An Interpretation," *The Development of Fundamental Theology*, ed. Johannes B. Metz, Concilium 46 (New York: Paulist Press, 1969), pp. 5–28.

50. *Theology of the World*, p. 107.

51. "Politische Theologie," pp. 268–79.

52. For Metz the process initiated with the Enlightenment is of capital importance for theological reflection; see the work done with Moltmann and Willi Oelmüller and recently published, *Kirche im Prozess der Aufklärung, Aspekte einer neuen "politischen Theologie"* (Munich: Kaiser, 1970).

53. "Politische Theologie," p. 270.

54. Marcel Xhaufflaire, "Les grandes lignes de la théologie politique selon J. B. Metz," in *La Lettre*, no. 150 (February 1971), p. 26. According to the author of this fine presentation of Metz's thought, the distinction to which we refer "allows political theology to be articulated in the political sphere, understood henceforth not as the sphere of the establishment of sovereignty, powers, or domination, but rather as the democratic 'public' place of the mediation of liberty or the liberation of men (the general welfare of society, not the particular welfare of the Church)."

55. "Politische Theologie," p. 271; italics in the original.

56. *Ibid.*, p. 268. For the sociological aspects of their analyses, Metz and some of his disciples often take their inspiration from the works of Jürgen Habermas. See his *Strukturwandel der Oeffentlichkeit* (Neuwied: Luchterhand, 1962) and *Technik und Wissenschaft als "Ideologie"* (Frankfurt: Suhrkamp, 1969).

57. Metz, *Theology of the World*, p. 108.

58. *Ibid.*, p. 109. Schleiermacher had already reacted in this way to the problems posed by the Enlightenment when he insisted that sentiment was the characteristic trait of religion (cf. Karl Barth, *Protestant Thought: From Rousseau to Ritschl* [New York: Harper & Brothers, Publishers, 1959], pp. 306–54). But at the opposite extreme is Hegel, who accepted the questions posed by the Enlightenment and sought to understand the relationship between revelation and reason on the basis of history.

59. Metz, *Theology of the World*, p. 110. The opposition to Bultmann is translated clearly into the neologism which expresses this first task of political theology. Metz is indeed very critical of the "existential interpretation of the New Testament," which is based on the philosophy of Heidegger and seems to Metz to imply a serious and dangerous individualism. Not unrelated to this critique is the influence of the social and historical thought of Bloch. Indeed it is his work *Das Prinzip Hoffnung* which is suggestively presented by Harvey Cox (for whom in the secular era politics ought to replace metaphysics as the language of theology; see *The Secular City*, p. 255) as the most serious alternative to the "Being and Time" of Heidegger for theological thinking ("Afterword" of *The Secular City Debate*, (ed. Daniel J. Callahan [New York: Macmillan, 1966], p. 200). Bloch himself criticizes Bultmann for having stripped the faith of any social weight (*Atheismus im Christentum*, pp. 69–72). On this theological level we have a situation which

is familiar to us in contemporary philosophy and can be illustrative. Marxism and existentialism have been engaged for some years in a harsh debate regarding the values of freedom and personal decision and the social and historical decisions of human existence (See Garaudy, *Perspectives de l'homme* and the letter from Sartre to Garaudy included in this work; Sartre has attempted a synthesis in *Critique de la raison dialectique* [Paris: Éditions Gallimard, 1960]). If we go a little deeper we discover the antagonistic thinking of Kierkegaard and Marx. Both are at least partially reacting to the Hegelian system which in one way or another is still a point of reference for contemporary thought. Perhaps therefore we should go upstream toward the source, that is to Hegel, to better situate the debate between political theology and "privatizing" theology.

60. "Politische Theologie," p. 272.

61. Metz, *Theology of the World*, p. 111.

62. "The so-called fundamental hermeneutic problem of theology is not the problem of how systematic theology stands in relation to historical theology, how dogma stands in relation to history, but what is the relation between theory and practice, between understanding the faith and social practice" (*Theology of the World*, p. 112).

63. *Ibid.*, p. 114.

64. "Politische Theologie," p. 289.

65. *Theology of the World*, p. 114. The expression *eschatological proviso (réserve eschatologique)* had already been used in a sense similar to Metz's by Heinrich Schlier, *Le temps de l'Église* (Tournai: Casterman, 1961), pp. 19–20.

66. Metz, *Theology of the World*, p. 116; the italics are ours.

67. *Ibid.*

68. *Ibid.*, p. 120.

69. Robert Spaemann believes that the political action of Christians has no need of a theological benediction; see "Theologie, Prophetie, Politik. Zur Kritik der politischen Theologie," *Wort und Wahrheit* 24 (1969): 491.

70. See Karl Lehmann, "Die 'politische Theologie': Theologische Legitimation und gegenwärtige Aporie," in *Diskussion zur "politische Theologie,"* pp. 185–216.

71. See Henri de Lavalette, "La théologie politique allemande," *Recherches de Science Religieuse* 58, no. 3 (July–September 1970): 321–50. Throughout this article the author is quite ambiguous concerning the ideas of Metz.

72. See Hans Maier, "Politische Theologie? Einwände eines Laien," in *Diskussion zur "politische Theologie,"* pp. 1–25. The author affirms the possibility—for lay people—of autonomous political and apostolic activity. But to defend his ideas Maier engages in a rearguard battle, still necessary it seems in some cases and situations, but on which the future of the Church does not depend today: the confrontation between the laity and the hierarchy. This issue has been transcended among Christians occupied with less intraecclesial problems.

73. Karl Rahner believes that "the concept of a 'political theology' is still not established in an absolutely clear manner," and he states, "I am not completely sure that I myself understand what is meant by it." And he goes on to say that he is in accord with a political theology understood as "the simple explicit valorization of the social implications of all the theological enunciations" ("L'avenir de la théologie," *Nouvelle Revue Théologique* 93, no. 1 [January 1971]:24). As we have seen Metz's effort goes beyond this. But Rahner is correct when he says that further clarification is still necessary.

74. See Trutz Rendtorf, "Politische Ethik oder 'politische Theologie'?," in *Dis-*

kussion zur "politische Theologie," pp. 217–30. Metz accepts this criticism and distinguishes between his effort and political ethics: "Political theology, as eschatological theology, is able to determine its orientation to praxis in an indirect manner mediated through the path of a political ethic" ("Politische Theologie," p. 280). Hugo Assmann challenges him for having adopted this distinction: *Teología de la liberación,* pp. 39–40; and "Teología política," in *Perspectivas para el Diálogo,* no. 50 (December 1970), p. 307.

75. Marcel Xhaufflaire and Frans van den Oudenrijn, "Bulletin informatif," in *Les deux visages de la théologie de la sécularisation,* pp. 74-75.

76. K. Levêque, "De la théologie politique à la théologie de la révolution," *Frères du Monde,* no. 46 (1970), p. 34.

77. This experience is fruitful for theological reflection; see Juan Luis Segundo, "Desarrollo y subdesarrollo: polos teológicos," pp. 76–80.

78. In this regard see the studies included in *Les deux visages.*

79. See above Chapter 6.

80. Another thing which must be avoided is that the new political theology contribute to an evasion of real and effective commitment to the historical present. A certain theoretical recovery at the level of language of the problems of the world today as well as the abstention which the term *eschatological proviso (Vorbehalt)* seems to imply—against the manifest intention of the author—are both an invitation to this.

81. *Théologie de la révolution* (Paris: Éditions Universitaires, 1970), p. 236.

82. See Robert Eisler, *The Messiah Jesus and John the Baptist* (New York: The Dial Press, 1931), which makes Jesus a Zealot. S. G. F. Brandon, *The Fall of Jerusalem and the Christian Church* (London: S. P. C. K., 1951), does not go to this extreme but does strongly emphasize Jesus' ties with the Zealot movement. Oscar Cullmann perceptively and carefully analyzes the matter in *The State in the New Testament* (London: SCM Press Ltd, 1957). Because of contemporary concerns regarding the political sphere this matter has been taken up again with a new vigor; see Martin Hengel, *Die Zeloten* (Leiden:E. J. Brill, 1961), and Samuel Georg Frederick Brandon, *Jesus and the Zealots* (Manchester: Manchester University Press, 1967); this author believes that the Gospels—especially Mark—have a tendency to depoliticize the life of Jesus. See also the recent work of Oscar Cullmann, *Jesus and the Revolutionaries,* trans. Gareth Putnam (New York: Harper & Row, 1970); of Martin Hengel, *War Jesus revolutionär?* (Stuttgart: Calwer Verlag, 1970); and of Georges Crespy, "Recherche sur la signification politique de la mort du Christ," *Lumière et Vie* 20, no. 101 (January–March 1971): 89–109.

83. *State,* p. 17. See the demonstration of this assertion, pp. 14–17. See also Crespy, "Recherche," pp. 100–01, and Brandon, *Jesus and the Zealots,* pp. 203–05.

84. This act of Jesus is considered as a Zealot gesture by Étienne Trocmé, "L'expulsion des marchands du Temple," in *New Testament Studies* 15, no. 1 (October 1968): 1 ff., cited by Cullmann, *Jesus and the Revolutionaries,* p. 18, no. 5.

85. Regarding these concurrences, see Cullmann, *Jesus and the Revolutionaries,* pp. 8–10. This author believes that Jesus rejected anything which might give a triumphal and political character to his entrance into Jerusalem; thus he rides on an ass and not a horse "in the manner of a warlike Messiah" (p. 43). But Crespy, following W. Vischer, *Die evangelische Gemeinde Ordnung-Mattheus 16, 13–20, 28* (Zurich: Evangelische Verlag, 1946) points out that if to understand its meaning Mark 11:10 is translated from the Greek to the Hebrew the text could be, "Save us! Blessed is he who comes in the name of the Lord. Blessed is the

kingdom that comes, the kingdom of David, our Father. Save us from the Roman!" With this correction, writes Crespy, the text would be coherent: "The kingdom of the Son of David comes through victory over the pagan occupier. On the other hand, the relationship of the forms explains the translation 'in the highest,' and the softening of the text is based on an identifiable grammatical fact." The cry of the people would then be a seditious, *Zealot* act; this would help explain the fear and the reprobation of the priests and scribes according to Matt. 21:16: "Do you hear what they are saying?" (pp. 101–02).

86. The Jewish historian Josephus presents the movement created by Jesus as a Zealot movement; see Cullman, *State*, p. 49.

87. "In relation to this plan," writes Comblin, "it is clear that the Zealot is essentially conservative. What did the Zealots want? To assure Israel complete political independence, to isolate the Jews from the others in a most complete fashion, to achieve an extreme Judaism, an extreme isolationism.... To follow the Zealots was to adopt a regression into the past" (*Théologie de la révolution*, pp. 240–41).

88. See Matt. 4:1–11. In this regard Cullmann correctly points out that "one is tempted only by the things which stand near him" (*State*, p. 24). Regarding the meaning of the temptations of Jesus, see Duquoc, *Christologie*,pp. 52–71. "Jesus rejects a political messianism. But he confronts the political power; he takes a stand in relation to it; and his message has inevitable political implications" (Augustin George, "Jésus devant le problème politique," *Lumière et Vie* 20, no. 105 [November–December 1971]:5).

89. See Pierre Benoit, *The Passion and Resurrection of Jesus Christ*, trans. Benet Weatherhead (New York: Herder and Herder, 1969), pp. 176–77; and Lucien Cerfaux, *Jésus aux origins de la tradition* (Paris: Desclée, deBrouwer, 1968), p. 199.

90. *State*, p. 43; see also p. 12; and *Jesus and the Revolutionaries*, p. 31; as well as Crespy, p. 99.

91. *State*, pp. 47–48, Heinrich Schlier speaks of Barabbas as "a Messianic revolutionary" (*The Relevance of the New Testament* [New York: Herder and Herder, 1968], p. 221). Paul Blanquart, in an exegesis which is unique to him, believes that "by entering the prison which he enabled the *guerrilla* Barabbas to leave, Jesus, in the same action, entered into his death and resurrection . . . and liberated politics—in the person of Barabbas. . . . He enabled it to be itself, by entrusting it to the reason and love of men" ("L'acte de croire et l'action politique," *Lumière et Vie* 19, no. 98 [June–July 1970]: 26).

92. Regarding the "trial of Jesus" see Josef Blinzer, *The Trial of Jesus*, trans. Isabel and Florence McHugh, (Westminster, Md.: The Newman Press, 1959); X. Léon-Dufour, *Supplément au Dictionnaire de la Bible*, s. v. "Passion" cols. 1419–92; Benoit, *Passion and Resurrection;* and the fine treatment of the state of this question of Wolfgang Trilling, *Jésus devant l'histoire*, trans. Joseph Schmitt (Paris: Les Éditions du Cerf, 1968), pp. 175–88. See also S. G. F. Brandon's most recent study, *The Trial of Jesus*, 2nd ed. (London: Paladin, 1971), which claims for Jesus a place of honor in the long history of martyrs of Israel (p. 14). See the interesting observations of Augustin George, "Comment Jésus a-t-il perçu sa propre mort?" *Lumière et Vie* 20, no. 101 (January–March 1971): 34–59. This article also includes a copious bibliography on this theme.

93. "Recherche," p. 105.

94. Schlier, *Relevance*, p. 215. This is also Bultmann's position in his interpreta-

tion of the Gospel of John. A good number of authors undertake to demonstrate that Jesus was innocent of the charges that were imputed to him (See Blinzer, Léon-Dufour, Benoit). It is not clear what the object of these attempts is. Innocent before what justice? Before the justice of the power groups of the Jewish people and the Roman oppressors, Jesus was guilty precisely because he challenged their legitimacy, in the name not of some partisan option, but of a message of love, peace, freedom, and justice. This message undermined the very bases of religious formalism, unjust privileges, and social injustice which supported the order of the power groups of the Jewish people and the Roman authority.

95. *Jesus and the Revolutionaries*, pp. 20 and 51.

96. *Ibid.*, p. 13; italics in the original.

97. *Ibid.*, p. 55. Cullmann qualifies these somewhat abrupt conclusions with considerations on the need for the Christian to commit himself to the world of today. But the basic thrust of this commitment is given by what we have just recalled. For example, he had said, "We could extend Jesus' line of thought and show that the social question would actually be solved already in this age if every individual would become as radically converted as Jesus demands" (p. 28). This makes us fear that there has been no real understanding of the political sphere. This certainly influences his interpretation of the attitude of Jesus in this regard.

98. See Werner Georg Kümmel, *Promise and Fulfillment: The Eschatological Message of Jesus* (London: SCM Press Ltd, 1961). Contrary to Albert Schweitzer, Cullmann believes that Jesus foresaw a time between his death and the parousia, a time which he had calculated, nevertheless, at the most in decades. See his work *Christ and Time*, rev. ed., trans. Floyd V. Filson (Philadelphia: The Westminster Press, 1964), pp. 148–50.

99. Bultmann also affirms the belief of Jesus in a proximate arrival of the end of time, but he thinks that this is secondary. The important thing would be the present personal decision for the Kingdom. The "difficult" texts are Matt. 10:23 and Mark 9:1 and 13:30. Rudolf Schnackenburg concludes a study of these texts by affirming: "We have arrived at the following position. A broad stream of tradition testifies that Jesus announced the coming of God's reign, and correspondingly of the Son of Man, for a near future but without further specification of the time, indeed with an explicit refusal to provide more precise details. Against this, only a few passages contain a definite time reference, to the generation then alive. It was not possible to explain these passages. It would seem that the early Church was uncertain how to fit these awkward pieces neatly into the eschatological discourse of Jesus. This attitude of the Church may well point to the best method for ourselves: namely, to nourish a living eschatological hope from the urgent prophetic preaching of Jesus without drawing false conclusions about that prophecy from individual passages" (*God's Rule and Kingdom*, p. 212). See also Trilling, *Jésus devant l'histoire*, pp. 143–66.

100. See Anton Grabner-Haider, "Zur Kultkritik im Neuen Testament," *Diakonia* 4 (1969): 138–46.

101. See above Chapter 10.

102. "In my opinion," writes Crespy, "it is too early to speak of the political meaning of the life and death of Jesus without equivocation" ("Recherche," p. 89). In reality it will always be too soon—and too late. Indeed for some time now a political meaning has been given to the life and death of Jesus; the problem cannot be avoided by speaking of the matter in the name of his alleged apoliticism. Exegetes are not always aware of the political presuppositions of their interpretation of Scripture. Notwithstanding his initial assertion, however, Crespy proposes

an interesting reflection on the political meaning of the testimony of Jesus.

103. Wolfhart Pannenberg, "Die politische Dimension des Evangeliums," in *Die Politik und das Heil* (Mainz: Matthias-Grünewald, 1968), p. 19.

104. See above Chapter 9. See also the observations of Jacques Guillet in "Jésus et la politique," *Recherches de Sciences Religieuses* 59, no. 4 (October–December 1971): 544.

105. Gustav Landauer was perhaps the first to consider—although in a perspective which suffered from a certain romanticism—the notion of utopia in our time. Landauer distinguishes between "topia"—stabilizing and even reactionary, "a broad, general conglomeration of common life in a state of relative stability"—and "utopia"—revolutionary, "a conglomeration of aspirations and tendencies of the will," which overturns the "topia," the previous order. See his work *Die Revolution* (Frankfurt: Rütten and Loening, 1907); the quoted texts are taken from the Spanish translation, *La revolución* (Buenos Aires: Proyección, 1961), p. 27. See also the classic work of one of the creators of the sociology of knowledge: Karl Mannheim, *Ideology and Utopia*, trans. Louis Wirth and Edward Shils (New York: Harcourt, Brace, and World, 1966); this work was first published in 1929. Regarding the notion of utopia, its impreciseness, its theoretical difficulties, and the present state of the question, see the texts gathered and presented by Arnhelm Neüssus in *Utopia* (Barcelona: Barral, 1971); this work also contains a copious bibliography on the subject. Orlando Fals Borda has attempted to interpret Colombian history from the perspective of utopian thought: *Subversion and Social Change in Colombia*, trans. Jacqueline D. Skils (New York: Columbia University Press, 1969). Paul VI has recently recognized the role that utopia plays in "the political problem of modern societies" (*Octogesima adveniens*, no. 37).

106. See Jean Servier, *Histoire de l'Utopie* (Paris: Éditions Gallimard, 1967).

107. Referring to the misunderstandings regarding this notion of utopia and the new conditions created in our time, Herbert Marcuse writes, "I believe that this restrictive conception must be revised, and that the revision is suggested, and even necessitated, by the actual evolution of contemporary societies. The dynamic of their productivity deprives 'utopia' of its traditional unreal content: what is denounced as 'utopian' is no longer that which has 'no place' and cannot have any place in the historical universe, but rather that which is blocked from coming about by the power of the established societies" (*An Essay on Liberation*, pp. 3–4).

108. Regarding the work of Thomas More see Concilium General Secretariat, "Utopia," *The Problem of Eschatology*, Concilium 41, pp. 149–65, which also includes a copious bibliography on the subject.

109. "Education as Cultural Action: An Introduction," in Louis M. Colonnese, ed., *Conscientization for Liberation* (Washington, D.C.: Division For Latin America, United States Catholic Conference), p. 119.

110. *Essay*, p. ix; regarding Marcuse see above Chapter 2.

111. See the works we have already cited by Ernst Bloch as well as an earlier one, *Geist der Utopie* (Frankfurt: Suhrkamp, 1964); this was first published in 1917. On this aspect of Bloch's work see P. Furter, "Utopia e marxismo segundo Ernst Bloch," in *Tempo Brasileiro*, October 3, 1965.

112. Thus José Carlos Mariátegui proposes with a certain amount of irony "to classify men no more as revolutionary and conservative but rather as imaginative and without imagination" (*El alma matinal*, 2nd ed. [Lima: Empresa Editora Amauta, 1959], p. 39).

113. Paul Ricoeur, "Tâches de l'éducateur politique," in *Ésprit* 33, no. 340 (July–August 1965): 91.

114. Paul Blanquart, "A propos des rapports science-ideologie et foi-marxisme," in *Lettre*, nos. 144–45 (August–September 1970), p. 36.

115. "Utopia is present, though in a hidden way, in scientific production itself whose dynamism it constitutes; it does not appear under normal circumstances but rather in periods of crisis, between two moments of science: the one worn out, insufficient, and the other yet to be made, more satisfactory. Thus in the same movement it is the expression of the inadequacy of the existing theoretical instrument and the crucible of the new reason" (*ibid.*).

116. *Ibid.*, p. 35.

117. *Ibid.*

118. See Hans Barth, *Wahrheit und Ideologie* (Zurich: Manesse Verlag, 1945); and Mannheim, *Ideology and Utopia*.

119. Louis Althusser has pointed this out very clearly; see his *For Marx* and *Reading Capital*, coauthored with Etienne Balibar, trans. Ben Brewster (New York: Pantheon Books, 1971). Althusser has recently taken up this theme again, trying to elucidate the relationships between ideology and the category of subject; see "Ideologie et appareils ideologiques d'Etat," in *La pensée*, no. 151 (June 1970), pp. 3–38.

120. Mannheim's distinction between utopia and ideology is well-known. Utopian are those "orientations transcending reality ... which, when they pass over into conduct, tend to shatter, either partially or wholly, the order of things prevailing at the time" (*Ideology and Utopia*, p. 173). On the other hand, those ideas are ideological which are appropriated for determined stages of existence "as long as they [are] 'organically' and harmoniously integrated into the worldview characteristic of the period (i.e. [do] not offer revolutionary possibilities)" (*ibid.*, p. 174). This does not mean that ideology cannot place the existing order into a relationship with ideals which are not found within it; but what is characteristic of ideology is that it does so in such a way that these ideals do not provoke real transformations in the established order. For a critique of Mannheim's thought see Franz Hinkelammert, *Ideologías del desarrollo y dialéctica de la historia* (Buenos Aires: Editorial Paidos, 1970), pp. 85–89.

121. As Blanquart points out, this distinction between utopia and ideology is not found in Althusser ("Science-ideologie et foi-marxisme," p. 36 and "Acte de croire," p. 20). For Althusser there is only ideology and science; the "epistemological rupture" between the works of Marx's youth and his maturity, which Althusser justifiably points out, are seen as the precondition for the transition from ideology to science. Althusser has vigorously and correctly indicated that what is proper to Marx is to have created a science of history. It is a question of a healthy reaction, thanks to an effort of true mental hygiene, against any interpretation of Marx's thought which is ideologizing and claims to be "humanistic." But the rigidity of this position and the consignment of every utopian element to ideology prevents seeing the profound unity of the work of Marx and consequently duly understanding his capacity for inspiring a radical and permanent revolutionary praxis. Ernest Mandel has shown the evolution, and therefore the continuity, of the notion of alienation in Marx (*The Formation of the Economic Thought of Karl Marx*, pp. 154–86); Althusser considers this notion pre-Marxist. Blanquart proposes the concept of appropriation (a notion taken from Henri Lefebvre, who presents it as the appropriation of nature and of his own nature by social man in *Marx: Sa vie, son oeuvre* [Paris: Presses Universitaires de France, 1964], p. 71), the negation of alienation, to signify the utopia that runs throughout Marx's work (Blanquart, "Acte de croire," p. 20).

122. See "Tercer Mundo y teología, in *Perspectivas para el Diálogo,* no. 50 (December 1970), pp. 304–05.

123. See above Chapter 2.

124. "Acte de croire," p. 25. The theologies of revolution and violence do not escape this danger. If at a given moment they presented a certain attraction it was because they were a useful attempt to break with the conception of a faith spontaneously linked to the established order (see the presentation of this theme in M. Peuchmaurd, "Esquisse pour une théologie de la révolution," *Parole et Mission* 10, no. 39 [October 1967]: 629–62 and the works already cited of Richard Shaull). But these approaches easily tended to belittle the theological and political questions involved. They also ran the risk—notwithstanding the intention of their initiators—of "baptizing" and in the long run impeding the revolution and counter-violence, because they furnished an *ad hoc* Christian ideology and ignored the level of political analysis at which these options are in the first instance being exercised. Here we are far from the theology of revolution. Our attempt at theological reflection moves within another frame of reference.

125. "The evangelical message," writes Schillebeeckx, "gives us no direct program of social and political action, but, on the other hand, is socially and politically relevant in an indirect way, namely, in a 'utopian' sense" ("The Magisterium and the World of Politics," Concilium 36, p. 32). See also "Dio e 'colui che verrà,' Per una nuova immagine di Dio nel mondo secolarizzato," in *Processo alla religione,* p. 155. Blanquart, who has worked out precisely the notion of utopia, is more categorical: "In this space of utopia, faith and political action enter into relationship: it is the point of contact, the place of (paschal) Passover and of Covenant" ("La foi et les exigences politiques," in *Croissance des jeunes nations,* June 1969, p. 25; see also "Acte de croire," p. 29).

126. See above Chapter 6.

127. Connected with this perspective is the role which Che Guevara gives in economic activity to moral stimulus: "sense of duty, the new revolutionary consciousness," as opposed to material stimulus, "the residue of the past," which "comes from capitalism" and "will have no part in the new society."

128. "Tâches de l'éducateur," p. 90. Today this approach, according to Ricoeur, is twofold: "on the one hand, to affirm humanity as a totality; on the other, to affirm the person as a singularity"; the first aspect is "the horizon of all our debates regarding inequality in the world"; the second aspect is important "regarding the anonymity and dehumanization of relationships among individuals in the midst of industrial society" (*ibid.,* pp. 90–91). In a similar vein, Blanquart believes that utopia, "constitutive of reason in our times," can be expressed in the formula "the integral and complete development of every man and of the whole man" ("Acte de croire," p. 22). This specifies the utopian notion of appropriation, the basis of "the only action which is really revolutionary; in the face of a single and diversified system, it can be only total and multiform; that is to say, it is at the same time universal (against exploitation—inequalities, injustice, segregations) and integral or multidimensional (against dehumanization)" (*ibid.,* p. 21).

129. This is clearly affirmed by Blanquart in the articles cited. The vocabulary is less resolute in Schillebeeckx; see the works mentioned in note 125.

THE CHRISTIAN COMMUNITY AND THE NEW SOCIETY

We have already attempted to see the relationship between faith, love, and hope on the one hand and the preoccupations of contemporary man on the other. What we have said concerning the meaning of the Gospel message lays the groundwork for an understanding of the meaning and mission of the Church in the world. The Church as a visible community is often being challenged in our times. Going beyond the achievements, the transformations, and the hopes of a postconciliar reformism, many Christians are asking themselves how they can be Church today. In this a determining role is played by the awareness of the comprehensiveness of the political sphere. The implications of the Gospel in this area have been perceived, as well as the role the Church has played up to now in relation to the existing social order. The roots of this approach thus go beyond the borders of the institutional Church; they are to be found in contemporary man's task of building a new society. All this has an effect on the mission of the Church and leads to a deepening of what it means to belong to the Church.[1] The problem cannot be permanently resolved by the expediency of making a distinction between institution and community. The existence of a necessary and fruitful tension between these two is one thing; it is quite another to have a situation of the moral failure of an institution which seems to be on the verge of bankruptcy.

A radical revision of what the Church has been and what it now is has become necessary. The initial impulse for this has

perhaps already been given by the Council—especially for the
great majority of Christians. But now the movement has a
dynamism all its own and to a certain extent autonomous. For
there have converged in this movement other currents which
the Council seemed to have assimilated and channeled; but
these currents did not lose their energy and are now seen in
their full light. The attempt at *aggiornamento* of the Church
has provided better conditions for entering into fruitful contact
with these forces, but it has not suppressed the challenges that
they bring with them. Rather it has strengthened and deepened
them. So much the better. Not only do we gain nothing by trying
to avoid them, but we lose much by not facing them straight
on. To confront these challenges, moreover, is nothing more
than a posture of humility before the facts.

The issue has caused alarm and concern.[2] For many there
has even been a kind of evaporation of any meaning of the
Church. And there are those who believe that this is the
Church's inevitable destiny.[3] At the same time, however, we are
witnessing both a rediscovery of the communitarian dimension
of the faith as well as new ways of living it. The search—at
times painful or wavering—has begun.[4] There is more than one
indication that "that community called Church"—to use the
expression of Juan Luis Segundo—has a persistent life. But this
will be so only if there is a substantial transformation. If this
does not happen with the hoped for rhythm and authenticity
it is not only because of bad or insufficient will, as some would
have it. Also, and perhaps more than anything, it is because
the path to be followed is not clearly discerned and because
there is not a complete understanding of the historical and
social factors which are obstacles to this transformation. What
the Church needs today goes beyond authoritarian or desperate
attitudes, beyond mutual accusations, and beyond personal disputes, all of which are only an expression of an inviable situation
and an attitude of personal insecurity; what it needs is a
courageous and serene analysis of the reasons for these situations and attitudes. This courage and serenity will be the
opposite of a facile emotionalism which leads to arbitrary
measures, superficial solutions, or evasions, but avoids the
search for radical changes and untrodden paths. At stake in
all this is the Church's faithfulness to its Lord.

The task is beyond us in this work and with our possibilities.

This is what always happens: it is easier to point out what must be done than to do it. Two points, however, might help us to situate these questions. The first has to do with certain aspects of the very meaning of the Church and its mission in the world; the second with a primordial and inescapable condition for fulfilling that mission.

NOTES

1. Paul Blanquart correctly points out that "the problem underlying this crisis of the Church is the problem of politics and its relationship to the faith. We should not be surprised: if politics is a new problem for humanity, why should it not be for the Church?" ("L'acte de croire," p. 29).

2. We refer to only one of the studies representative of this concern: Henri de Lubac, "L'Église dans la crise actuelle," Nouvelle Revue Théologique 91, no. 6 (June–July 1969): 580–96.

3. "It seems to me," said Althusser in a "diagnosis" of the Church, "that the crisis in the Church is going to become worse. On the one hand, the decadence of theological thought is manifest and irremediable. It is not the 'theologies of revolution' or the 'theologies of violence' that can restore a genuine theological thinking which is now moribund. On the other hand, the political and ideological crisis is evident. With its structures inherited from a long past having a political role at the service of the ruling classes and the whole tradition resulting from this, one cannot see how the Church can 'reconvert' to the service of the workers in the class struggle" (Lumière et Vie 18, no. 93 [May–June 1969]: 29; italics in the original).

4. As regards Latin America, see above Chapter 7. For other aspects of this process, see Cecilio de Lora, José Marins, and Segundo Galilea, Comunidades cristianas de base (Bogota: Indo-American Press Service, 1970), and Edgard Beltrán, Pastoral de conjunto y comunidades de base (Bogota: Indo-American Press Service, 1971); for an excellent theological reflection see Eduardo Pironio, La Iglesia que nace entre nosotros (Bogota: Indo-American Press Service, 1970).

CHAPTER TWELVE

THE CHURCH:
SACRAMENT OF HISTORY

Because the Church has inherited its structures and its life style from the past, it finds itself today somewhat out of step with the history which confronts it. But what is called for is not simply a renewal and adaptation of pastoral methods. It is rather a question of a new ecclesial consciousness and a redefinition of the task of the Church in a world in which it is not only *present*, but of which it *forms a part* more than it suspected in the past. In this new consciousness and redefinition, intraecclesial problems take a second place.

UNIVERSAL SACRAMENT OF SALVATION

The unqualified affirmation of the universal will of salvation has radically changed the way of conceiving the mission of the Church in the world. It seems clear today that the purpose of the Church is not to save in the sense of "guaranteeing heaven."[1] The work of salvation is a reality which occurs in history. This work gives to the historical becoming of mankind its profound unity and its deepest meaning.[2] It is only by starting from this unity and meaning that we can establish the distinctions and clarifications which can lead us to a new understanding of the mission of the Church. The Lord is the Sower who arises at dawn to sow the field of historical reality before we establish our distinctions. Distinctions can be useful for what Liégé calls "the new initiatives of God in the history of men,"

255

but as he himself says, "Too great a use of them, however, threatens to destroy the sense of a vocation to a single fulfillment toward which God has not ceased to lead the world, whose source he is."[3] The meaning and the fruitfulness of the ecclesial task will be clear only when they are situated within the context of the plan of salvation. In doing this we must avoid reducing the salvific work to the action of the Church. All our ecclesiology will depend on the kind of relationship that we establish between the two.

A New Ecclesiological Perspective

The perspective we have indicated presupposes an "uncentering" of the Church, for the Church must cease considering itself as the exclusive place of salvation and orient itself towards a new and radical service of people. It also presupposes a new awareness that the action of Christ and his Spirit is the true hinge of the plan of salvation.

Indeed, the Church of the *first centuries* lived spontaneously in this way. Its minority status in society and the consequent pressure that the proximity of the non-Christian world exercised on it made it quite sensitive to the action of Christ beyond its frontiers,[4] that is, to the totality of his redemptive work. This explains why, for example, the great Christian authors of that time affirmed without qualification the liberty of man in religious matters as a natural and human right and declared that the state is incompetent to intervene in this area. Because they had confidence in the possibility of salvation at work in every man, they saw liberty not so much as a risk of wandering from the path as the necessary condition for finding the path and arriving at a genuine encounter with the Lord.[5]

The situation of the Christian community changed in *the fourth century*. Instead of being marginated and attacked, Christianity was now tolerated (Edict of Milan, 313 A.D.) and quickly became the religion of the Roman state (Decree of Thessalonica, 381 A.D.). The proclamation of the Gospel message was then protected by the support of political authority, and the Christianization of the world of that time received a powerful impulse. This rapid advance of Christianity brought about a change in the manner of conceiving the relationship of mankind to salvation. It began to be thought that there were only two kinds of people: those who have accepted faith in Christ and those who have culpably rejected it. The Fathers continued to teach the doctrine of the universal will of salvation and held that this could not occur without the free acceptance on the part of man. But they asserted that there was no longer any excuse for ignorance of the Savior, for thanks to the ministry of the Church, the voice of the Gospel had come in one way or another to all men.[6] Neither Jews nor gentiles had any excuse. These ideas, which were presented with hesitation and even anguish in the fourth and fifth centuries, gradually gained ground. By the Middle Ages, when the Church was coextensive with the known world of that time and deeply pervaded it, Christians had the vital experience of security and tranquillity that "outside the Church there is no salvation." *To be for or against Christ came to be fully identified with being for or against the Church.* Therefore it is not strange that there was no longer any mention of bits of truth which could be found beyond the frontiers of the Church; there was no longer any world outside the Church. The Church was regarded as the sole repository of religious truth. In a spontaneous and inevitable fashion there arose an ecclesiocentric perspective which centered more and more on the life and reflection of the Church—and continues to do so even up to the present time.

From that time on, therefore, there was a subtle displacement of religious liberty as "a human and natural right" of all men by "the liberty of the act of faith"; henceforth, the right of liberty in religious matters would be synonymous with the right not to be coerced by the forced imposition of the Christian faith.[7] In a parallel fashion there occured another important displacement: no longer was it a question of the "incompetence" of political power in religious matters; rather it was a question of the state's "tolerance"—which presupposed an "option" for the truth—toward religious error. The reason for these two displacements is the same: the position of strength of a Church which had begun to focus on itself, to ally itself with civil power, and to consider itself as the exclusive repository of salvific truth.

This condition of the Church began to change in the *modern period*, with the internal rupture of Christendom and the discovery of new peoples. But at the beginning of this period the ecclesiocentric perspective persisted, with a few exceptions. In the matter of religious liberty, which we have focused on here, it was the period of "religious tolerance": what Thomas Aquinas considered valid for the Jews was extended to the descendents of Christians who had "culpably" separated themselves from the Church. In the nineteenth century religious toleration gave rise to the by-product of the theory of the thesis and the hypothesis; this theory sought to respond to the ideas born in the French Revolution by giving a new impulse to the development of toleration. But fundamentally the condition continued being the same: salvific truth could be found only in the Church. It is for this reason that "modern freedoms" endangered the eternal destiny of man.[8]

The effects of the new historical situation in which the Church found itself began to be felt more strongly in the nineteenth century and even more so in recent decades. Vatican II did not hesitate to place itself in the line of a full affirmation of the universal will of salvation and to put an end to the anachronistic theological and pastoral consequences deduced from the ecclesiocentrism which we have already mentioned.[9] This explains the change of attitude regarding religious liberty. The declaration dedicated to this subject tried to achieve a consensus by placing itself simply on the level of the dignity of the human person. But this position implies a change of position with regard to deep theological questions having to do with the role of the Church in the encounter between God and man.[10]

We might speak here of a return to the posture of the Church in the first centuries.[11] Without being inexact, however, this affirmation tends to schematize the process. There is never a pure and simple regression. The process which began in the fourth century was not simply an "accident." It was a long and laborious learning experience. And that experience forms part of the contemporary ecclesial consciousness; it is a factor which explains many phenomena today. It also cautions us against what might happen again. What was spontaneously and intuitively expressed in the first centuries must manifest itself today in a more reflective and critical fashion.

Sacrament and Sign

Thanks to the process which we have just reviewed, Vatican II was able to set forth the outlines of a new ecclesiological perspective. And it did this almost surprisingly by speaking of the Church as a sacrament.[12] This is undoubtedly one of the most important and permanent contributions of the Council.[13] The notion of sacrament enables us to think of the Church within the horizon of the salvific work and in terms radically different from those of the ecclesiocentric emphasis. The Council itself did not place itself totally in this line of thinking. Many of the texts still reveal the burden of a heavy heritage; they timidly point to a way out from this turning in of the Church on itself, without always accomplishing this. But what must be emphasized is that in the midst of the Council itself, over which hovered an ecclesiocentric perspective, new elements arose which allowed for a reflection which broke with this perspective and was more in accord with the real challenges to the Christian faith of today.[14]

In theology the term *sacramentum* has two closely related meanings. Initially it was used to translate the Greek work *misterion*. According to Paul, *mystery* means *the fulfillment and the manifestation of the salvific plan*: "the secret hidden for long ages and through many generations, but now disclosed" (Col. 1:26). The Gospel is, therefore, "that divine secret kept in silence for long ages but now disclosed ... made known to all nations, to bring them to faith and obedience" (Rom. 16:25–26).[15] This mystery is the love of the Father, who "loved the world so much that he gave his only Son" (John 3:16) in order to call all men, in the Spirit, to communion with him. Men are called together, as a community and not as separate individuals, to participate in the life of the Trinitarian community, to enter into the circuit of love that unites the persons of the Trinity.[16] This is a love which "builds up human society in history."[17] The fulfillment and the manifestation of the will of the Father occur in a privileged fashion in Christ, who is called therefore the "mystery of God" (Col. 2:22; see also Col. 1:27; 4:3; Eph. 3:3; 1 Tim. 3:16).[18] For the same reason Sacred Scripture, the Church, and the liturgical rites were designated by the first Christian generations by the term *mystery*, and by its Latin translation, *sacrament*. In the sacrament the salvific plan is fulfilled and revealed; that is, it is made present among men and for men. But at the same time, it is through the sacrament that men encounter God. This is an encounter *in* history, not because God comes *from* history, but because history comes from God. The sacrament is thus the efficacious revelation of the call to communion with God and to the unity of all mankind.

This is the primordial meaning of the term *sacrament* and

it is in this way that it is used in the first centuries of the Church. At the beginning of the third century, however, Tertullian introduced a nuance which gradually gave rise to a second meaning derived from the first. This African Father began to use the term *sacrament* to designate the rites of Baptism and the Eucharist. Gradually the two terms, *mystery* and *sacrament*, became distinct. The first referred more to the doctrinal mysteries; the second designated what we commonly call sacraments today. The theology of the Middle Ages recovered the meaning of sacrament, in the strict sense, in the formula *efficacious sign of grace*. The sign marks the character of visibility of the sacrament, by means of which there occurs an effective personal encounter of God and man. But the sign transmits a reality from beyond itself, in this case the grace of communion, which is the reason for and the result of this encounter.[19] This communion is also an intrahistorical reality.

To call the Church the "visible sacrament of this saving unity" (*Lumen gentium*, no. 9) is to define it in relation to the plan of salvation, whose fulfillment in history the Church reveals and signifies to men. A visible sign, the Church imparts to reality "union with God" and "the unity of all mankind" (*Lumen gentium*, no. 1). The Church can be understood only in relation to the reality which it announces to men. Its existence is not "for itself," but rather "for others." Its center is outside itself; it is in the work of Christ and his Spirit. It is constituted by the Spirit as "the universal sacrament of salvation" (*Lumen gentium*, no. 48); outside of the action of the Spirit which leads the universe and history towards its fullness in Christ, the Church is nothing. Even more, the Church does not authentically attain consciousness of itself except in the perception of this total presence of Christ and his Spirit in humanity. The mediation of the consciousness of the "other"—of the world in which this presence occurs—is the indispensable precondition of its own consciousness as community-sign. Any attempt to avoid this mediation can only lead the Church to a false perception of itself—to an ecclesiocentric consciousness.

Through the people who explicitly accept his Word, the Lord reveals the world to itself. He rescues it from anonymity and enables it to know the ultimate meaning of its historical future and the value of every human act.[20] But by the same token the Church must turn to the world, in which Christ and his

Spirit are present and active; the Church must allow itself to be inhabited and evangelized by the world. It has been said for this reason that a theology of the Church in the world should be complemented by "a theology of the world in the Church."[21] This dialectical relationship is implied in the emphasis on the Church as sacrament. This puts us on the track of a new way of conceiving the relationship between the historical Church and the world. The Church is not a non-world; it is humanity itself attentive to the Word. It is the People of God which lives in history and is orientated toward the future promised by the Lord. It is, as Teilhard de Chardin said, the "reflectively Chris-tified portion of the world." The Church-world relationship thus should be seen not in spacial terms, but rather in dynamic and temporal ones.[22]

As a sacramental community, the Church should signify in its own internal structure the salvation whose fulfillment it announces. Its organization ought to serve this task. As a sign of the liberation of man and history, the Church itself in its concrete existence ought to be a place of liberation. A sign should be clear and understandable. If we conceive of the Church as a sacrament of the salvation of the world, then it has all the more obligation to manifest in its visible structures the message that it bears. Since the Church is not an end in itself, it finds its meaning in its capacity to signify the reality in function of which it exists. Outside of this reality the Church is nothing; because of it the Church is always provisional; and it is towards the fulfillment of this reality that the Church is oriented: this reality is the Kingdom of God which has already begun in history.[23] The break with an unjust social order and the search for new ecclesial structures—in which the most dynamic sectors of the Christian community are engaged—have their basis in this ecclesiological perspective. We are moving towards forms of presence and structure of the Church the radi-cal newness of which can barely be discerned on the basis of our present experience. This trend, at its best and healthiest, is not a fad; nor is it due to professional nonconformists. Rather it has its roots in a profound fidelity to the Church as sacrament of the unity and salvation of mankind and in the conviction that its only support should be the Word which liberates.

We must recognize, nevertheless, that the ecclesiocentric point of view is abandoned more rapidly in the realm of a certain theological reflection than in the concrete attitudes of the majority of the Christian community. This presents not a few difficulties, for what is most important is what happens at this second level. To dedicate oneself to intraecclesial problems—as is often done in certain forms of protest in the Church, especially in the developed countries—is to miss the point regarding a true renewal of the Church. For this renewal cannot be achieved in any deep sense except on the basis of an effective awareness of the world and a real commitment to it. The changes in the Church will be made on the basis of such awareness and commitment. To seek anxiously after the changes themselves is to pose the question in terms of survival. But this is not the question. The point is not to survive, but to serve. The rest will be given.

In Latin America the world in which the Christian community must live and celebrate its eschatological hope is the world of social revolution; the Church's task must be defined in relation to this. Its fidelity to the Gospel leaves it no alternative: the Church must be the visible sign of the presence of the Lord within the aspiration for liberation and the struggle for a more human and just society. Only in this way will the message of love which the Church bears be made credible and efficacious.

EUCHARIST AND HUMAN BROTHERHOOD

The place of the mission of the Church is where the celebration of the Lord's supper and the creation of human brotherhood are indissolubly joined. This is what it means in an active and concrete way to be the sacrament of the salvation of the world.

"In Memory of Me"

The first task of the Church is to celebrate with joy the gift of the salvific action of God in humanity, accomplished through the death and resurrection of Christ. This is the Eucharist: a memorial and a thanksgiving. It is a memorial of Christ which presupposes an ever-renewed acceptance of the meaning of his life—a total giving to others. It is a thanksgiving for the love of God which is revealed in these events. The Eucharist is a feast, a celebration of the joy that the Church desires and seeks to share. The Eucharist is done within the Church, and simultaneously the Church is built up by the Eucharist. In the Church "we celebrate," writes Schillebeeckx, "that which is achieved outside the Church edifice, in human history."[24] This work, which creates a profound human brotherhood, gives the Church its reason for being.

In the Eucharist we celebrate the cross and the resurrection of Christ, his Passover from death to life, and our passing from sin to grace. In the Gospel the Last Supper is presented against the background of the Jewish Passover, which celebrated the liberation from Egypt and the Sinai Covenant.[25] The Christian Passover takes on and reveals the full meaning of the Jewish Passover.[26] Liberation from sin is at the very root of political liberation. The former reveals what is really involved in the latter. But on the other hand, communion with God and others presupposes the abolition of all injustice and exploitation. This is expressed by the very fact that the Eucharist was instituted during a meal. For the Jews a meal in common was a sign of brotherhood. It united the diners in a kind of sacred pact. Moreover, the bread and the wine are signs of brotherhood which at the same time suggest the gift of creation. The objects used in the Eucharist themselves recall that brotherhood is rooted in God's will to give the goods of this earth to all people so that they might build a more human world.[27] The Gospel of John, which does not contain the story of the Eucharistic institution, reinforces this idea, for it substitutes the episode of the washing of the feet—a gesture of service, love, and brotherhood. This substitution is significant: John seems to see in this episode the profound meaning of the Eucharistic celebration, the institution of which he does not relate.[28] Thus the Eucharist appears inseparably united to creation and to the building up of a real human brotherhood. "The reference to community," writes Tillard, "does not therefore represent a simple consequence, an accidental dimension, a second level of a rite that is in the first place and above all individual—as the simple act of eating is. From the beginning it is seen in the human context of the meal as it was conceived in Israel. The Eucharistic rite in its essential elements is communitarian and orientated toward the constitution of human brotherhood."[29]

A text in Matthew is very clear regarding the relationship between worship and human brotherhood: "If, when you are bringing your gift to the altar, you suddenly remember that your brother has a grievance against you, leave your gift where

it is before the altar. First go and make your peace with your
brother, and only then come back and offer your gift" (Matt.
5:23–24).[30] This is not a question of a scrupulous conscience, but
rather of living according to the demands placed on us by the
other: "If ... you suddenly remember that your brother has
a grievance against you." To be the cause of a fracture of
brotherhood disqualifies one from participation in that worship
which celebrates the action of the Lord which establishes a profound community among men. "The Christian community," said
Camilo Torres, "cannot offer the sacrifice in an authentic form
if it has not first fulfilled in an effective manner the precept
of 'love of thy neighbor.'"[31] The separation of sacrifice from the
love of neighbor is the reason for the harsh criticism which
Jesus—speaking from a strong prophetic tradition—addressed
to all purely external worship. For if "our relationship of service
to our neighbor in the world (a relationship profoundly expressed in prayer and the liturgy) were in fact absent, then in
this case the prayer and the whole liturgy, as well as our speaking of God ... would fall into a vacuum and degenerate into a
false and useless superstructure."[32] This is how Paul understood
it. Before recounting the institution of the Eucharist he
indicated the necessary precondition for participation in it when
he reproached the Corinthians for their lack of fraternal charity
in their gatherings to celebrate the Lord's Supper (1 Cor.
11:17–34; cf. James 2:1–4).

The profound unity among the different meanings of the term
koinonia in the New Testament both expresses and summarizes
these ideas. Congar has pointed out that *koinonia* simultaneously designates three realities.[33] First it signifies the common
ownership of the goods necessary for earthly existence: "Never
forget to show kindness and to share what you have with others,
for such are the sacrifices which God approves" (Heb. 13:16; cf.
Acts 2:44; 4:32). *Koinonia* is a concrete gesture of fraternal charity. Thus Paul uses this word to designate the collection
organized on behalf of the Christians in Jerusalem; the
Corinthians glorify God because of their "liberal contribution
to their need and to the general good" (2 Cor. 9:13; cf. 2 Cor.
8:3–4; Rom. 15:26–27). Second, *koinonia* designates the union of
the faithful with Christ through the Eucharist: "When we bless
'the cup of blessing,' is it not a means of sharing in the blood
of Christ? When we break the bread, is it not a means of sharing

in the body of Christ?" (1 Cor. 10:16). And third, *koinonia* means
the union of Christians with the Father—"If we claim to be sharing in his life while we walk in the dark, our words and our
lives are a lie" (1 John 1:6; cf. 1:3)—, with the Son—"It is God
himself who calls you to share in the life of his Son" (1 Cor.
1:9; cf. 1 John 1:3)—, and with the Spirit—"The grace of the
Lord Jesus Christ, and the love of God, and fellowship in the
Holy Spirit, be with you all" (2 Cor. 13:14; cf. Phil. 2:1).

The basis for brotherhood is full communion with the persons
of the Trinity. The bond which unites God and man is celebrated—that is, effectively recalled and proclaimed—in the
Eucharist. Without a real commitment against exploitation and
alienation and for a society of solidarity and justice, the
Eucharistic celebration is an empty action, lacking any genuine
endorsement by those who participate in it. This is something
that many Latin American Christians are feeling more and
more deeply, and they are thus more demanding both with
themselves and with the whole Church.[34] "To make a remembrance" of Christ is more than the performance of an act of
worship; it is to accept living under the sign of the cross and
in the hope of the resurrection. It is to accept the meaning of
a life that was given over to death—at the hands of the powerful
of this world—for love of others.

Denunciation and Annunciation

The primary task of the Church, as we have said, is to celebrate with joy the salvific action of the Lord in history. In the
creation of brotherhood implied and signified by this celebration, the Church—taken as a whole—plays a role which is
unique, but varies according to historical circumstances.

In Latin America to be Church today means to take a clear
position regarding both the present state of social injustice and
the revolutionary process which is attempting to abolish that
injustice and build a more human order. The first step is to
recognize that in reality a stand has already been taken: the
Church is tied to the prevailing social system. In many places
the Church contributes to creating "a Christian order" and to
giving a kind of sacred character to a situation which is not
only alienating but is the worst kind of violence—a situation
which pits the powerful against the weak. The protection which

the Church receives from the social class which is the beneficiary and the defender of the prevailing capitalist society in Latin America has made the institutional Church into a part of the system and the Christian message into a part of the dominant ideology.[35] Any claim to noninvolvement in politics—a banner recently acquired by conservative sectors—is nothing but a subterfuge to keep things as they are.[36] The mission of the Church cannot be defined in the abstract. Its historical and social coordinates, its here and now, have a bearing not only on the adequacy of its pastoral methods. They also should be at the very heart of theological reflection.

The Church—with variations according to different countries—has an obvious social influence in Latin America.[37] Without overestimating it, we must recognize that numerous facts have demonstrated this influence, even up to the present day. This influence has contributed, and continues to contribute, to supporting the established order. But this is no longer the entire picture. The situation has begun to change. The change is slow and still very fragile, but in this change are involved growing and active minorities of the Latin American Christian community. The process is not irreversible, but it is gradually gaining strength. It is still afflicted with many ambiguities, but the initial experiences are beginning to provide the criteria by which these ambiguities can be resolved. Within these groups—as might have been expected—there has arisen a question; on its answer will depend to a large degree the concrete path to be followed. The question is should the change consist in the Church's using its social influence to effect the necessary transformations? Some fear a kind of "Constantinianism of the Left," and believe that the Church should divest itself of every vestige of political power.[38] This fear is opportune because it points out a genuine risk which we must keep in mind. But we believe that the best way to achieve this divestment of power is precisely by resolutely casting our lot with the oppressed and the exploited in the struggle for a more just society. The groups that control economic and political power will not forgive the Church for this. They will withdraw their support, which is the principal source of the ambiguous social prestige which the Church enjoys in Latin America today. Indeed, this has already begun. Moveover, formulated in this way the question is somewhat artifical. How can the Church preach the Word, incarnated where the pulse of Latin American history throbs, without putting this social influence at stake? How can it perform a disappearing act with the situation which—with all its ambiguities—is the Church's own? How can it denounce the unjust order of the continent and announce the Gospel outside of the concrete position which it has today in Latin American society? Indeed, it is not a question of whether the Church should or should not use its influence in the Latin American revolutionary process. Rather, the question is in what direction and for what purpose is it going to use its influence: for or against the established order, to preserve the social prestige which comes with its ties to the groups in power or to free itself from that prestige with a break from these groups and with genuine service to the oppressed?[39] It is a question of social realism, of becoming aware of an already given situation, to start from it, and to modify it; it is not a question of creating that situation. The situation is already there and is the concrete, historical framework for the task of the Latin American Church.

Within this framework the Latin American Church must make the prophetic *denunciation* of every dehumanizing situation, which is contrary to brotherhood, justice, and liberty. At the same time it must criticize every sacralization of oppressive structures to which the Church itself might have contributed. Its denunciation must be public, for its position in Latin American society is public. This denunciation may be one of the few voices—and at times the only one—which can be raised in the midst of a country submitted to repression. In this critical and creative confrontation of its faith with historical realities—a task whose roots must be in the hope in the future promised by God—the Church must go to the very causes of the situation and not be content with pointing out and attending to certain of its consequences. Indeed, one of the most subtle dangers threatening a "renewed" Church in Latin America is to allow itself to be assimilated into a society which seeks certain reforms without a comprehensive critique. It is the danger of becoming functional to the system all over again, only this time to a system which tries to modernize and to suppress the most outrageous injustices without effecting any deep changes.[40] In Latin America this denunciation must represent a radical critique of the present order, which means that the Church must also criticize itself as an integral part of this order. This horizon will allow the Church to break out of its narrow enclosure of intraecclesial problems by placing these problems in their true context—the total society and the broad perspective of commitment in a world of revolutionary turmoil.

It has been pointed out, and rightly so, that this critical function of the Church runs the risk of remaining on a purely verbal and external level and that it should be backed up with clear actions and commitments. Prophetic denunciation can be made validly and truly only from within the heart of the struggle for a more human world. The truth of the Gospel, it has been said, is a truth which must be done. This observation is correct and necessary. This presupposes, we should recall, that given the concrete conditions in which the Church finds itself in Latin American society, a precise and opportune denunciation on the part of the Church is not only a "word" or a "text"; it is an action, a stand. Because of its very social influence, its words —if they are clear and incisive—will not be hollow. When the Church speaks, it can cause the old underpinnings of the established order to fall, and it can mobilize new energies. This is so much the case that simply because of their "speaking" or "making statements," certain organisms of the Church and many Christians have undergone severe attacks and serious difficulties at the hands of the representatives of the established order—including the loss of liberty and even the loss of life. It is not at all our purpose to overestimate the word and so to diminish the value of concrete actions; but simply to be realistic we should remember that at times the word is also an important gesture of commitment. In this regard, the critical function of the Church in Latin America—given its historical and social coordinates—has preconditions for its exercise and possibilities for action in relation to the process of liberation which are not found elsewhere. Therefore, its responsibility is all the greater.

The denunciation, however, is achieved by confronting a given situation with the reality which is *announced*: the love of the Father which calls all men in Christ and through the action of the Spirit to union among themselves and communion with him. To announce the Gospel is to proclaim that the love of God is present in the historical becoming of mankind. It is to make known that there is no human act which cannot in the last instance be defined in relation to Christ. To preach the Good News is for the Church to be a sacrament of history, to fulfill its role as community—a sign of the convocation of all men by

God. It is to announce the coming of the Kingdom. The Gospel message reveals, without any evasions, what is at the root of social injustice: the rupture of the brotherhood which is based on our sonship before the Father; the Gospel reveals the fundamental alienation which lies below every other human alienation. In this way, evangelization is a powerful factor in personalization.[41] Because of it men become aware of the profound meaning of their historical existence and live an active and creative hope in the fulfillment of the brotherhood that they seek with all their strength.

Moreover, the personalization stimulated by the annunciation of the Gospel can take on—in cases like Latin America—very particular and demanding forms. If a situation of injustice and exploitation is incompatible with the coming of the Kingdom, the Word which announces this coming ought normally to point out this incompatibility. This means that the people who hear this message and live in these conditions by the mere fact of hearing it should perceive themselves as oppressed and feel impelled to seek their own liberation. Very concretely, they should "feel their hunger" and become aware that this hunger is due to a situation which the Gospel repudiates. The annunciation of the Gospel thus has a conscienticizing function, or in other words, a politicizing function. But this is made real and meaningful only by living and announcing the Gospel from within a commitment to liberation, only in concrete, effective solidarity with people and exploited social classes. Only by participating in their struggles can we understand the implications of the Gospel message and make it have an impact on history. The preaching of the Word will be empty and ahistorical if it tries to avoid this dimension.[42] It will not be the message of the God who liberates, of "Him who restores," as José María Arguedas says.

Some years ago, a pope who is beyond any suspicion of "horizontalism," Pius XII, then Cardinal Pacelli, said that the Church civilizes by evangelizing. And this assertion was accepted without opposition. In the contemporary Latin American context it would be necessary to say that the Church should politicize by evangelizing. Will this expression receive the same acceptance? Probably not. To many it will seem offensive; they will perhaps accuse it of "humanizing" the Gospel message or of falling into a deceitful and dangerous "temporalism." This reaction can be explained in part by the fact that there are still many who—lacking a realistic and contemporary conception of the political sphere—do not wish to see the Gospel "brought down" to a level which they believe is nothing more than partisan conflict. But the more severe attacks will doubtless come from those who fear the upsurge of a true political consciousness in the Latin American masses and can discern what the contribution of the Gospel to this process might be. When it was a question of "civilizing," they had no objection because this term was translated as the promotion of ethical, cultural, and artistic values and at the most as a very general and uncommitted defense of the dignity of the human person. But "to politicize," "to conscienticize"—these terms have today in Latin America a deeply subversive meaning. Can we say that the struggle against the "institutionalized violence" endured by the weak and the struggle for social justice are therefore less human, less ethical, less "civilizing" than the promotion of moral, cultural, and asthetic values which are bound to a given social system? Girardi is correct when he says that "institutionalized violence generally goes along with institutionalized hypocrisy."[43]

When we affirm that the Church politicizes by evangelizing, we do not claim that the Gospel is thus reduced to creating a political consciousness in men or that the revelation of the Father—which takes on, transforms, and fulfills in an unsuspected way every human aspiration—is thereby nullified. We mean that the annunciation of the Gospel, precisely insofar as it is a message of total love, has an inescapable political dimension, because it is addressed to people who live within a fabric of social relationships, which, in our case, keep them in a subhuman condition. But did those who think in this way believe that Pius XII was reducing the Gospel to a civilizing work? If they did not believe it before, why do they think so now? Let us speak openly: to "civilize" does not seem to challenge their privileged situation in *this* world; to conscienticize, to politicize, to make the oppressed person become aware that he is a man—do challenge that privilege.

This conscienticizing dimension of the preaching of the Gospel, which rejects any aseptic presentation of the message, should lead to a profound revision of the pastoral activity of the Church. Thus this activity should be addressed effectively and primarily to those who are oppressed in the oppressed nations and not—as is presently the case—to the beneficiaries of a system designed for their own benefit. Or still better, the oppressed themselves should be the agents of their own pastoral activity. The marginated and the dispossessed still do not have their own voice in the Church of him who came to the world especially for them.[44] The issue is not accidental. Their real presence in the Church would work a profound transformation in its structures, its values, and its actions. The owners of the goods of this world would no longer be the "owners" of the Gospel.

It would be naive, nevertheless, to claim that the revolutionary exigencies in Latin America do not bring with them the danger of oversimplifying the Gospel message and making it a "revolutionary ideology"—which would definitively obscure reality. But we believe that the danger is not averted simply by noting its presence. It is not evaporated by a climate of alarm. It is necessary to look at it face to face and lucidly to analyze its causes as well as the factors which make it important for the Christians committed to the social struggle. Are we not in this position because we have tried to hide the real political implications of the Gospel? Those who—without stating so—neutralized these implications or oriented them for their own benefit are those who now have the least authority for giving lessons in evangelical "purity." We cannot expect the true and opportune counsel today to come from those who are "verticalists" in theory and "horizontalists" in practice. The problem exists, but the solution can come only from the very roots of the problem. It is where the annunciation of the Gospel seems to border on submersion into the purely historical realm that there must be born the reflection, the spirituality, and the new preaching of a Christian message which is incarnated—not lost—in our here and now.[45] To evangelize, Chenu has said, is to incarnate the Gospel in time. This time today is dark and difficult only for those who ultimately do not know how or hesitate to believe that the Lord is present in it.

The concrete measures for effecting the denunciation and the annunciation will be discerned little by little. It will be necessary to study carefully in a *permanent* fashion the signs of the times (*Gaudium et spes*, no. 4), responding to specific situations without claiming to adopt at every step positions valid for all eternity. There are moments in which we will advance only by trial and error.[46] It is difficult to establish ahead of time—as we have perhaps tried to do for a long time—the specific guidelines which ought to determine the behavior of the Church, taken as a whole, in these questions. The Church should rise to the demands of the moment with whatever lights it has at that moment and with the will to be faithful to the Gospel. Some chapters of theology can be written only afterwards.

But the incertitude and apprenticeship involved in this task should not lead us to disregard the urgency and necessity of taking stands nor to forget what is permanent—that the Gospel annunciation opens human history to the future promised by God and reveals his present work. On the one hand, this annunciation will indicate that in every achievement of brotherhood and justice among men there is a step toward total communion. By the same token, it will indicate the incomplete and provisional character of any and every human achievement. The Gospel will fulfill this function based on a comprehensive vision of man and history and not on partial focuses, which have their own proper and effective instruments of criticism. The prophetic character of the Christian message "always works from an eschatological option and affirmation. According to it, history—as long as it has not achieved its eschatological end—will not achieve its total maturity. Therefore every historical period always has new possibilities before it."[47] On the other hand, by affirming that brotherhood among men is possible and that it will indeed be achieved, the annunciation of the Gospel will inspire and radicalize the commitment of the Christian in history. In history and only in history is the gift of the love of God believed, loved, and hoped for.[48] Every attempt to evade the struggle against alienation and the violence of the powerful and for a more just and more human world is the greatest infidelity to God. To know him is to work for justice. There is no other path to reach him.

Christian Brotherhood and Class Struggle

Human brotherhood, which has as its ultimate basis our sonship before God, is built in history. Today history is characterized by conflict which seems to impede this building of brotherhood. There is one characteristic in particular which holds a central place: the division of humanity into oppressors and oppressed, into owners of the means of production and those dispossessed of the fruit of their work, into antagonistic social classes. But this is not all; the division brings with it confrontations, struggles, violence. How then are we to live evangelical charity in the midst of this situation? How can we reconcile the universality of charity with the option for a particular social class? Unity is one of the notes of the Church and yet the class struggle divides men; is the unity of the Church compatible with class struggle?

These questions are being posed to the Christian conscience with a growing insistence. On them depend very concretely the meaning of the presence of the Church in the world, a central theme of the Council. In the case of Latin America this means a presence in a world in revolutionary turmoil and in which violence takes on the most varied forms, from the most subtle to the most open.

The Council broke open a new path on which there is no turning back: openness to the world. In the conciliar texts this world appears above all in its positive and irenic aspects, but gradually the Church became more clearly aware of the conflicts and confrontations involved in it. The Church began to realize that this service to the world, into which it had thrown itself so joyfully, confronted it with demands and challenges beyond what it had foreseen. The class struggle is one of the cardinal problems of the world today which challenge the life and reflection of the Christian community and which can no longer be avoided.

It is undeniable that the class struggle poses problems to the universality of Christian love and the unity of the Church. But any consideration of this subject must start from two elemental points: the class struggle is a fact, and neutrality in this matter is impossible.

The class struggle is a part of our economic, social, political, cultural, and religious reality. Its evolution, its exact extent, its nuances, and its variations are the object of analysis of the social sciences and pertain to the field of scientific rationality.[49]

Recognition of the existence of the class struggle does not depend on our religious or ethical options. There are those who have claimed that it is something artificial, foreign to the norms which guide our society, contrary to the spirit of "Western Christian civilization," and the work of agitators and malcontents.

Perhaps in spite of those who think this way, there is one thing that is true in this viewpoint: oppression and exploitation, and therefore the experience of the class struggle, are endured and perceived first of all by those who have been marginated by that civilization and do not have their own voice in the Church. Although there is an awareness of the class struggle on the periphery, this does not mean that the struggle does not exist at the center of society: the dispossessed exist because of those who direct and govern this society. The class struggle is the product of demented minds only for those who do not know, or who do not wish to know, what is produced by the system. As the French bishops stated some years ago, "The class struggle is first of all a fact which no one can deny." And they continue, "At the level of those responsible for the class struggle, the first are those who voluntarily keep the working class in an unjust situation, who oppose their collective advancement, and combat their efforts to liberate themselves."[50]

Those who speak of class struggle do not "advocate" it—as some would say—in the sense of creating it out of nothing by an act of (bad) will. What they do is to recognize a fact and contribute to an awareness of that fact. And there is nothing more certain than a fact. To ignore it is to deceive and to be deceived and moreover to deprive oneself of the necessary means of truly and radically eliminating this condition—that is, by moving towards a classless society. Paradoxically, what the groups in power call "advocating" class struggle is really an expression of a will to abolish its causes,[51] to abolish them, not cover them over, to eliminate the appropriation by a few of the wealth created by the work of the many and not to make lyrical calls to social harmony. It is a will to build a socialist society, more just, free, and human, and not a society of superficial and false reconciliation and equality. To "advocate" class struggle, therefore, is to reject a situation in which there are oppressed and oppressors. But it is a rejection without deceit or cowardliness; it is to recognize that the fact exists and that it profoundly divides men, in order to be able to attack it at its roots and thus create the conditions of an authentic human community. To build a just society today necessarily implies the active and conscious participation in the class struggle that is occurring before our eyes.

In the second place, we must see clearly that to deny the fact of class struggle is really to put oneself on the side of the dominant sectors. Neutrality is impossible. It is not a question of admitting or denying a fact which confronts us; rather it is a question of which side we are on. The so-called "interclassist doctrine," writes Girardi in a well-known article on this question, "is in fact very classist: it reflects the point of view of the dominant class."[52] When the Church rejects the class struggle, it is objectively operating as a part of the prevailing system. By denying the existence of social division, this system seeks to perpetuate this division on which are based the privileges of its beneficiaries. It is a classist option, deceitfully camouflaged by a purported equality before the law. The history of this refusal is long,[53] and its causes many and complex.[54] But the ever more acute awareness that the oppressed have of their situation and the increasing participation of Christians in the class struggle are raising new questions in the Church which are more authentic and real.

The class struggle is a fact and neutrality in this question is not possible. These two observations delimit the indicated problems, prevent us from getting lost in facile solutions, and provide a concrete context for our search. More exactly, the questions raised with regard to the universal character of love and the unity of the Church are real questions precisely because the class struggle confronts us as a fact and because it is impossible not to take part in it.

The Gospel announces the love of God for all people and calls us to love as he loves. But to accept class struggle means to decide for some people and against others. To live both realities without juxtapositions is a great challenge for the Christian committed to the totality of the process of liberation. This is a challenge that leads him to deepen his faith and to mature in his love for others.

The universality of Christian love is only an abstraction unless it becomes concrete history, process, conflict; it is arrived at only through particularity. To love all men does not mean avoiding confrontations; it does not mean preserving a fictitious harmony. Universal love is that which in solidarity with the oppressed seeks also to liberate the oppressors from their own power, from their ambition, and from their selfishness: "Love for those who live in a condition of objective sin demands that we struggle to liberate them from it. The liberation of the poor

and the liberation of the rich are achieved simultaneously."[55]
One loves the oppressors by liberating them from their inhuman
condition as oppressors, by liberating them from themselves.
But this cannot be achieved except by resolutely opting for the
oppressed, that is, by combatting the oppressive class.[56] It must
be a real and effective combat, not hate. This is the challenge,
as new as the Gospel: to love our enemies. This was never
thought to be easy, but as long as it was only a question of
showing a certain sweetness of character, it was preached without difficulty. The counsel was not followed, but it was heard
without any uneasiness. In the context of class struggle today,
to love one's enemies presupposes recognizing and accepting
that one has class enemies and that it is necessary to combat
them. It is not a question of having no enemies, but rather of
not excluding them from our love. But love does not mean that
the oppressors are no longer enemies, nor does it eliminate the
radicalness of the combat against them. "Love of enemies" does
not ease tensions; rather it challenges the whole system and
becomes a subversive formula.

Universal love comes down from the level of abstractions and
becomes concrete and effective by becoming incarnate in the
struggle for the liberation of the oppressed. It is a question of
loving all people, not in some vague, general way, but rather
in the exploited person, in the concrete person who is struggling
to live humanly. Our love for him does not "abstract" him, it
does not isolate him from the social class to which he belongs,
so that we can have "pity" on him. On the contrary, our love
is not authentic if it does not take the path of class solidarity
and social struggle. To participate in class struggle not only
is not opposed to universal love; this commitment is today the
necessary and inescapable means of making this love concrete.
For this participation is what leads to a classless society without
owners and dispossessed, without oppressors and oppressed.[57]
In dialectical thinking, reconciliation is the overcoming of conflict. The communion of paschal joy passes through confrontation and the cross.

The fact of class struggle also challenges the unity of the
Church and demands a redefinition of what we understand by
this unity.

The Church is in a world divided into antagonistic social
classes, on a universal scale as well as at the local level. Because

it is present in our society, the Church cannot attempt to ignore a fact which confronts it. What is more, this fact exists within the Church itself. Indeed, Christians belong to opposing social classes, which means that the Christian community itself is split by this social division. It is not possible to speak of the unity of the Church without taking into account its concrete situation in the world.[58]

To try piously to cover over this social division with a fictitious and formalistic unity is to avoid a difficult and conflictual reality and definitively to join the dominant class. It is to falsify the true character of the Christian community under the pretext of a religious attitude which tries to place itself beyond temporal contingencies. In these conditions, to speak, for example, of the priest as "the man of unity" is to attempt to make him into a part of the prevailing system. It is to attempt to make him a part of an unjust and oppressive system, based on the exploitation of the great majorities and needing a religious justification to preserve itself. This is especially true in places like Latin America, where the Church has a great influence among the exploited masses.

Understood in this way, the unity of the Church is rightly considered by Althusser as a myth which must disappear if the Church is to be "reconverted" to the service of the workers in the class struggle: "For this to happen," he asserts, "it would be necessary that the myth of the 'Christian community' disappear, for it prevents the recognition of the division of society into classes and the recognition of class struggle. One can foresee serious divisions occurring in the Church precisely around the theme of the *recognition* and the *understanding* of social classes and the class struggle, the recognition and the understanding of a reality which is incompatible with the *peculiarly religious* myth of the 'community of the faithful' and the (catholic) universality of the Church."[59] The author does not seem very convinced of the possibility for this "reconversion." Nevertheless there are growing numbers of Christians who challenge the mythical notion of the Christian community alluded to by Althusser and who believe that the authentic unity of the Church necessarily implies the option for the oppressed and exploited of this world.[60]

Unity is a gift of God and a historical conquest of man. Unity is not something already given. It is a process, the result of overcoming all that divides men. The promise of unity is at the heart of the work of Christ; in him men are sons before the Father and brothers among themselves. The Church, the community of those who confess Christ as their Lord, is a sign of unity among men (*Lumen gentium*, no. 1). The unity of the Church is not truly achieved without the unity of the world. In a radically divided world, the function of the ecclesial community is to struggle against the profound causes of the division among men. It is only this commitment that can make of it an authentic sign of unity. Today, in Latin America especially, this unity implies the option for the oppressed; to opt for them is the honest, resolute way to combat that which gives rise to this social division. The Church itself will become more and more unified in this historical process and commitment to the liberation of the marginated and exploited.[61] Unity will thus be forged not among those who only say, "Lord, Lord," but among those who "do the will of the Father." For the ecclesial community to recognize the fact of class struggle and to participate actively in it will not be therefore a negation of the message of unity which it bears; rather it will be to discover the path by which it can free itself from that which now prevents it from being a clear and true sign of brotherhood.

This perspective is, among other things, changing the focus of the concerns of ecumenism. Christians of different confessions are taking similar positions regarding the misery and injustice in Latin America, and this unites them more strongly than intraecclesial considerations. Christian unity thus begins to present questions very different than those we receive from Europe.[62] Because of a more realistic focus for its presence in the world and its commitment to the disinherited, Christians in Latin America are united and divided in ways and for reasons very different than in past years.[63] The paths which lead to accepting the gift of unity in Christ and his Spirit in history are going through unecclesiastical places. A new kind of ecumenism is being born.[64]

If the historical and social coordinates of the Christian community are not taken into account, any reflection will not be critical or sound and will serve only to preserve the status quo and justify attitudes which evade reality. On the other hand, if we start from the concrete realities of the presence of the Church in a society which is divided and conflictual and which at the same time is engaged in creating a more human world, then we might be able to indicate new directions for ecclesiology.

NOTES

1. The theme has been studied especially in missionary circles. See the provocative article of Joseph Comblin, "Le but de la mission: sauver l'homme," *Spiritus* 9, no. 34 (May 1968): 171–79.

2. See above Chapter 9.

3. "Church of the World," in the work written in collaboration with Nikos A. Nissiotis and Philip Maury, *Discerning the Times: The Church in Today's World*, trans. Sister Agnes Cunningham, SSCM (Techny, Illinois: Divine Word Publications, 1968), p. 150.

4. Let us recall, for example, the words of Gregory of Nazianzen at the death of his father, who was a Christian convert: "Even before he entered our fold he was one of us. Just as many of our own are not with us because their lives alienate them from the common body of the faithful, in like manner many of those outside are with us, in so far as by their way of life they anticipate the faith and only lack in name what they possess in attitude. My father was one of these, an alien branch, but inclined toward us by his way of living"*(Funeral Orations by Saint Gregory Nazianzen and Saint Ambrose*, Fathers of the Church, vol. 22 [New York: Fathers of the Church, Inc., 1953], no. 6, p. 123).

5. "It is the law of mankind and the natural right of each individual to worship what he thinks proper" (Tertullian, "To Scapula," in *Tertullian, Apologetical Works, and Minucius Felix, Octavius*, Fathers of the Church, vol. 10 [New York: Fathers of the Church, Inc., 1950], p. 152). "It is in religion alone that liberty dwells. . . . No one can be made to adore what he does not wish"(Lactantius, "Epitome divinarum institutionum," 54, in *Patrologiae Latinae*, 6:1061).

6. Ambrose of Milan expresses this idea very clearly: "Where the preacher has not been present, the sound and the report of his voice has come" (Commentaria in epistolam ad romanes" [10:17–18] in *Patrologiae Latinae*, 17:146b).

7. This helps us to understand the famous distinction between pagans and Jews, who have not had access to the faith, and heretics, who have abandoned it after having accepted it. For the former there is the necessity of a free acceptance of the faith, and so there will be a more tolerant attitude. The latter, on the other hand, will be considered culpable for turning their backs on the truth after having received the gift of faith; for them, severe treatment is appropriate. This position is summarized in a well-known text of Saint Thomas: "Acceptance of the faith is a matter of the will, whereas keeping the faith, when once one has received it, is a matter of obligation" (*Summa Theologica*, II-II, q. 10, a. 8, ad 3).

8. This is the real reason why the popes of the nineteenth century opposed religious liberty: to proclaim the civil equality of truth and error is to go against the salvation of men. See the texts reproduced in Giovanni Lo Grasso, *Ecclesia et Status: Fontes selecti* (Rome: Apud Aedes Pontif. Universitatis Gregorianae, 1952).

9. This "uncentering" begun by the Council has been emphasized by many, including G. Martelet, "Horizon théologique de la deuxième session du Concile," *Nouvelle Revue Théologique* 86, no. 5 (May 1964): 449–68, and Edward Schillebeeckx, *L'Église du Christ et l'homme d'aujourd'hui selon Vatican II* (Le Puy: Éditions Xavier Mappus, 1965), pp. 122–35.

10. Here we have been considering ideas more thoroughly treated in Gustavo Gutiérrez, "Libertad religiosa y diálogo salvador," pp. 13–43.

11. Han Urs von Balthasar writes in this respect, "Centuries of wasted opportunity are being made good; and fundamental Christian truths are being formulated which once expressed appear so right and obvious, that it is difficult to conceive how they can have been overlooked or forgotten for so long. Bridges which should never have been severed are being re-built.... Consequences that should have been drawn long ago are being drawn from premises which have always been there: for example, that if all men are called to supernatural salvation, grace must be active in them in some sense or other; that a dialogue between Christian and non-Christian is possible and necessary within that grace.... Truths such as these appear overwhelmingly great to the Christians of today— and so they are. But that they should appear *new* is, for anyone who knows the Fathers, for example, somewhat surprising; for at bottom they are not new" (*Love Alone* [New York: Herder and Herder, 1969], pp. 122–23).

12. In this regard the most important texts are *Lumen gentium*, nos. 1 and 48; see also nos. 9 and 59; *Gaudium et spes*, no. 45; *Sacrosanctum concilium*, nos. 5 and 26; and *Ad gentes*, no. 9.

13. "In our opinion, the most important milestone of Vatican II in the field of dogmatic theology is to have designated the Church as 'sacrament,' that is, as a visible sign of salvation through the Holy Spirit sent by Christ" (H. Mühlen, "Das Verhältnis zwischen Inkarnation und Kirche in den Assagen des Vaticanum II," *Theologie und Glaube* 55 [1965]: 171). Karl Rahner says that the Christian of tomorrow, when he studies the history of the Council, "will be astonished that this statement was made at the Council quietly and spontaneously without opposition, without surprise, without anyone's appearing to notice just what was being said. *Sacramentum salutis totius mundi:* sign of the salvation of the world" (*The Christian of the Future*, p. 82). Years before the Council Otto Semmelroth had dedicated a substantial study to this theme: *Die Kirche als Ursakrament* (Frankfurt: J. Knecht, 1953); and Rahner himself had also provided a valuable contribution: *The Church and the Sacraments* (New York: Herder and Herder, 1963). Nevertheless, this approach did not win the acceptance of all theologians, for it was feared that it would lead to "reducing ecclesiology to the study of outward elements" (Jerome Hamer, *The Church is a Communion* [New York: Sheed and Ward, 1964], p. 88; the point is treated on pp. 87–90).

14. See Metz, *Theology of the World*, p. 81, and *Risposta dei teologi*, p. 62. Along the same lines see Karl Rahner, *Risposta*, pp. 61–62.

15. See the old but important study of D. Deden, "Le mystère paulinien," *Ephemerides Theologicae Lovanienses* (1936), pp. 405–42.

16. The decree *Ad gentes*, in one of the texts of greatest theological importance of Vatican II, links closely the plan of salvation and the Church's task in that plan to the Trinitarian missions (nos. 1–5).

17. Juan Luis Segundo, *Nuestra idea de Dios* (Buenos Aires: Lohlé, 1970), p. 91; English version to be published by Orbis Books as one in the series entitled *A Theology for Artisans of a New Humanity.*

18. See Edward Schillebeeckx, *Christ, The Sacrament of the Encounter with God* (New York: Sheed and Ward, 1963).

19. See Mühlen, *Ésprit dans l'Église*, 2:84–114; Piet Smulders, "La Iglesia como sacramento de salvación"; and Edward Schillebeeckx, *La mission de l'Église*, pp. 42–48.

20. "The Church," writes Christian Duquoc, "does not give human love its worth; rather it proclaims and signifies its eschatological dimension" (L'Église et le monde," *Lumière et Vie* 14, no. 73 [May–July 1965]: 65).

21. Clement, "Ensayo de lectura," *Iglesia en el mundo*, p. 663.

22. "Church and world definitely should be situated in dynamic terms within one salvific plan as two stages or two times" (Liégé, *Église de Jésus-Christ*, p. 164). "The decisive relationship between the Church and the world is not spatial but temporal" (J. B. Metz, *Theology of the World*, p. 94). From a somewhat different viewpoint Gustave Martelet had already attempted a fruitful reinterpretation of the temporal-spiritual distinction according to *Lumen gentium*: "La Iglesia y lo temporal: hacia una nueva concepción," *La Iglesia del Vaticano II*, 1:559–77; French version: "L'Église et le temporel," in *L'Église de Vatican II*, 2: 517–40. See also Lucio Gera, "La Iglesia y el mundo," *La Iglesia y el país* (Buenos Aires: Ediciones Búsqueda, 1967), pp. 9–19.

23. "The Church, if only she be rightly understood, is living always on the proclamation of her own provisional status and of her historically advancing elimination in the coming Kingdom of God" (Karl Rahner, "The Church and the Parousia of Christ," in *Theological Investigations*, vol. 6, [Baltimore: Helicon Press, 1969], p. 298).

24. "Dio e 'colui che verra,'" in *Processo alla religione*, p. 151.

25. The Exodus and the Covenant form a single unity. The God who established the Covenant is the same God who brought Israel "out of Egypt, out of the land of slavery" (Exod. 20:2; Deut. 5:6). As we have already recalled (see above Chapter 9), this liberation is above all a political act. On the basis of this liberation we can interpret correctly the meaning of the Exodus and the Covenant which are celebrated in the paschal meal. Joseph Blenkinsopp can therefore write that an "effect of this better understanding of the political dimension of early Israel's faith is that scholars are less inclined to accept the historical separation between covenant-traditions and exodus-tradition proposed by Von Rad." And he continues, "The founding event begins with a community in an intolerable economic and political situation and deals in the first place with their economic and political salvation—'Yahweh brought them out from there'" ("Scope and Depth of Exodus Tradition in Deutero-Isaiah 40–55," *The Dynamism of Biblical Tradition*, ed. Pierre Benoit and Roland E. Murphy, Concilium 20 [New York: Paulist Press, 1967], pp. 41–42).

26. See Joseph Ratzinger, "La destinée de Jésus et l'Eglise," in *L'Église aujourd'hui*, ed. Yves Congar (Paris: Desclée et Cie, 1967), pp. 43–45; Luc Dequeker and William Zuidema, "The Eucharist and St. Paul (1 Cor. 11, 17-34)," in *The Breaking of the Bread*, ed. Pierre Benoit, Roland E. Murphy, Bastiaan van Iersel, Concilium 40 (New York: Paulist Press, 1969), pp. 48–59. Blenkinsopp notes that the theme and the language of the Exodus are applied in the New Testament to the life and death of Jesus ("Scope and Depth," p. 50).

27. See J. M. R. Tillard, "L'Eucharistie et la fraternité," *Nouvelle Revue Théologique* 91, no. 2 (February 1969): 113–35.

28. C. H. Dodd believes that this episode "corresponds to the Synoptic account

of the Last Supper," and he explains its omission in John "probably because the evangelist will not divulge the Christian 'mystery'" (*The Interpretation of the Fourth Gospel* [Cambridge: The University Press, 1955], p. 393).

29. "Eucharistie," p. 121. Rafael Ortega has pointed out with solid Biblical basis the threefold meaning of the sacrifice of the cross: paschal sacrifice, the liberation from all servitude (Exod. 12; 1 Cor. 5:6–8; 1 Pet. 1:18); sacrifice of Covenant which restores the former pact of union between God and his people (Exod. 19:5; 24:1; Gal. 4:4; 1 Cor. 11:25; Heb. 9:15–28); and sacrifice of expiation, of the elimination of sin (Lev. 16; 1 John 2:1–2; Rom. 3:23–25), in *Biblia y penitencia, Cuestiones litúrgicas*, no. 8 (Medellín); see also Stanislas Lyonnet and Léopold Sabourin, *Sin, Redemption, and Sacrifice* (Rome: Biblical Institute Press, 1970), pp. 170–74.

30. This is one of the few texts attributed to Jesus which Bultmann considers authentic; see *Theology of the New Testament*, trans. Kendrick Grobel (New York: Charles Scribner's Sons, 1951), 1:17 ff.

31. This text is found in the declaration made public by Camilo Torres on June 24, 1965. He asked to be relieved from his "clerical obligations," and this was granted. In this idea Camilo found the basis for his pathetic decision of sacrificing "one of the rights that I love most dearly—to be able to celebrate the external rite of the Church as a priest—in order to create the conditions that make the cult more authentic" (Camilo Torres, *Revolutionary Writings*, pp. 163–64). This act by Camilo unmercifully revealed a reality hidden beneath a mountain of words and good intentions. And it also helped give birth to the hope of building a Church that does not present this kind of a dilemma to the best of its members.

32. Schillebeeckx, "Dio e 'colui che verrà,'" p. 150. L. M. Alonso Schökel has recalled the bond between the redemptive work of Christ and solidarity among men in "La redemption ouevre de solidarité," *Nouvelle Revue Théologique* 93, no. 5 (May 1971): 449–72.

33. "Les biens temporels de l'Église d'après sa tradition théologique et canonique," in *Église et pauvreté*, pp. 247–49.

34. "The hour has come," declared a group of Ecuadorian priests, "for us as servants of the People of God in Ecuador, to unite our voices to the cry of the people and the voice of the apostle Paul: we cannot continue calmly to celebrate the event of liberation in the Eucharist, in which the oppressors and the oppressed eat the same bread and drink the same wine—without any true reconciliation" ("Declaración de la segunda convención nacional de presbíteros del Ecuador," *NADOC*, no. 204 [May 1971], p. 169).

35. "In Latin America the awareness is spreading—even among Christians —that Christianity has contributed to producing the cultural alienation that is seen today. The Christian religion has served, and continues to serve, as an ideology justifying the domination of the powerful. In Latin America Christianity has been a religion at the service of the system. Its rites, temples, and works have contributed to channeling popular dissatisfaction toward another world totally disconnected from this one. Thus Christianity has checked popular protest against an unjust and oppressive system" (*Juventud y cristianismo en América Latina*, final document of the seminar on the problems of youth organized by the Department of Education of CELAM [Bogota: Indo-American Press Service 1969], p. 22).

36. Responding to accusations that the Church was "meddling in political affairs," the bishops and the Presbyteral Council of Lima recently stated that "every human action has an inescapable socio-political dimension. Evangelical

preaching and witness, without entering into technical or partisan aspects of political activity, have a deep human duty to transform society by promoting the establishment of true justice among men" (statement of May 13, 1971, in *El Comercio* [Lima], May 14, 1972, p. 10).

37. The observations made by Arend van Leeuwen at lectures given in Buenos Aires concerning the loss of the influence of Christianity in the revolutionary spirit of the West are not entirely valid for Latin America (*Desarrollo y revolución* [Buenos Aires: La Aurora, 1967], p. 155; in English see his *Development through Revolution* [New York: Charles Scribner's Sons, 1970]).

38. This is a controversial point in Latin America; see above Chapter 8 and Assmann, *Teología de la liberación*, pp. 44–45.

39. In this service the Church—even the groups in the Church which might be considered in the vanguard— must avoid regressing toward any kind of politico-religious messianism, the danger of which we indicated at the end of the last chapter. As the Church must be aware of its responsibilities in these matters, so too it must be aware of the limit of its activity. As Hector Borrat correctly indicates, "Every word, every action of the Church that appears to be a 'pronouncement' in political matters has the weight and the presumed objectivity of an institution which by its very nature can claim no power; but it also has the weakness that by itself it cannot fully achieve what it seeks. . . . The Church is not an alternative to power, but this does not mean that it does not participate in the political process" ("¿La Iglesia para qué?" *Cristianismo y Sociedad*, no. 22 [1970], pp. 13–18).

40. In this regard, although in a different social context, see the perceptive observations of Marcel Xhaufflaire, "L'Église de demain," *Lumière et Vie* 19, no. 99 (August–October 1970): 133–54, especially pp. 139–45.

41. See Carlos Alvarez Calderón, *Pastoral y liberación humana* (Lima: CEP, 1970).

42. The pastoral activity of the Latin American Church is moving more and more in this direction; see Segundo Galilea, *La vertiente política de la pastoral* (Quito: Instituto Pastoral Latinoamericano, 1970), pp. 7–16. "Here we must observe," J. B. Metz points out, "that the Church, insofar as it is a historico-social phenomenon, always has a political dimension. This is so even before it sets up criteria by which it guides its activity and before taking a stand with regard to specific situations. To insinuate, as is being done today, that the Church is and ought to be a priori 'neutral' either manifests a lack of critical judgment or serves only to camouflage existing political alliances" ("Presencia de la Iglesia en la sociedad," *Concilium* [December 1970], p. 248).

43. "Amore cristiano e violenza rivoluzionaria," *La violenza dei cristiani* (Assisi: Cittadella, 1969), p. 110.

44. "There has still not emerged," writes Pedro Negre from Bolivia, "a Church in the center of oppression and margination" ("Biblia y liberación," *Cristianismo y Sociedad*, tercera y cuarta entrega [1970], p. 70).

45. In this regard see the perceptive observations of Hector Borrat, "¿La Iglesia para qué?" pp. 26–29.

46. Moreover, these modalities will be different according to their situation in the People of God. In the case of the ecclesiastical magisterium it will be necessary to accept that, given the issues involved, there will be some positions taken which will be very much marked by the specific characteristics of given situations. It is a question of being situated at the level of historical decisions without claiming

to establish rigid norms based on abstract principles which can be applied to any situation. Rather than diminishing the value of the actions of ecclesiastical authority, this will make them more fruitful. The texts of the Bishops' Conference at Medellín are a good example of trying to interpret the Word of God *today* and in a *given situation* as well as trying to preach it opportunely and at the same time "inopportunely." "In the meantime," writes Schillebeeckx in an article dedicated to this point, *"this* specific pronouncement will hold *here and now* for the ecclesiastical community" ("The Magisterium and the World of Politics," Concilium 36, p. 37).

47. Lucio Gera, "Reflexión teológica," *Sacerdotes para el Tercer Mundo* (Buenos Aires: Ed. del Movimiento, 1970), p. 141. Later he writes, "Prophecy not only desacralizes every place, temple, race, or nation; it also desacralizes every time. It does not set up as the final and definitive goal any empire that supplants another, any level of civilization—no matter how Jewish or Christian it might be—or any political, economic, or social system" (p. 142).

48. Schillebeeckx has pointed out this dual function of the faith which both relativizes and radicalizes the building of the city of man; see "Foi chrétienne et attente terrestre," *L'Église dans le monde de ce temps* (Tours: Mame, 1967), pp. 151–58. See also W. Kasper, "Faut-il encore la mission extérieure?" *Église et Mission,* no. 180 (October 1970), pp. 180–92.

49. Here there is much that needs to be clarified. Because of very different situations the analyses of one social formation cannot be unqualifiedly transposed to other situations. Any schematization impoverishes the reality. But the studies which still must be made concern the precise manner in which the class struggle occurs in a given situation, prescinding from the central place that it holds in contemporary society.

50. A letter from the Comisión Episcopal del Mundo Obrero, October 1968 (quoted in R. Poterie, "Lutte de classes," *Masses Ouvrières,* no. 271 [June–July 1970], p. 9). See also "Hacia una definición," a document of the "Iglesia joven" of Santiago de Chile, in *NADOC,* no. 9 (November 1968).

51. In a famous text Marx points out very precisely his contribution to the class struggle: not the discovery of its existence, but rather the analysis of its causes and an indication of the path to a classless society. "As for me," he writes, "mine is not the merit to have discovered either the existence of classes in modern society or the struggle between them. Much before me bourgeois historians had described the historical development of this class struggle and the bourgeois economists had studied its economic anatomy. What I did that was new was demonstrate (1) that the *existence of the classes* is linked only to *stages of the determined historical development of production;* (2) that the class struggle necessarily *leads* to the *dictatorship* of the proletariat; (3) that this dictatorship itself constitutes but a transition to *the abolition of all classes* and a classless society ... " (Letter to J. Weydemeyer, March 5, 1852, in Karl Marx and Friedrich Engels, *Études philosophiques* [Paris: Éditions Sociales, 1961], p. 151; italics in the original). The class struggle is inherent in the classist organization of society. The objective which Marx proposes is to abolish that which gives origin to the very existence of social classes. But the causes of the class struggle cannot be overcome without first becoming aware of the struggle and its demands in the process of building a new society.

52. "Cristianismo, pastoral y lucha de clases," in *La vertiente política de la pastoral,* p. 94.

53. See L. Pelissier, "L'Église et la lutte des classes," *Frères de Monde*, nos. 40–41 (1966), pp. 99–126.

54. Girardi, "Cristianismo, pastoral y lucha de clases," pp. 93–95.

55. Girardi, "Amore cristiano e violenza rivoluzionaria," *Violenza dei cristiani*, p. 122.

56. "We must love everyone, but it is not possible to love everyone in the same way: we love the oppressed by liberating them; we love the oppressors by fighting them. We love the oppressed by liberating them from their misery, and the oppressors by liberating them from their sin" (Girardi, "Cristianismo, pastoral y lucha de clases," p. 98).

57. "We Christians must be committed both personally and collectively ... to the building of a new society. This new society must be a classless society in which there is collective ownership of the means of production" ("Cristianos en un mundo de injusticia," from the conclusions of the "Primer encuentro por una Iglesia solidaria," in *Expreso* [Lima], May 7, 1971).

58. These considerations are usually not sufficiently treated in dealing with the issue of the unity of the Church. For example this point of view is not to be found in three recent and important studies: Mühlen, *Esprit dans l'Église*; Kung, *Church*; and Congar, *L'Église: Une, sainte, catholique et apostolique* (Paris: Éditions du Cerf, 1970).

59. "Diagnostics," *Lumière et Vie* (May–June 1969), p. 29; italics in the original.

60. In an old and little known text, Althusser, after a careful study of the position of the Church in the class struggle on a worldwide scale, concludes his article with statements which are somewhat surprising but seem to us to have relevance in Latin America today: "The future of the Church depends on the number and the strength of the Christians who recognize the need for the struggle and join the files of the world proletariat ... The Church will live through those who by the struggle and in the struggle itself rediscover that the Word has been born among men and has lived among men and who give it a human place among men" (Reply to a study on "the real conditions of Evangelization" in *Jeunesse de l'Église* [Paris], no. 10 [1949], p. 24).

61. "As long as the Church is still on its pilgrimage in this world, even though it is already 'one,' it nevertheless always does penance for its imperfect unity and strives for a greater unity. Unity, like peace, is something which must be constantly done" (Gera, "Reflexión teológica," p. 125).

62. See the note of Jorge Mejía, "El encuentro anglicano-católico romano de Bogotá," *Criterio*, 1615, March 11, 1971, pp. 111–14.

63. In this regard see the observations by Noel Olaya, "Unidad cristiana y lucha de clases," *Cristianismo y Sociedad*, tercera y cuarta entrega, 1970, pp. 61–68.

64. This matter did not escape the alert spirit of Yves Congar: "Do the New Problems of our Secular World make Ecumenism Irrelevant?" in *Post-Ecumenical Christianity*, ed. Hans Kung, Concilium 54 (New York: Herder and Herder, 1970), pp. 11–21.

CHAPTER THIRTEEN

POVERTY:
SOLIDARITY AND PROTEST

For some years now we have seen in the Church a recovery of a more authentic and radical witness of poverty.[1] At first this occurred within various recently founded religious communities. It quickly went beyond the narrow limits of "religious poverty," however, raising challenges and questions in other sectors of the Church. Poverty has become one of the central themes of contemporary Christian spirituality and indeed has become a controversial question. From the concern to imitate more faithfully the poor Christ, there has spontaneously emerged a critical and militant attitude regarding the counter-sign that the Church as a whole presents in the matter of poverty.

Those who showed this concern—with John XXIII at the head—knocked insistently at the doors of Vatican II. In an important message in preparation for the opening of the Council, John opened up a fertile perspective saying, "In dealing with the underdeveloped countries, the Church presents herself as she is and as she wants to be—as the Church of all men and especially the Church of the poor."[2] Indeed, from the first session of the Council the theme of poverty was very much in the air.[3] Later there was even a "Schema 14," which on the issue of poverty went beyond "Schema 13" (the draft for *Gaudium et spes*). The final results of the Council, however, did not correspond to the expectations. The documents allude several times to poverty, but it is not one of the major thrusts.[4] Later,

Populorum progressio is somewhat more concrete and clear with
regard to various questions related to poverty. But it will remain for the Church on a continent of misery and injustice to
give the theme of poverty its proper importance: *the authenticity
of the preaching of the Gospel message depends on this witness.*[5]
The theme of poverty has been dealt with in recent years,
especially in the field of spirituality.[6] In the contemporary
world, fascinated by a wealth and power established upon the
plunder and exploitation of the great majorities, poverty
appeared as an inescapable precondition to sanctity. Therefore
the greatest efforts were to meditate on the Biblical texts which
recall the poverty of Christ and thus to identify with Christ
in this witness.

More recently a properly theological reflection on poverty has
been undertaken, based on ever richer and more precise exegetical studies. From these first attempts there stands out clearly
one rather surprising result: poverty is a notion which has
received very little theological treatment and in spite of everything is still quite unclear.[7] Lines of interpretation overlap; various exegeses still carry weight today, even though they were
developed in very different contexts which no longer exist; certain aspects of the theme function as static compartments which
prevent a grasp of its overall meaning. All this has led us onto
slippery terrain on which we have tried to maneuver more by
intuition than by clear and well-formulated ideas.

AMBIGUITIES IN THE TERM "POVERTY"

Poverty is an equivocal term. But the ambiguity of the term
does nothing more than express the ambiguity of the notions
themselves which are involved. To try to clarify what we understand by *poverty*, we must clear the path and examine some
of the sources of the ambiguity. This will also permit us to
indicate the meaning we will give to various expressions which
we will use later.

The term *poverty* designates in the first place *material
poverty*, that is, the lack of economic goods necessary for a
human life worthy of the name. In this sense poverty is considered degrading and is rejected by the conscience of contemporary man. Even those who are not—or do not wish to be—

aware of the root causes of this poverty believe that it should be struggled against. Christians, however, often have a tendency to give material poverty a positive value, considering it almost a human and religious ideal. It is seen as austerity and indifference to the things of this world and a precondition for a life in conformity with the Gospel. This interpretation would mean that the demands of Christianity are at cross purposes to the great aspirations of people today, who want to free themselves from subjection to nature, to eliminate the exploitation of some people by others, and to create prosperity for everyone.[8] The double and contradictory meaning of *poverty* implied here gives rise to the imposition of one language on another and is a frequent source of ambiguities. The matter becomes even more complex if we take into consideration that the concept of material poverty is in constant evolution. Not having access to certain cultural, social, and political values, for example, is today part of the poverty that people hope to abolish. Would material poverty as an "ideal" of Christian life also include lacking these things?

On the other hand, poverty has often been thought of and experienced by Christians as part of the condition—seen with a certain fatalism—of marginated peoples, "the poor," who are an object of our mercy. But things are no longer like this. Social classes, nations, and entire continents are becoming aware of their poverty, and when they see its root causes, they rebel against it. The contemporary phenomenon is a collective poverty that leads those who suffer from it to forge bonds of solidarity among themselves and to organize in the struggle against the conditions they are in and against those who benefit from these conditions.

What we mean by material poverty is a subhuman situation. As we shall see later, the Bible also considers it this way. Concretely, to be poor means to die of hunger, to be illiterate, to be exploited by others, not to know that you are being exploited, not to know that you are a person. It is in relation to this poverty—material and cultural, collective and militant—that evangelical poverty will have to define itself.

The notion of *spiritual poverty* is even less clear. Often it is seen simply as an interior attitude of unattachment to the goods of this world. The poor person, therefore, is not so much the one who has no material goods; rather it is he who is not attached to them—even if he does possess them. This point of view allows for the case of the rich man who is spiritually poor as well as for the poor man who is rich at heart. These are extreme cases that distract attention toward the exceptional and the accessory. Claiming to be based on the Beatitude of Matthew concerning "the poor in spirit," this approach in the long run leads to comforting and tranquilizing conclusions.

This spiritualistic perspective rapidly leads to dead ends and to affirmations that the interior attitude must necessarily be incarnated in a testimony of material poverty. But if this is so, questions arise: What poverty is being spoken of? The poverty that the contemporary conscience considers subhuman? Is it in this way that spiritual poverty should be incarnated? Some answer that it is not necessary to go to such extremes, and they attempt to distinguish between destitution and poverty. The witness involves living poverty, not destitution. But then, as we have said, we are not referring to poverty as it is lived and perceived by people today, but rather to a different kind of poverty, abstract and made according to the specifications of our spiritual poverty. This is to play with words—and with people.

The distinction between evangelical counsels and precepts creates other ambiguities. According to it, evangelical poverty would be a counsel appropriate to a particular vocation and not a precept obligatory for all Christians. This distinction kept evangelical poverty confined incommunicado for a long time within the narrow limits of religious life, which focuses on "the evangelical counsels."[9] Today the distinction is only another source of misunderstandings.[10]

Because of all these ambiguities and uncertainties we have been unable to proceed on solid ground; we have wandered along an unsure path where it is difficult to advance and easy to wander. We have also fallen into very vague terminology and a kind of sentimentalism which in the last analysis justifies the status quo. In situations like the present one in Latin America this is especially serious. We see the danger, for example, in various commentaries on the writings of Bossuet regarding "the eminent dignity of the poor in the Church"; or in symbolism like that which considers the hunger of the poor as "the image of the human soul hungering for God"; or even in the expression "the Church of the poor," which—in spite of the indisputable purity of intention of John XXIII—is susceptible to an interpretation smacking of paternalism.

Clarification is needed. In the following pages we will attempt to sketch at least the broad outlines. We will try to keep in mind that—as one spiritual writer has said—the first form of poverty is to renounce the idea we have of poverty.

BIBLICAL MEANING OF POVERTY

Poverty is a central theme both in the Old and the New Testaments. It is treated both briefly and profoundly; it describes social situations and expresses spiritual experiences communicated only with difficulty; it defines personal attitudes, a whole people's attitude before God, and the relationships of people with each other. It is possible, nevertheless, to try to unravel the knots and to clear the horizon by following the two major lines of thought which seem to stand out: poverty as a scandalous condition and poverty as spiritual childhood.[11] The notion of evangelical poverty will be illuminated by a comparison of these two perspectives.

Poverty: A Scandalous Condition

In the Bible poverty is a scandalous condition inimical to human dignity and therefore contrary to the will of God.

This rejection of poverty is seen very clearly in the vocabulary used.[12] In the Old Testament the term which is used least to speak of the poor is *rash*, which has a rather neutral meaning.[13] As Gelin says, the prophets preferred terms which are "photographic" of real, living people.[14] The poor person is, therefore, *ébyôn*, the one who desires, the beggar, the one who is lacking something and who awaits it from another.[15] He is also *dal*, the weak one, the frail one; the expression *the poor of the land* (the rural proletariat) is found very frequently.[16] The poor person is also *ani*, the bent over one, the one laboring under a weight, the one not in possession of his whole strength and vigor, the humiliated one.[17] And finally he is *anaw*, from the same root as the previous term but having a more religious connotation—"humble before God."[18] In the New Testament the Greek term *ptokós* is used to speak of the poor person. *Ptokós* means one who does not have what is necessary to subsist, the wretched one driven into begging.[19]

Indigent, weak, bent over, wretched are terms which well express a degrading human situation. These terms already insinuate a protest. They are not limited to description; they take a stand.[20] This stand is made explicit in the vigorous rejection of poverty. The climate in which poverty is described is one of indignation. And it is with the same indignation that the cause of the poverty is indicated: the injustice of the oppressors. The cause is well expressed in a text from Job:

> Wicked men move boundary-stones
> and carry away flocks and their shepherds.
> In the field they reap what is not theirs,
> and filch the late grapes from the rich man's vineyard.
> They drive off the orphan's ass
> and lead away the widow's ox with a rope.
> They snatch the fatherless infant from the breast
> and take the poor man's child in pledge.
> They jostle the poor out of the way;
> the destitute huddle together, hiding from them.
> The poor rise early like the wild ass,
> when it scours the wilderness for food;
> but though they work till nightfall,
> their children go hungry.
> Naked and bare they pass the night;
> in the cold they have nothing to cover them.
> They are drenched by rain-storms from the hills
> and hug the rock, their only shelter.
> Naked and bare they go about their work,
> and hungry they carry the sheaves;
> they press the oil in the shade where two walls meet,
> they tread the winepress but themselves go thirsty.
> Far from the city, they groan like dying men,
> and like wounded men they cry out; ...
> The murderer rises before daylight
> to kill some miserable wretch (Job 24:2–12, 14).

Poverty is not caused by fate; it is caused by the actions of those whom the prophet condemns:

> These are the words of the Lord:
>   For crime after crime of Israel

> I will grant them no reprieve
> because they sell the innocent for silver
>   and the destitute for a pair of shoes.
> They grind the heads of the poor into the earth
>   and thrust the humble out of their way ...
>   (Amos 2:6–7).

There are poor because some people are victims of others. "Shame on you," it says in Isaiah,

> you who make unjust laws
> and publish burdensome decrees,
> depriving the poor of justice,
> robbing the weakest of my people of their rights,
> despoiling the widow and plundering the orphan (10:1–2).[21]

The prophets condemn every kind of abuse, every form of keeping the poor in poverty or of creating new poor people. They are not merely allusions to situations; the finger is pointed at those who are to blame. Fraudulent commerce and exploitation are condemned (Hos. 12:8; Amos 8:5; Mic. 6:10–11; Isa. 3:14; Jer. 5:27; 6:12), as well as the hoarding of lands (Mic. 2:1–3; Ezek. 22:29; Hab. 2:5–6), dishonest courts (Amos 5:7; Jer. 22:13–17; Mic. 3:9–11; Isa. 5:23, 10:1–2), the violence of the ruling classes (2 Kings 23:30, 35; Amos 4:1; Mic. 3:1–2; 6:12; Jer. 22:13–17), slavery (Neh. 5:1–5; Amos 2:6; 8:6), unjust taxes (Amos 4:1; 5:11–12), and unjust functionaries (Amos 5:7; Jer. 5:28).[22] In the New Testament oppression by the rich is also condemned, especially in Luke (6:24–25; 12:13–21; 16:19–31; 18:18–26) and in the Letter of James (2:5–9; 4:13–17; 5:16).

But it is not simply a matter of denouncing poverty. The Bible speaks of positive and concrete measures to prevent poverty from becoming established among the People of God. In Leviticus and Deuteronomy there is very detailed legislation designed to prevent the accumulation of wealth and the consequent exploitation. It is said, for example, that what remains in the fields after the harvest and the gathering of olives and grapes should not be collected; it is for the alien, the orphan, and the widow (Deut. 24:19–21; Lev. 19:9–10). Even more, the fields should not be harvested to the very edge so that something remains for the poor and the aliens (Lev. 23:22). The Sabbath, the day of the Lord, has a social significance; it is a day of rest for the slave and the alien (Exod. 23:12; Deut. 5:14). The triennial tithe is not to be carried to the temple; rather it is for the alien, the orphan, and the widow (Deut. 14:28–29; 26:12). Interest on loans is forbidden (Exod. 22:25; Lev. 25:35–37; Deut. 23:20). Other important measures include the Sabbath year and the jubilee year. Every seven years the fields will be left to lie fallow "to provide food for the poor of your people" (Exod. 23:11; Lev. 25:2–7), although it is recognized that this duty is not always fulfilled (Lev. 26:34–35). After seven years the slaves were to regain their freedom (Exod. 21:2–6) and debts were to be pardoned (Deut. 15:1–18). This is also the meaning of the jubilee year of Lev. 25:10ff.[23] "It was," writes de Vaux, "a general emancipation ... of all the inhabitants of the land. The fields lay fallow: every man re-entered his ancestral property, *i.e.* the fields and houses which had been alienated returned to their original owners."[24]

Behind these texts we can see three principal reasons for this vigorous repudiation of poverty. In the first place, poverty contradicts the very meaning of *the Mosaic religion*. Moses led his people out of the slavery, exploitation, and alienation of Egypt[25] so that they might inhabit a land where they could live with human dignity. In Moses' mission of liberation there was a close relationship between the religion of Yahweh and the elimination of servitude:

> Moses and Aaron then said to all the Israelites, "In the evening you will know that it was the Lord who brought you out of Egypt, and in the morning you will see the glory of the Lord, because he has heeded your complaints against him; it is not against us that you bring your complaints; we are nothing." "You shall know this," Moses said, "when the Lord, in answer to your complaints, gives you flesh to eat in the evening, and in the morning bread in plenty. What are we? It is against the Lord that you bring your complaints, and not against us" (Exod. 16:6–8).

The worship of Yahweh and the possession of the land are both included in the same promise. The rejection of the exploita-

tion of some people by others is found in the very roots of the
people of Israel. God is the only owner of the land given to his
people (Lev. 25:23, 38); he is the one Lord who saves his people
from servitude and will not allow them to be subjected to it
again (Deut. 5:15; 16:22; Lev. 25:42; 26:13). And thus
Deuteronomy speaks of "the ideal of a brotherhood where there
was no poverty."[26] In their rejection of poverty, the prophets,
who were heirs to the Mosaic ideal, referred to the past, to the
origins of the people; there they sought the inspiration for the
construction of a just society. To accept poverty and injustice
is to fall back into the conditions of servitude which existed
before the liberation from Egypt. It is to retrogress.

The second reason for the repudiation of the state of slavery
and exploitation of the Jewish people in Egypt is that it goes
against *the mandate of Genesis* (1:26; 2:15). Man is created in
the image and likeness of God and is destined to dominate the
earth.[27] Man fulfills himself only by transforming nature and
thus entering into relationships with other men. Only in this
way does he come to a full consciousness of himself as the subject of creative freedom which is realized through work. The
exploitation and injustice implicit in poverty make work into
something servile and dehumanizing. Alienated work, instead
of liberating man, enslaves him even more.[28] And so it is that
when just treatment is asked for the poor, the slaves, and the
aliens, it is recalled that Israel also was alien and enslaved in
Egypt (Exod. 22:21–23; 23:9; Deut. 10:19; Lev. 19:34).

And finally, man not only has been made in the image and
likeness of God. He is also *the sacrament of God*. We have already
recalled this profound and challenging Biblical theme.[29] The
other reasons for the Biblical rejection of poverty have their
roots here: to oppress the poor is to offend God himself; to know
God is to work justice among men. We meet God in our encounter
with men; what is done for others is done for the Lord.

In a word, the existence of poverty represents a sundering
both of solidarity among men and also of communion with God.
Poverty is an expression of a sin, that is, of a negation of love.
It is therefore imcompatible with the coming of the Kingdom
of God, a Kingdom of love and justice.

Poverty is an evil, a scandalous condition,[30] which in our times
has taken on enormous proportions.[31] To eliminate it is to bring

closer the moment of seeing God face to face, in union with other men.[32]

Poverty: Spiritual Childhood

There is a second line of thinking concerning poverty in the Bible. The poor person is the "client" of Yahweh; poverty is "the ability to welcome God, an openness to God, a willingness to be used by God, a humility before God."[33]

The vocabulary which is used here is the same as that used to speak of poverty as an evil. But the terms used to designate the poor person receive an ever more demanding and precise religious meaning.[34] This is the case especially with the term *anaw*, which in the plural *(anawim)* is the privileged designation of the spiritually poor.

The repeated infidelity to the Covenant of the people of Israel led the prophets to elaborate the theme of the "tiny remnant" (Isa. 4:3; 6:13). Made up of those who remained faithful to Yahweh, the remnant would be the Israel of the future. From its midst there would emerge the Messiah and consequently the first fruits of the New Covenant (Jer. 31:31–34; Ezek. 36:26–28). From the time of Zephaniah (seventh century B.C.), those who waited the liberating work of the Messiah were called "poor": "But I will leave in you a people afflicted and poor, the survivors in Israel shall find refuge in the name of the Lord" (Zeph. 3:12–13). In this way the term acquired a spiritual meaning. From then on poverty was presented as an ideal: "Seek the Lord, all in the land who live humbly by his laws, seek righteousness, seek a humble heart" (Zeph. 2:3). Understood in this way poverty is opposed to pride, to an attitude of self-sufficiency; on the other hand, it is synonymous with faith, with abandonment and trust in the Lord.[35] This spiritual meaning will be accentuated during the historical experiences of Israel after the time of Zephaniah. Jeremiah calls himself poor *(ébyôn)* when he sings his thanksgiving to God (20:13). Spiritual poverty is a precondition for approaching God: "All these are of my own making and all these are mine. This is the very word of the Lord. The man I look to is a man down-trodden and distressed, one who reveres my words" (Isa. 66:2).

The Psalms can help us to understand more precisely this religious attitude. To know Yahweh is to seek him (9:11; 34:11), to abandon and entrust oneself to him (10:14; 34:9, 37:40), to hope in him (25:3–5, 21; 37:9), to fear the Lord (25:12, 14; 34:8, 10), to observe his commandments (25:10); the poor are the just ones, the whole ones (34:20, 22; 37:17–18), the faithful ones (37:28; 149:1). The opposite of the poor are the proud, who are the enemy of Yahweh and the helpless (10:2; 18:28; 37:10; 86:14).

Spiritual poverty finds its highest expression in the Beatitudes of the New Testament. The version in *Matthew*—thanks to solid exegetical studies—no longer seems to present any great difficulties in interpretation. The poverty which is called "blessed" in Matt. 5:1 ("Blessed are the poor in spirit") is spiritual poverty as understood since the time of Zephaniah: to be totally at the disposition of the Lord. This is the precondition for being able to receive the Word of God.[36] It has, therefore, the same meaning as the Gospel theme of spiritual childhood. God's communication with us is a gift of love; to receive this gift it is necessary to be poor, a spiritual child. This poverty has no direct relationship to wealth; in the first instance it is not a question of indifference to the goods of this world. It goes deeper than that; it means to have no other sustenance than the will of God. This is the attitude of Christ. Indeed, it is to him that all the Beatitudes fundamentally refer.[37]

In *Luke's* version ("Blessed are you poor" [6:20]) we are faced with greater problems of interpretation.[38] Attempts to resolve these difficulties follow two different lines of thinking. Luke is the evangelist who is most sensitive to social realities. In his Gospel as well as in Acts the themes of material poverty, of goods held in common, and of the condemnation of the rich are frequently treated. This has naturally led to thinking that the poor whom he blesses are the opposite of the rich whom he condemns; the poor would be those who lack what they need. In this case the poverty that he speaks of in the first Beatitude would be *material poverty*.

But this interpretation presents a twofold difficulty. It would lead to the canonization of a social class. The poor would be the privileged of the Kingdom, even to the point of having their access to it assured, not by any choice on their part but by a socio-economic situation which had been imposed on them. Some commentators insist that this would not be evangelical and would be contrary to the intentions of Luke.[39] On the opposite extreme within this interpretation are those who claim to avoid this difficulty and yet preserve the concrete sociological mean-

ing of poverty in Luke. Situating themselves in the perspective
of wisdom literature, they say that the first Beatitude opposes
the present world to the world beyond; the sufferings of today
will be compensated for in the future life.[40] Extraterrestrial salvation is the absolute value which makes the present life insig-
nificant. But this point of view implies purely and simply that
Luke is sacralizing misery and injustice and is therefore preaching resignation to it.

Because of these impasses, an explanation is sought from
another perspective: Matthew's. Like him Luke would be referring to *spiritual poverty*, or to openness to God. As a concession
to the social context of Luke there is in this interpretation an
emphasis on real poverty insofar as it is "a privileged path
towards poverty of soul."[41]

This second line of interpretation seems to us to minimize
the sense of Luke's text. Indeed, it is impossible to avoid the
concrete and "material" meaning which the term *poor* has for
this evangelist. It refers first of all to those who live in a social
situation characterized by a lack of the goods of this world and
even by misery and indigence. Even further, it refers to a marginated social group, with connotations of oppression and lack
of liberty.[42]

All this leads us to retrace our steps and to reconsider the
difficulties—which we have recalled above—in explaining the
text of Luke as referring to the materially poor.

"Blessed are you poor for yours is the Kingdom of God" does
not mean, it seems to us: "Accept your poverty because later
this injustice will be compensated for in the Kingdom of God."
If we believe that the Kingdom of God is a gift which is received
in history, and if we believe, as the eschatological promises—so
charged with human and historical content—indicate to us, that
the Kingdom of God necessarily implies the reestablishment of
justice in this world,[43] then we must believe that Christ says
that the poor are blessed *because* the Kingdom of God has begun:
"The time has come; the Kingdom of God is upon you" (Mark
1:15). In other words, the elimination of the exploitation and
poverty that prevent the poor from being fully human has
begun; a Kingdom of justice which goes even beyond what they
could have hoped for has begun. They are blessed because the
coming of the Kingdom will put an end to their poverty by creating a world of brotherhood. They are blessed because the Mes-

siah will open the eyes of the blind and will give bread to the hungry. Situated in a prophetic perspective, the text in Luke uses the term *poor* in the tradition of the first major line of thought we have studied: poverty is an evil and therefore incompatible with the Kingdom of God, which has come in its fullness into history and embraces the totality of human existence.[44]

AN ATTEMPT AT SYNTHESIS: SOLIDARITY AND PROTEST

Material poverty is a scandalous condition. Spiritual poverty is an attitude of openness to God and spiritual childhood. Having clarified these two meanings of the term *poverty* we have cleared the path and can now move forward towards a better understanding of the Christian witness of poverty. We turn now to a third meaning of the term: poverty as a commitment of solidarity and protest.

We have laid aside the first two meanings. The first is subtly deceptive; the second partial and insufficient. In the first place, if *material poverty* is something to be rejected, as the Bible vigorously insists, then a witness of poverty cannot make of it a Christian ideal. This would be to aspire to a condition which is recognized as degrading to man. It would be, moreover, to move against the current of history. It would be to oppose any idea of the domination of nature by man and the consequent and progressive creation of better conditions of life. And finally, but not least seriously, it would be to justify, even if involuntarily, the injustice and exploitation which is the cause of poverty.

On the other hand, our analysis of the Biblical texts concerning *spiritual poverty* has helped us to see that it is not directly or in the first instance an interior detachment from the goods of this world, a spiritual attitude which becomes authentic by incarnating itself in material poverty. Spiritual poverty is something more complete and profound. It is above all total availability to the Lord. Its relationship to the use or ownership of economic goods is inescapable, but secondary and partial. Spiritual childhood—an ability to receive, not a passive acceptance—defines the total posture of human existence before God, men, and things.

How are we therefore to understand the evangelical meaning of the witness of a real, material, concrete poverty? *Lumen gen-*

tium invites us to look for the deepest meaning of Christian poverty *in Christ:* "Just as Christ carried out the work of redemption in poverty and under oppression, so the Church is called to follow the same path in communicating to men the fruits of salvation. Christ Jesus, though He was by nature God ... emptied himself, taking the nature of a slave (Phil. 2:6), and being rich, he became poor (2 Cor. 8:9) for our sakes. Thus, although the Church needs human resources to carry out her mission, she is not set up to seek earthly glory, but to proclaim humility and self-sacrifice, even by her own example" (no. 8). The Incarnation is an act of love. Christ became man, died, and rose from the dead to set us free so that we might enjoy freedom (Gal. 5:1). To die and to rise again with Christ is to vanquish death and to enter into a new life (cf. Rom. 6:1–11). The cross and the resurrection are the seal of our liberty.

The taking on of the servile and sinful condition of man, as foretold in Second Isaiah, is presented by Paul as an act of voluntary impoverishment: "For you know how generous our Lord Jesus Christ has been: He was rich, yet for your sake he became poor, so that through his poverty you might become rich" (2 Cor. 8:9). This is the humiliation of Christ, his *kenosis* (Phil. 2:6–11). But he does not take on man's sinful condition and its consequences to idealize it. It is rather because of love for and solidarity with men who suffer in it. It is to redeem them from their sin and to enrich them with his poverty. It is to struggle against human selfishness and everything that divides men and enables there to be rich and poor, possessors and dispossessed, oppressors and oppressed.

Poverty is an act of love and liberation. It has a redemptive value. If the ultimate cause of man's exploitation and alienation is selfishness, the deepest reason for voluntary poverty is love of neighbor. Christian poverty has meaning only as a commitment of solidarity with the poor, with those who suffer misery and injustice. The commitment is to witness to the evil which has resulted from sin and is a breach of communion. It is not a question of idealizing poverty, but rather of taking it on as it is—an evil—to protest against it and to struggle to abolish it. As Ricoeur says, you cannot really be with the poor unless you are struggling against poverty. Because of this solidarity—which must manifest itself in specific action, a style of life, a break with one's social class—one can also help the poor and exploited to become aware of their exploitation and seek liberation from it. Christian poverty, an expression of love, is solidarity *with the poor* and is a protest *against poverty*.[45] This is the concrete, contemporary meaning of the witness of poverty. It is a poverty lived not for its own sake, but rather as an authentic imitation of Christ; it is a poverty which means taking on the sinful condition of man to liberate him from sin and all its consequences.[46]

Luke presents the community of goods in the early Church as an ideal. "All whose faith had drawn them together held everything in common" (Acts 2:44); "not a man of them claimed any of his possessions as his own, but everything was held in common" (Acts 4:33). They did this with a profound unity, one "in heart and soul" (*ibid.*). But as J. Dupont correctly points out, this was not a question of erecting poverty as an ideal, but rather of seeing to it that there were no poor: "They had never a needy person among them, because all who had property in land or houses sold it, brought the proceeds of the sale, and laid the money at the feet of the apostles; it was then distributed to any who stood in need" (Acts 4:34–35). The meaning of the community of goods is clear: to eliminate poverty because of love of the poor person. Dupont rightly concludes, "If goods are held in common, it is not therefore in order to become poor for love of an ideal of poverty; rather it is so that there will be no poor. The ideal pursued is, once again, charity, a true love for the poor."[47]

We must pay special attention to the words we use. The term *poor* might seem not only vague and churchy, but also somewhat sentimental and aseptic. The "poor" person today is the oppressed one, the one marginated from society, the member of the proletariat struggling for his most basic rights; he is the exploited and plundered social class, the country struggling for its liberation. In today's world the solidarity and protest of which we are speaking have an evident and inevitable "political" character insofar as they imply liberation. To be with the oppressed is to be against the oppressor. In our times and on our continent to be in solidarity with the "poor," understood in this way, means to run personal risks—even to put one's life in danger. Many Christians—and non-Christians—who are committed to the Latin American revolutionary process are running these risks. And so there are emerging new ways of living poverty which are different from the classic "renunciation of the goods of this world."

Only by rejecting poverty and by making itself poor in order to protest against it can the Church preach something that is uniquely its own: "spiritual poverty," that is, the openness of man and history to the future promised by God.[48] Only in this way will the Church be able to fulfill authentically—and with any possibility of being listened to—its prophetic function of denouncing every injustice to man. And only in this way will it be able to preach the word which liberates, the word of genuine brotherhood.[49]

Only authentic solidarity with the poor and a real protest against the poverty of our time can provide the concrete, vital context necessary for a theological discussion of poverty. The absence of a sufficient commitment to the poor, the marginated, and the exploited is perhaps the fundamental reason why we have no solid contemporary reflection on the witness of poverty.

For the Latin American Church especially, this witness is an inescapable and much-needed sign of the authenticity of its mission.

NOTES

1. This chapter summarizes a series of classes given at the University of Montreal in July 1967 on "The Church and the Problems of Poverty." The ideas have been revised and the bibliography has been brought up to date.

2. Radio Message of September 11, 1962, in *The Pope Speaks* 8, no. 4 (Spring 1963): 396.

3. "We will not respond to the truest and deepest demands of our time nor to the hope of unity shared by all Christians if we treat the theme of the evangelization of the poor as one of the many themes of the Council. This is not a theme like others; in a way, it is *the* theme of our Council" (Speech of Cardinal Lercaro, December 6, 1962; the text is in *La Documentation Catholique* 60, no. 1395 [March 3, 1963], col. 321, n. 2).

4. Most of the references are to be found in *Lumen gentium* (sixteen) and *Gaudium et spes* (fourteen). The most important text is *Lumen gentium*, no. 8.

5. See the Medellín document on "Poverty of the Church" and the other statements of the Latin American Church quoted above in Chapter 7.

6. See, for example, the works of Pie-Raymond Régamey, O.P., *Poverty: An Essential Element in the Christian Life*, trans. Rosemary Sheed (New York: Sheed & Ward, 1950); R. Voillaume, *Seeds of the Desert* (Notre Dame: Fides Publishers Association, 1955); Paul Gauthier, *Christ, the Church and the Poor*, trans. Edward Fitzgerald (Westminster, Md.: The Newman Press, 1965).

7. "The uncertainties regarding poverty are such today that it is necessary to reconsider the question from the beginning" (A. Hayen and Pie-Raymond Régamey, "Une anthropologie chrétienne" in *Église et pauvreté*, p. 83).

8. In reference to the society of the future Mounier wrote perceptively, "After we have experienced poverty of the spirit amid material poverty, perhaps humanity is called to the difficult task of practicing it amid material abundance" ("La révolution personaliste" in *Oeuvres completes*, 1:413).

9. In religious life poverty is often very closely linked to obedience. To be poor is to have no *personal* control over economic goods; on a *communal* level, things are very different, as we know.

10. See the remarks concerning the notion of the evangelical counsel in Hayen and Régamey, "Anthropologie," pp. 106–12. See also H. Feret, *L'Église des pauvres, interpellation des riches* (Paris: Les Éditions du Cerf, 1965), pp. 201–28; Yves Congar, O.P., "Poverty, in Christian Life amidst an Affluent Society," *War, Poverty, Freedom*, ed. Franz Bockle, Concilium 15 (New York: Paulist Press, 1966), pp. 52–53; and Karl Rahner, "Theologie de la vie religieuse" in *Les religieuses aujourd'hui et demain* (Paris, 1964), p. 71.

11. These two lines of thought were indicated and studied by Albert Gelin, P.S.S., in his pioneer work, *The Poor of Yahweh*, trans. Mother Kathryn Sullivan, R.S.C.J. (Collegeville, Minnesota: The Liturgical Press, 1964); they are treated with great clarity by González Ruiz in *Pobreza evangélica*.

12. Regarding the terminology, see Gelin, *Poor*; A. George, "Pauvre," in *Supplément au Dictionnaire de la Bible*, 1966, cols. 387–406; Jacques Dupont, *Les béatitudes*, vol. 2, *La Bonne Nouvelle* (Paris: J. Gabalda et Cie Editeurs, 1969) pp. 19–34; Ernst Bammel, "Ptokós" in *Theological Dictionary of the New Testament*, ed. Gerhard Friedrich, trans. and ed. Geoffrey W. Bromiley (Grand Rapids, Mich.: Wm. B. Eerdmans Publishing Company, 1968), 6:885–915; Jesús María Liaño, "Los pobres en el Antiguo Testamento," *Estudios Bíblicos* 25, no. 2 (April–June 1966): 162–67.

13. *Rash* is used twenty-one times in the Old Testament, especially in Proverbs.

14. See Gelin, *Poor*, p. 19.

15. *Ebyón* is used sixty-one times in the Old Testament, especially in the Psalms and the Prophets. See P. Humbert, "Le mot biblique ébyôn," *Revue d'Histoire et de Philosophie Religieuse* (1952), pp. 1–6.

16. *Dal* is used forty-eight times in the Old Testament, especially in the Prophets, Job, and Proverbs.

17. This is the most common term; it is found eighty times in the Old Testament, especially in the Psalms and the Prophets.

18. *Anaw* is found twenty-five times in the Old Testament (only once in the singular), especially in the Psalms and the Prophets.

19. *Ptokós* is used thirty-four times in the whole New Testament; in most cases it refers to the indigent person, one lacking what is necessary. Only on six occasions does this term have a spiritual meaning, but even then the poor person is found at the side of the blind, the mutilated, the leper, and the sick, providing a very immediate concrete context.

20. "Poverty was never something to which the prophets could be indifferent. When they spoke of it, they protested against the oppression and injustice of the rich and the mighty. Naturally, they found expressions consonant with their feelings" (Van der Ploeg, "Les pauvres d'Israël et leur piété," in *Oudtestamentische Studiën* 7 [1950]: 258, quoted in Gelin, *Poor*, p. 19).

21. "You ought to give judgement for the weak and the orphan, and see right done to the destitute and downtrodden, you ought to rescue the weak and the poor" (Ps. 82:3–4).

22. See Gelin, *Poor*, pp. 17–18.

23. See also Deut. 23:16–21; 24:5–22.

24. Roland de Vaux, O.P., *Ancient Israel:: Its Life and Institutions*, trans. John McHugh (New York: McGraw-Hill Book Company, Inc., 1961), p. 175. The author believes, however, that there is little indication that this legislation was faithfully observed (pp. 175–77).

25. Exod. 1:9–14 speaks of a dominant class that benefits from the dehumanizing work of the exploited masses.

26. Gelin, *Poor*, p. 16.

27. See Von Rad, *Old Testament Theology*, 1:139–48; and C. Spicq, O.P., *Dieu et l'homme selon le Nouveau Testament* (Paris: Les Éditions du Cerf, 1961), pp. 179–213.

28. See above Chapter 9.

29. See above Chapter 10.

30. "Neither wealth nor poverty ... ," Thomas Aquinas said long ago, "is in itself man's good" ("Neque divitiae neque paupertas ... est secundum se hominis bonum"; *Summa Contra Gentiles*, 3:134).

31. "Poverty belongs to the sphere of privation and want and is an intolerable scandal" (González Ruiz, *Pobreza evangélica*, p. 32).

32. Gelin points out that in the Bible there are also other, less important lines of thought regarding poverty. The relationship between poverty and sin and the ideal of an intermediate state between wealth and poverty are both considered. (*Poor*, pp. 23–26). Nevertheless, the dominant theme is the one we have indicated; moreover, it alone provides the basis for an adequate interpretation of the secondary themes.

33. *Ibid.*, p. 26.

34. "Words that once denoted a sociological reality came to mean an attitude of soul" (*ibid.*, p. 26). Something similar occurs with the term *justice;* in the Bible it first designates a social situation. Gradually—without losing its original sense —it is enriched by a spiritual meaning: justice as a synonym for sanctity.

35. George, "Pauvre," col. 393.

36. "Spiritual poverty is above all this power of being open to the will of God" (Pierre Ganne, "Aujourd'hui, la béatitude des pauvres," *Bible et Vie Chrétienne* 37 [January–February 1961]: p. 74).

37. This idea has been strongly emphasized by Bonhoeffer in *The Cost of Discipleship*, rev. ed. (New York: The Macmillan Company, 1963).

38. Jacques Dupont, *Les béatitudes: Le problème littéraire, Le message doctrinal* (Bruges: Éditions de l'Abbaye de Saint-André, 1954), pp. 82 and 122–23, and L. Vaganay, *Le problème synoptique* (Tournai: Desclée, & Co., 1954), pp. 255 and 291–92, believe that Luke is closer to the sources. Gelin, on the other hand, holds for the archaic character of the text in Matthew (*Poor*, p. 107).

39. "Does this mean that we must believe that Jesus 'beatified a social class'? ... [The Gospel] canonizes no sociological state, nor places it in direct relation with the Kingdom" (Gelin, *Poor*, p. 107). See Dupont, *Béatitudes* (1954), p. 242. See also the references to the hypothesis of ebionism and "socialism" in Luke on p. 215, n. 1. Léon-Defour also seems to situate himself in this line of interpretation; according to him if the exegete "selects only Luke, he tends to beatify a sociological condition; if he selects only Matthew, he runs the risk of having the Beatitude evaporate into a spirit of poverty, which the rich are supposed to possess" ("L'exégète et l'événement historique," *Recherches de Sciences Religieuses* 58, no. 4 [October–December 1970]:559).

40. "In the Beatitudes of Luke, the basic perspective ... is that of retribution after death. ... [Luke] sees in Christianity the inescapable obligation of choosing against the present life and for the future life" (Dupont, *Béatitudes* [1954], pp. 213–18).

41. Gelin, *Poor*, p. 108. The author has a clear tendency to spiritualize the Biblical theme of poverty. For a similar perspective see George, "Pauvre," col. 402. Dupont, *Béatitudes* (1969), pp. 141–42, refutes—and rightly so—a variation on this interpretation: that the poor—materially speaking—will be blessed because in them there occur more easily certain spiritual dispositions toward acceptance of the Kingdom. Karel Truhlar, S.J., notwithstanding the title of his article, also puts himself in a "spiritualist" perspective: "The Earthy Cast of the Beatitudes," *The Gift of Joy*, ed. Christian Duquoc, O.P., Concilium 39 (New York: Paulist Press, 1968), pp. 33–43.

42. The term *poor (ptokós)* occurs ten times in Luke (4:18; 6:20; 7:22; 14:13, 21; 16:21, 22; 18:22; 19:8; 21:3). The meaning we have just considered is seen very clearly if we keep in mind the context in which the expression occurs. Moreover, the first three Beatitudes in Luke form a unity and should be interpreted as a whole. "The afflicted" and "the hungry" are very concrete realities not subject to spiritualization (See Dupont, *Béatitudes* [1969], pp. 49–51 and 139).

43. See above Chapter 9.

44. Dupont includes the prophetic perspective in his interpretation of the text in question (See *Béatitudes*, [1954], p. 212). But he believes that Luke departs from it to adopt the point of view of the Wisdom Tradition (p. 213). Nevertheless Dupont seems to modify this position in his most recent work (*Béatitudes* [1969]).

45. Although he is speaking in a somewhat different context, Régamey remarks with lucidity and realism that "the spiritual fullness of the Beatitudes does not replace its messianic meaning. ... Christianity will always have the mission of taking on itself the hope of the poor. The task of the Messiah becomes the task of Christians. It is of utmost importance to maintain at the very core of the meaning of the Beatitudes their messianic significance. This must be translated to fit the changing circumstances which offer the challenge of fulfilling—according to Christ—the just aspirations of all people, just as the Beatitudes announced the fulfillment of the just aspirations of the Jews twenty centuries ago" (*Le portrait spirituel du chrétien* [Paris: Les Éditions du Cerf, 1963], p. 26).

46. "Perfection, however, does not consist in the renunciaton itself of temporal goods; since this is the way to perfection" (Thomas Aquinas, *Summa Theologica*, II-II, q. 19, a. 12).

47. "Los pobres y la pobreza en los Evangelios y en los Hechos," *La pobreza evangélica hoy* (Bogota: Secretariado General de la CLAR, 1971), p. 32.

48. The Medellín document on "Poverty of the Church" distinguishes among three meanings of the term *poverty* and describes the mission of the Church in terms of that distinction. It might be useful to quote here the entire paragraph: "(a) Poverty, as a lack of the goods of this world necessary to live worthily as men, is in itself evil. The prophets denounce it as contrary to the will of the Lord and most of the time as the fruit of the injustice and sin of men. (b) Spiritual poverty is the theme of the poor of Yahweh (cf. Zeph. 2:3; Luke 1:46–55). Spiritual poverty is the attitude of opening up to God, the ready disposition of one who hopes for everything from the Lord (cf. Matt. 5:3). Although he values the goods of this world, he does not become attached to them and he recognizes the higher value of the riches of the Kingdom (cf. Amos 2:6–7; 4:1; Jer. 5:28; Mic. 6:12–13; Isa. 10:2 et passim). (c) Poverty as a commitment, through which one assumes

voluntarily and lovingly the conditions of the needy of this world in order to bear witness to the evil which it represents and to spiritual liberty in the face of material goods, follows the example of Christ Who took to Himself all the consequences of men's sinful condition (cf. Phil. 2:5-8) and Who 'being rich became poor' (cf. 2 Cor. 8:9) in order to redeem us.

"In this context a poor Church: —Denounces the unjust lack of this world's goods and the sin that begets it; —Preaches and lives in spiritual poverty, as an attitude of spiritual childhood and openness to the Lord; —Is herself bound to material poverty. The poverty of the Church is, in effect, a constant factor in the history of salvation" (nos. 4-5).

49. In this regard it is necessary to rethink seriously the meaning of the assistance that the churches of the wealthy countries give to the churches of the poor countries. This assistance could very well be counterproductive as regards the witness to poverty that these poor churches should be giving. Moreover it might lead them into a reformist approach, resulting in superficial social changes which in the long run serve only to prolong the misery and injustice which marginated peoples suffer. This assistance can also provide a satisfied conscience —at low cost—for Christians who are citizens of countries which control the world economy. In this regard see the famous article of Ivan Illich, "The Seamy Side of Charity, *America* 116, no. 3 (January 21, 1967): 88–91.

CONCLUSION

The theology of liberation attempts to reflect on the experience and meaning of the faith based on the commitment to abolish injustice and to build a new society; this theology must be verified by the practice of that commitment, by active, effective participation in the struggle which the exploited social classes have undertaken against their oppressors. Liberation from every form of exploitation, the possibility of a more human and more dignified life, the creation of a new man—all pass through this struggle.

But in the last instance we will have an authentic theology of liberation only when the oppressed themselves can freely raise their voice and express themselves directly and creatively in society and in the heart of the People of God, when they themselves "account for the hope," which they bear, when they are the protagonists of their own liberation. For now we must limit ourselves to efforts which ought to deepen and support that process, which has barely begun. If theological reflection does not vitalize the action of the Christian community in the world by making its commitment to charity fuller and more radical, if—more concretely—in Latin America it does not lead the Church to be on the side of the oppressed classes and dominated peoples, clearly and without qualifications, then this theological reflection will have been of little value. Worse yet, it will have served only to justify half-measures and ineffective approaches and to rationalize a departure from the Gospel.

We must be careful not to fall into an intellectual self-satisfaction, into a kind of triumphalism of erudite and advanced "new" visions of Christianity. The only thing that is really new is to accept day by day the gift of the Spirit, who makes us love—in our concrete options to build a true human brotherhood, in our historical initiatives to subvert an order of injustice—with the fullness with which Christ loved us. To paraphrase a well-known text of Pascal, we can say that all the political theologies, the theologies of hope, of revolution, and of liberation, are not worth one act of genuine solidarity with exploited social classes. They are not worth one act of faith, love, and hope, committed—in one way or another—in active participation to liberate man from everything that dehumanizes him and prevents him from living according to the will of the Father.

INDEX OF BIBLICAL REFERENCES

OLD TESTAMENT

NEW TESTAMENT

311

GENERAL INDEX

Abelard, 5
Abraham, 160–61
Agency for International Development (AID), 92 n.3
Aggiornamento, 52 n.9, 252
Aguiar, César, 133, 141 n.10
Albert the Great, Saint, 5
Alliance for Progress, 39 n.16, 92 n.3
Althusser, Louis, 97 n.40, 249 n.121, 277
Alves, Rubem, 182 n.41, 217
America, 96 n.32, 142 n.12
Anamnesis, 213
Anaw, Anawim, 208, 291, 296
Ani, 291
Annunciation, 233–34, 265–72
Anonymous Christianity, 71
Anthropology, 7–8, 67, 189
Anthropophany, 213
Apologetics, 9
Apostolic Nuncios, 105
Aquinas, Saint Thomas, 5–6, 39 n.21, 55, 69, 258
Argentina, 59 n.8, 82, 110, 111, 118, 121 n.15, 122 n.16, 129 n.78
Arguedas, José María, 195, 269
Aristotelian categories, 5
Aristotle, 217
Ark of the Covenant, 190–92
Atheism, 34, 152, 240 n.16
Augustine of Hippo, Saint, 6, 42 n.53, 186 n.89, 193
Awareness, in Freud, 30–31

Bachelard, Gaston, 29
Bandung Conference, 23
Baptism, 260
Bara, 155
Barabbas, 229
Barth, Karl, 7, 162
Being, 69, 162
Bernanos, Georges, 10
Bishops:
    of Brazil, 123 n.22
    and Christendom mentality, 54
    commitment to liberation of, 106–07
    of Cuba, 125 n.36
    of El Salvador, 108
    of France, 274
    of Latin America, 108, 113–14, 118
    and lay apostolate, 103
    of Mexico, 115
    and New Christendom, 55
    of Paraguay, 124 n.23
    of Peru, 108, 113, 114–15
    and priest groups, 105
    of Third World, message of, 35, 109
    See also CELAM, Medellín Conference
Blanquart, Paul, 234, 236
Bloch, Ernst, 216–17, 220, 224, 243 n.59
Blondel, Maurice, 9, 70
Body, 209 n.12
Bolivia, 106, 109, 117
Bonald, Louis, 221

Bonhoeffer, Dietrich, 36, 67, 206
Bossuet, Jacques, 290
Bouillard, Henri, 13
Brandão, Dom Avelar, 141 n.5
Brazil, 73 n.5, 82, 97 n.36, 106, 120
  n.5, 120 n.6, 122 n.16, 123 n.22
Brotherhood:
  and class struggle, 272–79
  and Eucharist, 262–79
  See also Charity
Bukharin, Nikolai Ivanovich, 86
Bultmann, Rudolf, 243–44 n.59
Buñuel, Luis, 199–200

Cajetan, Cardinal Tommaso de Vio,
  69
Camara, Dom Helder, 89, 123 n.21
Camus, Albert, 50, 218
Canaan, 191
Capitalism:
  and Church, 133, 137, 266
  critique of, 39 n.18, 111–12,
    127 n.53, 127 n.55
  and dependence, 84–88, 110–11
  and development, 24, 109, 127 n.50
  Guevara on, 250 n.127
  Marcuse on, 32
  Marx on, 29–30
  Schumpeter on, 23
Cardoso, Fernando Henrique, 82, 83,
  85, 87
Casalis, G., 157
Castro, Fidel, 98 n.43, 120 n.10,
  123 n.20
Catholic Action, 56, 103. *See also*
  Laity, Lay Apostolic Movements
Catholic liberalism, 55
CELAM (Consejo Episcopal
  Latinoamericano), 109, 141 n.5
Celibacy, 122–23 n.18
Charity, 198–203, 238
  and class struggle, 275–76
  and faith, 219–20
  and freedom, 36
  and liberation, 204
  political, 202
  and revolution, 98 n.45
  and theology, 6–7
  See also Brotherhood
Chenu, M. D., 8, 47, 202, 271
Chile, 82, 112–13, 121 n.15
Christ:
  death of, 218, 262–63, 265

and liberation, 168–78
and neighbor, 198–203
and poverty, 300
and salvation, 151–52, 158
as temple of God, 192–93
See also Incarnation, Jesus,
  Messiah, Son of Man
Christendom:
  mentality of, 53–54
  "without the name," 71
Christianity:
  Anonymous, 71
  of the Beyond, 218
  of the Future, 218
  as ideology, 57, 238
  meaning of, 49–50, 143
Christian-Marxist Dialogue, 9–10,
  104, 137
Christian state, 221
Church:
  and assistance, 306 n.49
  and capitalism, 133, 137, 266
  and change, 140 n.1
  and Christendom mentality, 53–54
  and class struggle, 137–38, 253 n.3,
    276–79
  critical function of, 114–16, 223,
    268, 302
  and Kingdom of God, 11, 261
  and liberation, 101–131
  as *locus theologicus*, 8, 12
  mission of, 57, 138, 150, 169, 262,
    266, 305–06 n.48
  in New Christendom, 55
  and politics, 49, 54, 56, 65–66, 115,
    134, 265–72
  and poverty, 117, 130 n.80, 139–40,
    287, 290, 301–02, 305–06 n.48
  and repression, 139, 142 n.10
  and revolution, 116, 133, 138, 262
  as sacrament, 255–85
  and salvation, 53, 150, 256–58
  structures of 107, 117–18, 261
  and ties with established order,
    58, 65–66, 105, 108, 115, 118,
    120 n.11, 129 n.78, 130 n.80, 133,
    137, 138–40, 143, 224–25, 253 n.3,
    265–72
  unity of, 65, 137–38, 276–79
  and violence, 142 n.10
  wealth of, 130–31 n.91
  and world, 12, 43–77, 260–61, 273
"Circular flow," 23
City of God, The, 6

314

Ecuador, 121 n.15
Ecumenism, 104, 130 n.84, 278
Edict of Milan, 256
Egypt, liberation from. *See* Exodus
"Electoral path," 89
Elisha, 191
El Salvador, 108
England, 24
Enlightenment, 221-22
Epangelia, 160
Eschatological joy, 189, 207
Eschatological promises, 160-68, 298
Eschatological proviso, 223, 245 n.80
Eschatological radicalism, 229
Eschatologist theologians, 215
Eschatology, 137, 161-65
    Consequent, 230
    etymology of, 162
    and Exodus, 157
    and politics, 213-50
    and theology, 10
    transcendental, 162
Established order. *See* Church, and ties to established order
Eternity, 162
Ethical prophecy, 210 n.26
Eucharist, 137, 260, 262-79
Eucharistic Congress, 134
Europe, 68, 278
Evangelical Churches, 120 n.11, 141 n.7
Evangelical counsels, 290
Evangelical precepts, 290
Evangelion, 160
Evangelization, 57, 74 n.20, 116-17, 269-71
Evolution, 32
Exchange et Dialogue, 122 n.18
Exile, 192
Existentialism, 244 n.59
Existentialist theology, 222
Exodus, 116, 155-59, 163, 173, 182 n.41, 263, 294-95

Faletto, Enzo, 82, 83, 85
Fanon, Frantz, 41 n.35, 182 n.34
Fast, 196
Fathers of the Church, 4, 257, 280 n.11
Felipe, Leon, 211 n.45
Feuerbach, Ludwig, 216, 219-20
First Christian generation, 136, 208

Fragoso, Dom Antonio, 168
France, 59-60 n.13, 60 n.15, 274
Freedom, 29, 36, 221. *See also* Liberty
Freire, Paulo, 91-92, 213, 233, 234, 235
French Revolution, 28-29, 46, 55, 258
Freud, Sigmund, 30-31
Frings, Joseph, 170
Future, 213-15, 241 n.33
    Christianity of the, 218
    and eschatology, 161-65, 167, 230
    Jesus on, 185 n.79, 218
    and promise, 161
    theology of, 14
    See also Eschatology

Galileo, 39 n.20
Gaudium et spes
    on Church and world, 46, 58
    on development, 33
    on "integral," 71-72
    on liberation, 33-34
    on Kingdom of God, 168-72
    on poverty, 287
    on signs of the times, 8
    and Teilhard de Chardin, 76 n.35
Gelin, Albert, 157, 160, 291
Gentiles, 257
Geulah, 158
Gilson, Etienne, 28
Girardi, Giulio, 270, 275
Goel, 157
Golconda movement, 121 n.15, 128 n.57
González Ruiz, José María, 175, 189
Grace:
    efficacious sign of, 260
    and Eucharist, 263
    as historical, 167
    and nature, 55, 69-72, 169-72
    and salvation, 150, 151, 280 n.11
    and social movements, 8
Gramsci, Antonio, 13
Great I, 210-11 n.36
Great Refusal, 31, 233
Grelot, Pierre, 166, 180 n.14
Gross, G., 201
Guatemala, 121 n.15, 122 n.16
Guerrillas, 89
Guevara, Ernesto Che, 91, 211 n.45, 236, 250 n.127

Hamartiosphere, 175
Heaven, 191, 255
Hegel, Georg W. F., 219–20
  on alienation, 187 n.96
  on America, 96 n.32, 142 n.12
  on conflict and awareness, 30–31
  and contemporary thought,
    244 n.59
  on economics, 40 n.30
  on history, 28–29, 39 n.23
  on Marcuse, 31
  on philosophy, 11
  on work, 29, 40 n.36
Heidegger, Martin 243–44 n.59
Heretics, 279 n.7
Héring, J., 201
Hermeneutics, political, 13
Herod Antipas, 228
Hierarchy. See Bishops
Hinkelammert, Franz, 86
Hobson, J. A., 85
Holland, 122–23 n.18
Holtzmann, Heinrich Julius, 197
Holy of Holies, 191–192
Hope, 215–20, 238. See also
  Eschatology
Horeb, Mount, 164
Horizontalism, 8, 199, 200, 269, 271
Humanization, 160
Husserl, Edmund, 39 n.20

Iconization, 225
Ideology, 12, 48, 57, 234–35, 238, 266,
  271
Ignatian spirituality, 7
Imitation of Christ, 4
Immanence, 239 n.8
Imperialism, 27, 34, 85–86. See also
  Dependence
Incarnation, 8, 161, 185 n.83, 192,
  193, 196, 217, 239 n.8, 300.
  See also Christ
Incarnationalist theologians, 215
Indo-American socialism, 90
Inductive method, 58
Ingelaere, Jean-Claude, 197, 201
Innovation, 23, 95 n.27
Integral, as term, 71
Integral development, 33, 72, 171–72
Integral vocation, 72
Inter-American Development Bank
  (IDB), 39 n.16, 92 n.3

Interclassist doctrine, 275
International Monetary Fund
  (IMF), 39 n.16, 92 n.3
International organizations, 26, 82
ISAL (Iglesia y Sociedad para
  América Latina), 121 n.11,
  127 n.55, 128 n.57
Italy, 54
I-Thou relationship, 202

Jerusalem, 191, 264
Jesus:
  and eschatology, 185 n.79
  and external worship, 264
  as king, 227, 229
  and kingdom, 229–30
  and political world, 225–32
  and revolution, 230
  trial of, 229
  See also Christ
Jews:
  judgment of, 197
  liberation of, 231
  leaders of, 228–29, 231
  and meal, 263
  and salvation, 257, 258, 279 n.7
  See also Exodus
John XXIII, Pope, 8, 33, 287, 291
Joy, 189, 207–08, 262
Judas Iscariot, 227
Judgment, Last, 196–203

Kant, Immanuel, 28, 39 n.20, 39 n.23,
  147, 162
Kenosis, 300
Kierkegaard, Soren, 244 n.59
King, Jesus as, 227, 229
Kingdom of God:
  and Church, 11, 261
  and distinction of planes, 57
  hermeneutics of, 13
  as historical reality, 167
  and hope, 238
  Jesus and, 229–30
  and justice, 112, 135–36, 167–68,
    231–32, 269, 295
  and poor, 297–99
  and promise, 161
  and revolution, 103, 135
  and temporal progress, 168–74,
    176–77
  and theology, 15
  Zealots and, 227

317

Kingdom of Israel, 161
Koinonia, 264–65

Labor. *See* Work
Lagrange, Marie Joseph, 197
Laity, 54, 55–56, 57, 102–04, 118,
244 n.72
of Argentina, 110
of El Salvador, 108
spirituality of, 5, 7
See also Lay Apostolic
Movements
Larraín, Don Manuel, 141 n.5
Last Supper, 263
Last things, 162. *See also*
Eschatology
Latin American Episcopal Council.
See CELAM
Law, Zealots and, 227
Lay Apostolic Movements, 57–58,
63–64, 102–04
Lenin, N., 86
Leopard, 140
Leo the Great, 143
Liberation, three levels of, 36–37, 45,
176–78, 235–36
Liberty, religious, 59 n.6, 256–58
Liégé, Pierre-Andre, 255
Lima Vaz, Enrique de, 120 n.4
Liturgy. *See* Worship
Locus theologicus, 8, 12, 79
Loisy, Alfred, 197
Lord-bondsman dialectic, 29
Love. *See* Charity
Lumen gentium, 58, 299–300
Luther, Martin, 197
Luxemburg, Rosa, 85-86

Mannheim, Karl, 249 n.120
Manson, T. W., 201
Marcel, Gabriel, 215
Marcuse, Herbert, 31–32, 233
Mariátegui, José Carlos, 90
Maritain, Jacques, 54–55, 56, 120 n.4
Martelet, Gustave, 71
Marx, Karl, 219–20
and Bloch, 216
and class struggle, 284 n.51
and Hegel, 40 n.26, 40 n.30
and Kierkegaard, 244 n.59
and Marcuse, 31
originality of, 40 n.29
and religion, 222

and science of history, 29–30,
249 n.121
and sin, 187 n.98
Marxism:
and bishops, 106–07
Castro on, 123 n.20
and development, 25
and existentialism, 244 n.59
Mariátegui on, 90
and Metz, 224
and priests, 141 n.2
and theology, 9–10
See also Christian-Marxist
Dialogue
Mater et Magistra, 33
Materialism, 216, 220
Mathematics, Greek, 39 n.20
Meal, 263
Medellín Conference (Second
General Conference of Latin
American Bishops):
on Church, 66, 118
compared with Vatican II, 134–35
on conflict, 136
on conscienticizing evangelization, 116, 117
on education, 110
on injustice, 195
on liberation, 35
on new civilization, 214
on pastoral approach, 114
on poverty, 115, 117, 139,
305–306 n.48
on prophetic denunciation, 114
significance of, 105, 107, 134–35,
284 n.46
on "sinful situation," 109, 175
Memoria Christi, 223
Memorial, 262
Méndez Arceo, Bishop Sergio, 111
Mendicant Orders, 7
Messiah, 229, 245 n.85, 296, 298–99,
305 n.45
Messianism, 227–28, 236, 238,
283 n.39
Metz, Johannes B., 46, 72, 143,
220–25
Mexico, 82, 115, 121 n.15
Mission. *See* Church, mission of
Misterion, 259
Mixed Life, 7
MOAC (Workers' Catholic Action
Movement of Chile), 112
Modernization, 26, 56, 83

318

Moltmann, Jürgen, 14, 162, 182 n.41, 216–18, 220
Montini, Giovanni Battista, 169. *See also* Paul VI, Pope
More, Saint Thomas, 232, 233
Moses, 156, 159, 190–191, 294–95
Mountain, and encounter with God, 190–91, 193
Mühlen, Heribert, 197
Multinational corporations, 85, 88
Mystery, 259–60
Mystics, 206
Myth, of Christian unity, 277

Naaman, 191
Nathan, 191, 192
Nationalism, 227, 232
Natural and supernatural, 69–72, 169–72
Nature:
  domination of, 172, 214, 299
  and grace, 55, 69–72, 169–72
  and man, 9, 28, 295
Nazarín, 199–200
Neher, André, 158, 159
Neighbor, 47, 194–203, 204–05
Neo-colonialism, 109
Neoplatonic categories, 4
New Christendom, 54–56, 63, 102
New political theology, 220–25
"New theology," 8
Newton, Isaac, 39 n.20
Non possumus, 54
Novelty, 146
Nun, José, 85

Obedience, 303 n.9
Octogesima adveniens, 42 n.48
Onganía, Juan Carlos, 129 n.78
ONIS (Oficina Nacional de Investigación Social), 113, 121 n.15, 126 n.43
Opiate, religion as, 116
Oppressed, role in liberation of, 91, 113–14, 235, 271
Organization of American States (OAS), 92 n.3
Origen, 197
Orthodoxy, 10, 203
Orthopraxis, 10

Pacem in terris, 33
Pagans, 150, 197, 227, 279 n.7

Pannenberg, Wolfhart, 216–17, 220, 240–41 n.23
Parable, 209 n.16
Paraguay, 124 n.23, 129–30 n.79
Parousia, 167, 183 n.58, 241 n.33, 247 n.98
Pascal, Blaise, 165, 308
Passover, 158, 176, 207, 250 n.125, 263
Pastoral Activity, 11–12, 63–66, 270–71
Pastors, 8–9
Paul VI, Pope, 41 n.46, 42 n.48, 42 n.51, 51 n.9, 128 n.57, 200. *See also* Montini, Giovanni Battista
Paz Zamora, Nestor, 98 n.45, 212 n.47
Peasants, 89, 103
Peguy, Charles, 160, 218
Pereira, Henrique, 123 n.19
Perroux, François, 25
Persecution, theology of, 141 n.10
Personalist theology, 222
Personalization, 269
Peru, 108, 113, 114, 116, 121 n.15
Peter, Saint, 227
Pharisees, 228–29
Philosophy, 9, 11, 15 n.1, 28–30, 39 n.20
Pius XII, Pope, 33, 202, 269–70
Plato, 39 n.20
Platonic categories, 4
Pleasure principle, 40 n.32
Political Augustinism, 53
Political charity, 202
Political parties, 54, 59 nn.11–12, 88, 102
Political sphere, scope of, 47–49
Political theology, 45, 220–25
Politicization, 47, 104, 269–70
Politics:
  and Church, 49, 54, 56, 65–66, 115, 134, 265–72
  and development, 87–88
  and eschatology, 213–50
  and Jesus, 225–32
Pontius Pilate, 229
Populist movements, 82, 88–89
Populorum progressio, 33, 34–35, 110, 171–72, 288
Poverty:
  ambiguities in term, 288–91
  Biblical meaning of, 291–99
  and Christ, 300

Rockefeller Report, 133
Romans, 227, 229, 246 n.85, 256
Rostow, Walt W., 38 n.8
Russian Revolution, 46

Sabbath, 294
Sacerdotes para el Tercer Mundo. *See* Priests for the Third World Movement
Sacrament:
  Church as, 255–85
  man as, 295
  of neighbor, 202
  of salvation, 255–62
  and sign, 258–62
Sacramentum, 259
Sacrifice, 196, 264, 282 n.29
Sadducees, 228
Saint-Exupéry, Antoine de, 199
Salvation:
  as central theme of Christian mystery, 149–52
  and Christendom mentality, 53
  Church and, 53, 150, 256–58
  and creation, 153–60, 173
  gratuitousness of, 69, 205–07
  and Jews, 257, 258, 279 n.7
  and justice, 122 n.18, 238
  and liberation, 45, 72, 149–87
  and New Christendom, 55
  of pagans, 150
  qualitative notion of, 151–52
  quantitative notion of, 150–51
  as re-creation and complete fulfillment, 157–60, 173
  single call to, 69–72, 255–56
  universality of, 69–72, 150–52, 255–58, 280 n.11
  universal sacrament of, 255–62
Samaritans, 227
Sanhedrin, 228, 229
Sartre, Jean Paul, 9
Schema of Ariccia, 169–71, 175, 186 nn. 89–90
Schema 14, 287
Schema 13, 169, 287
Schema of Zurich, 169
Schillebeeckx, Edward, 10, 13, 72, 263
Scholasticism, 5–6
Schumpeter, Joseph A., 23
Schweitzer, Albert, 162, 230

Science:
  of history, 29–30
  and nature, 9, 28, 172, 173, 214
  and philosophy, 39 n.20
  and secularization, 67
  theology as, 6–7
  and utopia, 234, 235, 238
  See also Social sciences
Second General Conference of Latin American Bishops. *See* Medellín Conference
Secularism, 74 n.16
Secularization, 66–68, 72, 224
Segundo, Juan Luis, 252
Shekinah, 190
Sign, and sacrament, 258–62
Signs of the times, 6, 8–9, 35, 101, 271
Simon the Zealot, 227
Sin, 175–76
  in Augustine, 42 n.53
  of Church, 124 n.27
  and class struggle, 265–76
  and Eucharist, 263
  as historical reality, 152, 167, 172
  and injustice, 35, 109, 110, 114, 175, 231
  Jesus and, 231
  and liberation, 237
  Marx on, 187 n.98
  and poverty, 295, 300–01, 304 n.32
  and salvation, 150, 152, 158
Sinai, Mount, 190, 191, 263
"Sinful situation," 109, 114, 175, 231
Sino–Soviet split, 89
Socialism:
  and class struggle, 274, 285 n.56
  Colombian priests on, 128 n.57
  Guevara on, 236
  ISAL on, 128 n.57
  Latin American, 90–91
  Latin American Christians and, 111–13
  and liberation, 27, 30
  Marcuse on, 32
  Paul VI on, 128 n.57
  and psychological liberation, 31
  variety of, 127 n.53
Social sciences, 5, 85, 86–87, 136, 224, 273
Socialists, True, 220
Sociology, 95 n.28
Socius, 47
Solomon, 191
Son of Man, 197, 201, 211 n.36, 228